BODY TALK

RHETORIC OF THE HUMAN SCIENCES

General Editors

David J. Depew

Deirdre N. McCloskey

John S. Nelson

John D. Peters

Body Talk

RHETORIC, TECHNOLOGY, REPRODUCTION

EDITED BY MARY M. LAY, LAURA J. GURAK

CLARE GRAVON, AND CYNTHIA MYNTTI

THE UNIVERSITY OF WISCONSIN PRESS

The University of Wisconsin Press
2537 Daniels Street
Madison, Wisconsin 53718

3 Henrietta Street
London WC2E 8LU, England

Library of Congress Cataloging-in-Publication Data
Body talk : rhetoric, technology, reproduction / edited by Mary M. Lay . . . [et al.].
    326 pp.   cm. — (Rhetoric of the human sciences)
    includes bibliographical references and index.
    ISBN 0-299-16790-9 (cloth: alk. paper)
    ISBN 0-299-16794-1 (paper: alk. paper)
    1. Human reproductive technology—Social aspects   2. Rhetorical criticism.
  3. Feminist criticism.   4. Women—Health and hygiene.   I. Lay, Mary M.
  II. Series.
    RG133.5.B63   2000
    616.69'206—dc21   99-006903

CONTENTS

Contents

FOREWORD

There has never been a shortage of experts ready to pronounce on women's nature and women's bodies. The biological revolution of the second half of the twentieth century has, however, raised the stakes. Now multiple instruments and technologies, as well as hidden players like genes, stand behind the words of the experts. Promising to help women realize their dreams, to mend what they say is broken, to bypass what they say is defective, today's experts stand ready to assist women into a world of reproductive options. Techno-science and technomedicine permeate private lives, turning intimacy inside out, appropriating even the language of the self. If we listen only to the experts, a vista of expanding human control over nature is optimistically displayed. If we listen also to the women who are targets of the new knowledge, a more ambiguous future and a more and conflicted discursive landscape displace the clinical cheer. This book analyzes these multiple voices to show the complexity and unpredictability of the implementation and reception of the new biomedical technologies.

Reading these evocative and persuasive chapters provoked sparks of recognition and memories of unarticulated disquiet that demonstrate how intimately the academic and personal are linked in our lives. The authors in this collection open up discussions about women's gendered bodies at specific locations where reproduction is, in fact, a preoccupation for many women and their families. Case studies and narratives, along with quite sophisticated tools of analysis and recourse to important theoretical constructs, make the accounts in these chapters especially effective rhetorical counterpoints to the clinical language and authoritative pronouncements that are at the core of medical science. We hear women's voices, in sometimes great variety, amid the institutional, often male, voices that seek to influence women's thinking and their lives.

As in most feminist scholarship, the chapters are interdisciplinary and attend layers of experience, including ideology, practice, and public policy. These discussions of reproduction create enlightening places for discourse by and about women's lives that inevitably intersect with other conversations about gender. Most studies in this book are situated in North America—the exceptions are Greece and Australia—and consciously relate to the lives of white women, with relevant commentary about class and race. At issue in most chapters are the claims of expert knowledge and authority in relationship to women's experiences. In such analyses, informed by a variety of theorists, authors interrogate the language, metaphors, images, and broadly defined rhetorics that position various discussants. At stake are critically important issues around fertility and infertility, delivery by midwives or physicians, genetic information, the effects of implants, maintenance of a healthy body and spirit while pregnant, and the myriad phenomena related to women's fertility, health, and life cycles. Inevitably, perhaps, the intensity and the personal nature of this culturally rooted discourse affect individual women; themes of guilt, failure, and anxiety are common threads in these women's voices, coming as they do from a technological society that constructs and contests normality.

The sources tapped as material for these chapters reflect the pervasiveness of discussions of women's reproduction. Contributors use an array of such primary sources as oral interviews, individual questionnaires, popular women's magazines, cookbooks, prescriptive self-help books, scientific reports, clinical records, policy statements, and legal documents. The plethora of images and metaphors nonetheless underscores the tendency toward a technocratic outlook in which "normal" is the presumed goal, yet individual deviation is so common that ambiguity and anxiety are commonplace. Many chapters discuss women's uneasy collaboration with and about themselves and their highly gendered bodies. Palpable in the stories recounted here is the sense of alienation from their own bodies for women who are unable to conceive, for those directed away from sports during menstruation, women who are dealing with the loss of a breast during cancer treatment, or those who are confronting genetics in an abortion or sterilization decision. In the fast-paced world of biotechnology women receive information about external possibilities but live with a private sense of limitation. Common and medical vocabulary reinforces their personal sense of inadequacy and flawed bodies: "incompetent uterus," "hostile cervical environment," "psychosomatic abortion," "ovarian failure," "disorderly cycles," "abnormal period," "deficient genes," and so forth. Women even adopt this language themselves, viewing their own bodies as mechanisms that have failed them. The linguistic paradigms for men are more typically neutral and impersonal, such as "antibody reaction" rather than "hostile testicles" following the reversal of a vasectomy. Genetic models, however, may be less discriminating in their suggestion that altered or problematic genes in both men and women "trigger" cancer and related diseases.

The roles that women have played in shaping the practices around reproduction complicate some accounts. Progressive eighteenth-century midwives, for example, staved off male physicians and carved a niche for their craft in part by criticizing and thus limiting some of their less well-educated peers. Even today the compromises allowing some (almost inevitably women) midwives to practice are so complex that no two states have precisely the same policies governing their use of instruments and drugs. Gym teachers also mediated between their students and external authorities in ways that acknowledged problems for some of their charges during menstruation while emphasizing that "periods" were normal and not unhealthy in general. Women writing books to advise pregnant women about reproduction similarly negotiate, in some cases drawing distinctions between women and the fetus within them and sometimes allowing attention and concern for the latter to overshadow health, sexual, and other personal needs of the women themselves. What is important, however, is that these and other practices seem to vary by culture, making it essential to locate our discussions about clinical practitioners, women under scrutiny, and women activists in particular times and places.

The roots of this book go back to a conference entitled "Women, Gender, and Science: What Do Research on Women in Science and Research on Gender and Science Have to Do with Each Other?" held at the University of Minnesota in 1995. Several sessions on rhetoric and science, coordinated by program committee member Mary Lay, paid close attention to health and reproduction. Their success stimulated attendees to pursue the subjects further and in conjunction with one another. Some chapters are considerable extensions of those conference papers, whereas others represent responses to a general call for contributions to this book. The four editors showed imagination and resourcefulness in bringing this volume to fruition. As cochairs of that conference, which involved historians, philosophers, rhetoricians, biologists, physicists, teachers, activists, and others, we are particularly pleased that the conference served as a catalyst for this important project.

SALLY GREGORY KOHLSTEDT AND HELEN E. LONGINO

ACKNOWLEDGMENTS

The editors wish to thank the colleagues and associates who provided support and assistance for this project. First and foremost, we thank the individual authors who worked diligently and with patience throughout the writing and revising process. Their chapters represent exceptional scholarship, and we appreciated the opportunity to work with each of them. We thank Elizabeth C. Britt for her suggestions on the early drafts of the introduction. We also thank Raphael Kadushin, Scott Lenz, and the other associates at the University of Wisconsin Press. In addition, our thanks go to Amy Koerber for her research assistance. We are also grateful for the support of the University of Minnesota's Agricultural Experiment Station and the Center for Advanced Feminist Studies, both of which provided partial assistance for the research involved with this project.

BODY TALK

INTRODUCTION

THE RHETORIC

OF REPRODUCTIVE TECHNOLOGIES

MARY M. LAY, LAURA J. GURAK,

CLARE GRAVON, AND CYNTHIA MYNTTI

In the past one hundred years, we have seen an amazing rise in reproductive technologies. Recently, these technologies have assumed major status on our cultural landscape. In-vitro fertilization, contraceptive devices and vaccines, and diagnostic tools define human reproduction in ways never imagined at the turn of the twentieth century. In 1998, the Centers for Disease Control and Prevention estimated that about 15 percent of all women had received some type of infertility services. From Viagra to multiple births resulting from fertility treatment, the rhetoric of reproductive technologies surrounds us.

However, although popular perceptions of these technologies often focus on the device, drug, or procedure, critics have long realized that these technologies are more than simply tools to assist human birth: human reproduction and related technologies also provide a focus by which to understand and critique culture. Reproductive technologies and the rhetoric that a culture uses to communicate about them—what we call "body talk"—can reveal a range of social features, such as ownership and control of knowledge, access to tools and techniques of science and technology, place and power of experts and professionals, societal definitions of normality and pathology, definitions of the self, the rights granted to the embodied citizen, and views about the relationship between technology and religion.

Although the rhetoric surrounding human reproduction provides a lens for viewing these features, it also points toward future developments, providing a "terrain for imagining new cultural futures and transformations" (Ginsburg and Rapp 1995:2). These developments point out conflicts about the uses of technology in relation to human conception and birth; yet what often gets reported and thus communicated to society at large is a mix of technological determinism and wonder, with little critical perspective.

For example, the births of the McCaughey septuplets in 1997 and the Chukwu octuplets in 1998 (in both cases, the babies were conceived via fertility treatments) were primarily reported in wondrous terms, with the parents claiming that their successful multiple births were primarily acts of God, not science. Yet in reality these births are both wondrous and frightening—acts of God and acts of science and technology, trends that provide hope and raise grave concerns about the viability and long-term health of so many babies. A December 1998 editorial in the *New York Times* noted this conflict:

> It is tempting to regard the eight babies born to a Houston mother [Nkem Chukwu] as a holiday season miracle, the fruit of a woman's fervent desire to have children and of modern medicine's ability to assist reproduction in those otherwise unable to conceive. Who does not root strenuously for the survival of the world's only known living octuplets as they cling tenuously to life in a neonatal intensive care unit? But this is not an event that should be overly sentimentalized or glamorized. It is instead a mixed blessing, illustrating the limitations of high-tech medicine as it strives to bring sound, healthy babies into the world without generating a crowd of fragile newborns. ("Too Much of a Good Thing":26)

This conflict of medicine, technology, and culture can be considered in light of what philosopher Michel Foucault characterized as "bio-power" (1990). The era of bio-power, according to Foucault's *Sexuality,* began with "an explosion of numerous and diverse techniques for achieving the subjugation of bodies and the control of populations" (140). Through science, society could control, monitor, and make more efficient the individual body, recast in this era as a machine, and harness and direct the entire population, a sort of species body. Therefore, individuals and their bodies became parts of the entire system of knowledge, power, and discourse within a society; cultural ideologies and norms filtered the choices of individuals and their needs. Moreover, when internalized by society's citizens, bio-power has normalizing and regulatory functions. Culturally derived truths about the body, according to Foucault, can confirm that life is an object of knowledge. According to this view, once science understands life's mechanics, unlimited possibilities exist for control and intervention into such processes as reproduction. Certain experts begin to represent this bio-power; these experts are individuals who successfully claim "authoritative knowledge"—what anthropologist Brigitte Jordan defines as any kind of knowledge that gains "ascendance and legitimacy" within a society or group, regardless of whether it is "correct" (1997:56). As bio-power and authoritative knowledge grow, they create a framework for how one should best live, reproduce, maintain health, and even die. If, in the case of multiple births, experts (which include not only medical experts but newsmagazines, television, the Internet, and other sources of communication) create a rhetoric of wonder and hope instead of a rhetoric of concern and ethical considerations, the former will become the dominant discourse, setting the stage for increased funding, future technologies, and often ill-fated human hope.

Bio-power does its work through a concept that Foucault called "normalizing," as experts divide the normal from the abnormal and as they define, compare, and rank risks, abnormalities and diseases, and treatments. Normalizing, operating on both the level of the individual and on the level of the population, creates and perpetuates a distinction between the normal and abnormal, and, because the normal is always defined in contrast to the abnormal, experts are continuously identifying new abnormalities. Within these normalizing arguments, although women are certainly subjects or creators of knowledge, they also become objects of knowledge. Their bodies may be fragmented into mechanical parts, and their reproductive functions may become medical conditions, to be fixed or rehabilitated if they fall outside the norm. This fragmentation, as identified by anthropologist Emily Martin, enables medical science to treat the person as a machine and to "assume the body can be fixed by mechanical manipulations," thereby ignoring other aspects of the self, such as emotions and personal relationships and support systems (1992:19–20).

As an example, authoritative knowledge within traditional medical communities may argue that after a woman delivers her baby through cesarean section, subsequent vaginal births will be high risk. For example, four Boston medical childbirth specialists recently warned that some hospitals were going "too far" in trying to reduce the cesarean rate and were endangering the lives of women and infants (Brody 1999: A25). The experts warned that 1 percent of women attempting to have a vaginal birth after an earlier cesarean delivery (VBAC) could suffer a ruptured uterus and hemorrhage or the baby could suffer brain damage or die (A25). In contrast, within the midwifery community, authoritative knowledge about birth may argue that if the midwife is experienced in helping with VBACs or if the mother herself is confident about attempting a vaginal delivery, risk to mother and baby is low. The Boston medical experts reasserted the authoritative knowledge of medical experts, rather than that of the midwives or the mothers themselves, in the belief that once women have had cesarean sections, most should deliver the rest of their babies through this procedure.

Rhetorical analysis of arguments such as these identify authoritative knowledge, within midwifery and within the medical community, as not true knowledge but instead as discursive constructs. However, an additional consequence of legitimizing authoritative knowledge is the devaluation or silencing of other systems of knowledge. As Jordan says, "Those who espouse alternative knowledge systems then tend to be seen as backward, ignorant, and naïve, or worse, simply as troublemakers" (1997:56). Discursive efforts to constitute authoritative knowledge contribute to power relationships, and people begin to see this social order as the natural order, adding to the persuasive power of authoritative knowledge. They not only accept such knowledge as valid but also consciously and unconsciously contribute to its production and reproduction (57–58). The knowledge systems of high-tech medicine often devalue women's experiential and embodied knowledge, that is, their unique experience with birthing their children and their knowledge of their own bodies' signs and needs.

This book is about bio-power and its relationship to authoritative knowledge systems, what we call body talk—how language constructs bodies and reproductive technologies. The editors and contributors believe that, by examining the discourse surrounding reproduction and technology, we can reveal, explicate, and even shake up that discourse. We can recall women's experiential and embodied knowledge; we can illuminate how language normalizes certain reproductive choices. As we move forward into a new century and the many new reproductive and bodily "miracles" that loom, we hope this book provides a much needed critical framework on matters of urgency for men and women who live in this new high-reprotech landscape.

Rhetoric, Discourse, and Power

Before discussing the chapters in this book, we must take a moment to discuss what we mean by "rhetoric" and why rhetorical analysis is a powerful critical tool for understanding social and cultural views about reproductive technologies. The contributors use a method known broadly as "rhetorical criticism" or "rhetorical analysis" to analyze discourse related to women's reproductive technologies. Their purpose is to examine closely word choice, arguments, warrants, claims, motives, and other purposeful, persuasive features of language, visuals, and various artifacts to understand how such discourse not only creates our social conceptions of women's bodies and reproduction but also defines the policies and knowledge systems that are available to women and men. For it is through discourse that we come to accept as "givens" these various technologies and their effects. As sociologist Judy Wajcman notes, "The literature on reproductive technology is rife with technological determinist arguments which assume that changes in technology are the most important cause of changes in society" and that these technologies "are seen as having directly transformed women's lives for the better" (1994:155). By using rhetorical theory as an analytical tool, we can tell the other side(s) of these determinist stories by illustrating subtexts that may not be readily apparent to the casual reader, listener, or viewer but nonetheless are part of the messages. These chapters look at how discourse creates realities and perceptions, empowers and marginalizes certain voices, shapes bodies and technologies, and frames public policy. Discourse is thus an artifact whose metaphors, definitions, and vocabulary help us understand "the complexities of the production and use of meanings" and the "underlying social forces" linked to these rhetorical processes (Condit 1990:5). In addition, some chapters look not only at discourse but at the technologies themselves, in essence analyzing the techniques and technologies as arguments.

For example, when qualified by modalities of time, place, and speaker, statements are usually open to debate: "At this time, we suspect that estrogen replacement therapies may offset the development of osteoporosis in some women." When the speaker drops the qualifiers, a statement becomes fact or part of that community's authoritative knowledge about birth: "Artificial replacement of estrogen in the postmenopausal woman offsets the development of osteoporosis." Therefore, knowledge, including what we accept to be fact, is a matter of language far more than it is an observation of some external reality (Latour and Woolgar 1986). This concept is not new and is related not only to the study of reproductive technologies. Evelyn Fox Keller (1985), the historian and philosopher of science, studied the language of Francis Bacon, who labeled nature as female and charged his fellow scientists to "conquer" and "control" her, whereas he defined science by the adjectives *objective* and *logical,* which his culture used to describe men or masculinity. As Keller says,

> It may have taken the lens of feminist theory to reveal the popular association of science, objectivity, and masculinity as a statement about the social rather than the natural (or biological) world, referring not to the bodily and mental capacities of individual men and women, but to a collective consciousness; that is, as a set of beliefs given existence by language rather than by bodies, and by that language, granted the force to shape what individual men and women might (or might not) do. (1992:25)

Thus studying the language and the technologies used to describe and represent the body, and those reproductive technologies that diagnose, treat, and control it, reveals essential cultural and social attitudes toward women and reproduction. Moreover, it affords the opportunity to identify when women function as subjects and creators of knowledge and how they interpret their own experience.

But what exactly are the components and methods of rhetorical analysis? And how might rhetorical analysis differ from or extend the studies of reproduction and reproductive technologies conducted by anthropologists, historians, sociologists, biologists, and political scientists? Although it may be the oldest of the humanities, rhetoric has suffered a much maligned career throughout its more than two-thousand-year history. "Mere rhetoric" is a common phrase among politicians and the popular press. Yet rhetoric is anything but mere. The Greeks developed theories of rhetoric in Western culture in the fourth and fifth centuries B.C.E. to help provide heuristics for making persuasive discourse, which was a central component of their newly emerging democracy. They viewed rhetoric as central to a society in which citizens needed to express various opinions and all citizens had a voice in government. Rhetoric remains equally important today in any democracy; citizens need an understanding of what makes effective discourse in order to participate fully in their governments.

Long after the Greeks (and later the Romans) began to explore the power of language implicit in rhetoric, scholars noticed that the concepts from rhetoric so effective in forming effective discourse were also valuable critical tools. One could use aspects of rhetorical theory to create a speech or essay, but one could also use those same tools to critique speeches, writing, and other forms of discourse. Noting this distinction, Brock, Scott, and Chesebro remind us that "historically and currently, [rhetoric] has been and is used in both senses" (1989:14). The rhetorical appeal of *ethos* provides an example. In classical rhetoric, ethos is one of three appeals, or methods of creating an effective argument (the other two are *logos*—argument based on logic—and *pathos*—argument based on emotional appeal). Aristotle called ethos "the controlling factor in persuasion" (1991:I.2.1356a), recognizing that a speaker's character plays an important role in how audiences view his or her argument. Thus one uses the notion of ethos to create an effective speech, essay, brochure, or television program by injecting aspects that build credibility. Yet along with this heuristic role, one can also use the concept of ethos to critique discourse. S. Michael Halloran (1984), for example, uses ethos to help explain how Watson and Crick made a convincing and credible argument in their published paper announcing the discovery of the double-helical structure of DNA. In a similar use of rhetoric as a critical tool, Kathleen Welch (1990) uses rhetoric's fifth canon (delivery) to explain the rhetorical power of new communication technologies.

Yet the classical tradition, which has dominated rhetorical criticism, has recently been critiqued as overly masculinist. With its roots in Aristotle's culture, where women were not citizens, classical rhetoric has often ignored women and feminist concerns. Even contemporary rhetorical theory, drawing on scholars such as Kenneth Burke or I. A. Richards, has been criticized for not including women's voices. To address this obvious gap, feminist rhetoricians have explored ways to create feminist rhetorics; for example, Karlyn Kohrs Campbell has argued that rhetorical scholars need to study more speeches and works by women, arguing that this approach is important for both political and scholarly reasons (1989:212). In an approach that not only includes women's voice but also revisits classical theory in terms of contemporary feminist thought, Susan Jarratt (1991) has examined the sophists, ancient teachers of rhetoric before Aristotle, and argues for feminist applications of these theories. Likewise, Lisa Ede, Cheryl Glenn, and Andrea Lunsford have argued for a feminist approach to rhetoric, noting that "rhetoric offers feminism a vibrant process of inquiring, organizing, and thinking, as well as a theorized space to talk about effective communication; feminism offers rhetoric a reason to bridge differences, to include, and to empower, as well as a politicized space to discuss rhetorical values" (1995:401).

Examples of feminist rhetorical criticism abound; some examples that are related to body talk include the work of Emily Martin (1996), who explores the elaborate romance metaphor constructed within medical textbooks, which rely on seemingly universal feminine and masculine traits to depict the passive role of the egg in interaction with the sperm. Also, Carol Cohn (1996) explicates how the phallic and war metaphors used in the nuclear weapons industry reflect and shape the ideologies of U.S. nuclear strategy and minimize the effects of nuclear destruction (see also Keller 1992). In a related historical study, Londa Schiebinger (1993) analyzes how defining mammals by using a term linked to the female reproductive system supported social views of proper masculinity and femininity in eighteenth-century Europe. Paula Treichler describes what she calls the linguistic capital—"the power to establish and enforce a particular definition of childbirth" (1990:116)—of medical discourse communities within the United States, which determine that most births occur within hospital settings and that childbirth is a medical event, supported by technological control and intervention. This linguistic capital leads physicians, "already oriented toward scientific progress, decisive clinical action, and professional sovereignty," to reject definitions of childbirth as natural (118). Therefore, childbirth, as Treichler proposes, is not a simple label for a real event but instead is rhetorically determined; the word *childbirth* "inscribes" the event, "makes the event intelligible to us," and influences public policy (132). We thus believe that rhetorical theory, particularly from a feminist perspective, can help articulate important cultural questions more fully and thereby function as a powerful lens through which to view and understand reproductive technologies.

Yet the critical role of rhetoric is not all that is significant here. As noted earlier, rhetoric can also be used as a heuristic, suggesting alternatives to dominant discourse. The discourse of citizenship, for example, often excludes women from the public spaces where alternatives are framed and debated. Using the words of Evelyn Fox Keller (1988), Kathleen Jones observes, "Women cannot be seen in public spaces as women citizens who act politically on their own ground, with their full being-female because the discourse of citizenship is itself gendered. The dominant conceptualization of citizenship displaces 'women, their work, and the values associated with that work from the culturally normative definitions of objectivity, morality, and citizenship, and even, of human nature'" (1990:782). Contributors to this book use rhetorical analysis to reveal the gendered nature of our societal, personal, and medical attitudes about reproduction and reproductive technologies and suggest possibilities for new rhetorics of reproduction. The vocabulary, definitions, narratives, and metaphors, as well as the warrants and models that underlie these messages, signal which knowledge systems take on authority within our culture, which communities have more credibility within a public debate, and which images of birth, motherhood, and bodies direct our choices and actions. Whether they are using the theories of Foucault, Burke, Leff, Perelman and Olbrechts-Tyteca, or more generic forms of textual analysis, the contributors demonstrate the capacity of language to create meaning and direct social action. In doing so, they enable us to question that meaning and recapture voices and systems of knowledge that have been silenced within public discourse about women's bodies and the role of reproductive technologies.

Body Talk: The Language of Reproduction

By viewing reproductive technologies through the lens of their rhetorical features, the chapters reveal a variety of discussions and topics regarding bodies, reproduction, and technologies. The chapters herein are rich in their uses of primary source material (texts, interviews), and each has some resonance with all the others. Certain chapters dovetail quite naturally, and others provide a broader picture that enhances or recasts certain studies. Although the chapters resist somewhat the essential task of being categorized (and we invite the reader to find new themes), we nonetheless wish to speak to certain commonalities that seem important from our point of view.

First, several chapters address technology as a cultural force. This line of thinking proposes that society has used technology to confirm and support women's subordinate position, illustrating the ideological link between technology and masculinity. Such work debates whether society has used technologies to free women (e.g., from housework), whether new technologies have given more women choices (e.g., to become pregnant later in life and detect birth defects in the womb), whether society has used technologies to oppress women (e.g., work technologies have enabled employers to raise the standards for production so high that they cause repetitive stress injuries such as carpal tunnel syndrome), or whether society continues to use the ideology of technology to exclude women (e.g., telling girls in some subtle and not-so-subtle ways that they are not "as good" at math and computers as boys are). Visual and verbal messages reinforce or reflect the ideology of technology, its symbolic and social link to masculinity, and its application to the socially assigned place of women, including their reproductive roles. Moreover, as Wajcman says, "Nowhere is the relationship between gender and technology more vigorously contested than in the sphere of human biological reproduction" (1991:54). Thus our society wonders whether reproductive technology is neutral, a key to women's liberation or a reflection of patriarchal domination, an opportunity to form new identities and knowledge systems or an activity to negate identities and knowledges that do not fit into the norm.

With the arrival of the twenty-first century, reproductive technologies place additional pressure on families, women, physicians, and state officials to reconsider the place of human reproduction locally and globally. More and more we begin to realize that technologies are never neutral tools but are instead, as Snow comments, "chosen, designed, evaluated and promoted by select (and often different) political communities, and they manifest the values and interests of those communities" (1994:148). Wajcman confirms this social aspect of technology: "Technology is not simply the neutral product of rational technical imperatives; rather, it is the result of a series of specific decisions made by particular groups of people in particular places at particular times for their own purposes" (1994:154). Societies must ask who has access to reproductive technologies, how women and their physicians can use these technologies to promote health and human values, what potential for abuse these technologies bring, and how these technologies affect knowledge production and the distribution of power.

The history of reproductive technology contains significant examples of how the technologies created new categories of knowledge and new assignments of power. For example, the Chamberlen family of England created the first such reproductive technology, the forceps, in 1598 and promoted it as the best way to end prolonged labor and maternal and infant death. The Chamberlens owned this technology, and they allowed only men to use these tools, a boundary that some scholars believe marked the end of women's monopoly over birth. With the invention and use of the forceps, what was women's craft became a predominantly male profession. However, the forceps and other similar reproductive technologies became broader sites of contention. Female midwives believed that their craft, their herbs, and their sense of touch better administered to the pregnant and laboring woman and ensured her safety against the intrusion of what midwives considered brutal and unsafe devices. They fought against having their knowledge, procedures, and experience discounted in the birth room. In what became a clear division by gender, they argued for the value of women's knowledge and expertise. Thus the introduction of new reproductive technologies into a culture raises additional questions of access, power, and knowledge: whose knowledge and experience counts, who has access to the new technology, and who gains economic and political power by claiming expertise in the new technology?

In this book the work of Chloé Diepenbrock (chapter 4) extends our understanding of how technology constructs social norms about birth. She uses Burke's theory of the pentad to explore a new narrative form, the modern gynecological case history. She proposes that through repetition and, for some, almost daily reinforcement, stories of miracle babies cause infertile women to become "consumers" of technology. These stories provide a model for behavior, a "selective view of reality," as they relate fantastical and happy endings to women's pursuit of a healthy baby. The new mothers within the stories seem willing participants in experimental technologies and justify the cost and pain of giving birth to their biological offspring. Society portrays physicians as Merlin-like magicians who guide the woman with perseverance to motherhood through the use of reproductive technologies. As Diepenbrock notes, these mothers enter a modern version of the cult of true womanhood as they are "linguistically engineered" into a newly extended caste system.

Taking another angle, Mary Lay discusses how the legal language that defines traditional midwifery in the United States in the 1990s addresses midwives' attitudes toward and access to scientific and technological tools. In chapter 10 she analyzes the legal definitions of birth, safety, risk, and normality within legislative rules that govern midwifery. In meeting their charge to protect the health and well-being of citizens, states that have addressed the regulation of traditional midwifery practice must decide whether the midwives' experiential and embodied knowledge enables them to perform procedures such as emergency episiotomies and to administer such drugs as pitocin to control postpartum hemorrhages. At the same time, midwives must decide whether using such techniques fits into their ideology of practice, which includes a belief in the natural process of birth and a reliance on hands and herbs rather than intervention through technology. Questions about the place of technologies in the centuries-old practice of midwifery reveal whose voices count in normalizing birth within our culture.

Other chapters examine the concept of women's bodies as objects of scientific knowledge. These explore and apply Foucault's proposition (1990) that once a subject becomes a focus of discussion within a knowledge system, that subject takes on a certain legitimacy or truth. Technologies can enhance and even make possible such discussions—if we can see, measure, define, rank, and categorize a function or activity, we can more easily give that function or activity legitimacy and primacy. As an example, Bernice Hausman (1995) argues that the development of certain medical technologies made transsexualism as a subject of discussion possible. Moreover, these technologies made possible our contemporary definitions of gender. In deciding whether to use medical technologies to enable the intersexual person to become male or female, physicians had to rely on a person's "sense of self as sex"—his or her gender (7).

However, one result of being able to better define and see aspects of the body through technology is that bodies themselves may become mechanical objects of study. Donna Haraway (1990) has proposed, for example, that the boundaries between human flesh and technology have become blurred. Such devices as ultrasound imaging seem to merge our sense of our bodies with technology's image of our bodies— we have become cyborgs, combinations of machines and flesh. However, *cyborg* is a term that Haraway also uses to disrupt the male-female binary, and she sees that the body's becoming a cyborg is not necessarily a bad thing. Other scholars agree; for example, Jana Sawicki (1991) proposes that new reproductive technologies create new norms and goals to which women aspire but that these goals are not necessarily or uniformly bad for the individual or for the population. Other scholars express more discomfort with the effects of technology on cultural views of the body. For example, once social discourse removed the human body from the "purviews of religion and philosophy, as well as superstition and ignorance," Robbie Davis-Floyd cautions that to then "conceive of the body as a machine was to open it up to scientific investigation and get on with the research" (1992:49). In other words, the body becomes an object of study, subject to all the norms of scientific reasoning. Scholars of reproductive technologies then complicate the division of nature and culture and avoid asserting that women's experiential knowledge and the natural processes are always better for women, but such scholars also must document the results of negating that experiential knowledge and the advent of cultural respect and reliance on technologies of the body.

Chapter 1, by Jeanette Herrle-Fanning, marks the period in the history of midwifery when the female reproductive body became a legitimate object of medical and scientific knowledge, a key aspect of male practitioners' campaign to professionalize midwifery. Medical men had to overcome the culture of modesty they encountered when they first entered the birth room with their anatomical knowledge and new reproductive technologies. They had to argue that failure to intervene in difficult pregnancies would spell certain death, a proposition that women and their midwives were sometimes reluctant to accept. Herrle-Fanning relies on Foucault's definitions of bio-power to explore the metaphors that early physicians and male midwives used to mechanize the body and its functions and to support the anatomical knowledge systems of the growing profession of male midwives and medical practitioners. She contrasts two midwifery texts to mark the change from reliance on women's experiential and embodied knowledge to men's anatomical knowledge, their "hierarchization of detail, analysis of component parts, and development of an abstract, standardized model of Woman that encouraged the development of a mechanical metaphor of parturition." Sarah Stone's case histories, published in 1737, demonstrate a reliance on personal experience and experiential midwifery knowledge, whereas the 1797 Martha Mears text portrays the body as requiring professional medical management.

Similarly, Martha Verbrugge explores in chapter 3 the persuasive power of labeling menstruation as not only a pathology but also a defining feature of womanhood. Academia identifies the normal female body as a legitimate object of study but contests the range of normality. Verbrugge explores the debate about the definition of normal between physicians and female physical educators during the nineteenth and twentieth centuries and contrasts the two views of women's bodies. She marks a point at which the voices of female physical educators won authority in discussions about the place of recreation and exercise in women's lives. During the nineteenth century, most girls learned about menstruation from their mothers and other adult women, much as midwives and the female community controlled the seventeenth- and eighteenth-century birth room. However, between 1900 and 1940, gym teachers began to conceptualize menstruation in ways that enhanced their authority over the female body. To them menstruation was a natural phenomenon, but they embraced the more mechanical effect of menstruation, rather than the biological causes, in order to gain professional leverage to broaden the range of normal. In doing so, they countered medical intervention with sensible living.

In addition, chapters 6, 7, and 11 reveal how culture tends to define *woman* according to her reproductive abilities and to divide women's bodies into parts, functions, and processes. The discourse that identifies the female body as a legitimate object of scientific knowledge, scholars note, often defines the female body, indeed women's lives, according to reproductive functions and abilities. Moreover, the discourse tends to divide that body into distinct parts and, to a great extent, distinguish them from the activities of the mind. For example, Rosalind Petchesky and Karen Judd, in their international study of reproductive rights, note that women's "reproductive careers" were "lifelong and highly gender-specific" (1998:9). Therefore, women's childbearing and childrearing functions identified their lives. However, society also determined this identification, "as forms of social labour done for others and demanding considerable organization, energy and skill" (9).

Women have indeed demanded the development of reproductive technologies because of their desire to bear healthy children. In doing so, they have often been willing to become living laboratories, undergoing painful testing and invasion to extract unfertilized eggs and insert fertilized ones, for example, and their partners have masturbated to produce the sperm to fertilize those eggs, often supplying it in a small cup and with the help of pornographic materials in a physician's back room. However, ironically, women's demand for these reproductive technologies has in essence increased the cultural value of having one's own child, thus reaffirming the reproductive function of women. Moreover, because reproductive technologies can determine abnormalities in utero, women and their partners ask that the child be healthy. The assumption that birth is a safe and natural process has shifted to the assumption that the baby "may not be right—a doubt which, once sown, can only be satisfactorily removed by undergoing a series of tests" (Wajcman 1994:166). Finally, the woman who becomes pregnant while using fertility drugs may declare that the multiple fetuses she might bear are the result of both her physician's expertise and God's will—a characterization that assigns even greater authority to those who control reproductive technologies and greater identification of her body with its reproductive abilities. Physicians take on the role of experts who possess technical knowledge, while at the same time technology "plays a major role in consolidating the distancing of the doctor from a necessarily passive patient, leading to the dehumanization of health care" (Wajcman 1994:164–65). The two recent multiple births noted earlier illustrate well how faith and modern technology are often linked. However, the woman who fails to become pregnant through such means might consider herself less of a true woman and a failure as a person, rather than a person whom technology has failed.

In all historical and current discussions of human reproduction and reproductive technologies, women and their bodies become a central focus. After technology became part of the birth room and entered the private sphere, women seemed to become their bodies—or parts of their bodies such as the uterus, the ovaries, and the breasts. Those who wished to argue against women's entering the public sphere, the workplace, or even the athletic field proposed that such activities were inappropriate for people so controlled by their reproductive organs and that these activities would threaten those organs, causing them to atrophy or go wildly out of control. As Webb comments, "Women continue to be defined as appendages of their genital organs, with personalities which are inherently less active, ambitious, rational and intellectual than those of men" (1987:44). When women's feelings and experiences conflict with the advice of their physicians, powerful diagnostic and prescriptive technologies often trump these feelings and experiences.

Also, women can suffer alienation from their bodies, which Emily

Martin characterizes as, "a fragmentation of the unity of the person" (1992:19). A type of Cartesian mind-body dualism often accords men the functions of the mind and women the functions of the body. As Susan Bordo puts it, although our cultures have granted some groups subject status, others "have been denied those protections, becoming for all medical and legal purposes pure *res extensa*, bodies stripped of their animating, dignifying, and humanizing 'subject-ivity'" (1993:73). Bordo proposes that, rather than being invested with "personal meaning, history, and value," these bodies have become sites of "quantifiable processes that can be assessed objectively" (73–74). Thus Laura Shanner's chapter on infertility clinics (chapter 6) reveals how women within these settings become less than whole persons as they become their bodies, alienated from their minds, feelings, and personal histories. On a linguistic level, women therefore become associated with their bodies; infertile women feel like patient-as-failure, rather than as part of a couple that must confront a problem or challenge. Thus Shanner finds that although in-vitro fertilization is a therapy for male as well as female infertility, women assume the physical risks because their bodies are the sites for the technology. The medical establishment may attribute undesirable personality traits to women's body parts, such as the "incompetent cervix." This associates women with and objectifies their flawed bodies.

In her chapter on surgical sterilization Lyn Turney explains how doctors expect that after such procedures women will feel better, because they are free of the body parts that caused them discomfort and inconvenience. Turney explores in chapter 7 the capacity of language to create meaning and direct social action by contrasting the embodied knowledge of women after sterilization with the knowledge systems of the clinic. The vocabulary of the clinic understates the seriousness, permanency, and intrusiveness of surgical intervention and argues for the option of surgical contraception. Therefore, lost within the messages about these procedures are women's individual feelings and sensations. For example, women often feel sad because of the ways in which sterilization affects their sexual feelings. But the medical establishment dismisses women's own accounts as nonscientific, even as women complain that they were ill informed or had illusions about reversal of the procedures, failure rate, risk for ectopic pregnancies, physical discomfort, menstrual disturbance and pain, and decreased sexual enjoyment. Thus they feel alienated from their bodies while they receive messages that their reproductive parts are dispensable once childbearing is complete. At the same time, as Beverly Sauer describes in chapter 11, so-called fertile women, able to bear children, observe the societal emphasis on their bodies and reproductive functions. Sometimes this emphasis or marking takes on a political force, through public policy that is designed to protect women's reproductive capabilities but leave other populations at risk. Sauer uses the theories of rhetoricians Perelman and Olbrechts-Tyteca to illustrate how markings gave definition to the reproductive "value" of women's bodies. Thus Sauer sees both the female lobster and the female human as marked in the controversy about dioxin-polluted lobster consumption in Maine.

Several chapters also discuss the emerging definition of the fetus as a separate self and the pregnant woman as the environment in which that fetus grows or fails. As new reproductive technologies permit the pregnant woman, with the guidance of her physician, to see, monitor, measure, and even alter the baby growing within her, the fetus takes on a separate self. No longer seen as flesh growing from the flesh of the woman as part of her body, the fetus becomes an embodied person, identified first by the ultrasound imaging device rather than the quickening sensations perceived by the woman. As Barbara Rothman puts it, such technologies as ultrasound and amniocentesis, which permit prenatal diagnosis, selective abortion, and even in-utero corrective surgery, cast women as "untrusted, unskilled workers" whose task it is to transform a seed into a baby (1993:x). Thus the essence of the pregnant woman is "her biological, purely mechanical role in preserving the life of another" (Bordo 1993:78). The womb becomes an incubator or, if the woman makes what society and her physician consider unwise decisions (such as to smoke, drink excessively, or take certain drugs), a prison for the unborn child (85). Such technologies as ultrasound enable the physician to treat the fetus as a separate person whom they can treat directly despite its residence in the womb. However, as Bordo states, "the disturbing fact remains that increased empathy for the fetus has often gone hand in hand with the decreased respect for the autonomy of the mother" (1993:86; see also Oakley 1984:171). As Anne Balsamo has noted, "This leads some obstetricians to claim that the fetus is actually the *primary* obstetrics patient" (1996:90).

Eugenia Georges and Lisa Mitchell's chapter on the use of ultrasound and the printed material that defines motherhood within Canada and Greece demonstrates how women may be reduced to fetal environments. In chapter 8 Georges and Mitchell illuminate the metaphorical images of the fetus and the mother in two culturally distinct locations and demonstrate how these images, particularly ones interpreted through ultrasound fetal imaging, discipline women to become certain kinds of mothers. They find that to be considered modern and progressive, many Greek women seek the aid of reproductive technologies to determine the viability and identity of their fetuses. To be considered responsible future parents for the unborn child, many Canadian women seek the help of reproductive technologies to reduce risks, maintain self-control, and protect the vulnerable fetus. Thus, although motherhood is defined differently in Greece and Canada, the key to a successful pregnancy in both cultures is to learn more about the fetus, with the help of ultrasound and other prenatal diagnostic tools.

These messages about protecting the fetus from uninformed and perhaps irresponsible and unskilled women carry over into other areas. For example, Mary Thompson's analysis of the Maryland public debate about the dangers and benefits of silicone-gel breast implants shows how language may portray women as beings whose physiology controls their emotional state. In exploring in chapter 12 the rhetorical strategies used to defend these devices, Thompson discovers how the ideograph of free choice affected the hearings. Relying on the testimony of breast cancer survivors, those defending the safety and need for the devices linked their arguments to women's right to choose and the necessity to safeguard women's femininity. This argument proposes that women have the right and the need to have breasts so they still feel like women. Thus the image of the technologically gendered female body, with breasts enhanced with implants or replaced by implants after mastectomy, reinscribes women into what Thompson considers the hegemonically familiar role of being associated with the body. At the same time, breast implant technology denaturalizes that gendered body, and the body becomes cyborg (to use again Haraway's term).

Another set of themes is the growing identification of issues involving fertility and pregnancy as pathologies or diseases and the challenge of the increasing amount of information that women and couples must use to determine the viability of pregnancies. As the fetus takes on a separate identity—an embodied self that must be protected from the faulty functionings and decisions of the uninformed woman—the medical establishment once again depicts aspects of pregnancy and fertility as pathologies and diseases. It becomes the woman's duty to be fully informed about all possible risks to her child and to make emotionally difficult decisions to terminate her pregnancy if medicine cannot eliminate or manage these risks. Again, Herrle-Fanning traces in chapter 1 the transformation of pregnancy from a natural process aided by the experiential and embodied knowledge systems of midwives and mothers to the authoritative knowledge systems of a medical community that claims exclusive jurisdiction over scientific and technological development and discourse. With this transformation came what Davis-Floyd calls the "production of the 'perfect baby'"—

a result of the "combination of the technocratic emphasis on the baby-as-product with the new technologies available to access fetal quality" (1992:57). Again, as Georges and Mitchell found, in accepting this new technology and image of birth, women feel less vulnerable to the "caprices" of the natural process of birth and more like modern and progressive participants in their cultures (Davis-Floyd 1992:283). However, with these new technologies and knowledge systems comes the burden of making responsible decisions, a challenge for the physician and an emotional burden for the woman. As Rothman notes, when women contemplate what future problems a baby with an extremely damaging genetic makeup might have, "women anguish over these questions and then, virtually all, decide they cannot knowingly go through with it, deliberately bring a child into the world knowing what they know, however limited, about what the child will face" (1993:xii). The information women use to make these decisions may often be incomplete, the "bits, dribs and drabs of partial information genetic decoding" that assesses risk and probability (xii). Given the trauma that most women experience even after a so-called necessary abortion for a severely damaged fetus, Rothman says, "we are asking mothers to become the gatekeepers of life" (xii). Moreover, these mothers also rely on reproductive technologies to help them make these decisions.

In chapter 9 Elizabeth C. Britt argues that a Massachusetts statute that mandates insurance coverage for infertility is an example of a technology of bio-power that normalizes both fertility and infertility. Seeing the norm as a cultural argument, Britt argues that being identified as "abnormal" on a range of fertility is both comforting and stigmatizing: comforting in that established authorities are giving serious attention to this condition, which has previously been blamed on women's conscious or unconscious desire to avoid pregnancy; stigmatizing in that treatment (mostly in the form of assisted reproductive technology) seeks to create pregnancies but rarely "cures" the condition. The creation of norms gives individuals (particularly women, who receive most of the treatment) something to aspire to; middle-class American women are particularly likely to aspire to these norms because of their tendency to operate through the cultural logic that success comes through hard work. The creation of norms also serves to distinguish and perpetuate the distinction between the very poles it purports to eliminate. For this reason, we can see that the failure of infertility treatment to "cure" most of the condition, and the failure of many patients to even become pregnant, are part of the normalizing process, not oppositions to it.

The Human Genome Project represents this message as well, as Celeste Condit explains in chapter 5. If human bodies are flawed from the moment of conception and if the inadequacies of a fetus's own constitution cause illness, given the genetic model of medicine, the woman must be fully informed about the health and genetic makeup of her unborn child. Using the rhetorical analytical techniques inspired by Michael Leff, Condit first analyzes a speech by geneticist Paul Berg, then shares her observations of genetic counseling. She discusses how the genetic theory of medicine, with its assumptions that human bodies can be flawed from conception, is replacing the germ theory of medicine, with its assumptions that the body becomes ill only upon invasion by disease-causing factors. This ideological transformation to the genetic model has assigned women substantial responsibility for ensuring the health of their children through prenatal testing. However, Condit's observations of genetic counseling in various clinics suggest that the information and testing offered to women differ according to particular state and medical perceptions. For example, officials did not encourage women in detox clinics to undergo prenatal testing, Condit found. In contrast, major research hospitals encouraged women to use these tests, and they sought every tool possible to gather information and make decisions. Thus Condit proposes that women must not only make informed choices about genetic selection based on highly technical information, often difficult to understand, but also that medical authorities do not always present information uniformly and according to women's values.

Part of the problem with sorting through this information stems from the persuasive discourse that argues for a particular model or knowledge system or labels a reproductive function as pathological. For example, these discourse communities may use what Condit calls an "ultimate term" or a word linked to the constitutional commitments or ideographs of a community, such as life, liberty, and property. Or they may rely on myths or stories that illustrate the gains or losses resulting from accepting or rejecting their argument, and within these narratives, they may depict universal agents, acts, scenes, purposes, and methods to characterize their stories (Condit 1990:13). In chapter 2 Kathleen Dixon uses Condit's concept of the ideograph to illustrate how physician C. T. Javert relied on the ideograph of the optimization of human life to define miscarriage and to alert the medical community to its causes and consequences. By preventing miscarriage, Javert hoped to enable women to reach the "culmination" of their adult roles—motherhood. Dixon therefore explores the social construction of disease or the morbidization of recurrent miscarriage and how, through the metaphors of triage, Javert created a heightened sense of vulnerability and fetal peril to persuade others to accept his model of reproduction.

Finally, rhetorical analyses of gendered representations of reproduction and the body reveal how race, class, and ethnicity influence and are influenced by these discursive formations. For example, Deborah Grayson (1998) explores the discourse about racial identities and mothering identities in court cases dealing with surrogacy. In cases such as *Johnson v. Calvert,* a dispute about surrogacy and maternity, the "total ownership of the fetus depended on the condition of genetic ancestry" (Grayson 1998:531). Anna Johnson, an African American woman, bore a child from Mark and Crispina Calvert, of white and Filipina ancestry. After the relationship between the Calverts and Johnson broke down, Johnson sued for custody of baby Christopher. Grayson found that to make Johnson the legal and natural mother of Christopher, the court would have had to decide that the baby was black, or "to say that Johnson could be a mother to baby Christopher would be to indicate a willingness on the part of the courts and the public to relinquish or, at minimum, to blur, racial-familial boundaries" (545). Grayson found that the new reproductive technologies provide a vocabulary to "reaffirm the primacy of a closed, privatized, and homogenous family," an image that carries with it and reaffirms certain cultural assumptions about race, class, and ethnicity (546). Three chapters deal with issues of race, ethnicity, and class. Condit's (chapter 5) includes women in two types of clinical settings, one of which attends to women in a lower economic class who are given different choices and information about reproduction than are their middle-class counterparts. Georges and Mitchell (chapter 8) note the cultural differences in Greek and Canadian clinics and how these cultural differences influence attitudes toward ultrasound and other technologies. Diepenbrock (chapter 4) crosses ethnic boundaries to describe how women in the United States, England, and Australia regard the narratives about perfect babies and mothers that women's service magazines offer. These three chapters, along with very recent studies such as that by Grayson, suggest the work that must be done next as we consider cultural discursive formations of reproduction and the body. Race, socioeconomic status, and ethnicity will complicate our future studies of reproductive technologies.

Though these and many other overlapping concepts and themes create a variety of configurations for these essays, ultimately, we chose to arrange the chapters around what we felt was the most intuitive and accessible structure for readers, as it groups the essays into three general categories rather than several small and specialized ones. We begin with a historical perspective as Herrle-Fanning, Dixon, Verbrugge, and Diepenbrock explore attitudes toward women and reproduction over several decades and even centuries. Although some of these first chapters, such as Herrle-Fanning's and Verbrugge's, trace a transformation in attitudes about reproduction and technologies, we suspect that the reader will also become aware of how more contemporary arguments still cast women into roles created for them during these earlier times.

The chapters in part 2 address the major models of how we think about reproduction and how these models or perspectives inform such practices as prenatal testing, contraception, and infertility treatment. These practices, created or aided by reproductive technologies, seem to reinforce the societal messages that most women want very much to become pregnant but that many need help to become so, that women must be informed about the genetic makeup of their unborn children to decide whether to carry to term, and that, once the childbearing years are over, women's reproductive parts are easy to remove without consequence if they prove troublesome.

In part 3 the contributors offer case studies of specific issues involving reproduction and technologies. They demonstrate the discursive power of naming and defining such conditions as infertility, the persuasive strategies offered in debates about breast implants, and the ways of assessing risk in regard to women's reproductive abilities and choices. These essays recall how, even with increasing development and use of reproductive technologies, society still casts women into roles determined long ago. This final section reveals the gendered nature of legal and policy decisions related to women's reproduction and allows us to consider how we might promote change in public policies to make them more responsive to women's needs. As Sapiro notes, Americans base decisions about public policy and health on accepted scientific knowledge and standards, yet this canon ultimately derives from a system imbued with value judgments and assumptions on the part of the scientists—assumptions that are often based on gender biases (1985: 47–48). Society then uses such knowledge to construct standards that define and normalize female reproduction, resulting in policies and laws that reinscribe the traditional sex-gender system.

Throughout this book, then, contributors analyze the discourse of reproduction and technology, offer critical readings of what they find, and explore variations to the dominant discourse, variations that might imply new design decisions, alternative technologies, and changed public policies. We hope this book inspires women and their supporters to enter public debates about reproductive technologies in a more informed and empowered way and to challenge standard, authoritative readings on this subject. The *New York Times* editorial, cited at the beginning of this introduction, ends on this note: "Until scientists come up with a better way to limit multiple births, the only hope for improvement is the common sense of doctors and their patients. That can best be brought to bear in an atmosphere that recognizes that these events, however wondrous they may seem, are really medical mishaps that few doctors or patients desire" ("Too Much of a Good Thing": A26).

How to create such an atmosphere? The common sense called for here is actually, we would argue, a much needed cry for more critical explanations and readings of these high-tech reproductive events. We hope this book makes a contribution toward this very important end.

REFERENCES

Aristotle. 1991. *On rhetoric: A theory of civic discourse.* Translated by G. A. Kennedy. New York: Oxford University Press.

Balsamo, Anne. 1996. *Technologies of the gendered body: Reading cyborg women.* Durham, N.C.: Duke University Press.

Bordo, Susan. 1993. *Unbearable weight: Feminism, Western culture, and the body.* Berkeley: University of California Press.

Brock, B. L., R. L. Scott, and J. W. Chesebro. 1989. An introduction to rhetorical criticism. In B. L. Brock, R. L. Scott, and J. W. Chesebro, eds., *Methods of rhetorical criticism: A twentieth-century perspective,* pp. 10–22. Detroit: Wayne State University Press.

Brody, Jane E. 1999. Warning on drop in caesarean births: Four top specialists challenge government's goal, citing dangers. *New York Times,* January 1, p. A25.

Campbell, Karlyn Kohrs. 1989. The sound of women's voices. *Quarterly Journal of Speech* 75:212–58.

Cohn, Carol. 1996. Nuclear language and how we learned to pat the bomb. In Evelyn Fox Keller and Helen E. Longino, eds., *Feminism and science,* pp. 173–84. Oxford: Oxford University Press.

Condit, Celeste M. 1990. *Decoding abortion rhetoric: Communicating social change.* Urbana: University of Illinois Press.

Davis-Floyd, Robbie E. 1992. *Birth as an American rite of passage.* Berkeley: University of California Press.

Ede, Lisa, Cheryl Glenn, and Andrea Lunsford. 1995. Border crossings: Intersections of rhetoric and feminism. *Rhetorica: A Journal of the History of Rhetoric* 13:401–42.

Foucault, Michel. 1990. *The history of sexuality: An introduction.* Vol. 1. Translated by Robert Hurley. New York: Vintage.

Ginsburg, F. D., and Rayna Rapp. 1995. Introduction. In F. D. Ginsburg and Rayna Rapp, eds., *Conceiving the new world order,* pp. 1–17. Berkeley: University of California Press.

Grayson, Deborah. 1998. Mediating intimacy: Black surrogate mothers and the law. *Critical Inquiry* 24:525–46.

Halloran, S. Michael. 1984. The birth of molecular biology: An essay in the rhetorical criticism of scientific discourse. *Rhetoric Review* 3:70–83.

Haraway, Donna. 1990. A manifesto for cyborgs: Science, technology, and socialist feminism in the 1980s. In L. J. Nicholson, ed., *Feminism/postmodernism,* pp. 190–233. New York: Routledge.

Hausman, Bernice L. 1995. *Changing sex: Transsexualism, technology, and the idea of gender.* Durham, N.C.: Duke University Press.

Jarratt, Susan. *Re-reading the sophists: Classical rhetoric refigured.* Carbondale: Southern Illinois University Press.

Jones, Kathleen B. 1990. Citizenship in a woman-friendly polity. *Signs* 15:781–812.

Jordan, Brigitte. 1997. Authoritative knowledge and its construction. In Robbie E. Davis-Floyd and C. F. Sargent, eds., *Childbirth and authoritative knowledge: Cross-cultural perspectives,* pp. 55–79. Berkeley: University of California Press.

Keller, Evelyn Fox. 1985. *Reflections on gender and science.* New Haven, Conn.: Yale University Press.

Keller, Evelyn Fox. 1988. Feminist perspectives on science studies. *Barnard Occasional Papers on Women's Issues* 3:10–36.

Keller, Evelyn Fox. 1992. *Secrets of life/secrets of death: Essays on language, gender, and science.* New York: Routledge.

Latour, Bruno, and Steve Woolgar. 1986. *Laboratory life: The construction of scientific facts.* Princeton, N.J.: Princeton University Press.

Martin, Emily. 1992. *The woman in the body: A cultural analysis of reproduction.* Boston: Beacon.

Martin, Emily. 1996. The egg and the sperm: How science has constructed a romance based on stereotypical male-female roles. In Evelyn Fox Keller and Helen E. Longino, eds., *Feminism and science,* pp. 103–17. Oxford: Oxford University Press. Reprinted from *Signs* 16 (1991):485–501.

Oakley, Ann. 1984. *The captured womb: A history of the medical care of pregnant women.* Oxford: Basil Blackwell.

Petchesky, Rosalind P., and Karen Judd, eds. 1998. *Negotiating reproductive rights: Women's perspectives across countries and cultures.* London: Zed.

Rothman, Barbara K. 1993. *The tentative pregnancy: How amniocentesis changes the experience of motherhood.* New York: Norton.

Sapiro, Virginia. 1985. Biology and women's policy: A view from the social sciences. In Virginia Sapiro, ed., *Women, biology, and public policy,* pp. 41–64. Beverly Hills, Calif.: Sage.

Sawicki, Jana. 1991. *Disciplining Foucault: Feminism, power, and the body.* New York: Routledge.

Schiebinger, Londa. 1993. *Nature's body: Gender in the making of modern science.* Boston: Beacon.

Snow, R. C. 1994. Reproductive technologies: For whom, and to what end? In Gita Sen and R. C. Snow, eds., *Power and decision: The social control of reproduction,* pp. 145–51. Boston: Harvard Center for Population and Development Studies.

Too much of a good thing. 1998. *New York Times,* December 23, p. A26.

Treichler, Paula A. 1990. Feminism, medicine, and the meaning of childbirth. In Mary Jacobus, Evelyn Fox Keller, and Sally Shuttleworth, eds., *Body/ politics: Women and the discourses of science,* pp. 113–38. New York: Routledge.

Wajcman, Judy. 1991. *Feminism confronts technology.* University Park: Pennsylvania State University Press.

Wajcman, Judy. 1994. Delivered into men's hands? The social construction of reproductive technology. In Gita Sen and R. C. Snow, eds., *Power and decision: The social control of reproduction,* pp. 154–75. Boston: Harvard Center for Population and Development Studies.

Webb, C. A. 1987. Defining women and their health—The case of hysterectomy. In Jean Orr, ed., *Women's health in the community,* pp. 39–56. New York: Wiley.

Welch, Kathleen E. 1990. Electrifying classical rhetoric: Ancient media, modern technology, and contemporary composition. *Journal of Advanced Composition* 10:22–38.

PART ONE

HISTORICAL BASES

OF REPRODUCTIVE DISCOURSE

1

FIGURING THE

REPRODUCTIVE WOMAN

THE CONSTRUCTION

OF PROFESSIONAL IDENTITY

IN EIGHTEENTH-CENTURY

BRITISH MIDWIFERY TEXTS

JEANETTE HERRLE-FANNING

As is now well known, the eighteenth century marks a significant turning point in the history of British midwifery: the increasing presence of men in an occupation formerly dominated by women recasts what was a vaguely defined traditional craft as a nascent profession (Donnison 1977; Moscucci 1990; Cody 1993; Lord 1995; Wilson 1995). At this time the number of midwifery texts published in Britain increased significantly, and the predominantly oral transmission of midwifery knowledge between women was eclipsed by the burgeoning written discourse of male practitioners seeking to establish midwifery as a legitimate medical specialty. In this chapter I argue that the female body becomes a site for the production of professional identity by the practitioner-authors of midwifery publications. These authors represent the body and its reproductive functions in accordance with the particular kind of "knowledge" that they believe distinguishes them from rival practitioners. I will demonstrate how the construction of the female reproductive body as an object of medical and scientific knowledge was a key aspect of the male practitioners' campaign to professionalize midwifery and that it severely curtailed the discursive options for self-representation open to midwives. These efforts critically shaped the Anglo-American obstetrics of our own day, most notably in the discursive dichotomy that divides traditional midwives and the medical community and is reflected in their significantly different representations of childbirth, as Mary M. Lay's analysis in chapter 10 demonstrates. By referring to selected eighteenth-century midwifery texts, and in particular two publications written by female practitioners, I hope to shed light on the birth of what remains a very influential professional discourse.

The Body as an Object of Knowledge

In the 1771 volume of the English medical journal *Medical Observations and Inquiries,* John Lynn, a surgeon at Woodbridge in Suffolk, described the case of a pregnant woman suffering from the eventually fatal inability to urinate as a consequence of a retroverted uterus.[1] Of particular interest is the author's description of his efforts and those of another surgeon, first to obtain an accurate diagnosis and then to correct this disorder:

> From an imperfect idea and recollection of the case of an inverted uterus, communicated by Dr. *Hunter* to his pupils, at lecture on the twenty-first of *October* 1754, I suspected this to be of the same nature; and being very desirous of investigating the true cause, I was confirmed in my suspicion by passing a finger up the *vagina,* which was pushed towards the *ossa pubis* by a tumor (as big as a small child's head) lying behind the *vagina,* almost in the *perinaeo;* so likewise, it was found impossible to pass the finger any length up the *rectum,* the same tumor pressing strongly on that bowel. . . . Many efforts were made to reduce the *uterus,* by placing the woman on her knees and elbows, with her head downwards; and by introducing one hand up the *vagina,* attempting to draw it forwards, at the same time, with two fingers of the other hand *in ano,* we endeavoured to push up the *fundus uteri,* according to the method recommended and attempted by Dr. *Hunter,* and the surgeon who desired his advice. (1771:390–91)

We learn nothing of the patient's reaction to these procedures other than that she submitted to them. However, she did subsequently resist the surgeons' proposal to puncture her bladder, "determining rather to submit to fate" (392).

Although the surgeons made no incisions, it is impossible not to recognize that the manipulations so coolly described are acutely invasive procedures. The tension between this graphic description of bodily penetration and the underlying themes of the narrative—intellectual curiosity, the attempt to put theory into practice, the effort to redress what ultimately became a fatal disorder—prompts two important questions. First, why is the account of such a scenario tolerable in a medical journal, when it would most likely be classified as pornographic in any other context? In an age that placed such a high premium on female modesty, how could medical men legitimize the performance, let alone the representation, of such "indelicate" manual interventions? Second, why is the strategy of investigation and corrective action so compelling when, as the patient herself eventually makes clear, there always remains the choice of not knowing, of "submitting to fate"? The desire to survive is not of itself sufficient to account for this—subsequent details of the narrative indicate that the woman did not share the surgeon's certainty that the failure to intervene would result in death.

ANATOMY AND "OBJECTIVE" KNOWLEDGE

In Britain at the beginning of the eighteenth century, when midwifery was still emphatically the private business of women, what little midwifery literature existed bore the stigma of an ambiguous status because such works were seen to cater to lewd tastes, despite their avowals of didactic intent (Eccles 1977). Even after midcentury, critics of man-midwifery voiced their outrage at the indecency of such publications: "That man-midwives may think foolishly, and act wantonly, is no more than I can easily conceive, but that a man midwife should sit down and write, and publish a serious book, and give therein serious directions relative to the practice of midwifery, so contrary to reason, so void of judgment, and so alarming to modesty, is astonishing beyond expression!" (Thicknesse 1764: 5).

Remarkably, the fine points of man-midwifery came to have a place in polite knowledge, despite such objections. Everything from public exhibitions of wax anatomical figures to the *Encyclopaedia Britannica* unveiled the mysteries of the female reproductive body. In 1774 the same Dr. Hunter mentioned by Lynn, perhaps the most eminent midwifery practitioner and lecturer of his day, published a highly regarded obstetrical atlas that, as Ludmilla Jordanova remarked, "showed female genitals in unrelenting detail," its life-sized engravings revealing "to open view what was normally concealed" (1985:401).[2]

This contrast reflects the success with which men-midwives promoted the textual and visual representation of the female reproductive body as both permissible and necessary. If we return to Lynn's case history, we see how the rhetorical strategies these practitioners adopted allowed them to achieve this goal. The most notable characteristic of the passage is the distancing effect produced by the fragmentation of the patient's body into anatomical loci. This intense focus on Lynn's efforts to chart the topography of this woman's reproductive organs distracts from the image of a woman on all fours being probed by two men. Lisa Cody has suggested that male practitioners of obstetrics were especially motivated to represent the female body in a "socially decontextualized and desexualized way" in order to overcome suspicion of sexual impropriety (1993:263). The rational, "objective" vision of the body that they promoted functions within its own closed self-referential system of anatomical description, so that "ultimately, the most decontextualized of obstetric statements were tautological, for descriptions of the body and its processes always referred back to the body itself, by comparing one bone to another, stating that the color or smell of a certain muscle or specific fluid was like another bodily part" (Cody 1993:295).

TAKING CHARGE OF LIFE: BIO-POWER AND THE LOGIC OF INTERVENTION

The persuasive power of this objective, anatomical vision of the body lies in its promise of perfectability, of control. In his *History of Sexuality* the French philosopher Michel Foucault posed a question with regard to European attitudes toward sexuality from the seventeenth century onward that parallels some of my queries: in what is allegedly an age of sexual repression, why is there nonetheless "a steady proliferation of discourses concerned with sex" (1978:18)? In addressing this question, Foucault advanced the notion of "bio-power," a power that produces "truths" about the body, which, when internalized, have a "normalizing" and "regulatory" function (1978). For Foucault, the emergence of bio-power is a distinctive development of Western modernity: "For the first time in history, no doubt, biological existence was reflected in political existence; the fact of living was no longer an inaccessible substrate that only emerged from time to time, amid the randomness of death and its fatality; part of it passed into knowledge's field of control and power's sphere of intervention. . . . it was the taking charge of life, more than the threat of death, that gave power its access even to the body" (1978:143).

Thus as survival became less random, the conceptual possibility of "taking charge of life," of applying expertise to quotidian existence, opened a new space for the operation of power relations. If life can be made an object of knowledge and its mechanics laid bare, the possibilities for manipulation, intervention, and fine-tuning are endless. The ancient juridical power to take life, to rule by force, was now complemented by a power that cultivates life, prescribes how best to live by hypostatizing norms of existence: public health, public education, psychiatry, sexology, and all such endeavors are the manifestations of this new possibility to order and regulate life. The discourses that proliferate with such vigor in the new era of bio-power are those of experts and professionals who propose to make things better than before.

If both patient and practitioner have accepted an anatomical understanding of the body, simply "submitting to fate" is an almost unthinkable option: thus the irresistibility of the man-midwife's logic of manual or surgical intervention, despite the violation of sexual taboos and bodily boundaries that are invariably a feature of such procedures. However, in order to appreciate the novelty of this outlook, which is so close to our own, we need to look back at how cultural attitudes toward childbirth changed during the course of the eighteenth century.

From "Women's Secrets" to Public Knowledge

WOMEN'S SECRETS

In Britain at the beginning of the eighteenth century, the management of childbirth was social rather than medical in nature and entirely the business of women. This is not to say that expectant women did not anticipate complications; most would have known someone who had died in childbirth, and a number seem to have feared their approaching deliveries (Lewis 1986:74). Nonetheless, childbirth was viewed as a rite of passage that most women experienced, a time of trial requiring moral fortitude: we have some evidence that one office performed by the midwife was leading the woman and her friends in prayer (Otten 1993). As the author of the most recent and comprehensive study of childbirth in this period, Adrian Wilson, has demonstrated, the exclusively female, collective ritual of the "lying-in" had clearly defined procedures: the summoning of the woman's female friends, relatives, and neighbors; the creation of an enclosed and ritually demarcated space through the darkening of the room and the sealing of all apertures; the preparation of a special beverage, the caudle; and the postpartum month of confinement with its carefully graduated stages of bed rest, "upsitting," and so forth (Wilson 1995:25–30). This ritual structure, according to Wilson, "defined the horizons of both male knowledge and male ambitions in midwifery": medical knowledge of the anatomy and physiology of pregnancy and birth was sketchy at best, and medical men appeared in the bedchamber only as the last resort, performing the emergency extraction of dead infants in what was merely an unremarkable subset of surgical practice (1).

The nonprofessional status of such women's practices meant that childbirth was not identified with any single *group* of practitioners, and the office of midwife might be executed by any number of women, from an experienced friend or neighbor to the highly skilled, accomplished midwife whose training included a lengthy apprenticeship (Evenden 1993; Hess 1993). Although there is evidence that midwives were considered experts in women's matters (to the extent that physicians consulted them regarding women's and children's diseases and midwives functioned as expert witnesses in cases of illegitimacy, antenuptial fornication, rape, and infanticide), midwives did not enjoy an official corporate identity comparable to the male medical occupations of apothecary, surgeon, or physician (Harley 1993:35–39). All these circumstances point to the predominantly moral orientation of the lying-in ritual as an act of collective witnessing. Midwifery was of public concern only to the extent of its capacity to monitor (or subvert) moral concerns such as paternity, infanticide, and baptism. Thus the erratically enforced ecclesiastical licensing of midwives—contingent on character witnesses rather than a formal examination of skill—was more concerned with moral qualifications than technical competence as a practitioner (Harley 1993: 29–30). Although some midwives put forth proposals for more formal education and organization (Jane Sharp, Elizabeth Cellier), it seems that the most important credential a midwife could have was acceptance by the local community of women, whose informal referral networks brought midwives the bulk of their clientele (Evenden 1993; Hess 1993).

A NEW PROFESSIONAL IDENTITY

The rise of the man-midwife, beginning in the 1730s, marked a "revolution in obstetrics" in that it represented a profoundly different vision of midwifery practice, emphasizing an entirely different set of priorities. The men-midwives proposed a professional identity that was grounded in a technical expertise derived from a formal, anatomical knowledge of the body. The dramatic nature of this change was most clearly apparent in the marked increase in the number of midwifery publications after the publication of the forceps design in 1733 (Wilson 1995:6). Despite conflicting views among historians as to whether forceps represented the medical miracle that paved the men-midwives' path to the bedchamber, I think one can safely suggest that the publication of the forceps design promulgated the *conceptual possibility* that male practitioners could deliver infants alive, thus promoting the elevation of effective physical intervention as a criterion for competence in midwifery.[3]

Although undoubtedly part of the overall surge in medical and scientific publication at this time, this torrent of publications attested to the emergence of a new conception of midwifery and its practitioners. Midwives tended not to publish books; the small body of midwifery literature extant before the 1730s consisted, for the most part, of manuals that surgeons wrote to instruct midwives, or translations of Continental works. As Robert Erickson (1982) has demonstrated, the midwifery manuals of the seventeenth century were packed with agricultural imagery, reproductive lore, and quasi-magical "secrets" culled from ancient and modern "authorities." Their descriptions of the reproductive body and its functions are more analogical than analytical, and the interventions they recommend appeal to magic, custom, or experience, rather than reference to an anatomical conception of the body.

Such works were supplanted by lectures, syllabi, systematic textbooks, collected case histories, tables of anatomical plates, and research monographs: medical, scientific, and academic genres characterized by specialized terminology and concepts, reflecting the new model of midwifery expertise rooted in a medical knowledge of the female body and its reproductive functions. These works grew out of a newly formed institutional milieu, a network of private lecturing and hospital-based education that the men-midwives established in the larger urban centers to remedy the absence of midwifery from the traditional curricula of academic medicine. The application of anatomical thinking to the reproductive body facilitated these novel modes of education and publication. It permitted the hierarchization of detail, analysis of component parts, and development of an abstract, standardized model of Woman that encouraged the development of a mechanical metaphor of parturition. This new kind of midwifery literature was in part the result of the male practitioners' traditional focus on the resolution of abnormal or obstructed births, but it also reflected their need to join theory and practice, to create a *medical* literature in order to counter opposition from more traditional medical men who dismissed midwifery as mere "women's work."

WEDDING THEORY AND PRACTICE:
THE MECHANICAL METAPHOR

The shift from oral to textual transmission of mid-wifery knowledge had a significant impact on the manner in which the body and its processes were represented. Having forsaken the traditional mode of one-on-one apprenticeship in favor of the lecture series, male practitioners needed to find a way to communicate their expertise to a mass audience. William Smellie, the most influential of the London midwifery lecturers, was among the first to arrive at a satisfactory method. Having schematized his observations and subsequently reduced the extraction of a child to "the rules of moving bodies in different directions," he was delighted to find that he could convey to his pupils "a more distinct idea of this art in this mechanical light than in any other" (1752:251). Indeed, his proved to be the strategy for the representation of the body most amenable to the widespread dissemination of midwifery knowledge, because its introduction of anatomical and physiological "norms" harmonized theory and practice in a persuasive manner and provided compelling grounds for the claim to professional status. In the introductory lecture to his midwifery course, John Leake articulated this correlation for his pupils:

> Without a previous and distinct knowledge of all these, no one deserves the name of *Accoucheur;* for if he ventures to give advice or assistance which is not founded on rational theory and the established rules of his profession, he will act like a bungling mechanic, who attempts to repair a complex machine, without being acquainted with the several wheels and springs which compose it, or the principles upon which its motion depends. (1776:50)

Over the course of the eighteenth century the "norms" thus established eventually outgrew the mechanical metaphor and came to be identified as the truths of nature itself. As men-midwives' attendance at uncomplicated (i.e., nonemergency) births became more commonplace, and therefore the necessity to intervene less frequent, they placed an increasing emphasis on their supervisory capacity. Publications concerned largely with the dissemination of manual and surgical techniques gave way to a more theoretical kind of writing, offering a blueprint of normative reproductive processes. The latter stress the "naturalness" of pregnancy and birth but nonetheless depict "normal" childbirth as tentative, conditional on the supervising practitioner's capacity to protect the woman from the pathology incipient in her body. The realization of what should occur naturally thus depends on the practitioner's capacity to intervene when necessary, based on his theoretical knowledge of the natural course of events.

The novelty of the man- midwives' formulation of midwifery expertise is reflected not only in their schematic approach to the body but in its implicit claim that the transformation of this body into an object of medical and scientific knowledge had legitimate grounds in the *humanitarian* benefits it would provide. The analytic quality of the new types of midwifery writing aligns it with what Thomas Laqueur has identified as a new literary genre in the eighteenth century, "the humanitarian narrative" (1989:177). According to Laqueur, the accretion of vast quantities of detail renders the body intelligible in narrative modes such as the case history, the autopsy, the social inquiry, and the novel. In these narratives minute observation of the body reveals a history of specific causes and their effects, as well as the steps that might have been taken to prevent these outcomes. By exposing "the lineaments of causality and human agency," these narratives make apparent not only a specific logic of intervention but also the ethical obligation to take corrective action: "Ameliorative action is represented as possible, effective, and therefore morally imperative" (178).

The men-midwives often explicitly made the connection between the medical and moral imperative to improve the lot of pregnant women, underscoring the significance of their expertise for the population at large as well as the individual. At the opening of his *Lecture Introductory to the Theory and Practice of Midwifery,* Leake proclaimed: "The subject of this LECTURE relates to a branch of medical science, in which we are all interested; not only as men appointed to discharge the important duties of their profession, but also as members of society, who ought to look on the exercise of it as a relative obligation, tending to the preservation of that amiable part of the creation from whom we derive our being and our greatest happiness" (1776:1).

It appears that this scientifically grounded humanitarian rhetoric appealed to the literate and increasingly sentimental upper classes that provided men-midwives with the bulk of their paying clientele. Although it is difficult to account for the many factors that may have contributed to the men-midwives' success in colonizing midwifery as a male medical profession, some historians of the family have convincingly argued that aristocratic men, seeking to reconcile a desire for progeny with a newfound affectionate concern for the health of their wives, were attracted to the notion of expert medical supervision (Trumbach 1978; Lewis 1986). Wilson has suggested that the traditional lying-in ritual enshrined a notion of universal female suffering and subordination that effaced class differences in a way that increasingly made upper-class women uncomfortable (1995:185–92). If these classes did indeed come to reject more fatalistic attitudes toward reproduction, this may explain why the accusations that men-midwives violated female modesty fell on deaf ears.

It should be noted that by the end of the century men-midwives had managed substantially to redefine midwifery and become the accepted experts in "women's matters," *without* ever achieving anything close to a monopoly on practice (Loudon 1986:87). Therefore, I choose to illuminate these eighteenth-century developments by reference to the publications of two female midwives: Sarah Stone's *Complete Practice of Midwifery* (1737) and Martha Mears's *Pupil of Nature* (1797). A brief analysis of these two works and the differences that separate them will allow me to demonstrate the influence that the efforts of male practitioners to secure midwifery as a *professional* domain had on the manner in which midwives represented themselves and their work.

Sarah Stone

Sarah Stone's *Complete Practice of Midwifery* (1737) was published shortly after her move to the capital. Despite her new London address, she chose the forty case histories that comprise this work from her thirty-five-year practice in the towns and countryside of Somerset. Addressing her "Sisters of the Profession," Stone declared her intention to instruct them that "it may be in their power to deliver all manner of Births with more ease and safety, than has hitherto been practis'd by many of them, and without exposing the Lives of their Women and Children to every boyish Pretender" (1737:xiv). Perhaps the move to the more competitive London milieu prompted the publication of this work, an unusual strategy for a midwife, although it was an increasingly popular mode of self-advertisement for male practitioners. But Stone *was* an unusual practitioner. Her efforts to claim the traditional male domain of emergency calls for midwives, even as she criticized most of her female peers as superstitious and ignorant, inspired Wilson to characterize her as a practitioner who transcended the "female/male division" (1995:57). Another scholar has attempted to capture the paradoxical aspect of Stone's self-fashioning by dubbing her an "Enlightenment midwife" (Grundy 1995).

Stone used a humanitarian rhetoric in her work similar to that of the men-midwives. As Grundy (1995) has observed, each narrative turns on Stone's capacity as a troubleshooter. In all the cases recounted, she appears as a specialist in difficult labors who is called in when the primary midwife can do no more: she consistently represents her timely, well-considered interventions as changing the course of events, often dramatically bringing the laboring woman back from the brink of death. The terms by which Stone distinguished herself from other midwives—technical incompetence, attempts to cover up mistakes, failure to take action—are perhaps the clearest sign that she shared the humanitarian premise and interventionist logic of the new professional discourse that the male practitioners were promoting.

However, the professional identity she proposed is not necessarily that of a medical practitioner. Stone scorned the men-midwives' reliance on tools in obstructed labors, using instead the traditional midwife's technique of cervical manipulation in combination with a singularly effective manual maneuver, which, as Wilson has observed, duplicates the action of the vectis, an instrument that male practitioners commonly used (1995:59). In their details, the case histories also articulated a vision of midwifery as women's work, *outside* the realm of medicine. Stone set her narratives in the all-female world of the traditional lying-in ritual, and the only men who gained Stone's approbation were those "grave and sedate" practitioners who respected the boundary between medical and nonmedical practice by confining themselves to a consulting role in matters of physic (i.e., traditional scholastic, humoral medicine). She summarily dismissed the male practitioners' claims to superior practice on the basis of their greater anatomical knowledge for the same reason, asserting: "For dissecting the Dead, and being just and tender to the Living, are vastly different; for it must be supposed that there is a tender regard one Woman bears to another, and a natural Sympathy in those that have gone thro' the Pangs of Childbearing; which doubtless, occasion a compassion for those that labour under those circumstances, which no man can be a judge of" (1737:xiv–xv).

For Stone, judgment in matters of midwifery included recourse to an experiential knowledge to which no man was privy, whereas purely medical knowledge was largely superfluous to practice. Thus she declined to "fill any part of this book, with needless discourses on the Parts of Generation, nor the Reasons of Conception," asserting that "all the Disorders of Teeming Women do not belong to midwives; but they ought to commit themselves to the Care of a Physician; a Midwife's business being only to be well instructed in her Profession" (xix).

Stone characterized medical knowledge as largely irrelevant to the midwife's mastery of her art, because in her view competence in this business cannot be defined in terms of an abstract body of knowledge—it is organically tied to the midwife's personal experience, both as a woman and as a midwife. She emphasized the importance of compassion in midwifery practice and was uniquely sensitive to bodily boundaries: as Wilson has observed, she was the only writer to note the pain caused the woman by the internal use of the hand (1995:59). The substance of her argument against the medicalization of midwifery was that male practitioners had introduced a new set of standards that threatened not only the livelihood of midwives but also the lives of their patients: "These young Gentlemen-Professors put on a finish'd assurance, with pretence that their Knowledge exceeds any Woman's, because they have seen, or gone thro', a Course of Anatomy: and so, if the Mother, or the Child, or both die, as it often happens, then they die *Secundem Artem*, for a Man was there and the Woman-Midwife bears all the blame" (xi).

For Stone, the male practitioners' emphasis on academic credentials and theory abstracted midwifery, alienating knowledge from experience. Under this new standard, adherence to theory, whether he practiced *"Secundem Artem,"* was the measure of a practitioner's competence, not the result of his efforts. Stone indicated that she was not intrinsically opposed to theoretical knowledge but to the implications of an overdependence upon it:

> I have seen several Women open'd; and 'tis not improper for all of the Profession to see Dissections, and read Anatomy, as I have done. But had I inspected into them all my life, and not been instructed in Midwifery by my Mother, and Deputy to her full six years, it would have signified but little; nor should I have dared to have undertaken such a Profession, lest any Life should have been lost thro' my ignorance. (xv)

In "an Art where Life depends," results are paramount and only long experience can guarantee the skill that will result in an acceptable record of good outcomes (xvii).

Stone therefore intended her book as a bulwark against the changes wrought by the entrance of men into regular midwifery practice. This is apparent not only in its explicitly stated aims (to eliminate altogether the custom of calling in men-midwives) but also in its formal arrangement. The forty cases are presented in a roughly chronological order rather than grouped thematically (for example, by diagnosis or treatment). *A Complete Practice of Midwifery* provides no diagrams, and the anatomical references are so sparing as to render the bodies in this book fairly obscure. Stone offered only what was relevant to the description of her manual techniques, and her casual mixing of Latin medical terminology and popular expressions ("Share-bone," "After-burthen") underscored the practical, rather than theoretical, import of her descriptions. By refusing to frame her case histories with a theoretical apparatus or to abstract general principles from her individual narratives (and instead integrating instruction directly into them), Stone provided a unique alternative, rendering the traditional apprenticeship model of instruction in textual form. But because her expertise cannot be divorced from the context in which it originated, she transmitted her knowledge in the only way possible: by narrating her life's experience.

Martha Mears

Sixty years after the appearance of the *Complete Practice of Midwifery,* another London midwife published a significantly different work. If the event of childbirth was at the center of Stone's book, the hysterical female body, especially the uterus, was the subject of Martha Mears's *Pupil of Nature* (1797). This work depicted the pregnant woman as a cluster of symptoms to be managed, particularly with regard to her psychological state, for Mears subscribed to the common notion that "irritability" of the pregnant woman's uterus induced heightened "sensibility." The organization and broad scope of the text mirrored this representation of the body as a bundle of potential pathologies: it offered (according to the subtitle) "candid advice to the fair sex, on the subjects of pregnancy, childbirth, the diseases incident to both, the fatal effects of ignorance and quackery, and the most approved means of promoting the health, strength and beauty of their offspring." The ten essays that constitute Mears's book informed her readers about everything from the state of the womb before and after conception to the effect of music on the nerves.

The Pupil of Nature provided its genteel readership with an abstract, generalized account of pregnancy and childbirth that emphasized the "natural" safety of the process when it falls within accepted norms. Mears's constant injunctions to "follow nature" were consistent with the notions prevailing in the male midwifery literature contemporary with her own work: in both, bringing the volatile pregnant body into line with Nature, that is, with its "normal" functioning, was the essence of professional management. Therefore Mears depicted herself as a mere transcriber of a wisdom immanent in nature itself, declaring: "I have little more to do than to copy some pages from the volume of nature!—happy, if I could preserve the beautiful simplicity of the original!—happier still, if I could impress upon the minds of my fair countrywomen a few of its salutary maxims!" (1797:2).

In fact, Mears often transcribed—word for word at times—the work of Thomas Denman, the leading London man-midwife of the 1790s, especially of his *Introduction to the Practice of Midwifery* (1788). Indeed, it soon becomes apparent that in *The Pupil of Nature*, this particular "pupil" most often apprehended "Nature" through the eyes of distinguished man-midwives and the established medical authorities to whose works she had continual recourse:

> Let it not be supposed that, after having spent some years under the most eminent professors of midwifery, and devoted a great part of my time to the perusal of the best treatises on the subject, such as those of a HARVEY, a LEAKE, a SMELLIE, and a DENMAN, I am now ungratefully endeavouring to bring their doctrines and their practice into disrepute. On the contrary, I would with heartfelt rapture strain my feeble voice to swell the note of public praise which they have so justly deserved. (1797:3)

After further rhapsodic praise—"I know not which most to admire"—Mears noted that these learned men themselves taught her to feel "a still higher reverence" for nature's wisdom (3). This conflation of Nature's dictates and a textual, medical knowledge—rendered as "the dictates of enlightened practice" (28)—was also in keeping with the prevailing tendencies of midwifery writing at the end of the century.

In fact, *The Pupil of Nature* did not disseminate its author's observations on practice or innovations in technique; rather it digested the current medical consensus on these subjects. We learn virtually nothing about Martha Mears or her practice as a midwife from this work: she recounted no case histories and gave little personal information. Mears openly stated that the purpose of her "little book" was not to enlarge on topics "already discussed by others with clearness, precision, and ability" (128). Instead it was to provide sufficient information to educate pregnant women, in order to guard them against the ill effects of their own ignorance and that of others: in effect, it was an eighteenth-century version of the popular prenatal guide *What to Expect When You're Expecting* (Eisenberg, Murkoff, and Hathaway 1984).

The exclusively lay orientation of Mears's publication and the educational project it proposed presumed the notion of self-identified medical subjects. Let us return for a moment to the case of the woman suffering from the effects of uterine retroversion described at the beginning of this chapter. Details of the account indicate that she was a poor woman (symptoms began as she stooped to glean corn [Lynn 1771: 389]). Her willingness to undergo the invasive procedures that the surgeons deemed necessary may therefore have been in part an effect of the socially superior status of the practitioners. However, although the coercive power of class alone might have been sufficient to overcome the issues of modesty and bodily privacy among the poor in the charity hospitals, dispensaries, and so forth, the exercise of persuasive power was more necessary to convince the upper and middle classes that constituted the paying clientele; they needed to be *educated*, enough so as to allow them to recognize the superior expertise of scientific midwifery.

In choosing to write a popular work for a lay audience, Mears was addressing the literate classes, which were at the vanguard of the "revolution in obstetrics." These were also the clients whom traditional midwives had lost: the traditional lying-in ritual gave way first among the women of these classes, who shunned the midwife in preference for male expertise. Mears was writing at a time when a new variety of midwife had appeared in London and some of the other major urban centers—midwives trained in the lying-in hospitals and dispensaries that sprung up after midcentury (Wilson 1995:201–2). By writing the kind of book she did, Mears opened a space for the educated midwife, suggesting she could play the unique and important role of counselor or what we might call "childbirth educator."

Although an admirable attempt to turn the prevailing conditions to her advantage, Mears's strategy ultimately backfired. With its heavy reliance on the "the dictates of enlightened practice," her role as "counselor" had the effect of undermining her competence as a midwife. Mears's educational mandate justified the comprehensive scope of her book, and in its breadth it did resemble the male-authored systematic textbooks of this period. Yet it was bereft of the concrete technical information that would solidly establish her expertise as a practitioner. *The Pupil of Nature* deprived its midwife-author of much of her authority by constantly deferring to other texts in technical matters, such as at the end of the ninth essay, where Mears simply stated: "Midwives will find in Dr. Osborn's Essays the best instructions on this head. . . . In the very same valuable performance, and in other works before recommended, they will likewise meet with the most accurate information on every other point of duty" (128).

Throughout the book the midwife appears more as a proxy than an expert in her own right. With the exception of the passage recommending Osborne's works, the figure of the midwife as *practitioner* is virtually absent from this book. Not only did Mears never explicitly propose a collective professional identity for midwives but she never succeeded in representing herself as more than the conveyor of an authoritative, text-based knowledge that was located outside of herself.

Two Midwives

The substantial difference in the works of Stone and Mears reflects the enormous changes that occurred in the sixty years that separated these two publications. In 1737, Stone was writing at a unique historical moment. Because the medical, professional discourse of male midwifery practice was still in its earliest stages of development, her publication was not immediately marginal. Although Stone astutely identified the threat that the increasing encroachment of male practitioners represented, she clearly thought an internal reform of female midwifery to be still a viable option. She wrote looking back at a country practice, a context in which the midwife retained a good part of her traditional authority and monopoly. Although a humanitarian rhetoric is evident in the structure of her arguments, for the population at large, childbirth still fell within the category of "women's matters" rather than matters of public and expert concern.

By 1797, however, Mears was not in a good strategic position to speak authoritatively. By the end of the century, men-midwives had consolidated their professional discourse, and their writings exercised considerable influence over the conceptualization of midwifery as a topic and a profession. This is not to say that midwifery's status as a *professional* discipline was fundamentally secure—physicians continually contested it, and to some degree it remained in question until the midnineteenth century. However, midwifery had been definitively transformed from a women's craft into a public science; it had become the clinical analysis of a mass phenomenon, "the re-production of the human species" (Mears 1797:28). These conditions severely constrained Mears's options for self-definition as a midwifery professional: her sex no longer credited her with special authority in a world in which midwifery expertise had come to exist independent of the practitioner's lived experience, as an abstract and public body of knowledge.

The Pupil of Nature attempted to capitalize on this development: scientific midwifery's construction of the female reproductive body as an object of knowledge, a knowledge that can and should be made available to the literate public, opened up the possibility of midwife as "childbirth educator." Yet this attempt was inevitably compromised: such a figure always remains a dilettante, at best a tolerated subordinate, in relation to the male professional discourse. Thus Mears ultimately failed to construct a professional identity for midwives that could effectively counter the now dominant male model. For what the men-midwives secured by the end of the century was more a monopoly on authority than on practice: what changed was not so much who practiced but who defined the profession.

Perhaps one of the most provocative aspects of Foucault's formulation of bio-power is his insistence that this is a form of power that does not impose itself from without (as does a repressive force) but instead channels behavior through disciplinary institutions and the propagation of authoritative discourses, producing individuals who have internalized its logic and reproduce its norms of their own accord. In its medical manifestations, bio-power derives an enormous persuasive capacity from its suggestion that one might evade death, disease, and suffering if one cleaves to what has been defined as the "norm." The prevention, regulation, and correction of abnormality depend on careful surveillance for signs of incipient pathology, a task that requires increasing expertise as the definition of the pathological expands to include irregularities that are perceived as potential antecedents of more serious conditions. The proliferation of professional discourses publicizes the "facts" as determined by the experts, further encouraging individuals to internalize these norms, in their self-interest.

The management of childbirth in present-day North America is a familiar example of this phenomenon in its conflation of "safety" and staying within "established norms." The routine assumption that "anything that can go wrong, will," makes obstetrics a "'just-in-case' game," as Suzanne Arms put it, which turns "sloppy old nature into a clean, safe science" (1975:53). The compulsion to submit to the better judgment of professionals is particularly amplified in the case of pregnancy and childbirth, because the question of survival is magnified to include the fetus ("you wouldn't want to harm your baby") and, by implication, the species at large (the obligation to act *responsibly*). Thus modern obstetrics is an obvious manifestation of Foucault's observation that sexuality's situation "at the juncture of the 'body' and 'population'" makes it particular focus of social control (1978:147).

I am by no means denying that obstetrics has made real advances since the eighteenth century; however, given that the vast majority of pregnancies and births are normal, it is striking how few women go through the process without some form of medical intervention, some of which is of questionable value. Conditioned by prenatal testing, genetic counseling, childbirth education, pregnancy literature such as

What to Expect When You're Expecting, and so forth, to conceptualize their state in terms of "risks" and "percentages," many pregnant women embrace "routine" invasive procedures such as amniocentesis, internal fetal monitoring, and cesarean section as the means of avoiding deviation from the norm, whether such deviations are unequivocally indicative of danger or not. In fact, as Barbara Katz Rothman has demonstrated, many of these deviations—"false labor," or "precipitate deliveries"—are the artifacts of statistical projections or institutional routine (1992: 255–74).

I believe that the aspects of modern North American obstetrics I have just described have their roots in the professionalization of British midwifery during the eighteenth century. The men-midwives of that era, struggling to legitimize their intrusion into "women's secrets," developed a professional discourse that had a substantial impact on cultural attitudes toward childbirth. They were also pioneers in the effective exploitation of the persuasive power inherent in doing things by the book, that is, defining *and* disseminating the norms, so that they gained what Paula Treichler has called a monopoly of "linguistic capital" (1990:116). The compelling authority of the medical professions therefore relies on the identification of their prescriptions with "what everyone knows" to be the proper mode of proceeding. As Lay demonstrates in chapter 10, in our own day both state agencies and large sectors of the populace have so thoroughly embraced the medical model that traditional midwifery is continually defined in terms of how it differs from the medical "norm." Although today's traditional midwives, like the men-midwives of the eighteenth century, have the ear of those in the elite, literate classes that are discontented with the status quo and searching for an alternative, their voices are not so easily heard. Their writings do not simply fill a textual vacuum but must compete with an entrenched professional discourse that pervades both institutional and popular conceptions of childbirth.

NOTES

1. For Lynn and his contemporaries a "retroverted" or "inverted" uterus meant a condition in which the uterus, tipped backward and down, has become locked into the restricted space of the pelvic cavity. The difficulty may be spontaneously resolved if the expanding uterus rises up and out of the pelvis early in the pregnancy. However, if it remains trapped in the pelvic cavity without sufficient room to expand, it will press on the neck of the bladder, making the emptying of the bladder increasingly difficult. In the case Lynn

described, the bladder eventually ruptured, a spontaneous abortion occurred, and the woman died.

2. The expensive and lavish nature of Hunter's folio, which featured engravings, ink, and paper of the highest quality, indicate that it was not directed exclusively or even primarily at a medical audience. In fact, in 1751, at the outset of this undertaking, Hunter publicly exhibited the first ten plates and solicited subscriptions.

3. The notion that the invention of the forceps alone explained the rise of man-midwifery is conventional in the traditional histories of obstetrics, especially those written by physicians. Wilson (1995) has been the most prominent dissenter on this point, arguing that the rejection of the forceps by a substantial number of prominent men-midwives (often in favor of other instruments, such as the vectis) undermines this thesis.

REFERENCES

Arms, Suzanne. 1975. *Immaculate deception: A new look at women and childbirth in America.* Boston: Houghton Mifflin.
Cody, Lisa. 1993. The politics of body contact: Disciplines of reproduction in Britain, 1688–1834. Unpublished Ph.D. diss., University of California, Berkeley.
Denman, Thomas. 1788. *Introduction to the practice of midwifery.* London: T. Bensley for J. Johnson.
Donnison, Jean. 1977. *Midwives and medical men: A history of interprofessional rivalries and women's rights.* New York: Schocken.
Eccles, Audry. 1977. The early use of English for midwiferies, 1500–1700. *Neuphilologische Mitteilungen* 78:377–85.
Eisenberg, Arlene, Heidi Murkoff, and Sandee Hathaway. 1984. *What to expect when you're expecting.* New York: Workman.
Erickson, Robert A. 1982. "The books of generation": Some observations on the style of the British midwife books, 1671–1764. In P.-G. Boucé, ed., *Sexuality in eighteenth-century Britain,* pp. 74–94. Manchester, U.K.: Manchester University Press.
Evenden, Doreen. 1993. Mothers and their midwives in seventeenth-century London. In Hilary Marland, ed., *The art of midwifery: Early modern midwives in Europe,* pp. 9–26. London: Routledge.
Foucault, Michel. 1978. *The history of sexuality: An introduction.* Vol. 1. Translated by Robert Hurley. New York: Vintage.
Grundy, Isobel. 1995. Sarah Stone, Enlightenment midwife. In Christopher Fox, Roy Porter, and Robert Wokler, eds., *Inventing human science: Eighteenth-century domains,* pp. 128–41. Berkeley: University of California Press.
Harley, David. 1993. Provincial midwives in England: Lancashire and Cheshire, 1660–1760. In Hilary Marland, ed., *The art of midwifery: Early modern midwives in Europe,* pp. 27–48. London: Routledge.

Hess, A. G. 1993. Midwifery practice among the Quakers in southern rural England in the late seventeenth century. In Hilary Marland, ed., *The art of midwifery: Early modern midwives in Europe*, pp. 49–76. London: Routledge.

Jordanova, Ludmilla. 1985. Gender, generation, and science: William Hunter's obstetrical atlas. In Roy Porter and W. F. Bynum, eds., *William Hunter and the eighteenth-century medical world*, pp. 385–411. Cambridge, U.K.: Cambridge University Press.

Laqueur, Thomas. 1989. Bodies, details, and the humanitarian narrative. In Lynn Hunt, ed., *The new cultural history*, pp. 176–204. Berkeley: University of California Press.

Leake, John. 1776. *A lecture introductory to the theory and practice of midwifery . . .* London: R. Baldwin.

Lewis, Judith Schneid. 1986. *In the family way: Childbearing in the British aristocracy, 1760–1860*. New Brunswick, N.J.: Rutgers University Press.

Lord, Alexandra M. 1995. "To relieve distressed women": Teaching and establishing the scientific art of man-midwifery or gynecology in Edinburgh and London, 1720–1805. Unpublished Ph.D. diss., University of Wisconsin–Madison.

Loudon, Irvine. 1986. *Medical care and the general practitioner, 1750–1850*. Oxford, U.K.: Clarendon.

Lynn, John. 1771. The history of a fatal inversion of the uterus, and rupture of the bladder, in pregnancy, by Mr. John Lynn, surgeon at Woodbridge in Suffolk, communicated by William Hunter, M.D. F.R.S. *Medical Observations and Inquiries* 4:388-99.

Mears, Martha. 1797. *The pupil of nature; or, candid advice to the fair sex . . .* London: author.

Moscucci, Ornella. 1990. *The science of woman: Gynaecology and gender in England, 1800–1929*. Cambridge, U.K.: Cambridge University Press.

Otten, Charlotte F. 1993. Women's prayers in childbirth in sixteenth-century England. *Women and Language* 16:18–21.

Rothman, Barbara Katz. 1991. *In labor: Women and power in the birthplace*. 2d ed. New York: Norton.

Smellie, William. 1752. *A treatise on the theory and practice of midwifery*. London: D. Wilson.

Stone, Sarah. 1737. *A complete practice of midwifery; consisting of upwards of forty cases or observations in that valuable art . . .* London: Printed for T. Cooper.

Thicknesse, Philip. 1764. *Man-midwifery analysed: And the tendency of that practice detected and exposed*. London: R. Davis.

Treichler, Paula. 1990. Feminism, medicine, and the meaning of childbirth. In Mary Jacobus, Evelyn Fox Keller, and Sally Shuttleworth, eds., *Body/politics: Women and the discourse of science*, pp. 113–38. New York: Routledge.

Trumbach, Randolph. 1978. *The rise of the egalitarian family: Aristocratic kinship and domestic relations*. New York: Academic Press.

Wilson, Adrian. 1995. *The making of man-midwifery: Childbirth in England, 1660–1770*. Cambridge, Mass.: Harvard University Press.

2 MINDING THE UTERUS

C. T. JAVERT AND

PSYCHOSOMATIC ABORTION

KATHLEEN MARIE DIXON

Medicine plays an important role in both social and personal constructions of the body. It takes us beneath the surface, charting the largely unseen realms of our physical being as humans: constructing the skeleton, establishing experiments and models that are thought to test or govern the physiological mechanisms of muscle, organ, nerve, or cell. Medicine offers itself as a guide and interpreter of our spaces. Although this could simply express the enormous complexity of our physical and mental systems, it might also whisper of undercurrents of fearful alienation. These roles of medicine take on new importance when illness or disease estranges us from our bodies, when mechanisms and processes that are normally hidden propel themselves into view and forcibly occupy our attention.

The optimization of human reproduction has been a long-standing interest of medicine. Physicians have scrutinized the mechanisms of conception, gestation, and parturition. Medicine has painstakingly constructed norms and analyzed defects or deviances, weighing models that explored their significance. This chapter traces the rhetorical evolution of C. T. Javert's psychogenic theory of spontaneous abortion (Javert 1957). (All subsequent references to Javert are to this work.) The task of this chapter is not to offer a social history or panoramic display of medical constructions of miscarriage. Instead it provides a detailed blueprint of the rhetorical and scientific strategies by which an intriguing researcher problematized recurrent miscarriage and both challenged and extended physiological accounts of spontaneous abortion. In such a way readers may come to appreciate both the theoretical complexities of arguments for psychosomatic causation and their pragmatic limitations. This strategy also affords readers more intimate glimpses into the emergence of scientific discourse, revealing the intersections between the motivations and commitments of individual researchers and the emerging content of specific theories.

The first section of the chapter introduces the man and his work. Javert's distinctiveness lies in his subspecialization in the treatment of women experiencing recurrent miscarriage and his advocacy of psychosomatology. His professional commitment was to exhaustive research of miscarriage. By preventing miscarriage he facilitated delivery of women to the responsibilities and pleasures of motherhood, the vocation Javert saw as the culmination of their adult roles.

The second section of the chapter chronicles Javert's efforts to rouse medical professionals from their languid response to miscarriage, establishing the exigency of spontaneous abortion. This effort reveals Javert's deep appreciation of the rhetorical situation, his strategic use of arguments of incidence and mortality to contest medical disinterest. Javert builds rapport with his audience through his rhetorical incorporation of the ideographs of Life and Property. I critically assess these strategies as well as Javert's implicit use of metaphors of triage.

Establishing the exigence of spontaneous abortion allowed Javert to turn his attention to the next major stage in the development of his ideas. The chapter follows the evolution of Javert's rhetorical strategies and familiarizes scholars with his scientific presentation and defense of the concept of psychosomatic abortion. Javert prepares the ground through selective presentations of physiological arguments that create a heightened sense of decidual vulnerability and fetal peril. It is a less difficult argumentative task to provide an account of the psychosomatic derangement of systems that are, at best, precariously balanced. In this third section, I identify and discuss initial problems with Javert's clinical research that hamper access to psychosomatic accounts of miscarriage.

Javert's rhetorical strategies reach their maturity with his accounts of psychosomatic mechanisms of miscarriage. Final portions of the chapter offer detailed explanations and critiques of his causal models. Javert capitalizes on earlier characterizations of decidual vulnerability, articulating endocrinous arguments that connect emotions such as anxiety, anger, sexual arousal, fear, or stress with decidual hemorrhage, which causes miscarriage. The chapter closes with an analysis of the limitations of Javert's theory. I critically assess Javert's performance with respect to three tests that can be used to establish psychosomatic mechanisms of abortion. Finally, I show that one of Javert's own rhetorical devices offers a significant threat to the integrity of his theory.

Javert's psychosomatic model merits careful consideration and thorough analysis. It offers scholars an outstanding illustration of the social construction of disease in the morbidization of recurrent miscarriage. It can also be used to identify and evaluate discourse patterns of science. Javert displays a variety of scientific and rhetorical strategies in his effort to promulgate a new and challenging theory of spontaneous abortion. If we can appreciate the vulnerabilities of arguments that articulate psychosomatic origins of disease, we can reconsider the connections between our minds and bodies. Such appreciation also allows us to analyze more fully and warily our roles and responsibilities in our quest for health and well-being.

Javert and the Problem of Spontaneous Abortion

Carl Theodore Javert received his medical education at the University of Buffalo. He completed a five-year residency in obstetrics and gynecology under Dr. Henricus J. Stander at the New York Hospital (ix). Javert first became interested in the study of miscarriage in 1936 when he was charged with the care of a forty-one-year-old woman who had three spontaneous abortions. The results of standard examinations and tests were all normal. Rather than provide the antisyphilitic treatments that eminent clinicians advocated on the ground that occult syphilis was probably responsible for miscarriages, the young physician recommended a vitamin- and mineral-rich diet and provided reassurance and emotional support. When these efforts were rewarded with a term delivery, young Javert campaigned for the development of a special clinic to study and treat miscarriage. The clinic's first patient arrived in 1940 (338–39).

Following wartime service in the U.S. Army Air Force, Javert accepted a position at Cornell University as an assistant professor of obstetrics and gynecology. He worked under Dr. Marchetti, the obstetric and gynecological pathologist at the Woman's Clinic or Lying-In Hospital of New York Hospital. Javert succeeded his mentor in this role (ix). An active researcher, pedagogue, and clinician, Javert was ultimately appointed professor of clinical obstetrics and gynecology at the College of Physicians and Surgeons, Columbia University, and director of obstetrics and gynecology of the Woman's Hospital in New York (iv).

Medical colleagues recognized Javert as an intrepid advocate of an emerging discipline, psychosomatology, which proceeded from a new holism to explore what Helen Flanders Dunbar called "the physics of emotion" (1947:83). Javert's commitment to psychosomatology is visible in his detailed explorations of the effects of anxiety, anger, sexual arousal, fear, and stress on the physiology of pregnancy. His theories reverse ancient themes of hysteria, detailing the effect of mental states on the uterine decidua. Psychosomatology applied the techniques and theories of psychoanalysis to American medicine. It offered catharsis of or preventatives for affect or emotional conditioning thought to derange physical and mental functioning. Although the work of the early psychosomatologists is no longer well known, we can trace current strategies in philosophical psychoanalysis and medical interventions to their concepts and theories. Javert's contributions to psychosomatology involved the articulation of psychogenic causes of "habitual abortion." He defined habitual abortion as at least three consecutive, spontaneous abortions before the twenty-second week of gestation, with a fetus weighing 500 grams or less (3). A more conventional way to describe the problem associated with this inflammatory title is "recurrent miscarriage."

Javert published many detailed pathological studies of maternal and fetal causes and cofactors of abortion. His works on pregnancy and prothrombin concentration, nutrition, cord lesions, and decidual hemorrhage established his reputation as a medical researcher. His major work, *Spontaneous and Habitual Abortion* (1957), is an encyclopedic presentation of fetal and maternal causes of spontaneous abortion, a critical appraisal of other professionals' preventative measures, and a thorough presentation and defense of his own methods (3). It offers an outstanding illustration of social constructionism that emphasizes the interplay of sex and gender roles in the morbidization of recurrent miscarriage.

Javert's gambit in the psychosomatic assessment and treatment of spontaneous abortion was to establish the exigence of miscarriage. Rhetorician Lloyd Bitzer described exigence as "an imperfection marked by urgency" (Hauser 1986:36). Once spontaneous abortion was problematized, other strategies could be employed that would present and defend the scientific foundations of the psychosomatic model. Javert could then integrate psychosomatology with new and promising medical emphases on pathophysiology.[1] Javert positioned psychosomatology's speech on the failure or silence of traditional approaches. He contributed a characterization to the literature, constructing a psychosocial profile of the "habitual aborter" (Condit 1990:14). Establishment of this clinical type displayed the features physicians could use to identify problem patients and justify clinical intervention. Javert offered physicians a therapeutic regimen for a population whose experiences resisted incorporation in traditional disease models. No anatomic anomalies could be demonstrated. These patients appeared to be physiologically normal, yet they persistently aborted (vi). Javert's rhetorical strategies thus extended the compass of pathophysiological argumentation, expanding the frontiers of obstetrics and gynecology.

The Exigency of Spontaneous Abortion

Javert's professional work demonstrates remarkable sensitivity to the rhetorical situation. Bitzer's appraisal of the rhetorical situation emphasizes the power of discourse to prompt resolution of potential or actual exigence (Hauser 1986:33). Javert understood that the strength of his response to the problem of spontaneous abortion set him apart from his medical colleagues. He considered miscarriage the "country's foremost health problem" (5) and clearly recognized the sources of medical inattention to miscarriage. Spontaneous abortions, by medical definition, resulted in nonviable fetuses. Physicians often attributed these losses to fetal pathology (8, v). The prevalence of miscarriage was also relatively low. Between 8 and 10 percent of all pregnancies ended in spontaneous abortion (11, 204–5, 369). Finally, when appropriately managed, miscarriage did not produce significant morbidity and mortality among women (369).

Medical responses to threatened miscarriage regularly consisted of "hopeful expectancy and masterful inactivity" (256). Completed abortions often met with putative professional bolstering of the patient that linked miscarriage and fetal malformations. Doctors told women they should be relieved rather than disturbed by the miscarriage as nature had probably cast off a "defective ovofetus" (v). They sent women home with the encouragement to "try, try again." Javert was not satisfied with his personal commitment as a researcher and clinician to the minimization of "fetal wastage." His career could be viewed as the effort to translate what might otherwise have been seen as a personal obsession into a professional and public exigence.

Javert's presentation of the exigence of miscarriage starts with the inscription of *Spontaneous and Habitual Abortion:*

> This book is dedicated to the millions of men, women, and children who escaped the fate of an abortus in their first struggle for existence (in utero) and are now engaged in their second struggle for life (ex utero) which, even with the additional hazards of war, marriage, pregnancy, accident, and disease, is much less dangerous.

With this witticism Javert begins to resensitize physicians to the perils of pregnancy, focusing their attention on the problem of miscarriage. Javert builds his strategy with statements that present and reframe the incidence of spontaneous abortion. He indicates that between 1947 and 1954 physicians at the New York Hospital delivered 30,788 pregnancies. They saw 2,545 spontaneous abortions, an incidence of 8.3 percent (3203–4). Javert argues that because many do not seek medical assistance for spontaneous abortions, the gross percentage of women experiencing miscarriages each year would be approximately 10 percent. Given the number of pregnancies occurring in the United States each year, this incidence gave Javert a foundation to claim that the threats to life and health posed by miscarriage matched those associated with recognized "killers"—cancer and cardiovascular disease. He writes:

> Spontaneous abortion is not only the most frequent complication of pregnancy, but is also the country's foremost health problem. Approximately 4,000,000 pregnancies occurred in America in 1955 and about 400,000 of these ended in spontaneous abortion, or more than 1,000 per day. In addition, these abortuses were cheated out of a life expectancy of 60 to 70 years. While this loss is immeasurable, the estimated medical cost to society is $120,000,000 for 1 year's crop of miscarriages. What Texan in the cattle business would put up with such staggering losses? The high fetal loss due to abortion ranks it with cardiovascular conditions and cancer as the leading causes of death. These latter two annually kill about 400,000 and 200,000, respectively, in a total population of 160,000,000. Spontaneous abortion affects fully half the adult (female) population of child-bearing age, which makes it our greatest public health problem in terms of incidence. We are not as complacent about the thousands of old people with cancer and heart disease who are treated at great suffering and expense, only to add a few weeks or months to their lives, as we are to the abortion problem. Realistically, it would be more appropriate to turn in the old model for a new one. (Javert 1957:5–6)

Appreciating the rhetorical force that this passage would have held for his audience may be difficult today. Feminists might question this strategy's naked interest in the optimization of fetal life and criticize its willingness to identify human reproductivity with commercial productivity (Dixon 1990). We might also find its Malthusian appraisal of spontaneous abortion particularly direct and vulgar. Javert's notable elision of women and their bodies would open him to derision. Women are first suggested as the terrain from which the crop of abortuses emerge, and then women are inserted as ground to the clinical field of spontaneous abortion. Many readers would also resist his dichotomous thinking, which encourages intergenerational battles for resources.

However, this strategy challenged medicine's inattention to spontaneous abortion. Javert presents his exigence in terms familiar to the average physician: numeric comparisons of incidence and outcome. The dramatic morbidity and mortality rates to which he refers rivet attention, albeit by switching the focus from maternal to fetal effects. Although some of his statements strike us as outrageous, he persuades by following low-risk, widely accepted methods and cadences. This is the format of the "in-service" presentation, acquainting physicians with events and theories outside their purview or subspecialties.

Javert sustains this strategy throughout his book. He extends his arguments by comparing incidences, effects, and medical responses to miscarriage, immature delivery, and premature delivery.[2] In Javert's study immature deliveries represent 1.2 percent of the total number of deliveries and premature deliveries constitute 4.7 percent (3). Javert raises the issue of the appropriateness of resource allocations within obstetrics and gynecology. He argues:

> It can be readily seen . . . that next to a full-term labor and delivery, spontaneous abortion ranks next in importance. As such, abortion is the commonest complication of pregnancy. Premature viable infants, with an incidence of 5 per cent, properly receive a tremendous amount of consideration in public health programs and hospitals throughout the country. This effort to salvage these babies is discussed by Kramer. The infantile mortality rate due to prematurity is around 20 per cent and it is the most frequent cause of fetal death. The lowering of maternal mortality rates in recent years has led to a reduction of infantile mortality of full-term infants to 1 to 2 per cent. However, the abortion problem, with an incidence of 8 to 10 per cent and fetal wastage or loss of 100 per cent has not received proportional attention. (204–5)

Javert continues to raise the stakes of argumentation, directly challenging apathetic physicians. He charges them with failure to fulfill the central mission of medicine: "During the past two decades, many people, including a few doctors have said to the author: 'There are too many people in the world now. Why do you worry about a few abortions?' The answer should be perfectly obvious: doctors try to be of help to those who need it. This includes every pregnant woman, especially those having a history of miscarriage and sterility" (368). Javert subsequently mitigates this blow, reducing its likelihood of alienating his audience by explicitly linking studies of abortion with the more widely recognized goals of enhancement of understanding and prevention of prematurity (368).

Javert is obviously disturbed by the absence of professional and public response to the problem of spontaneous abortion. He contrasts well-organized and well-funded national groups for the prevention of infantile paralysis, cancer, cerebral palsy, and heart disease with the absence of similar programs for spontaneous abortion (368–69). Javert's persistent contrast of miscarriage, cancer, and cardiovascular disease as causes of death suggests the discourse of triage. This implicit sorting of casualties, prioritizing some for treatment and neglecting others, would have enormous rhetorical power for a generation of physicians steeped in the experiences of war.

Javert's use of incidence and triage to problematize spontaneous abortion and challenge existing social resource allocations results in horrific rhetorical strategies. He decries the absence of a "Society for the Prevention of Spontaneous Abortion" when Americans support other specialized organizations. "There is a society for the advancement of colored people, who constitute only a fraction of our national population" (369). Javert uses arguments of incidence to claim that the needs and welfare of fetuses have greater importance than those of persons of color. The interests of predominantly white *potential* persons trump those of stigmatized and oppressed *persons.* Javert expostulates, "There is . . . even a Society for the Prevention of Cruelty to Animals, a hold-over from . . . primitive animalism" (369). The message is clear: our allocation patterns and values require review if we can respond energetically to other diseases, to the needs of stigmatized minorities, and to care for the welfare of nonhuman animals yet continue to ignore the problem of spontaneous abortion.

Javert largely avoids discussions of race or ethnicity. However, he does say that a disproportionate percentage of unwed mothers are "Negro" women (310). Javert describes unwed mothers as psychologically stable and unconflicted because they have met their basic needs through conception and maintenance of the pregnancy, even though they are "out of step with society" (310–11). He contrasts these women with the immature or neurotic "habitual aborters" who reject their pregnancies, preferring the ideas of love or motherhood to their pragmatic demands. Javert also identifies "mixed marriages" as sources of conflict and tension that can precipitate abortion (323–24, 329–30). However, for Javert this term encompasses any kind of obvious socioeconomic variance between marital partners (329–30). Although he presents one case of habitual abortion in an "interracial" marriage, Javert does not explicitly comment on the social, cultural, or psychological dynamics of this case (331). However, his antagonistic response

to the husband of another habitual abortion patient and his framing of
that case presentation suggest anti-Semitism (324–25).

Javert also stuns contemporary audiences with his cattle metaphors
(5, 7, 368–69). Although the identification of humans and bovines may
have shocked and amused his medical audiences, the dominant ideograph they present is Property. Rhetorician Celeste Condit describes
the ideograph as one of three units of discourse central to persuasion.
She writes:

> The first unit is a kind of "ultimate term"—special words or
> phrases that express the public values that provide the "constitu-
> tional" commitments of a community. These words or phrases are
> called *ideographs, and in the United States they include Life,
> Liberty, and Property. Unless an act can be justified under such
> constitutive values, it may be allowed but it cannot be defended
> as a right nor can a public agency be forced to act on it. (Condit
> 1990:13)

Javert's cattle metaphors suggest and reinforce ancient legal views of
children as chattel. A year's crop of abortuses can be assigned a dollar
value. He prods physicians to more serious responses to spontaneous
abortion by unfavorably comparing their management or husbandry
of fetal resources. Javert asks how Texas ranchers would react to cor-
responding rates of miscarriage among their cattle. A colleague jok-
ingly brings the point home by responding: "They would get a new
bull" (368).

Javert also makes extensive use of the ideograph of Life.[3] He suggests that optimization of life, particularly numerically, is a constitutive
American value. Javert contrasts the willingness of ancient societies
to practice infanticide or induce abortion as means of population control with contemporary American interests in "salvaging all viable infants" (369). Another application of this ideograph makes explicit use
of Javert's psychosomatic doctrines. He identifies social apathy regarding spontaneous abortion with the pathology of habitual aborters, arguing it represents "a psychologic rejection of pregnancy on a national
scale" (369).

The Presentation and Defense
of Psychosomatic Abortion

Once he established the exigence of spontaneous abor-
tion, Javert was free to undertake the second major phase of his rhetorical strategy: the scientific presentation and defense of the concept of

psychosomatic abortion. He defined psychosomatic abortion as "the expulsion of a product of conception from a normal uterus in a somatically normal woman who has experienced recent intrinsic or extrinsic psychologic stimuli or both of a stressful nature" (200–201). He offers an account of his burgeoning interest in psychosomatic abortions that emphasizes his orthodoxy, establishing a fundamental doctrinal and professional union between himself and his audience.[4] Javert repeatedly presents himself as having become interested in the potential of psychosomatic theories only when standard anatomic or physiological accounts of miscarriages failed (319, 323, 338–39). He writes:

> To be sure, many abortions are the direct result of actual fetal or maternal pathology, the description of which was the original purpose of this book, yet 22 per cent of the specimens studied were perfectly "normal," as indicated in Table 16. Then, why did they abort? What caused the uterus to expel a normal product of conception? Therefore, it seemed only logical to investigate the psychopathologic situation, if any, in the parental relationship, in an effort to understand "psychosomatic abortion." (323)

Javert's voice is so sure and soothing that it's easy to overlook the limitations of the argument he offers. He states that these women were somatically normal and nevertheless aborted. However, to do so he temporarily suppresses recognition and use of an important theory of spontaneous abortion to which he devotes considerable time and attention in his book. Javert presents detailed physiological arguments that link key vitamin and mineral deficiencies to decidual hemorrhage—bleeding in the uterine decidua vera or basalis—which he believes is a principal factor responsible for abortion. Indeed, information and arguments about the importance of these nutrients to bleeding and clotting mechanisms constitute the bulk of his crucial chapter on the mechanisms of decidual hemorrhage (290–99). Furthermore, provision of substantial doses of vitamins C, P, and K and calcium played pivotal roles in Javert's clinical prevention programs (343).[5]

Javert argues that studies measuring blood plasma levels reveal a correlation between vitamin C and decidual hemorrhage. When maternal plasma showed a deficiency in vitamin C, 66 percent of spontaneous abortion specimens were positive for decidual hemorrhage. When plasma levels were adequate, researchers observed decidual hemorrhages in only 40 percent of the specimens (292–93). Vitamin K, an antihemorrhagic, is necessary for the manufacture of fibrin, the most important part of blood clots (Javert 1957:296; *Dorland's* 1974:586). Javert also drew on his clinical experience to note that pregnant women with low serum calcium levels suffered from irritable uteri (231).

Javert's theory of psychosomatic abortion rests on claims that if "somatically normal women" abort, physicians will be able to find psychological explanations and causes of the miscarriages. Unfortunately, Javert failed to obtain nutritional surveys or tests on the vast majority of his subjects (162, 223). He indicates that he collected nutritional data for only 461 patients, whereas he treated 2,545 patients for spontaneous abortion in the seven-year study period (3–4, 162). He states that "accurate dietary data was available on only 26" of his 104 habitual abortion patients (162). Half these women's diets were nutritionally deficient (162). Of the women experiencing spontaneous abortion who received nutritional evaluations, 35 percent had deficient diets (223). Thus the clinical foundations of Javert's psychosomatic model of abortion are threatened at two early points. First, Javert's own data could not establish the women's "somatic normality." This undermines both the definition of psychosomatic abortion and the warrant for a psychogenic theory. Second, among "habitual aborters," the group Javert uses to most strongly shape and justify his psychosomatic theory, the nutritional data collected suggest little need for a psychogenic mechanism to account for a substantial percentage of the "unexplained" abortions. Javert's own nutritional mechanisms might have explained these fetal losses.

His next step in the presentation and defense of psychosomatic abortion was to argue for the primacy of decidual hemorrhage as a cause of miscarriage. He would ultimately link women's mental and emotional states to systemic and uterine physiological changes that produced abortion by means of decidual hemorrhage. Javert drew on his histological studies of habitual abortion patients, arguing that "decidual hemorrhage was the most frequent maternal lesion. . . . This lesion is dismissed in most studies of abortion" (169). With the incidence of decidual hemorrhage confirmed, he could explore its physiological role and significance to miscarriage. Javert needed to establish decidual hemorrhage as a primary mechanism, as a crucial cause of abortion rather than a secondary effect or by-product of fetal demise. He also had to demonstrate that it was not an artifact associated with the curettage sometimes required to complete an inevitable abortion. He accomplished the first objective by comparing decidual histological studies of missed abortions with those characteristic of the late stages of normal pregnancy (293).[6] He also called on his clinical experience with women admitted for threatened abortion. Tissue expelled during the early phases shows "slight decidual hemorrhage"; later, as the abortion becomes inevitable, the samples passed are increasingly hemorrhagic (293). Javert met the second end by presenting histological data from his control group, women who underwent therapeutic or unintentional abortions. Although they were curetted, only 10 percent experienced decidual hemorrhage (293).

To the extent that Javert can paint a portrait of substantial physiological vulnerability of the uterine decidua, his effort to substantiate the psychosomatic model becomes easier. Disrupting systems in precarious balance does not require dramatic or extensive intervention. Psychogenic pathology thus becomes a more plausible approach. He begins this strategy by discussing normal uterine and placental physiology. Maternal and fetal circulatory exchange occurs when fetal trophoblasts bore openings in decidual blood vessels, particularly arteriovenous (AV) shunts, providing blood to the intervillous spaces (34–35). Uterine peristalsis, the rhythmic autonomic contraction and relaxation of the pregnant uterus, drives the exchange of fluids across these spaces. Uterine muscle relaxation gives arterial blood free passage through the system. Contraction of the uterine muscle cuts off arterial flow (33–35).

Javert uses the physiology of uterine tidal flow to create an image of the decidua as a danger zone, a physiological fault line. He writes, "The rhythmic contractions of the uterus on the one hand, and those of the placenta on the other, keep the decidua in a constant state of flux. It is a trigger area for something to happen, i.e., the decidual hemorrhage. Therefore, the decidua basalis becomes a target area for the prevention of this vascular accident" (270). Javert extends this sense of decidual vulnerability by discussing the effects of uterine growth during pregnancy. The enormous increase in uterine size stretches the decidua thin (23). Javert draws on Ramsey's experiments with rhesus monkeys to argue that although the coiled spiral arterioles of the decidua can unwrap and weather this physiological shock, decidual veins and venules, which are straighter, can readily be stretched to the breaking point (288). This would produce decidual hemorrhage, which could result in premature separation of the placenta and miscarriage.

Javert heightens the sense of peril through a dark rendition of the fetal effects of these mechanisms. He presents the fetal environment as harsh, unforgiving. "The fetus lives in a state of anoxemia" (37). That is to say, the fetus lives in an environment in which there is a "reduction of oxygen content of the blood below physiologic levels" (*Dorland's* 1974:101). The scarcity of oxygen results in a situation that Eastman called "Mount Everest in utero" (Javert 1957:37). Once Javert suggests the image of the fetal climber, he makes it clear that exacerbation of its exquisitely vulnerable position could precipitate a "fall." Natural uterine peristaltic contractions implicitly become sources of tension and dread as they "challenge" fetal oxygen supplies.

Through these efforts Javert has fashioned a rhetorical environment hospitable to psychogenic theories of abortion. Beginning with standard physiological accounts of pregnancy and expressions of clinical orthodoxy, he builds professional coherence. He presents a definition of psychosomatic abortion that minimizes conflict with dominant professional paradigms. He establishes the primacy of decidual hemorrhage as a cause of abortion. He then carefully and selectively marshals anatomical and physiological data to instill an image of impending decidual crisis. Thus mental states that alter uterine blood flow by producing or strengthening uterine contractions can more plausibly shake the delicate pregnancy, the precarious hold of the fetus to the uterus.

Psychosomatic Mechanisms of Abortion

Javert's definition of psychosomatic abortion explicitly conjoins "intrinsic or extrinsic psychologic stimuli" with fetal expulsion (200–201). Javert obviously required a means of accounting for this connection. He constructed extensive endocrinous arguments that established a detailed physiological chain with causal connections between each link. The process begins with such stimuli as anxiety, anger, sexual arousal or orgasm, fear, and stress, whether internally or externally induced. These stimuli bring about physical stress reactions, including hyperventilation. Hyperventilation compresses the adrenal glands "located beneath the diaphragm and above the kidney," which results in the release of adrenal secretions (268). Although the adrenal cortex and medulla produce a variety of important hormones, Javert is most interested in epinephrine and norepinephrine. He argues that these hormones stimulate and exacerbate uterine contractions, causing decidual hemorrhage and ultimately abortion (272).

Javert carefully explores the physiological effects of epinephrine, thoroughly presenting and discussing the experimental literature.[7] He needed to be precise in marshaling the data because "the effect of epinephrine on uterine muscle contractility has been somewhat controversial" (270). Javert begins his discussion with references to a variety of animal studies, including one conducted by Robertson in which epinephrine produced strong uterine contractions in cats (270). Javert then reports his own observations of increased contractions in human uterine muscle strips suspended in a muscle bath and exposed to epinephrine solutions. Javert also notes his clinical trial of sorts, in which he gave weak intravenous epinephrine solutions to two women at term who were not in labor and produced strong uterine contractions and tachycardia (270). He presents other human studies that document increased uterine contractility as a response to adrenal hormones. Javert moves to secure his psychosomatic hypothesis, by reporting that Robertson conducted experiments on twenty patients with secretory endometrium and measured increased uterine contractions when he applied emotional stimuli. Javert also presents a study by Alvarez and Caldeyro-Barcia on a pregnant patient. When they told her she required surgery, her uterus responded with strong contractions (269). Javert summarizes this data by writing:

> One can conclude from the above evidence that hormonal secretions of the pituitary, adrenal, or ovarian glands serve to augment normal peristaltic uterine contractions. Epinephrine and *l*-norepinephrine are oxytocic to the human pregnant uterus under certain circumstances. The amount of endogenous epinephrine is increased by fright and excitement. The stress-epinephrine-hysterasthenia gravis hypothesis is proposed as one of the causes of spontaneous abortion. (272)[8]

Javert attempts to strengthen his arguments by presenting the cases of his patients whose abortions were preceded by emotional shocks, familial tensions, and disputes. He also indicates that he developed a preconception survey that he uses on the marital pair. It consists of two hundred questions divided into twenty major categories. The questionnaire is an effort to detect unresolved marital conflicts. Javert is not particularly interested in detail, depth, or development of narrative but instead compiles a checklist of marital "hot spots" (320–21). He then attempts to resolve such conflicts before the couple undertake a subsequent conception. Javert argues that "psychological or social stressors" such as domineering mothers, weak or distant fathers, religious or financial conflicts, "mixed marriages," failure to accept adult gender roles, or daily stress could, through the mechanisms described, produce abortion. He offers physicians management strategies for these patients, describing the psychosomatic components of his own treatment regimen for habitual abortion.

Problems with Javert's Theory of Psychosomatic Abortion

Psychosomatic arguments turn on the notion of psychological or social stresses. Arguments that assign causal roles to stress in abortion succeed by meeting one of three important challenges. To pass the first test, they must establish an exclusive connection between their cohorts and stress. Javert attempts this by arguing that women who experience spontaneous abortion are those who experience marital stress or tension and ambivalence about their pregnancies.[9] He argues that unwed mothers, whom he claims seldom miscarry, experience no psychologic stress because they are fulfilling their basic biological and emotional needs. As the men who impregnated them abscond, Javert argues, these women don't experience marital tensions (310–11). Their predominantly social stress begins when their pregnancies "show." Javert believes pregnancies are hardier at this point and claims that marriages without miscarriages are free of marital tension. He presents the interview "score" of a "Mr. and Mrs. M., the successful parents of 5 normal children, and no abortions. They had no conflicts in the marriage relationship" (321).

These arguments are subject to ready counterexample. Javert's use of Mr. and Mrs. M. scarcely establishes the logical connections he requires. Similarly, he can't secure his arguments by demonstrating that many habitual abortion patients who miscarried under stress went on to term when stresses were resolved. One could rebut with a reminder of the fallacy post hoc, ergo propter hoc. Instead Javert would have to prove that marriages without abortions were uniformly or predominantly free of stress or unresolved conflict, a difficult undertaking at best. Javert's lack of familiarity with or failure to appreciate the complex and varied responses and stresses of single mothers also substantially weakens his arguments.

A second means of establishing psychosomatic arguments for abortion would require researchers to demonstrate comparatively greater stresses among women who spontaneously abort. Proponents of psychosomatology would then have to offer a physiological account of a threshold mechanism, explaining why women miscarry when they surpass a specific level or severity of stress and not before. Javert attempts a related strategy in his arguments linking sex, specifically female orgasm, with habitual abortion. However, his data largely consist of anecdotal reports and extensions of and correlations with Kinsey's studies. Javert recognizes the speculative and perhaps unwarranted nature of some of these connections (207–8, 220ff., 304–18). He does not offer a threshold mechanism.

A third evidentiary strategy would be to argue for a characteristic physiological response that demarcates the target population. This would probably be most successful if subjects were limited to "habitual aborters." However, this would also restrict the value of theories or clinical findings generated. Javert notes that the 104 habitual abortion patients represent only 5.2 percent of the patients enrolled in his study (160). He explains that this is a relatively rare medical condition, writing,

> On our obstetric service, primary habitual abortion has an inci-
> dence of 1:300 and the secondary type has an incidence of 1:493,
> according to Javert, Finn, and Stander. At this rate, the average
> busy doctor usually sees only 1 or 2 of these cases a year. If one
> considers the matter on a national basis, there were approximately
> 13,000 cases in the United States on the basis of 4,000,000 deliv-
> eries in 1954. (159–60)

Javert further undermines his study by observing that very different
therapeutic protocols produce virtually identical rates of success. He
remarks on this situation, saying, "This-and-that-method produces 80%
success" (355, 338–39). Although he states that effective methods are
linked by their provision of "tender loving care" to pregnant women,
he does not furnish documentary support of this claim. This statement
also seems inconsistent with a number of Javert's critiques of rival programs. Unfortunately for Javert, his therapeutic regimen achieved only
an 81 percent success rate. Thus one could argue that he has failed to
demonstrate any unique clinical efficacy of psychosomatic programs.

A final criticism could be brought against Javert's theories. Javert
undermines accounts that make physicians culpable for miscarriage on
the ground that their pelvic or speculum examinations precipitate abortions. Here he draws on his own clinical experience, writing,

> Those who have performed a therapeutic abortion are fully
> aware of the considerable degree of physical force required to
> dilate the cervix and remove the conceptus. . . . If physical activ-
> ity, external uterine trauma, pelvic examinations, and so-called
> "abortifacient" drugs, etc., could easily produce an abortion, the
> medical profession would use these simple methods to induce
> therapeutic abortion instead of the intrauterine trauma shown in
> these illustrations. (182)

This argument could readily be turned on Javert. If stress is a reliable
cause of abortion, why subject patients to the hazards of a surgical procedure or drugs when one could simply say, "Have two arguments and
see me in the morning." More poignantly, however, if stress could reli-
ably induce abortion, women would not have had to resort to knitting
needles. Nor would they have had to subject themselves to the dangers
of unsanitary or illegal abortions. Neither would those needing abortion today be forced to confront hostile crowds of protesters or risk being caught in escalating clinic violence. Their very life difficulties and
stresses would have achieved their abortions. These women could have
privately anticipated spontaneous terminations at home.

NOTES

1. Cassell argues that the pathophysiological approach to disease supplanted doctrines of specific causation and medical theories that emphasized the role of macro- or microscopic anatomic changes in the development of disease (1991:4–12).

2. Spontaneous abortion is defined "the termination of pregnancy before the 22d week of gestation resulting in a fetus weighing 500 gm or less" (Javert 1957:8). Javert identifies immature deliveries as those occurring between the gestational ages of twenty-two and thirty weeks, with fetal weight ranging from 500 to 1,500 grams. Premature deliveries are those that occur between thirty and thirty-six weeks with fetal weights of 1,501 to 2,500 grams (8–9).

3. For discussions of this ideograph and its use in abortion rhetoric see Condit (1990).

4. Cassell quotes and defends Coulter's view that "professional coherence is engendered by doctrinal coherence" (1991:6).

5. Although discussions of the properties of "vitamin P" were common in Javert's era, more recent references are to the bioflavonoids. Javert argues that vitamin P's functions are similar to those of vitamin C (295).

6. Javert defines missed abortions as "a fairly common type in which the ovum, embryo, or fetus has died, yet is retained in utero for a period of days, weeks, months, or even years. . . . As time passes, the uterus fails to increase in size" (198).

7. Javert had long-standing interests in epinephrine. In his youth, he was a subject in some of the early experiments to determine its effects on human beings (270).

8. *Oxytocic* means "pertaining to, characterized by or promoting" rapid labor (*Dorland's* 1974:1116–17). To say something is endogenous is to refer to internal processes, those "developing or originating within the organism, or arising from causes within the organism" (*Dorland's* 1974:517). Javert writes, "Hysterasthenia gravis may be defined as hypertonicity and increased irritability of the pregnant uterus. This term is used to describe the uterus of some of the repeated abortion patients during a pregnancy" (276–77).

9. Javert argues that these married women often exhibit conditioned reflexes (i.e., nausea and vomiting) to their husbands' presence in the home and that these are misunderstood as "morning sickness" and an inability to tolerate the scents and sights of evening food preparation (236-37).

REFERENCES

Cassell, Eric. 1991. *The nature of suffering and the goals of medicine.* New York: Oxford University Press.

Condit, Celeste Michelle. 1990. *Decoding abortion rhetoric: Communicating social change.* Urbana: University of Illinois Press.

Dixon, Kathleen Marie. 1990. A case of surrogate pregnancy. *Journal of Family Practice* 30:19–26.

Dorland's illustrated medical dictionary. 1974. 25th ed. Philadelphia: Saunders.

Dunbar, Helen Flanders. 1947. *Mind and body: Psychosomatic medicine.* New York: Random House.

Hauser, Gerard A. 1986. *Introduction to rhetorical theory.* New York: Harper and Row.

Javert, Carl Theodore. 1957. *Spontaneous and habitual abortion.* New York: McGraw-Hill.

3

GYM PERIODS AND

MONTHLY PERIODS

CONCEPTS OF MENSTRUATION IN

AMERICAN PHYSICAL EDUCATION

1900–1940

MARTHA H. VERBRUGGE

From antiquity to the present, the normative female body has been a contested matter. Which structures and processes are thought to define women's physical "nature"? Who marks the boundary between function and dysfunction, between "health" and "abnormality"? How female biology is constructed—and by whom—has direct social significance. As various scholars have argued, theories about female physicality constitute "technologies" of the body; they support "knowledges, practices, and strategies" through which women's physical lives are monitored and regulated (Cole 1993:87; see also Bartky 1988; Bordo 1989; Hall 1996:49–68; Theberge 1991).

One important technology of the female body involves theories and customs associated with menstruation. How does a particular culture perceive menstruation? Who defines the contours of "normal" cycles and "disordered" ones? How are women expected to "behave" during their cycles? Concepts and practices related to menstruation are powerful constructs. They affect medical services, employment policies, and the ways in which women understand and experience their own bodies. Whoever controls menstrual rhetoric and rituals, then, exerts considerable power, in both public and private settings.

In the United States, control over menstrual discourse changed hands during the nineteenth and twentieth centuries (Brumberg 1993;

Bullough and Voght 1973; Cayleff 1992; Farrell-Beck and Kidd 1996; Smith-Rosenberg 1973). As Brumberg (1993) has shown, most girls in nineteenth-century America learned about the monthly cycle from their mothers and other adult women. In the early twentieth century, although some instruction remained private—especially in working-class communities—other, more public authorities gained influence. Increasingly, doctors, scientists, and a burgeoning hygiene industry directed how American girls and women thought about, prepared for, and "managed" their periods.

The process by which medical and commercial interests became dominant, though, was not uncontested. Between 1900 and 1940 other professionals competed for authority over menstrual discourse and practices. Among the more influential but least studied challengers were women physical educators. In schools, colleges, YWCAs, summer camps, and other settings, gym teachers—by choice and sometimes by default—educated thousands of girls and women about their monthly cycles. Some instruction was direct; on occasion, for example, gym teachers were responsible for classes in hygiene. Menstrual education could also be informal; gym teachers conveyed lessons about menstruation whenever they excused girls from class during their periods or responded to complaints about cramps. As the twentieth century progressed, menstrual education in the gym reached a wider range of females, with respect to age, class, and race; public schools joined colleges in requiring physical education, and organizations such as the YWCA expanded their recreational programs for children and adults.

Physical educators thought carefully about the information and advice they should impart about menstrual health. Specifically, how did posture, clothing, exercise, diet, and mental outlook affect the ease or difficulty with which females negotiated their monthly cycles? For many teachers the most pressing question about menstruation was its compatibility with exercise. On the one hand, did physical activity disturb the female cycle? Conversely, did menstruation affect motor skills and performance? Since the early 1900s, the relationship between gym periods and monthly periods has been a pivotal issue for female physical educators in the United States.

This chapter examines the question of exercise and menstruation in women's physical education in the United States during the early decades of the twentieth century, when the profession's concern about the topic intensified. The first section analyzes teachers' ideas about exercise and menstruation. I argue that physical educators conceptualized menstruation in terms that enhanced their authority over the female body while undermining the claims of other experts. Gym teachers solidified their power by enacting curricular rules about students' physical activities during the monthly cycle. I trace those policies in the second section of the chapter. Overall, I demonstrate that women physical educators used the issue of exercise and menstruation to construct—in both discursive and practical terms—what they regarded as a "normal" female body, thereby strengthening their authority over women's physicality. The teachers' claim on menstruation, in fact, was part of their general campaign for professional influence during the early development of physical education in the United States. Between 1900 and 1940, female teachers sought control over virtually all matters related to the physical training of girls and women.

This chapter adds to a growing literature on the history of menstruation and exercise (Dosch 1991; Lenskyj 1986:17–53; Pfister 1990; Vertinsky 1990:39–87, 132–67). My study highlights physical educators (rather than doctors) and draws upon an extensive base of both published and archival sources. I have surveyed the professional and popular writings of women physical educators, including textbooks, journals, reports, and official sports manuals. I also conducted research in more than thirty archives affiliated with schools, colleges and universities, YWCAs, and professional organizations. My archival work in postsecondary institutions has been especially diverse, covering both private and public, coed and single-sex, and white and historically black schools. Despite that range of sources, the primary figures in this essay are white middle-class teachers in secondary schools and colleges; published works and manuscript collections of white women in other settings and those of minority physical educators in most institutions are limited in number and difficult to find. In addition, the chapter focuses on women who were classroom teachers or administrators, rather than researchers. Though important in their own right, science-based physical educators had perspectives and agendas that differed from those of instructors (Park 1995).

Menstruation and Exercise: Theories and Language

To understand teachers' ideas about menstruation in the early 1900s, one must first consider the general history of Western attitudes about female physiology. Since antiquity, many philosophers, scientists, and other observers regarded menstruation as a defining feature of womanhood and speculated about its purpose and cause. Although explanatory models changed significantly over time, scientific discourse (as well as popular culture) usually pathologized menstruation; according to most observers, the monthly cycle not only constituted womanhood but signified female inferiority as well (Delaney, Lupton, and Toth 1988:45–53).

In the fourth century B.C.E., for instance, Aristotle's analysis of reproduction deemed male physiology to be superior to female functions. Men, he argued, had sufficient internal heat to transform nutriment into blood and then blood into semen; as the purest and most useful state of matter, semen contributed the active principle during reproduction. In women, however, the conversion of nutriment was incomplete; limited by their cold, moist nature, females could produce only blood. Except for nourishing a fetus during pregnancy, such matter was quite superfluous; it collected in women's blood vessels and, once a month, was expelled. Aristotle's theory regarded women's supposed lack of heat as a defect and, by corollary, declared menses to be the "outward sign of female inferiority" (Delaney, Lupton, and Toth 1988:46; see also Cadden 1993:21–26; Tuana 1989:147–53).

In succeeding eras, Western philosophers both elaborated on and modified Aristotelian concepts. In the second century C.E., for example, Galen developed the plethora theory of menstruation (Cadden 1993: 30–37; Tuana 1989:153–56). As its name suggests, the plethora model focused on the extra matter that accumulated in women's bodies—because of their supposedly inactive lives—and the periodic release of the excess through menstruation. Although Galen reduced the sexual polarities that dominated Aristotelian thought, he perpetuated the idea that menstrual blood demonstrated women's arrested development. During the Middle Ages, women's monthly discharge carried theological as well as physical meaning. Medieval scholars believed that menstruation restored the body's equilibrium by purging excess blood while also marking women's fall from spiritual grace (Cadden 1993: 170–77).

From the sixteenth through the eighteenth century, discoveries about female anatomy and physiology prompted new theories of menstruation. In particular, studies of the ovaries focused attention on the probable relationship between ovulation and menstruation: Did the ovaries regulate processes in the womb and, if so, by what mechanism? In the second half of the nineteenth century, many scientists adopted a neurophysiological model that posited that "ovarian influence on the uterus was . . . mediated through the central nervous system" (Valdiserri 1983: 69). Such speculations added to nineteenth-century fascination with women's small yet powerful ovaries and strengthened the assumption that females were essentially reproductive beings who bore no resemblance to males (Laqueur 1990:175–81, 207–27).

With the discovery of ovarian secretions in the late 1800s, scientists investigated the role of hormones in controlling women's monthly cycle. During the early decades of the twentieth century, this biochemical explanation of menstruation became increasingly detailed and persuasive (Corner 1933; Gruhn and Kazer 1989; Novak 1930, 1931). The sophisticated concepts and data of biomedicine, however, did little to reduce age-old biases about female physiology. Using economic metaphors, doctors compared the complex turmoil of hormonal cycles in women to disruptions in control and information during industrial production (Martin 1987:36–67).

The development of neurophysiological and biochemical models of menstruation had direct significance for professions that dealt with female health. Gynecologists and other clinicians, for example, had to apply new modes of monitoring and "correcting" women's physical condition (Oudshoorn 1994:42–64, 82–107). Scientific trends in the early twentieth century also impelled personnel in schools, colleges, and other institutions to consider in new terms how biological development affected the mental progress and physical well-being of their female students. Increasingly, institutions relied on physical educators for knowledge and services related to female health and maturation. In the early 1900s, therefore, gym teachers' ideas about the female body gained further importance.

What views about female physiology, especially menstruation, did women physical educators advance? The following discussion summarizes teachers' ideas about the monthly cycle, its "normal" and "abnormal" states, and methods of maintaining or restoring "regularity." How did teachers conceptualize menstruation, and what factors informed their particular rhetoric about the monthly cycle?

Between 1900 and 1940, most white female physical educators described menstruation as a natural, not pathological process. As Katharine Wells of Wellesley College declared in 1939, "[T]he menstrual period is a normal physiological function in women. The term 'sick period' should be forever banished" (48). Such optimism was especially common among women who had trained in both physical education and medicine (Bell 1938b, 1942; McKinstry 1916–17:21–25). Helen McKinstry, for instance, a physical educator and doctor at the Pratt Institute, argued that healthy cycles should be relatively uneventful—as routine and inconspicuous as digestion (25). Even teachers who viewed female physicality in conservative terms agreed that, ordinarily, menstruation might inconvenience a girl but should not incapacitate her (Lee 1937:259).

But were all versions of the menstrual cycle "normal"? White female physical educators asserted that moderate variations—in the frequency of periods and in amount and duration of flow—were common, within a woman's own life and between different women. On the question of frequency, for example, Helen McKinstry stated that a girl "may be perfectly normal . . . who menstruates regularly as often as every 21 days or as infrequently as every five weeks. Regularity of appearance is the important factor, but even this may be disturbed without any cause for alarm. Change of climate, a great mental or nervous strain, a radical change in habits of living may cause marked irregularities in the perfectly normal, healthy woman" (1916–17:18).

Next, McKinstry asked, "is a long period and a profuse discharge to be considered normal or abnormal?" (20). Although "any marked deviation from [one's] customary condition at menstruation" might warrant medical attention, she concluded, there was no standard length or amount of flow; patterns varied widely, according to a person's general level of health, "individual and racial peculiarities," body size, and even hair color (20). For other teachers too, labels such as "normal" and "average" did not mean "uniform" but encompassed a wide range of phenomena (see, for example, Bell 1938b:2; 1942:187).

By contrast, many American doctors tended to narrow the meaning of normality. Clinicians in the early 1900s often categorized menstrual variations as "irregularities" that required medical diagnosis and correction (Engelmann 1900:986–88; Ehrenfest 1937:699–713, 1053–63). Although more moderate views did appear by the 1940s (Bartelmez 1937:29–31, 32–33; Meaker 1941), some doctors continued to problematize menstrual phenomena that physical educators regarded as natural variations.

This is not to suggest, however, that teachers considered every menstrual pattern to be normal. They expressed concern about delayed onset, excessive flow, irregular or absent periods, and vaginal discharges. Above all, they worried about two conditions: disorders that jeopardized fertility and childbirth, and dysmenorrhea (that is, painful menstruation).

Teachers frequently discussed the relationship between physical activity and reproductive health, from puberty through adulthood. Because females are "responsible for the future of the race in the bearing of children," teachers reasoned, exercise and sports should protect, even strengthen, women's generative system (Bell 1925:66). The teachers' emphasis on reproduction was hardly unusual. During the early twentieth century, many white middle-class professionals and reformers in the United States equated female health and reproductive fitness. Fearing that birth rates among recent immigrants were outpacing those of American citizens, many doctors, social workers, and educators defined female health in terms of fertility and proposed measures to preserve, even improve, the reproductive fitness of white middle-class women.

The source of teachers' preoccupation with dysmenorrhea is less apparent. Between 1900 and 1940, they wrote extensively—and with obvious concern—about the prevalence, causes, and management of painful periods.[1] In all likelihood, the teachers' accounts of dysmenorrhea were accurate. Given cultural assumptions about menstruation at the turn of the century (Brumberg 1993), painful periods probably were an expected and thus commonly reported occurrence among young white middle-class females—the very population that white physical educators usually encountered.

Teachers attributed both reproductive problems and dysmenorrhea to the structural mechanics of women's pelvic system. Because only a few overworked ligaments held the uterus in place, they argued, the organ was inherently unstable and thus ill equipped to carry heavy loads. It was especially vulnerable before and during the menstrual flow. As Margaret Bell explained, "The small, pear-shaped, freely movable uterus—slung in bands of ligaments—is topheavy and engorged with blood during menstruation" (1942:208). Bell's shift from lyrical images to more ominous ones dramatized the vulnerability of the uterus before and during the menses.[2] Once menstrual blood was discharged, the organ regained some degree of stability.

According to this mechanical model, both dysmenorrhea and reproductive problems stemmed from undue uterine stress. Poor posture, restrictive clothing, insufficient or ill-advised exercise, and other faulty habits, teachers explained, weakened a woman's abdominal muscles and ligaments, making uterine cramps and spasms—that is, painful periods—more likely (see, for example, Bell 1925). Similarly, excess pressure on the womb compromised its structural integrity; the ensuing displacement or collapse could endanger fertility and childbirth. Teachers singled out competitive sports as activities that were especially risky; collisions, falling, and other accidents, they argued, were particularly dangerous before and during the menstrual flow (Frymir 1930b:22; Lee 1937:68–69). Alice W. Frymir, for instance, warned about the hazards of track and field events: "Girls should not be allowed to compete during the menstrual period nor to participate in the practice of any of the jumping events, or hurdling, as the uterus during this period is slightly heavier, and the jar may cause too great a pull on the ligaments sustaining this organ" (1930b:22).

The teachers' mechanical model of the female body owed little to the emerging paradigms of biomedicine. Scientific researchers focused on the biological causes and purpose of menstruation, conducted studies in laboratories and clinics, and invoked the language and theories of modern biomedicine. By contrast, physical educators were interested in how menstruation affected women's daily lives; their information came from gyms, homes, and workplaces; they relied on classical, not modern, concepts of physiology. Snubbing biomedical hypotheses about menstruation, the teachers' views harked back to the ancient plethora model of cyclic congestion and elimination.

Why did physical educators adopt that particular perspective? Their focus on mechanical effects rather than biological causes was a strategic choice. Similarly, their preference for a classical description of menstruation was an advantageous, not random, decision. Teachers conceptualized menstruation in terms that afforded them professional leverage in women's lives while weakening the role of other experts.

Every theory of menstruation specifies how "regular" cycles can be maintained and "disordered" ones can be prevented or corrected. Biomedical models of the early 1900s legitimized biomedical intervention: analgesics to suppress pain, hormone injections to regulate cycles, surgery to reposition the uterus (Ehrenfest 1937:719–27; Frank 1932). By corollary, many doctors were suspicious of nonmedical explanations and treatments (Miller 1930:1801–3). Biomedical paradigms granted physicians the exclusive authority to manage women's monthly cycles and precluded (or at least diminished) contributions from other professions, including physical education.

By contrast, the plethora theory of menstruation favored the involvement of gym teachers. According to the plethora model, girls and women could maintain normal cycles and avoid disordered ones by reducing mechanical strain in the womb. Effective measures for controlling uterine pressure included proper dress, hygiene, diet, and exercise. But how much physical activity, and of what sort, was safe or harmful during the monthly cycle? And to whom might women turn for sound advice about the topic?

Physical educators insisted that their profession was best equipped to counsel women about exercise and menstruation. Or, at least, that other presumed experts were not prepared for the job. For example, scientists could provide useful data on the subject, but current research seemed incomplete and inconclusive to physical educators (Coops 1933:51–53; Frymir 1930a:26, 239–40; Halsey 1925:495; Somers 1930:

131–32; Wayman 1925:153–54). And, indeed, it was. My reading of scientific studies of exercise and menstruation conducted between 1900 and 1940, both American and foreign, also revealed a lack of consensus among researchers; every extravagant report of dysfunction due to exercise was countered by equally zealous arguments that activity during menstruation was safe, even beneficial.

Who else might adjudicate the question of exercise and menstruation? Female teachers considered, and dismissed, a number of other possibilities. Male physical educators, for example, seemed unqualified for two reasons: they could not understand the physical dynamics of womanhood, nor would girls feel comfortable discussing their periods with men. As one female teacher explained in 1935, "A man can never supervise the health of girls as a woman can. . . . [I]t is imperative to have a trained woman who understands the physiology of girls, their problems and troubles; a woman in whom the girls can confide" (Bateman 1935:23).[3] Nor could one trust male sports promoters, the men who coached girls and women in interscholastic, municipal, and industrial athletic leagues; they were quite willing to exploit female players, sacrificing their health in pursuit of victories and trophies (Bateman 1935; Smith 1927). Finally, female teachers considered the decisions that girls and women themselves made about exercise and menstruation. Some teachers evidently trusted their students' judgment (Bell 1945; Frymir 1930a:26–27; Richards 1920:408; Somers 1930:28, 118–19). Most, however, were skeptical about girls' choices of physical activity during menstruation. On the one hand, students who enjoyed exercise might conceal their periods and overexert themselves (Cummings 1922; Norris 1914:72; Norris 1924a:513). On the other hand, females who disliked exercise might use their menstrual periods (real or alleged) as a reason to be excused from physical activity. At Stanford University, for instance, teachers were suspicious of the unusual frequency of their students' periods; as noted in the minutes for a department meeting on October 26, 1939, staff members believed that students' custom of skipping gym class with claims of menstrual distress had become a "racket." Asserting that scientific information was ambiguous and the judgments of male teachers, sports promoters, and women themselves were untrustworthy, female physical educators claimed the issue of gym periods and monthly periods as their own.

In sum, teachers conceptualized female physiology in terms that favored their professional authority. Grounded in classical rather than modern images, their mechanical model of menstruation brought women's cycles—both normal and disordered—within the purview of physical education. In their own estimation, gym teachers seemed best situated to evaluate women's experiences and to assist them in maintaining or restoring menstrual health. The teachers' arguments thus afforded them rhetorical and literal ownership of menstrual health while diminishing the role of doctors and other experts.

Menstruation and Exercise: Policies and Practices

Having seized the discourse of exercise and menstruation, women physical educators implemented their ideas through practical measures. This section examines the curricular policies and practices that teachers developed between 1900 and 1940 to regulate students' physical activity during their cycles. What rules about exercise and menstruation did teachers formulate, and how did they enforce their guidelines? What prompted teachers to devise particular regulations and to modify them over time? I argue that physical educators used curricular policies to extend and solidify their professional authority over women's bodies and exercise.

To identify teachers' recommendations about exercise and menstruation, a logical starting place is their professional literature, such as books, articles, and other professional material. Between 1900 and 1940, the writings of both individual teachers and professional organizations outlined standards for physical activity during different phases of the monthly cycle.[4] Such publications reveal a clear, nearly uniform position. In general, teachers advised girls and women to continue their usual routines, including moderate exercise, throughout the month. One need not—in fact, one should not—become inactive during the menstrual flow; light exercise during menstruation, they said, was not only possible but therapeutic. Both research and experience had demonstrated, teachers explained, that exercise strengthened women's abdominal muscles; better muscle tone stabilized the uterus, thereby alleviating, even preventing, menstrual cramps.[5]

At the same time, most physical educators insisted that girls and women avoid—before and during their menstrual flow—any strenuous activity. Vigorous exercise, the argument ran, could displace, even dislodge, a female's already overburdened uterus. Teachers were especially adamant about the hazards of athletic training and competition; sports that involved jumping, kicking, or hurdling or that exposed girls to collisions and falls, they asserted, were particularly dangerous while the uterus was accumulating or expelling menstrual blood (see, for example, Burchenal 1916; Frymir 1930b:22; Lee 1937:68–69; Somers

1930:118–19). Some teachers, however, suspected that the womb's vulnerability had been exaggerated (Bell 1933b; Perrin 1924:658–59). As researchers at the University of Wisconsin pointed out, ordinary women had endured the rigors of work and motherhood throughout history without deteriorating (Hellebrandt 1940:37–40; Hellebrandt and Meyer 1939:19–20). Nevertheless, most teachers strongly disapproved of vigorous exercise during menstruation.

That injunction applied to all females, regardless of age or condition. As Mabel Cummings of Wellesley College stated in 1927, "[N]o girl, however well and husky, should take part in the most vigorous exercise during her menstrual period." Physical educators were especially concerned about the vulnerability of adolescents; as girls' bodies and monthly cycles developed, they observed, the likelihood of overexertion, menstrual difficulties, and other problems was greater, and the long-term risks were more dire. "[T]he danger of strain is greater than after maturity," one teacher noted in 1917, "and exhaustion should be guarded against [so] that the development of the generative organs may not be retarded" (Cochran 1917:7; see also Anderson 1922:66; Burchenal 1916; Clark 1923; Frymir 1930a:22–29; Patrick 1917; Spindler 1931; Stoneroad 1910). Another teacher conveyed the point metaphorically, using the mechanical imagery so common among physical educators. Mary Channing Coleman of the Woman's College in Greensboro, North Carolina, compared the bodies of young girls (and boys) to newly constructed bridges. "We do not allow heavy loads to pass [over a bridge] until the structure has settled," Coleman observed. Like the engineers of a new bridge, she continued, teachers, principals, and parents must judge carefully if and when a youngster's structure had stabilized enough to accept heavy loads (1930:108).[6] Once girls matured, teachers said, their reproductive systems could handle somewhat larger, though never excessive, burdens (see, for example, Wright 1910).

Overall, published guidelines about exercise and menstruation charted a middle course between what one prospective teacher called "excessive caution" and "reckless disregard" (Waterman 1925:139). Girls and women need not (and should not) be immobilized during menstruation, nor should they invite trouble through willful misbehavior.[7] During their own periods, in fact, most gym teachers continued their usual routines but eliminated intense activities (Kidwell and Simpson 1929:88–89; Stoner 1917–18). In theory and practice, then, the "sane middle position" seemed the most sensible one, if only because science had yet to render a verdict about exercise and menstruation (Perrin 1924:660). As we await better data, one teacher advised, "we can best err on the side of safety" (Halsey 1925:495).

This policy of prudence was a visible and consistent theme in teachers' writings during the early decades of the twentieth century. Published guidelines, however, reveal only teachers' recommendations, not their actual practices. A crucial question remains: What rules about exercise and menstruation did physical educators enforce in the gym?

Tracking menstrual policies at "ground level" is no easy task. First, relevant information appears primarily in archival documents. The historian must "excavate" diverse materials, including the records of physical education departments, personal correspondence and other manuscripts, and official institutional publications, such as student handbooks. Second, there is no guarantee that such documents will reveal the desired information. Many institutions may have developed informal policies about exercise and menstruation but not codified them. Others, perhaps, recorded their regulations, but extant archives do not contain them.[8]

During research in more than thirty archives around the country, I have uncovered relatively few institutions (secondary schools, colleges, or YWCAs) that recorded explicit policies about exercise and menstruation. My search has been most successful at colleges and universities where national leaders in women's physical education oversaw departments. Examples include Wellesley College, Smith College, Stanford University, and the state universities of Michigan, Minnesota, Wisconsin, and Nebraska. The discussion that follows is based primarily on policies at those (and similar) institutions.

In general, colleges and universities codified menstrual regulations for their instructional or "general service" programs, rather than for extracurricular activities (that is, intramural sports or, in rare cases, intercollegiate events). Although teachers regarded vigorous sports as especially risky, the logistics of regulating participation in such events may have seemed too hard. Thus, departments focused on gym class itself: Was attendance during menstruation excused, voluntary, or mandatory? If attendance was required, which activities should a girl undertake or "sit out"?

To some extent, rules and practices varied by institution. Schools did not develop identical regulations about attendance, required activities, makeup sessions for missed classes, and other matters. Still, most colleges and universities—whether private or public, coed or female only—followed the same general pattern. Between 1900 and 1940, most schools changed from a lenient policy (which allowed girls to skip class during some or all of their menstrual flow) to more stringent rules (which mandated some level of participation throughout the month). In the process, most departments also instituted disciplinary systems, through which teachers monitored students' physical status and activities, encouraged compliance with attendance regulations, and imposed penalties for violations. Between 1900 and 1940, such arrangements became increasingly intricate and punitive.[9]

Policies at Smith College offer a good case study. The progression of rules at Smith, a private predominantly white women's college in New England, is representative of trends at other colleges and universities from the early 1900s to World War II. Moreover, the archival record of Smith's policies is especially detailed and complete.[10]

In the early twentieth century, regulations at Smith reflected traditional concerns about exercise during menstruation. From 1910 to 1915, the physical education department excused students from gym class during their periods; a girl could take as many menstrual days as she "conscientiously need[ed]" (Smith College, *Regulations* ca. 1913/14) and was not required to make up the work she had missed. Ordinarily, then, menstrual absences were automatic and "free." Students, however, could not disappear at will; they had to notify the department using the "excuse box" and, upon returning to class, had to explain their absence to the instructor (Smith College, *Regulations* ca. 1912/13, 1915). Moreover, unexplained or excessive absences led to serious penalties. Physical education was required of all first- and second-year students; because exercise classes were "regarded as academic requirements," the department warned, the college's usual reprimands for attendance violations applied, and penalties incurred for unexplained or excessive absences had to be removed promptly through appropriate makeup work (Smith College, *Regulations* ca. 1912/13). In egregious cases, delinquent girls could be banned from playing on intramural teams or from holding office in the students' athletic club; that was stiff punishment, given the school's spirited culture of sports in the early twentieth century (Smith College, *Regulations* ca. 1912/13, ca. 1913/14, 1915).

Between 1915 and 1920, Smith still required physical education of first- and second-year students, and penalties for poor attendance remained in effect. In two respects, though, regulations stiffened. First, menstrual excuses could not exceed three a month. Although the department had always discouraged excessive menstrual absences, it now specified a limit and directed girls who exceeded it to see their instructor, whose discretion about disciplining students had grown (Smith College, *Regulations* 1916, 1918). Second, girls were now required to make up work missed during regular (not just excessive) menstrual absences; otherwise, the department imposed a penalty (Smith College, *Regulations* 1916, 1918, 1920).

Overall, Smith's menstrual policies between 1910 and 1920 construed both women's bodies and behavior as problematic. By excusing girls from gym class during their periods, the department depicted menstruation as a perilous condition. At the same time, menstruation did not relieve students of personal responsibility. Strict rules about absences, notification, and makeup work imposed standards of discipline and accountability on the girls. In short, from 1910 to 1920, Smith College treated menstruation as a physical liability but not an ethical free ride.

Between 1920 and 1940, both attendance regulations and disciplinary systems changed considerably. In 1921 the department began requiring attendance in gym class throughout the month. At first, menstruating girls took "special supervised work" (probably light exercise). By 1927, students reported for regular class activities; as the department manual stated tersely, "work will be continued as usual" during menstruation (Smith College, *Department* 1927/28).

The change from automatic or approved menstrual excuses to required attendance reflected teachers' efforts to "naturalize" female physiology. In the view of staff members at Smith and other schools, the permissive policies of the early 1900s sent the wrong message; if one allowed, even required, girls to skip gym class during their periods, one reinforced popular myths about menstruation as a disabling, even pathological, event. By contrast, a policy of mandatory attendance construed menstruation as a fairly routine process, during which moderate activity was possible, safe, and beneficial. During the 1920s and 1930s, then, attendance rules coincided with (and enforced) teachers' conviction that menstruation was a normal phenomenon.

The transition to required attendance was rarely fast or smooth. At some institutions, physical education departments favored mandatory attendance but lacked sufficient staff or facilities to handle the growth in student participation that such a policy entailed (Norris 1924b). In addition, administrators, staff physicians, and parents often objected when departments moved to require class attendance during menstruation (Cummings 1924; Lee 1924; Trilling 1924). Such groups wondered whether physical exertion was safe and appropriate for girls during their periods.

To some extent, physical educators shared those apprehensions. Between 1920 and 1940, staff members at Smith, for example, allowed several exceptions to mandatory attendance. The college physician could grant special excuses to girls with serious menstrual disorders. Moreover, certain activities were off-limits to all Smith students during their periods. Between 1931 and 1936, menstruating girls were not permitted to ride horses but simply observed equitation class in their street clothes (Smith College, *Bulletin* 1931/32–September 1936). From 1932 to the early 1970s, students were not allowed to swim during their periods (Smith College, *Bulletin* 1932/33–1965/66).[11]

The injunction against riding reflected teachers' concerns about the mechanical instability of the uterus. The policy about swimming revealed a deep-seated belief that menstruation was unsanitary. Although many physical educators argued that menstrual blood was not impure, they usually advised girls not to swim during the menses. That admonition lasted—at Smith and elsewhere—long after tampons became commercially available following World War II.[12] Teachers also encouraged girls to bathe frequently in order to control the extra perspiration and odors that accompanied menstruation (Bell 1938b:5–6; 1942:187, 208). By restricting vigorous activity, riding, and swimming during menstruation, teachers at Smith stigmatized the monthly cycle.

Between 1920 and 1940, then, staff members at Smith (and other schools) regarded menstruation as a process that was both routine and encumbered, both natural and problematic. They designed attendance rules that expressed and enforced this perspective on female physiology. In short, menstrual policies were discursive strategies that articulated and advanced the teachers' views about women's bodies.

Menstrual regulations also served as disciplinary strategies (Zieff 1996:124). Rules about attendance, absences, and makeup work delineated correct behavior; departments monitored students' compliance and penalized delinquency. Although physical educators never allowed students much latitude, enforcement measures became increasingly complex and intrusive between 1920 and 1940.

Developments at Smith College illustrate the toughening of disciplinary systems during the interwar years (Smith College, *Bulletin* 1931/32, 1939/40). For example, the department's administrative scheme—whereby menstrual (and other) excuses were requested, approved, verified, and recorded—became increasingly elaborate. Given such arrangements, only the most pain-ridden (or determined) girls probably sought a menstrual excuse. Even if attained, a menstrual excuse was not "cost free." Menstrual absences were probably subject to the department's general rules for "excused absences," that is, ones granted by the college physician for medical reasons. Through the mid-1920s, girls with medically approved excuses had to complete the work they had missed; during the late 1920s and 1930s, however, they were exempt from makeup work. Finally, the department warned students that unexcused absences (and even excused absences when too numerous) would adversely affect their grades and might constitute grounds for an "Incomplete" or "Failure" in physical education. As before, such penalties were not trivial; given the college's two-year requirement in gym, students had to make up unsatisfactory work in later semesters. Only a very brave (or foolish) student would tempt such a fate through poor attendance.

To some extent, general policies and practices at Smith governed regulations in physical education. The school's rules about attendance and performance in academic programs typically applied to classes in physical education as well. The same held true at other colleges and universities in the United States during the early twentieth century. In fact, most institutions had extensive codes of conduct, covering every facet of student life from academic work to social behavior. During the 1920s and 1930s, such codes became increasingly detailed and conservative. As undergraduate populations became more heterogeneous and campus culture seemed more rowdy, many institutions—from private female colleges to coed state universities—regarded student deportment and discipline as an urgent problem (Solomon 1985:142–44, 146–48, 150–51, 157–71). Searching for a solution, administrators and faculty began to regulate student behavior more closely during the interwar years. Women's physical education reflected this general trend toward micromanagement. By mandating attendance throughout the monthly cycle, gym teachers could supervise what students did or did not do; although such authority was limited to a few hours per week in the gym, it was better than no control at all. By instituting complex schemes for menstrual excuses, makeup work, and penalties, gym teachers at Smith and other schools gained considerable knowledge of and control over their students' behavior.

Disciplinary systems, though, also derived from specific features of physical education. In particular, menstrual rules allowed female teachers to demarcate their professional turf. At coeducational schools, for instance, their emphasis on menstrual health (and sex differences in general) helped legitimize, and institutionalize, the separation of men's and women's departments of physical education (Verbrugge 1997). Menstrual policies also allowed women teachers—at both coed and female schools—to clarify the relationship between physical education and medicine. At many schools, the two professions interacted (and argued) during various functions, including physical examinations of students, hygiene instruction, and decisions about students' participation in physical education and sports (a girl's menstrual history was one consideration). Where and how should the jurisdictional lines between medicine and physical education be drawn in such matters? The answer for menstrual policy—however realized—was clear: at most institutions, teachers proposed menstrual regulations and enforced them;

school doctors certified which girls needed special dispensation in gym class for medical reasons. In teachers' minds, the arrangement was a favorable one; except for deferring to doctors' clinical expertise about the severity of a girl's condition (for instance, dysmenorrhea), physical educators determined which activities were appropriate for students at various stages of the monthly cycle. Women teachers thereby solidified their claim over menstrual policies and practices.

In sum, women physical educators in the United States adopted theories and policies about menstruation that enhanced their authority over the female body. By adopting a mechanical rather than biomedical model of physiology, gym teachers strengthened their involvement in women's lives while neutralizing the power of other experts. For the average woman, they claimed, sensible living, not medical intervention, was the best path to reproductive health. By asserting that the exercise-and-menstruation question was up for grabs—and then grabbing it—teachers positioned themselves as arbiters of female physicality. Both training and experience, they said, equipped their profession to supervise girls' and women's physical activities. Finally, by enacting curricular rules and procedures, teachers regulated if, when, how much, and in what way girls and women exercised during the monthly cycle. In effect, women teachers became menstrual police—marking and patrolling the border between female fitness and dysfunction.

Physical educators communicated their normative model of the female body every day—in the gym, the classroom, and the locker room. Did they perpetuate or reject long-standing prejudices about women's physiology and "nature"? With respect to menstruation, the answer is mixed: teachers both problematized and demythologized the monthly cycle.

On the one hand, teachers stigmatized menstruation as a perilous and unhygienic process. Their mechanical paradigm depicted the uterus in almost Aristotelian terms, as a fragile organ that, under duress, could wander or collapse. Female teachers also reinforced old stereotypes of menstruation as unsanitary by urging special precautions during the menses. Above all, the teachers' model gave greater priority to reproductive health than to physical activity. Physical educators rarely asked how the menstrual cycle affected women's physical abilities; for instance, did a girl's motor skills improve or decline during her period? Though immaterial to teachers, the topic stimulated many scientists between 1900 and 1940 to study the cyclic effects of menstruation on physical variables (including muscle efficiency, blood pressure, metabolism, and respiratory rate), as well as on women's mental abilities and temperament; researchers disagreed about the extent and cause of such variations.[13] The minute effects of menstruation, though, did not interest physical educators; instead, they focused on the opposite question: How do daily life and exercise affect menstrual health? Activities that endangered fertility and childbirth, they maintained, were forbidden; the fact of menstruation and the promise of pregnancy were more important to them than were athletic skill and performance. Simply put: no woman should trade reproductive health for an hour of basketball.

In part, teachers' conservative views about menstruation derived from their professional interests. As discussed earlier, they sought both rhetorical and literal control over female health and exercise. Of equal importance was the women's social locus. Physical educators of the early 1900s were reared and educated during the post–Civil War decades; their ideas about physicality and gender befit the conventions of their sex, race, and class in late Victorian America. Teachers who were white and middle class, for instance, understood and experienced their lives through the structures of white middle-class culture. Endorsing the norms of heterosexual femininity, white female teachers equated health with reproduction, considered women's bodies to be somewhat flawed, and frowned on masculine values, such as competitiveness (Verbrugge 1997). Their conservative opinions about menstruation and vigorous exercise were a logical, and probably comfortable, feature of their social background.

At the same time, physical educators challenged popular mythology about womanhood. Rejecting late Victorian standards of female frailty, they chose lives of activity and fitness, for themselves and their students. To some extent, they also redefined menstruation. By depicting the monthly cycle as a normal occurrence, teachers encouraged women to worry less and exercise more. "Most happily," one teacher cheered in 1916, "actual facts and statistics are absolutely disproving previous theories of woman's physical and mental inferiority and particularly this antiquated temporary shelving of woman for the menstrual period and permanent retirement to caps and knitting at 50" (McKinstry 1916–17: 22). Given long-standing claims about women's innate "liabilities," the teachers' positive philosophy is noteworthy, though often overlooked by historians. Just as significantly, teachers translated their optimism into curricular programs. Overturning the tradition of menstrual excuses, many teachers began in the 1920s to require that students attend class during their periods and undertake at least light exercise.

What enabled teachers to question old notions about the monthly "handicap"? Several factors were important. First, experience and observation probably taught physical educators that conventional ideas about menstruation were misguided. Teachers were living proof that women could be (even had to be) physically active and competent throughout the month. That conclusion was reinforced by a broader reconceptualization of "womanhood" in the United States during the early twentieth century. Within white middle-class culture, a new paradigm of active, healthy femininity gradually emerged during the very decades that these teachers were active professionals. White middle-class teachers both contributed to and benefited from that important (albeit limited) reformulation of women's "nature." Finally, a positive construction of menstruation enlarged the scope of their profession. If teachers merely comforted girls during menstruation or taught exercises that relieved pain, physical education accepted purely custodial and corrective roles. By naturalizing the monthly cycle, however, teachers could focus on more educative functions; menstruation was absorbed into students' general program of physical activity and personal development in the gym.

Women teachers were not the only figures in menstrual education in the United States during the early twentieth century. Many groups, including doctors and the hygiene industry, tried to influence how females thought about and "managed" their periods. To some extent, the initiatives of such "outsiders" intruded upon the gym: family doctors and school medical staffs determined which girls could or could not participate in class because of menstrual problems; hygiene companies supplied physical education departments with pamphlets and films about menstruation for in-class instruction. Few clues remain about how teachers regarded such efforts. There is no doubt, however, that women physical educators positioned their field to be an important force in menstrual education. They adopted language, concepts, and policies that staked their claim on the territory of exercise and menstruation and, more generally, on female physicality.

In recent decades, the controversy about exercise and menstruation has escalated in the United States. Articles about menstrual disturbances in active women have appeared regularly in medical and popular literature since the mid-1970s; professional organizations have issued position statements about female fitness and reproductive health; coaches and athletes now discuss the "female athlete triad," a combination of amenorrhea, osteoporosis, and disordered eating that some participants in sports may develop.

The current debate about exercise and menstruation both differs from and resembles the dispute of a half-century ago. On the one hand, women physical educators exert less influence today than do research-based professions, such as endocrinology, gynecology, exercise physiology, and sports medicine. Discourse and rules about exercise and menstruation have moved from the gym to the lab.

On the other hand, the issue of reproductive health still dominates discussions about women's physical activity. Since the 1970s, for example, the phenomenon of "exercise-associated amenorrhea," that is, the extended cessation of periods during intensive training, has provoked fervent debates about the reproductive futures of young female athletes. Long before researchers determined the causes or effects of "exercise-associated amenorrhea," scientific journals and popular media defined the condition as a reproductive risk. Evidence now suggests that menstrual dysfunction in active females is a multidimensional phenomenon with diverse forms, causes, and consequences; moreover, certain reproductive sequelae in such girls and women may be reversible, whereas nonreproductive conditions (such as osteoporosis) seem less tractable and more ominous (Otis et al. 1997; Shangold 1994). For many observers, however, these scientific complexities have not dislodged old, seemingly automatic, apprehensions about female exercise and reproductive health.

Overall, recent discourse about the subject has been both scholarly and nontechnical, its tone both serious and sensationalistic, its conclusions both balanced and hyperbolic. Whatever the rhetorical form, however, the underlying premise about exercise and menstruation remains a simple and familiar one: physical activity must not interrupt reproductive normality. Simply put: procreation still outranks recreation.

NOTES

Research for this paper was supported by a 1991–1992 Fellowship for College Teachers and Independent Scholars from the National Endowment for the Humanities (FB-28294-91), a 1994 faculty development stipend from Bucknell University, and a 1995–1996 award from the Small Research Grants Program of the Spencer Foundation. I presented an earlier version of this work at the sixty-ninth annual meeting of the American Association for the History of Medicine, May 1996, in Buffalo, New York. I am grateful to Catherine Blair (Bucknell University) and to colleagues at the Five College Women's Studies Research Center (Mount Holyoke College, 1995–1996) for helpful discussions and insights as this essay developed.

1. A typical example is Wayman (1925:153–56). Margaret Bell was especially prolific on the subject; see Bell (1930a, 1930b, 1933a, 1934), Bell and

Parsons (1931), and Bell, Parsons, and Schutz (1931). Dysmenorrhea was also a major concern among women doctors, especially those connected with college health services. Examples include Boynton (1932), Meredith (1920), Mosher (1911), and Scott (1931).

2. Elsewhere, Bell argued that, except for the first few days of menstrual flow, the uterus was fairly sturdy, and slight variations in its position were neither uncommon nor worrisome. See Bell (1933b, 1938b:3–4, 5–6; 1942:208).

3. It is worth noting that male teachers were both more liberal and more conservative than their female counterparts on the question of exercise and menstruation. For a liberal position, see Arnold (1914); Arnold later reversed his opinion (1924). For a cautious view, see Dearborn (1916).

4. The following discussion emphasizes works by individual teachers. Examples of organizational statements about menstruation and exercise (especially competitive athletics) include National Section on Women's Athletics of the American Physical Education Association (1937:40, 52), Women's Division of the National Amateur Athletic Federation (1930:3–4), Schoedler (1926:593), and annual official guides for girls' and women's sports published by American Sports, and later A. S. Barnes, in collaboration with women's committees of the American Physical Education Association. Local and state athletic leagues also established guidelines; for example, see Clark (1921:140).

5. For example, see Baer (1916), Bell (1933a, 1934:54–55, 61), Bell and Parsons (1931), Frost (1932), Halsey (1925:495), Plummer (1910), Spindler (1931:51, 55), Stearn and Mitchell (1931), and Wright (1917–18). Many women doctors also endorsed exercise; examples include Mosher (1914) and Ramsey (1935).

6. Coleman applied the metaphor, generally, to children's recreation. In other versions, the metaphor clearly involved the physical effects of puberty; see Coleman (n.d.).

7. Typical statements of the policy of prudence include Bell (1938a:27), Coops (1933:51–54), Frymir (1930a:22–29, 239–40), Halsey (1921–22:3; 1925:495), McKinstry (1916–17:25–26), Norris (1920:82), Perrin (1924, 1932), Somers (1930:28, 118–19), Stoneroad (1910:940), and Wayman (1928:56, 127–28, 163–66; 1938:165). Over time, some teachers' views became more liberal; for example, see Bell (1925:66–67; 1938a:26–27; 1947). By contrast, organizations that promoted elite sports for girls and women asserted that active training and competition did not impair the monthly cycle; for example, see Folsom (1933).

8. One can also learn about menstrual policies through surveys that physical educators themselves conducted about programs in secondary schools and/or colleges. The following surveys focused on participation in competitive sports during the menstrual period and show a trend toward fewer restrictions: Richards (1920:408), Von Borries (1926:6), Report (1926), Tapley (1933:7), Coops (1933:51–54), and White (1940:16–18). Other reports covered attendance and activities in gym class during the menstrual period and reveal cautious policies in the 1920s: Baird (1924), Bass, Emond, and Snell (1926:26–28), and Johnson (1927:53–62).

9. These two trends were apparent at the following colleges and universities.

Institutions are listed chronologically, according to the year by which they required class attendance during menstruation.

- Stanford University (by 1910). See Mosher (1915), Stanford University (1927/28–1940/41), and Zimmerli (1945:268).
- University of North Carolina at Greensboro (by 1917–18). See University of North Carolina (1917–18) and Coleman (ca. 1925).
- University of Wisconsin (by 1923). See Trilling (1916, 1924, 1925).
- Wellesley College (by 1924). See Cummings (1924, 1927).
- University of Michigan (ca. 1924). See Bell (1924), Evans (1916–17:31), University of Michigan (1928:20–21; 1930/31–1943/44).
- Radcliffe College (by 1924–25). See Radcliffe College (ca. 1924–25).
- State Normal Schools of Massachusetts (1925). See Women's Division of the National Amateur Athletic Federation (1925a, ca. 1925b).
- University of Nebraska (by 1926–27). See Lee (1924, 1924–26, 1926–27).
- Pembroke College (of Brown University) (by 1931–32). See Pembroke College (1927/28–1940/41).

My information about menstrual practices at other schools is less complete or conclusive. At Howard University, Agnes Scott College, and Sophie Newcomb College, girls probably reported to "corrective classes" during menstruation. At Spelman College and Tuskegee Institute, most students attended regular class (by the 1940s).

10. The discussion that follows derives primarily from documents in the records of the Department of Physical Education, housed in the archives of Smith College. Citations identify departmental document and publication date. I am grateful to archivist Margery Sly for her assistance during my research at Smith in 1995–1996.

11. Two retired teachers at Smith confirmed this information (Helen Russell and Rita Benson, interview by author, March 1, 1996, Northampton, Mass.).

12. By midcentury, some teachers were more open-minded about swimming and menstruation. For example, see Thwing (1943), and successive editions of Bell's *The Doctor Answers Some Practical Questions on Menstruation* (1938b, 1951, 1955).

13. I examined several dozen studies published between 1900 and 1940 about the effects of menstruation. Representative works that uncovered cyclic variations are Moore and Cooper (1923) and Eagleson (1927); research that argued effects were minimal or unrelated to menstruation include Bilhuber (1926) and Hollingworth (1914).

REFERENCES

Anderson, Mrs. Lou Eastwood. 1922. The high school age and the university age. In *Spalding's official basketball guide for women, 1922–23*, p. 66. New York: American Sports.

Arnold, E. H. 1914. The effect of school work on menstruation. *American Physical Education Review* 19:113–18.

Arnold, E. H. 1924. Athletics for women. *American Physical Education Review* 29: 452–57.

Baer, Clara G. 1916. Therapeutic gymnastics as an aid in college work, With some observations of specific cases. *American Physical Education Review* 21: 513–21.

Baird, Dorothy B. 1924. Summary of questionnaire on menstruation made by Dorothy B. Baird, instructor in girls' physical education, Placer Union High School, Auburn, Calif. Department of Women's Physical Education and Dance (School of Education, 82/50) Papers, Folder 18: Menstruation, Box 11. Steenbock facility, University of Wisconsin–Madison Archives.

Bartelmez, George W. 1937. Menstruation. *Physiological Reviews* 17:28–72.

Bartky, Sandra L. 1988. Foucault, femininity, and the modernization of patriarchal power. In Irene Diamond and Lee Quinby, eds., *Feminism and Foucault: Reflections on resistance,* pp. 61–86. Boston: Northeastern University Press.

Bass, Oneida, Marylyn Emond, and Catherine Snell. 1926. Questionnaire on the administration of the menstrual problem in colleges and universities of the United States. *Mary Hemenway Alumnae Association Bulletin,* no. 1 (March):26–28.

Bateman, Marjorie. 1935. Health aspects of girls' basketball. *Mind and Body* 42: 21–24.

Bell, Margaret, to Blanche Trilling. 1924 (December 18). Department of Women's Physical Education and Dance (School of Education, 82/50) Papers, Folder 18: Menstruation, Box 11. Steenbock facility, University of Wisconsin–Madison Archives.

Bell, Margaret. 1925. Why girls should play girls' basketball rules—Discussed from the physiological angle. In *Spalding's official basketball guide for women, 1925–26,* pp. 66–67. New York: American Sports.

Bell, Margaret. 1930a. Painful menstruation. *Sargent Quarterly* 15 (May–June): 17–19.

Bell, Margaret. 1930b. Painful menstruation. *Sargent Quarterly* 15 (July–August):18–19.

Bell, Margaret. 1933a. Study of physical education students—menstrual function, 1932–1933—175 cases [typescript]. Margaret Bell Papers, Folder: Articles and Talks, 1929–1939, Box 3. Bentley Historical Library, University of Michigan, Ann Arbor.

Bell, Margaret. 1933b. The biological and physiological aspects of soccer for girls and women [typescript, March 24]. Margaret Bell Papers, Folder: Articles and Talks, 1929–1939, Box 3. Bentley Historical Library, University of Michigan, Ann Arbor.

Bell, Margaret. 1934. A further study of dysmenorrhea in college women—University of Michigan: A detailed study of 1,550 college women. *Research Quarterly* 5:49–62.

Bell, Margaret. 1938a. The doctor advises. In *Official basketball guide for women and girls, 1938–39,* pp. 26–27. New York: A. S. Barnes.

Part One: Historical Bases of Reproductive Discourse

Bell, Margaret. 1938b. *The doctor answers some practical questions on menstruation.* Washington, D.C.: National Section on Women's Athletics of the American Association for Health, Physical Education, and Recreation.

Bell, Margaret. 1942. Answers to practical questions on menstruation. *Hygeia* 20:186–87, 208–9.

Bell, Margaret. 1945. Memo to the house heads [typescript, June 15]. Margaret Bell Papers, Folder: Articles, 1930–1944, Box 2. Bentley Historical Library, University of Michigan, Ann Arbor.

Bell, Margaret. 1947. The doctor discusses basketball. In *Official basketball and officials rating guide for women and girls, 1947–48,* pp. 36–39. New York: A. S. Barnes.

Bell, Margaret, and Eloise Parsons. 1931. Dysmenorrhea in college women. *Medical Woman's Journal* 38:31–35.

Bell, Margaret, Eloise Parsons, and Emeth Schutz. 1931. Data in menstrual variation at the University of Michigan. *Proceedings of the Twelfth Annual Meeting of the American Student Health Association* 15:77–84.

Bilhuber, Gertrude. 1926. The effect of functional periodicity on the motor ability of women in sports. D.P.H. diss., University of Michigan.

Bordo, Susan R. 1989. The body and the reproduction of femininity: A feminist appropriation of Foucault. In Alison M. Jaggar and Susan R. Bordo, eds., *Gender/body/knowledge: Feminist reconstructions of being and knowing,* pp. 13–33. New Brunswick, N.J.: Rutgers University Press.

Boynton, Ruth E. 1932. A study of the menstrual histories of 2,282 university women. *American Journal of Obstetrics and Gynecology* 23:516–24.

Brumberg, Joan Jacobs. 1993. "Something happens to girls": Menarche and the emergence of the modern American hygienic imperative. *Journal of the History of Sexuality* 4:99–127.

Bullough, Vern, and Martha Voght. 1973. Women, menstruation, and nineteenth-century medicine. *Bulletin of the History of Medicine* 47:66–82.

Burchenal, Elizabeth. 1916. Athletics for girls. In *Spalding's official basket ball guide for women, 1916–17,* pp. 82–89. New York: American Sports.

Cadden, Joan. 1993. *Meanings of sex difference in the middle ages: Medicine, science, and culture.* Cambridge, U.K.: Cambridge University Press.

Cayleff, Susan E. 1992. She was rendered incapacitated by menstrual difficulties: Historical perspectives on perceived intellectual and physiological impairment among menstruating women. In Alice J. Dan and Linda L. Lewis, eds., *Menstrual health in women's lives,* pp. 229–35. Urbana: University of Illinois Press.

Clark, Lydia. 1921. Illinois league of high school girls' athletic associations. *American Physical Education Review* 26:138, 140, 142.

Clark, Lydia. 1923. Games for the upper grades. In *Spalding's official basketball guide for women, 1923–24,* pp. 68–69. New York: American Sports.

Cochran, Helen F. 1917. Basket ball for high school girls? *Publication of the Physical Education Alumnae Association of Oberlin College* 4, no. 1 (December):6–7.

Cole, Cheryl L. 1993. Resisting the canon: Feminist cultural studies, sport, and technologies of the body. *Journal of Sport and Social Issues* 17:77–97.

Coleman, Mary Channing. ca. 1925. Notice from Mary Channing Coleman to students. Chancellor J. I. Foust Papers. Special Collections, Walter Clinton Jackson Library, University of North Carolina at Greensboro.

Coleman, Mary Channing. 1930. Games and athletics in the school program. *North Carolina Parent-Teacher Bulletin* 8:107–8, 111.

Coleman, Mary Channing. n.d. A balanced diet in physical education [speech ms.]. Mary Channing Coleman Papers, Folder: Selected Writings, Box 1. Special Collections, Walter Clinton Jackson Library, University of North Carolina at Greensboro.

Coops, Helen Leslie. 1933. *High school standards in girls athletics in the state of Ohio.* New York: Teachers College, Columbia University.

Corner, George W. 1933. The nature of the menstrual cycle. *Medicine* 12:61–82.

Cummings, Mabel, to Paul B. Williams. 1922 (May 19). Department of Hygiene and Physical Education Papers, Folder: Competition and Competition Policies, Box 14. Archives, Margaret Clapp Library, Wellesley College, Wellesley, Mass.

Cummings, Mabel, to Blanche Trilling. 1924 (December 17). Department of Hygiene and Physical Education Papers, Folder: Menstruation (1924–1927), Box 19. Archives, Margaret Clapp Library, Wellesley College, Wellesley, Mass. A nearly identical letter can be found in Department of Women's Physical Education and Dance (School of Education, 82/50) Papers, Folder 18: Menstruation, Box 11. Steenbock facility, University of Wisconsin–Madison Archives.

Cummings, Mabel, to Margaret Tyler. 1927 (March 25). Department of Hygiene and Physical Education Papers, Folder: Menstruation (1924–1927), Box 19. Archives, Margaret Clapp Library, Wellesley College, Wellesley, Mass.

Dearborn, George. 1916. More or less random notes on exercise. *Mind and Body* 23:365–73.

Delaney, Janice, Mary Jane Lupton, and Emily Toth. 1988. *The curse: A cultural history of menstruation.* Rev. ed. Urbana: University of Illinois Press.

Dosch, Nancy C. 1991. "The sacrifice of maidens" or healthy sportswomen? The medical debate over women's basketball. In Joan S. Hult and Marianna Trekell, eds., *A century of women's basketball: From frailty to Final Four,* pp. 125–36. Reston, Va.: American Alliance for Health, Physical Education, Recreation and Dance.

Eagleson, Helen E. 1927. Periodic changes in blood pressure, muscle coordination, and mental efficiency in women. *Comparative Psychology Monographs* 4 (serial no. 20).

Ehrenfest, Hugo. 1937. Menstruation and its disorders. *American Journal of Obstetrics and Gynecology* 34:530–47, 699–729, 1051–76.

Engelmann, George J. 1900. What is normal menstruation? *New York Medical Journal* 72:986–88.

Evans, Alice. 1916–17. Organization of the Department of Physical Training for

Women at the University of Michigan, Ann Arbor. *Mary Hemenway Alumnae Association Bulletin,* pp. 29–32.

Farrell-Beck, Jane, and Laura K. Kidd. 1996. The roles of health professionals in the development and dissemination of women's sanitary products, 1880–1940. *Journal of the History of Medicine and Allied Sciences* 51:325–52.

Folsom, Mrs. Richard S. 1933. Report of the National Women's Sport Committee, A.A.U. *Mind and Body* 39:300–302.

Frank, Robert T. 1932. Hormonal disturbances as a cause of functional menstrual disorders. *Proceedings of the Thirteenth Annual Meeting of the American Student Health Association* 16:69–77.

Frost, Lorraine. 1932. Dysmenorrhea and exercise. *Physiotherapy Review* 12:251–54.

Frymir, Alice W. 1930a. *Basket ball for women: How to coach and play the game.* New York: A. S. Barnes.

Frymir, Alice W. 1930b. *Track and field for women.* New York: A. S. Barnes.

Gruhn, John G., and Ralph R. Kazer. 1989. *Hormonal regulation of the menstrual cycle: The evolution of concepts.* New York: Plenum Medical.

Hall, M. Ann. 1996. *Feminism and sporting bodies.* Champaign, Ill.: Human Kinetics.

Halsey, Elizabeth. 1921–22. Physical education in the summer camp. *Mary Hemenway Alumnae Association Bulletin,* pp. 1–8.

Halsey, Elizabeth. 1925. The college curriculum in physical education for women. *American Physical Education Review* 30:490–96.

Hellebrandt, Frances A. 1940. The physiologist discusses hockey. In *Official field hockey guide for women and girls, 1940,* pp. 37–40. New York: A. S. Barnes.

Hellebrandt, Frances A., and Margaret H. Meyer. 1939. Physiological data significant to participation by women in physical activities. *Research Quarterly* 10:10–23.

Hollingworth, Leta Stetter. 1914. *Functional periodicity: An experimental study of the mental and motor abilities of women during menstruation* (Contributions to Education no. 69). New York: Teachers College, Columbia University.

Johnson, Georgia Borg. 1927. *Organization of the required physical education for women in state universities* (Contributions to Education no. 253). New York: Teachers College, Columbia University.

Kidwell, Kathro, and Dorothy Simpson. 1929. A study and investigation of the health of women teachers of physical education. *American Physical Education Review* 34:83–91.

Laqueur, Thomas. 1990. *Making sex: Body and gender from the Greeks to Freud.* Cambridge, Mass.: Harvard University Press.

Lee, Mabel, to Blanche Trilling. 1924 (December 15). Department of Women's Physical Education and Dance (School of Education, 82/50) Papers, Folder 18: Menstruation, Box 11. Steenbock facility, University of Wisconsin–Madison Archives.

Lee, Mabel. 1924–26. Menstrual period regulations [typescript]. Mabel Lee Papers, Folder: Public. N.S., Box CB4. Archives, American Alliance for Health, Physical Education, Recreation and Dance, Reston, Va.

Lee, Mabel. 1926–27. *Handbook of the Department of Physical Education for Women.* Mabel Lee Papers, Folder: Public. N.S., Box CB4. Archives, American Alliance for Health, Physical Education, Recreation and Dance, Reston, Va.

Lee, Mabel. 1937. *The conduct of physical education: Its organization and administration for girls and women.* New York: A. S. Barnes.

Lenskyj, Helen. 1986. *Out of bounds: Women, sport and sexuality.* Toronto: Women's Press.

Martin, Emily. 1987. *The woman in the body: A cultural analysis of reproduction.* Boston: Beacon.

McKinstry, Helen. 1916–17. The hygiene of menstruation. *Mary Hemenway Alumnae Association Bulletin,* pp. 15–27.

Meaker, Samuel R. 1941. Menstrual disorders in adolescent girls and young women. *Journal of Health and Physical Education* 12:12–15, 62–63.

Meredith, Florence. 1920. Functional menstrual disturbances. *Surgery, Gynecology and Obstetrics* 31:382–87.

Miller, Norman F. 1930. Additional light on the dysmenorrhea problem. *Journal of the American Medical Association* 95:1796–1803.

Moore, Lillian M., and Catherine R. Cooper. 1923. Monthly variations in cardiovascular activities and in respiration rate in women. *American Journal of Physiology* 64:416–23.

Mosher, Clelia Duel. 1911. Functional periodicity in women and some of the modifying factors. *American Physical Education Review* 16:493–507.

Mosher, Clelia Duel. 1914. A physiologic treatment of congestive dysmenorrhea and kindred disorders associated with the menstrual function. *Journal of the American Medical Association* 62:1297–1301.

Mosher, Clelia Duel. 1915. The physical training of women in relation to functional periodicity. *Woman's Medical Journal* 25:71–74.

National Section on Women's Athletics of the American Physical Education Association. 1937. Standards in athletics for girls and women: Guiding principles in the organization and administration of athletic programs— A report of Committee on Standards. *Research Quarterly* 8:17–72.

Norris, J. Anna. 1914. The necessity for supervision of basket ball. In *Spalding's official basket ball guide for women, 1914–1915,* pp. 71–72. New York: American Sports.

Norris, J. Anna. 1920. Exercise in colleges. In *Proceedings of the International Conference of Women Physicians, Vol. 1: General problems of health,* pp. 73–83. New York: Womans Press.

Norris, J. Anna. 1924a. Dangers in basket ball: Popular sport should be made safe for girls. *Child Health* 5:512–14.

Norris, J. Anna, to Blanche Trilling. 1924b (December 13). Department of Women's Physical Education and Dance (School of Education, 82/50) Papers, Folder 18: Menstruation, Box 11. Steenbock facility, University of Wisconsin–Madison Archives.

Novak, Emil. 1930. Recent advances in the physiology of menstruation. *Journal of the American Medical Association* 94:833–39.

Novak, Emil. 1931. The biologic significance of the female reproductive cycle. *Journal of the American Medical Association* 96:2173–76.

Otis, Carol, Barbara Drinkwater, Mimi Johnson, Anne Loucks, and Jack Wilmore. 1997. ACSM position stand on the female athlete triad. *Medicine and Science in Sports and Exercise* 29:i–ix.

Oudshoorn, Nelly. 1994. *Beyond the natural body: An archeology of sex hormones.* New York: Routledge.

Park, Roberta J. 1995. The contributions of women to exercise science and sports medicine, 1870–1994. *Women in Sport and Physical Activity Journal* 3:41–69.

Patrick, Augusta L. 1917. Athletics for girls and its problems in the high school. *American Physical Education Review* 22:427–31.

Pembroke College. 1927/28–1940/41. Rules and regulations of the Department of Physical Education. In *Student Handbook.* Providence, R.I.: Pembroke College.

Perrin, Ethel. 1924. Athletics for women and girls. *Playground* 17:658–61.

Perrin, Ethel. 1932. Health safeguards in athletics for girls and women [in Monograph on athletics for girls and women]. *Research Quarterly* 3:93–94.

Pfister, Gertrud. 1990. The medical discourse on female physical culture in Germany in the 19th and early 20th centuries. *Journal of Sport History* 17:183–98.

Plummer, Laura S. 1910. [Discussion]. *Addresses and Proceedings of the National Education Association,* pp. 941–42.

Radcliffe College. ca. 1924–25. *Physical Education Regulations.* Department of Physical Education Papers, Folder 54, Box 3. Archives, Radcliffe College, Cambridge, Mass.

Ramsey, F. Muriel. 1935. The effect of exercise on menstruation. *Medical Woman's Journal* 42:324–25.

Report of the survey of conditions of athletic competition for girls in high schools of Wisconsin. 1926 (February 12). W. Van Hagen Papers, Folder: High Schools. Archives and Historical Collection, Department of Human Biodynamics, University of California, Berkeley.

Richards, Elizabeth. 1920. Everyday problems in girls' basket ball. *American Physical Education Review* 25:407–14.

Schoedler, Lillian. 1926. Girls' athletics—Wise and otherwise. *Child Welfare Magazine* 20:591–95.

Scott, K. Frances. 1931. Dysmenorrhea in the college student. *Proceedings of the Twelfth Annual Meeting of the American Student Health Association* 15:70–77.

Shangold, Mona. 1994. Menstruation and menstrual disorders. In Mona Shangold and Gabe Mirkin, eds., *Women and exercise: Physiology and sports medicine,* pp. 152–71. 2d ed. Philadelphia: F. A. Davis.

Smith, Helen N. 1927. Athletic education. *American Physical Education Review* 32:608–11.

Smith College. ca. 1912–1924/25. *Regulations of the Department of Hygiene and Physical Education.* Department of Physical Education Papers, Box 1206, and Box: Undergraduate bulletins and scrapbooks. Archives, Smith College, Northampton, Mass.

Smith College. 1926/27–1930/31. *Department of Hygiene and Physical Education: Regulations and Instructions.* Department of Physical Education Papers, Box: Undergraduate bulletins and scrapbooks. Archives, Smith College, Northampton, Mass.

Smith College. 1931/32–1965/66. *Physical Education Bulletin.* Department of Physical Education Papers, Box 1206, and Box: Undergraduate bulletins and scrapbooks. Archives, Smith College, Northampton, Mass.

Smith-Rosenberg, Carroll. 1973. Puberty to menopause: The cycle of femininity in nineteenth-century America. *Feminist Studies* 1:58–72.

Solomon, Barbara M. 1985. *In the company of educated women: A history of women and higher education in America.* New Haven, Conn.: Yale University Press.

Somers, Florence. 1930. *Principles of women's athletics.* New York: A. S. Barnes.

Spindler, Evelyn. 1931. Prevalence of and correlations between physical defects and their coincidence with functional disorders. *Research Quarterly* 2:36–56.

Stanford University. 1924/25–1940/41. Department of Women's Physical Education Papers, Minutes, Folders: Minutes of staff meetings, Box 1. Department of Special Collections, Green Library, Stanford University, Stanford, Calif.

Stearn, Esther W., and Grace R. Mitchell. 1931. Important factors in directing the health of the college woman. *American Journal of Public Health* 21: 984–88.

Stoner, Elizabeth. 1917–18. Report of the effect of teaching gymnastics during the menstrual period. *Mary Hemenway Alumnae Association Bulletin,* pp. 70–72.

Stoneroad, Rebecca. 1910. Physical education of girls during childhood and pubescent period, or upper-grammar and lower-high-school age. *Addresses and Proceedings of the National Education Association,* pp. 936–41.

Tapley, Dorothy S. 1933. Report of questionnaire committee, May 13. In *Spalding's official basketball guide for women and girls, 1933–34,* pp. 6–7. New York: American Sports.

Theberge, Nancy. 1991. Reflections on the body in the sociology of sport. *Quest* 43:123–34.

Thwing, Grace. 1943. Swimming during the menstrual period. *Journal of Health and Physical Education* 14:154.

Trilling, Blanche, to Ina Gittings. 1916 (December 19). Department of Women's Physical Education and Dance (School of Education, 82/50) Papers, Folder 18: Menstruation, Box 11. Steenbock facility, University of Wisconsin–Madison Archives.

Trilling, Blanche, to Gertrude Dudley. 1924 (December 20). Department of Women's Physical Education and Dance (School of Education, 82/50) Papers, Folder 18: Menstruation, Box 11. Steenbock facility, University of Wisconsin–Madison Archives.

Part One: Historical Bases of Reproductive Discourse

Trilling, Blanche, to Laura Garrett. 1925 (February 27). Department of Women's Physical Education and Dance (School of Education, 82/50) Papers, Folder 18: Menstruation, Box 11. Steenbock facility, University of Wisconsin–Madison Archives.

Tuana, Nancy. 1989. The weaker seed: The sexist bias of reproductive theory. In Nancy Tuana, ed., *Feminism and science,* pp. 147–71. Bloomington: Indiana University Press.

University of Michigan. 1928. Department of Physical Education for Women. *Physical education activities for high school girls.* Philadelphia: Lea and Febiger.

University of Michigan. 1930/31–1943/44. Department of Physical Education for Women Papers, Annual reports, Boxes 4–5. Bentley Historical Library, University of Michigan, Ann Arbor.

University of North Carolina. 1917–18. Annual report, 1917–18: [ms.]. School of Health, Physical Education, Recreation, and Dance Papers, Folder: 1910–1920, Box 1. Special Collections, Walter Clinton Jackson Library, University of North Carolina at Greensboro.

Valdiserri, Ronald O. 1983. Menstruation and medical theory: An historical overview. *Journal of the American Medical Woman's Association* 38:66–70.

Verbrugge, Martha H. 1997. Recreating the body: Women's physical education and the science of sex differences in America, 1900–1940. *Bulletin of the History of Medicine* 71:273–304.

Vertinsky, Patricia. 1990. *The eternally wounded woman: Women, doctors and exercise in the late nineteenth century.* Manchester, U.K.: Manchester University Press.

Von Borries, Eline. 1926. Report of questionnaire committee for year 1925–26. In *Spalding's official basketball guide for women, 1926–27,* pp. 5–7. New York: American Sports.

Waterman, Emma F. 1925. The physiologic and anatomic basis for the selection and limitation of women's motor activities. M.A. thesis, Department of Hygiene and Physical Education, Wellesley College, Wellesley, Mass.

Wayman, Agnes R. 1925. *Education through physical education: Its organization and administration for girls and women.* Philadelphia: Lea and Febiger.

Wayman, Agnes R. 1928. *Education through physical education: Its organization and administration for girls and women.* Rev. ed. Philadelphia: Lea and Febiger.

Wayman, Agnes R. 1938. *A modern philosophy of physical education with special implications for girls and women and for the college freshman program.* Philadelphia: Saunders.

Wells, Katharine R. 1939. Overcoming periodic pain. *Parents Magazine* 14:26, 48, 52.

White, Christine. 1940. Report on basketball survey. In *Official basketball guide for women and girls, 1940–41,* pp. 15–20. New York: A. S. Barnes.

Women's Division of the National Amateur Athletic Federation. 1925a. Report of meeting of physical education teachers [F. Somers, typescript]. WD-NAAF Papers, Folder: Medical Advisory Committee, Box 2, Series 9.

Archives, American Alliance for Health, Physical Education, Recreation and Dance, Reston, Va.

Women's Division of the National Amateur Athletic Federation. ca. 1925b. Investigation of the relation of exercise to menstruation [typescript]. WD-NAAF Papers, Folder: Medical Advisory Committee, Box 2, Series 9. Archives, American Alliance for Health, Physical Education, Recreation and Dance, Reston, Va.

Women's Division of the National Amateur Athletic Federation (comp.). 1930. *Women and athletics*. New York: A. S. Barnes.

Wright, Elizabeth A. 1910. The physical training of post-adolescent girls. *Addresses and Proceedings of the National Education Association*, pp. 942–46.

Wright, Elizabeth A. 1917–18. Report on exercise as a factor in the relief of menstrual disturbances. *Mary Hemenway Alumnae Association Bulletin*, pp. 72–74.

Zieff, Susan G. 1996. *The medicalization of higher education: Women physicians and physical training, 1870–1920*. Ann Arbor: UMI.

Zimmerli, Elizabeth K. 1945. A history of physical education for women at Stanford University and a survey of the Department of Physical Education for Women in 1943–44. Ed.D. thesis, Stanford University, Stanford, Calif.

4

GOD WILLED IT! GYNECOLOGY

AT THE CHECKOUT STAND

REPRODUCTIVE TECHNOLOGY

IN THE WOMEN'S SERVICE

MAGAZINE, 1977–1996

CHLOÉ DIEPENBROCK

You may have read about me. . . . I am the woman who wanted desperately to have a baby.
Doris Del Zio, "I Was Cheated of My Test-Tube Baby,"
Good Housekeeping

I tried Prozac, a puppy, a litter of cats, and two baby goats; but after five miscarriages nothing helped.
Helen Bransford, "Surrogacy: A Mother's Story," *Vogue*

In 1978, Leslie Brown achieved her goal of becoming a biological mother when her doctor placed into her arms the baby he had created for her in his laboratory. This persistent Englishwoman, who had allowed her body to become an object of experimentation, uttered three words that have come to characterize and legitimize the practice of technological reproduction: "God willed it!" (Libman Block 1979:70). Today, in the United States alone, infertile couples spend approximately $2 billion annually on assisted reproduction. Though the U.S. infertility rate of 8.5 percent has not increased since 1965, the number of people seeking treatment for infertility tripled between 1968 and 1982. Since 1985, the number of fertility clinics has grown from thirty to more than three hundred (Wright 1998). Despite the financial, physical, emotional, and social costs of assisted reproduction, the popular media have represented these technologies as beneficial—even desirable—to potential clients. To understand how the media are conveying these messages to U.S. women, we must turn a critical feminist eye to a new narrative form—the modern gynecological case history—a text whose fairy-tale qualities have made it increasingly popular in the women's service magazine since the 1978 birth of Louise Joy Brown.[1]

Without powerful motivation, women do not participate in the type of human research that reproductive technology requires. They must be convinced, through a variety of messages, that allowing their bodies to be the focus of experimentation will bring them benefits that are crucial to their psychological well-being and that are unattainable through other means. By using the heuristic pentad created by U.S. philosopher-rhetorician Kenneth Burke (1969a) to investigate the rhetorical effect of the case history published in the women's service magazine, we can better understand how one very influential medium fosters some of the motivation women have for becoming willing experimental subjects in the fertility clinic. Using the pentad clarifies how the fairy-tale structure of the case history makes it a persuasive argument for reproductive technologies while omitting the financial, physical, emotional, and social problems associated with these gynecological practices.

Gynecological practices have been scrutinized by a wide variety of feminist critics. In her landmark attack on patriarchy, *Gynecology: The Metaethics of Radical Feminism,* Mary Daly characterizes gynecology as a "violent enforcement of the sexual caste system" (1978:227). Nearly ten years later journalist Gena Corea (1987) updated that characterization by speculating that twenty-first-century reproduction will be "a complicated intellectual and technical feat performed by teams of highly skilled men who use, as raw material for their achievements, the body parts of a variety of interchangeable females" (Rowland 1992:2). Corea also draws parallels between the methods used in animal husbandry and the "reproductive brothel" system (1987:39) that is evolving as human reproductive technologies create a hierarchy of procreational functions for women: social, genetic, and gestational.

Feminist critics like Mary Daly (1978), Gena Corea (1987), Robyn Rowland (1992), Jalna Hanmer (1985), Patricia Spallone (1989), Helen Holmes (1980), and Janice Raymond (1987) have discussed, from the viewpoint of the philosopher, journalist, psychologist, sociologist, biochemist, geneticist, and medical ethicist, the destructive and dehumanizing fetishizing of women's reproductive capabilities—what Daly calls medical science's "colonization of women's bodies" (1978:230). Their analyses consider the effects of reproductive technologies on women and on the brave new society that scientists are engineering in the laboratory. These critics have also commented on the transforming concept of normality that is being inculcated in women as they develop attitudes of acceptance toward the use of medical technology.

Unfortunately, while critical texts usually strive for an objective analysis of such issues, popular texts in women's magazines are often highly subjective and sensational. The deceptively positive and overly emotional portrayal of reproductive technologies in many popular texts means that the ethical and moral issues involved are edited into the margins, making it difficult for any reader—educated or not—to recognize the ways in which these texts operate to rewrite social values.

Because of its entrenched status in U.S. culture and the role it plays in defining American femininity, the women's service magazine is an excellent medium for what social psychologist Rowland calls "reprospeak": the medical jargon that "infiltrates media reporting of reproductive technology" in order to prepare us for practices we would not otherwise endorse (1992:230). The women's magazine industry has been "teaching" women how to be exceptional wives and mothers since the nineteenth century. One vehicle for these nineteenth-century lessons was a popularized form of the gynecological case history—already a staple of medical textbooks. Tales of medicalized births, along with doctors' advice columns, dispensed an earlier version of Rowland's reprospeak to our grandmothers and mothers, linguistically preparing them to accept the "normalcy" of narcotics-assisted hospital birth. Today, hospital birth is the standard, and modern versions of these gynecological case histories are indoctrinating our daughters and granddaughters with messages about the normality of assisted reproduction, inviting our collusion in the twenty-first-century scenario that Corea describes.

Why look for this indoctrinating influence in the case history? Burke tells us that "we must think of rhetoric not in terms of some one particular address, but as a general body of identifications that owe their convincingness much more to trivial repetition and dull daily reënforcement than to exceptional rhetorical skill" (1969b:26). The case history is daily fare in women's magazines. This "body of identifications" reaches and indoctrinates the largest audience of U.S. women to be found reading any print medium.

Women's Service Magazines

Of the "seven sister" publications in the women's service magazine category, three have been in publication for more than one hundred years: *McCall's* (1870), *Ladies' Home Journal* (1883), and *Good Housekeeping* (1885) (Wood 1956). The remaining four have been in publication since the first half of the twentieth century: *Redbook* (1903), *Better Homes & Gardens* (1922), *Family Circle* (1932), and *Woman's Day* (1938) (Garvey 1995; Wood 1956). The seven sisters have a combined circulation of more than thirty million (Katz and Katz 1995). Because the industry's standard practice is to multiply the number of subscribers by three to determine the number of actual readers for each magazine, we can assume that these seven publications are reaching approximately ninety million women. The four "little sisters"—the fashion magazines *Glamour, Vogue, Cosmopolitan,* and *Mademoiselle*— add another 22.5 million readers to this audience (Katz and Katz 1995) for a total of 112.5 million. For the sake of comparison, commentary magazines such as *Commentary* and the *New Republic,* which traditionally invite and publish critical commentary on a variety of topics, have an approximate combined monthly circulation of 45,000 (Katz and Katz 1995).

READERSHIP

Who is the woman reaching for the *Ladies' Home Journal* or *Good Housekeeping* as she waits at the checkout stand during her weekly shopping expedition? Depending upon which magazine she is reaching for, she may or may not be college educated and her age will range from twenty-five to fifty-five. According to 1994 figures supplied by *Redbook,* she is married, with an annual household income of $40,000 per year, and she works to help keep her family fed, housed, and financially secure (Margolis 1984). Today's woman appears to have more options than her grandmother did. The industrialization of the United States changed the turn-of-the-century woman's role. Rather than working to make products for her household, she was charged with selecting and purchasing the best manufactured products. If she and her husband were fortunate, she also had some disposable income to spend on "luxury" items. Today's turn-of-the-century woman has the opportunity to attend college, pursue a career, delay childbearing. She appears to have much more control over her life, but the twenty-first-century world into which she is moving is an increasingly complex one—one in which technology has created moral and ethical dilemmas that her grandmother would never have envisioned.[2]

Pursuing a career and establishing financial stability for her family often means that the woman at the checkout stand has delayed motherhood well into her thirties. According to Woloch, "If she had children, the young woman of the 1980s was likely to have them later than her mother had done. During the 1970s, fertility dropped precipitously among women in their early twenties although it increased among women a decade older" (1984:533). As a result of delaying reproduction, many women ready to start families have found that they cannot conceive. Extended use of birth control pills, untreated sexually transmitted diseases, pelvic inflammatory diseases, endometriosis, and the natural decline in fertility that comes with age are just some factors that contribute to what appears to be an increase of infertility in women. These factors often trace to women's behavior, and thus society may hold today's woman accountable for her "failure" to conceive. In chapter 6 Laura Shanner comments at length on the reproductive industry's depiction of infertile women as biological failures, whereas it minimizes the fact that at least 50 percent of the infertility problems experienced by couples are the result of male infertility. Because of this portrayal as biological failure, the late twentieth-century woman may feel terrible guilt and responsibility for her inability to conceive and therefore may feel even more compelled to take whatever steps are necessary to remedy the problem.

So, like early advertisers, medical science defines the problem and offers the solution. Just as industrial technology took over women's productive activities in the nineteenth century, medical technology is poised to take over twenty-first-century women's reproductive functions. Women's service magazines have added case histories promoting the latest marvels of medical technology—the "miracle babies" created in the nation's laboratories—to their advertisements promoting consumer goods. Today's aspiring mother now faces purchasing decisions about a variety of reproductive technologies available to her. Consumerism has come full circle: women (those who can afford it) can purchase the technology that creates babies; they may even purchase the use of another woman's body as the site of this technology and have their genetic child delivered into their open but unlabored arms.

The Case History
as Representative Anecdote

CASE HISTORY DATA

The primary research for this study includes eighty-five articles on assisted reproduction that were printed in the seven women's service magazines, four fashion magazines, and two weekly women's magazines over a period of twenty years (1977 to 1996). Of these articles, 52, or 61 percent, are case histories narrating the stories of women who received treatment for infertility. Of these case histories, 44, or 85 percent, are positive accounts of the experience. Ironically, this 85 percent success rate is almost the exact opposite of the average reported success rate for infertility treatment. A July 1994 study published in the *New England Journal of Medicine* quotes an average take-home baby rate of only 12 percent (Neumann, Soheyla, and Weinstein 1994:241). Magazines that are particularly likely to give potential fertility customers a skewed view of the efficacy of treatment include the three oldest: *Good Housekeeping, Ladies' Home Journal,* and *McCall's. Ladies' Home Journal (LHJ)* has the distinction of having printed the most articles on the topic (seventeen) and the most cases (sixteen); as of mid-1999, it is the only one of the seven sisters that has not published a critique of the fertility industry.

As it appears at the checkout stand, the case history masquerades as what Burke (1945) calls a representative anecdote. The representative anecdote is a model of behavior from which the researcher derives a vocabulary for discussing human motives. That discussion represents a selective view of reality (59). Burke warns that when selecting a representative anecdote, "if you don't select one that is representative in a good sense, it will function as representative in a bad sense" (324). An anecdote functioning in a bad sense represents a deflected view of reality. Clearly, the anecdotes presented in the women's magazine are bad representatives, for they do not match the statistics; instead the stories told in the women's magazine almost always relate happy endings, deflecting reality in favor of a highly sensational characterization of both motives and outcomes.

BURKE'S PENTAD

This study employs Burke's pentad (1945) to analyze the rhetorical dynamics of the classical author-reader-text relationship. Burke's pentad is a heuristic device that allows its user to consider the relationships among five elements of an event. These elements—act, agent, agency, scene, and purpose—are similar to the questions a journalist answers when reporting an event, except that Burke is more interested in the dramatic interaction between given elements. The elements are defined as follows: act is the action engaged in, physical or linguistic; agent is the actor who performs the act; agency is the means by which the act is performed; scene is the physical or rhetorical context for the act; and purpose is the motivation the agent has for performing the act.

For example, the rhetorician can use the pentad to examine how an agent or performer of an action responds within a given rhetorical context or scene. At the same time this influence can be reciprocal: the nature of the agent may shape the scene itself. How one defines the elements of an event can also shift. The narrator of the case history in the women's magazine can be defined as the agent in one set of relationships, giving her rhetorical authority over the text. Alternatively, she can be defined as the agency or tool of the magazine editors who choose to publish her narration because it fits with their larger purpose or motivation—to publish stories that will attract both readers and advertisers while continuing the century-old commitment to writing and revising a particular definition of femininity for the magazine's readership.

When the narrator is defined as the agent of the case history, the scene is defined very narrowly as the case itself. This analysis focuses on the pentadic definitions that result from narrowing the interpretation of scene in this manner. Doing so allows a detailed look at the relationships between the author-narrator, the text she creates, and the reader who becomes her audience. Knowing how the reader of the women's magazine is constructed textually is crucial to understanding how women become willing participants in experimental technologies. When the scene is interpreted as the case history, the agent can then be defined as the new mother whose purpose is both to proclaim her newfound status as a legitimate mother and to justify the costly and painful means to her end. She does this through the act of constructing a sensationalized narrative of her technosex experience for her reader.

Of particular interest is the agency or means by which the writer of the case history accomplishes the glorification of the technosex experience. This agency is the narrative structure that the case histories in this study share—a rich hybrid of cultural genres comprised of elements of the fairy tale, heroic quest, and religious miracle. Because this hybrid narrative structure draws on values and myths embedded in our culture, it is a highly effective tool for accomplishing the agent's purpose. The narrative structure allows the woman who participates in reproductive technologies to minimize—for herself and her reader—the physical and mental costs of attaining motherhood through assisted reproduction. At the same time, she sends the message to her reader that her ability to endure such hardships is the mark of the true woman's desire to reproduce. She sets a new standard for the "normal" woman, even as she argues that she is no different from the woman who has achieved motherhood in the old-fashioned way. Her quest also implies that without children, women cannot be complete.

To reinforce the degree to which the narrator appears to have control over her journey to self-fulfillment, the medical technology of which she makes use appears as a powerful transforming device that she herself has invoked. The wand of technology is a potent tool, its narrative roots growing from both alchemy and religion. The doctor who wields the wand is characterized as a benevolent, grandfatherly Merlin, devoid of any of the basest of human motivations. Greed, ambition, pride, and conceit are completely edited from his character. He is often depicted as the right hand of God, collaborating with his maker in the very creation of life.

Finally, the baby, or mythic boon, is always described as a perfect cherub, an angel sent from heaven. Quadruplets, quintuplets, sextuplets, and, recently, even septuplets and octuplets are photographed as stretched serenely along their mothers' all-inclusive arms, smiling at the camera, the picture of health, the months they spent in intensive neonatal care written into the fine print of the story.

THE CINDERELLA SYNDROME

Within the pages of the women's magazine, the narrator-agent of the case history tells her story in a variety of ways. Most often, she writes her own story, giving a first-person account of her emotional journey to motherhood. Alternatively, she tells her story to a professional writer who functions as a more literate scribe. Less common are articles in which a professional writer takes control of the story and relates the woman's experience through selected quotes. Despite the differing methods for telling these stories, the narrative characteristics remain remarkably constant, and the woman who tells of her experience with reproductive technology appears to have authority over the construction of her experience. This authority is complicated, however, by her portrayal of herself as the heroine of her fairy tale. By assigning herself a role within the narrative structure of the story, she redefines herself as an element of the agency as well.

To accomplish her purpose of legitimizing her status as a mother, the narrator draws on the archetypal characteristics of the fairy-tale heroine. She presents herself not as royalty but as an ordinary suffering woman, more akin to Cinderella than to Sleeping Beauty, waiting for childbirth to rescue her from the cinders of childlessness and make her complete. "Who cares about me? I'm a nobody from Plattsburg, N.Y.," says Doris Del Zio (1979:135). Leslie Brown tells the world, "'We're just two ordinary people with a simple ordinary name. We're the Browns'" (Libman Block 1979:71). Laurie Steel transforms herself into Cinderella-at-the-ball by dressing in a magical velvet gown. She wears this garb into Patrick Steptoe's operating room, hoping fervently that his magic wand will make the transformation permanent: "A tradition has developed among the women at Bourn Hall to dress for the occasion [implantation]. Laurie brushed her long blond hair, [and] put on makeup and a magenta velvet gown" (Remsberg 1982:106).

The fairy-tale heroine is also capable of enduring all physical obstacles that would prevent her from reaching her goal. Pain, inseparable from childbearing for as long as humanity can remember, is an expected characteristic of motherhood, but technological motherhood includes suffering inconceivable even to Eve in the midst of her worst labor pains. An example of the case history heroine's physical commitment to motherhood is evident in Leslie Brown's willingness to allow Steptoe to remove her fallopian tubes because they were "in the way" of the procedures he wanted to perform:

> Nothing slowed Leslie. Uncomplaining, she underwent dozens of tests and explorations. She permitted Dr. Steptoe to completely remove her *useless* Fallopian tubes. The operation was extremely painful and on the long train ride back to Bristol from Oldham the wound in her stomach began to bleed. Leslie was in agony until she reached home and John could gently pull away the layers of her clothes that had become glued to her by her clotting blood. (Libman Block 1979:66; emphasis added)

Doris Del Zio's description of her physical condition after three operations to open her blocked fallopian tubes is equally gruesome: "My abdomen now looked like a road map and my insides were a mass of adhesions. Sometimes they were so painful that I just couldn't straighten up" (1979:200). Arlette Schweitzer (who bore twins for her daughter) speaks of how painful it was to inject herself with hormones: "As long as you know there's an end to it, I think you can bear almost anything. For eighty-nine days, I think you could even walk on burning coals if you had to" (Nash 1991:58). Laurie Steel's perky reaction to hearing about Steptoe's in-vitro work sums up the new standard for motherly commitment: "I don't mind being a guinea pig" (Remsberg 1982:105).

THE QUEST FOR FULFILLMENT

As a feature of the agency of the case history, the mythical quest adds another strategy for legitimizing the technomom's position: emphasizing the requisite characteristic of perseverance. In the language of the fairy tale, freelance writer Bonnie Remsberg describes Laurie Steel as "a long-legged, suntanned California blonde, bursting with good health and honest charm" (1982:75). Despite a medical condition that prevented pregnancy, Steel tried to conceive for twelve years because she "simply, instinctively and profoundly wanted to have a baby, to love it, to meet the challenge of raising it, and to share it with Jon" (Remsberg 1982:75).

In another account that emphasizes the normality of this type of Odyssean tenacity, Claudia Franson says: "I don't think I was fanatical about having a baby. I just didn't want to give up without having tried everything'" (Baker 1980:50). "Everything" amounted to a seven-year quest. She took Clomid (a powerful hormone that stimulates ovulation), had surgery to remove an adhesion, was treated for a microscopic infection, and miscarried. Yet despite all of these impediments, shortly after the birth of a son, she and her husband were already preparing to try to conceive a second time.

Soap opera actor Deidre Hall's quest for motherhood took her twenty years and three husbands. Like the others, she subjected herself to the entire gamut of fertility treatments: "I injected myself with hormones, tried artificial insemination and had every hand in the medical profession up my skirt trying to figure out what was wrong with me" (Radovsky 1993:37).

Hall's "20-year struggle for son David" (Radovsky 1993:37) is profiled in a newer and less substantial women's magazine, *First for Women*, but after the birth of her second son (compliments of the same genetic-gestational mother), she tells her story, "What We Did for Love," in *LHJ* (Hall 1995). In an opening line that sends a disturbing message about the "appropriate" role of the 1990s woman, Hall explains how her life is now completely fulfilled as a result of her social role as mother: "I used to be a driven person, one of the baby boomers who live from goal to goal. But ever since I became a mother, that ambition has completely fallen away. Now I can't wait to rush home from work and hug my sons David, three, and Tully, who turns one next month" (74).

By writing herself as a suffering fairy-tale heroine, questing for the ultimate feminine fulfillment, the narrator of the case history achieves two objectives. The first is that she accomplishes her purpose of legitimizing her status as a mother. The second is perhaps not intentional; she has revised for her readers the definitions of some key characteristics of motherhood. Because she depicts herself as a heroine who begins as an ordinary woman desiring motherhood, she sets new standards for those ordinary women who make up her readership. The modern woman must show her commitment to motherhood by adding reproductive technologies to her repertoire of strategies for achieving her goal. Doing so means raising her capacity for physical endurance, pursuing her goal beyond all physical, emotional, and financial boundaries, and intensifying her belief that motherhood is the ultimate feminine achievement.

At the same time, technology is represented as the means by which infertile women may retake control over bodies characterized as failures. Such control, however, is arguably only an illusion in an industry that refers to female patients as "girls" and that routinely offers sexually objectified images of women in the form of the pornography that assists their male partners in semen production (see Shanner, chapter 6).

MAGIC WANDS, MIRACLES, AND TECHNOWIZARDS

No fairy tale is complete without magic, and in the case history the wand of reproductive technology draws its power from magic and miracle. The doctor-facilitator who waves it is a benevolent Merlin figure and God's creative colleague; his altruistic crusade to coax new lives into the world has God's full blessing. (Though the field does include a small percentage of female practitioners, the masculine and scientific aims of achieving control over those reproductive mysteries still locked inside women's bodies still dominate.) In her dual role as narrator-agent and heroine-agency, the narrator both summons and prays for the magical miracle of reproductive technology and submits to and is transformed by it. The case history depicts Steptoe as the kindly grandfather of the technology. Libman Block, who told Leslie Brown's story describes him as a "brilliant gynecologist" (1979:64). Remsberg, who told Laurie Steel's story, calls him the "genial, gray-haired doctor" (1982:105) and says he is "deeply devoted to the reproductive health and well-being of women" (104). Steptoe's more contemporary colleagues now appear in the women's magazine as expert advisers, warning the reader that if she is older than thirty-eight, she should not try to reproduce without medical assistance (McDowell 1993:31). The magazines conveniently provide the names and locations of the fertility clinics that these helpful advisers operate.

Perhaps the most compelling combination of the benevolent doctor working medical miracles through the magical powers of technology appears in Remsberg's narration of Steel's implantation by Steptoe. The scenario also illustrates Shanner's point about the blurring that occurs between sexuality and reproduction via medical intervention. Steel represents the Cinderella character: she dresses in a flowing magenta gown and prepares her hair and makeup in anticipation of the act of technosex in which she is about to participate. Entering the operating theater at night because Steptoe likes to do it "when the uterus is quiet," she waits while the embryo is carried in from the laboratory (Remsberg 1982:106). Steptoe takes the long tube that encases it—the wand of technology—and "places it through the cervix into the womb. He waits several minutes, then removes the instrument" (108). Magical doctor, phallic technology, miraculous transformation: it comes as no surprise to read that "when the procedure was over, Laurie felt hugely relieved" (108).

Children, once considered gifts from God, are now miraculous GIFTs (gamete intrafallopian tube transfer) from the fertility clinic. If God has willed that a technology be created, the aspiring mother is obliged to participate in it. Doris Del Zio explains: "I'm firmly convinced that there is a bond between science and religion. I always say a prayer for my doctor before I undergo surgery" (1979:200). Leslie Brown "reckon[s] that God wanted me to have this baby or He wouldn't have let that miracle of modern science happen to me" (Libman Block 1979:67). "Dick" and "Cynthia," the first ZIFT (zygote intrafallopian tube transfer) parents, make a similar connection: "Why would God have created the technology that made ZIFT surrogacy possible if He didn't want people to use it?" (Edmondson Gupta 1989:216). Arlette Schweitzer had a more difficult religious dilemma because she is a "devout Catholic" and her church opposes surrogacy (1992:189). She put her problem into "God's hands" (189). As a sort of double affirmation of her faith in both God and science, she conceived twins.

Two recent multiple births exemplify this reliance on faith: the first surviving set of septuplets, born to Bobbi and Kenny McCaughey in November 1997, and octuplets born to Nkem Chukwu and Iyke Louis Udobi in December 1998. In both cases the couples cited religious reasons for refusing to undergo "pregnancy reduction" when they learned of the multiple pregnancies. The parents believe that they were carrying out God's will in continuing to carry all the fetuses. The news coverage to date parallels that of the women's magazines in celebrating the women's strength and endurance as they spent months in the hospital, watching their stomachs grow to epic proportions. "Chukwu showed tremendous dedication to her unborn children, never complaining, even offering to stop eating if it would provide more room for the fetuses," the *Houston Chronicle* reported (Milling 1998:10A). When the parents invoke God's will as the reason for not aborting some of the fetuses, writers find it easier to set aside discussions of the terrible dilemmas created when women who conceive with fertility drugs find themselves forced to choose between aborting babies they desperately want and the inevitable medical risks to all concerned.

FAIRY GODMOTHERS

If the doctor plays the magician in these technological tales, the role of the fairy godmother goes to the surrogate mother. She contributes to the agency of the narrative structure by facilitating the happiness of the narrator-agent—just as Cinderella's fairy godmother helped her to attend the ball. The surrogate's magic lies in her ability to conceive: "I have babies so easily—they just pop out," says Elizabeth Kane (Markoutsas 1981:98). The use of the term *surrogate* implies that she is not really a mother at all but, as one writer puts it, a "human incubator" (Edmondson Gupta 1989:141). Because terms such as these allow us to remove the surrogate mother from the physical act in which she is participating, the woman who contracts out her motherhood becomes a safe character in the case history. This fairy godmother waves a magic linguistic wand that euphemizes her relationship with the child she is carrying.

For Karen Mills, who was acting as a "traditional" surrogate (i.e., supplying the egg and the womb), her baby was simply her "little passenger" while she was the "carrier" (Mills 1985:209). "Debbie" says she was "just a baby-sitter" (Edmondson Gupta 1989:215). The women claim to bond instead with the aspiring mothers who are their clients. "Kathy," who says she "had no emotional trouble giving up . . . twins," explains that her real bond is with the woman for whom she carried them (Edmiston 1991:237). Deidre Hall is proud that she and "Robin," who is both the genetic and gestational mother of her children, bonded in what she calls a "girlfriend process" (Radovsky 1993:38). Hall even believes that "having a child through a surrogate mother is more involving than having it come from your body, because you're forming a kinship with another woman as intimately as you can" (Radovsky 1993:38). The surrogate-godmother's role also receives God's blessing in the case history: one set of happy new parents believes that "Elizabeth Kane is a saint" and another nameless birth mother is a "crusader," according to Markoutsas (1981:96, 98). Hall says she believes that Robin "came from God with my name on her" (Radovsky 1993:37).

WICKED WITCHES

When surrogate mothers—genetic or gestational—refuse to honor the terms of their contracts, their surrogate's narrative roles are easily rewritten. Because she has purchased the surrogate's services, the narrator uses her authorial control to stake her emotional claim to the child by transforming the fairy godmother into the wicked witch. The best illustration of how the wicked witch image is used to reassure aspiring mothers in the case history is the highly publicized custody suit that was fought over Baby M. This battle made Mary Beth Whitehead-Gould, the child's genetic and gestational mother, the most famous "surrogate" mother since that other Mary gave birth in a stable two thousand years ago. Whitehead-Gould has become a mythic presence in the case history fairy tale: the personification of the selfish woman who went back on her promise to deliver up her child to an unfulfilled aspiring mother. Her depiction by the justice system as a bad mother complicates more than the legal definition of motherhood. Characterizing Whitehead-Gould's desire to keep her child as an obsession, the courts used her mothering instinct as evidence of her unfit status. Ironically, the only way she could have reversed this negative characterization was to agree to give up her child. The Whitehead case helped to establish a split definition of the good mother in the case history. When she signs a contract, the accepted nurturing role of the genetic and/or gestational mother begins and ends with supplying the genetic material and/or incubation necessary to create the child. Once the surrogate has played her part, only the social mother may nurture the child emotionally.

While the custody case was being fought, Whitehead-Gould did receive the opportunity to operate as agent and tell her story in the women's magazine. *Family Circle* printed excerpts from her book (1989a, 1989b). However, a more recent profile in *Redbook* (Squire 1994) portrays her as an obsessive mother. Since 1989, case histories have invoked Whitehead-Gould as the negative example against which all potentially problematic women may be measured. McDowell's 1993 account of the birth of Deidre Hall's first child reassured readers when they learned that Robin, the woman hired by Hall to give birth, showed the film made about Baby M to her children to convince them that, unlike the bad woman in the movie, she would be doing a good deed by giving their sibling away. A 1995 reference reaffirms that Whitehead's symbolic "wicked witch" status remains unchallenged: "Mary Beth Whitehead single-handedly poisoned the pot" (Bransford:177).

ANGELS FROM HEAVEN

When a mythic hero endures considerable suffering on a protracted odyssey, it is usually to gain a boon so great that even the risk of death is worth the reward. As the final element of the fairy-tale–myth–miracle narrative structure of the case history, the baby has to be represented as the ultimate boon in order to fill this crucial position. For her role in the agency, the baby is both mythic holy grail and the angelic manifestation of God's will. The births are reported in the hyperbolic miracle language that has become the standard for the women's service magazine: "She is a miracle" (Remsberg 1982); "Our miracle daughter" (Travaglini 1992); and "I'm living with a miracle" (Uchytil 1993). They are also always described as perfect. Louise Joy Brown is a "cooing, gurgling, blue-eyed beauty" (Libman Block 1979: 62). Laurie Steel's Samantha is "a beautiful baby . . . gorgeously healthy and rosy looking" (Remsberg 1982:108), and little Brent was born "healthy and robust, loudly protesting his rough introduction to life" (Baker 1980:46).

If one child is a boon, multiple births are multiple blessings. The heroine of the case history becomes truly epic if she faces the challenge of mothering a large group of same-age children. She has returned from her torturous journey with not one holy grail but four, five, six, or seven. In articles with titles like "Love (times) 5" (Fein 1993); "The Triplets Club" (Rock 1996); "A Quint-essential Christmas" (Williams 1988); and "Oh Baby, Baby, Baby, Baby!" (Davenport 1995), the narrator-agent offers her sage advice to her readers who may be following her quest.

Reading between the Lines

SHATTERED SLIPPERS

The narrator-agent of the case history uses her account of the pain she experiences to legitimize herself as a mother. In so doing, she glosses over the multiple costs of participating in reproductive experimentation. Most women who participate in these experiments do not go home with babies. For them, the physical price has no final fulfilling purpose. And the pain is quite real and intense. Raymond considers egg "harvesting" to be medical rape:

> In the 1980s, an Austrian female student-observer described the vaginal harvesting of eggs from a woman in full view of a medical

school class: "At each follicle puncture he [the doctor] retracted the needle and then drove it in hard. The woman asked him to stop, because she was in great pain. But Dr. M. would have none of that . . . and so [more] follicles were punctured against her will . . . again each puncture unmistakably resembled a penetration." (1991:32)

Reproductive technologies also exact costs that go far beyond the physical pain they produce. People spend their savings, mortgage their homes, and go deeply into debt to finance their extravagant quests. The average reader of the women's magazine has an annual income of only $40,000. In 1994 Neumann, Gharib, and Weinstein reported that the cost to create and deliver an IVF baby is $67,000 when the first attempt is successful; after six attempts the cost goes to $114,000 (1994:242). For older women and for men with infertility problems, the price increases dramatically: $160,000 for just one attempt and as much as $800,000 for six attempts (241). A more recent HMO cost analysis reports lower costs of $9,329 for a single birth, $20,318 for twins, and $153,335 for triplets (Hidlebaugh, Thompson, and Berger 1997:570). Women make this investment with the belief that the procedures they will endure are safe and effective. However, older women, who are arguably the most likely to be seeking help, spend more money, incur more physical risk, and are least likely to succeed. Recent medical research finds that IVF treatment is most effective with the first attempt; with subsequent attempts, the rate of conception actually goes down (Templeton, Morris, and Parslow 1996). These same researchers also found that age is the most significant factor in the success or failure of in-vitro technologies: "The success rates at ages 40 and 45 are only 7 percent and 2 percent" (1406). Medical researchers are also trying to determine whether a connection exists in the use of fertility drugs and an increased risk of breast and ovarian cancers (Venn et al. 1995). Although no one has answered this question definitively, fertility treatments do pose a host of other physical dangers to the women who participate in them, ranging from infections and hyperstimulation of the ovaries to high-risk multiple pregnancies (Kershner 1996). Multiple births also raise the financial costs of assisted reproduction (Brownlee 1994).

HIERARCHIZING HEROICS

The attitudes of the women profiled in these case histories reveal that they distinguish different types of motherhood as more and less valuable. The highest level of achievement is to bear a child genetically related to both aspiring parents. The next preference is to experience pregnancy and childbirth, even if this means the woman has to use an egg "donor." If this option is not possible, the aspiring parents hire a woman to carry a child created from their genetic material; the next option is to hire a woman who "donates" her own egg and undergoes fertilization with the contracting male's sperm. Finally, the last method on the list is adoption. Those who demand a biological connection do not consider this solution an option; for those who do choose it, adoption appears not to be as fulfilling as pregnancy and childbirth, nor does it seem to qualify the woman as a "true" mother.

Thus even if a woman has children in her life—her own but not her present husband's, his from a previous marriage, or adoptive children—if she has the opportunity to acquire a child with even a remote biological connection to her or her mate and/or she can gestate, she must do so to properly consider herself a mother. The more actively she quests for control over the act of creation, the closer to "true" motherhood she comes. The testimony of one woman who used an egg donor implies a work ethic: "I've gone through more than most women would go through to give this baby life. If you think of it that way, it's more mine than anyone else's, because I had to work at it more" (Liebmann-Smith 1989:178). Another woman's dedication to her struggle makes her almost Godlike: "I fought so hard to have this baby that I feel ninety-nine-point-nine percent the creator" (Liebmann-Smith 1989:178). Ironically, that control is an illusion; in the fertility clinic the manipulation of gametes is firmly in the hands of the medical practitioners, not the women who present themselves as research subjects.

Many of the women discussed here already had other children. Brown considered raising her stepdaughter as practice for the real thing (Libman Block 1979:65). Del Zio had a biological daughter but wanted a child with her present husband (1979:135). Mills had already adopted a Korean girl, but she thinks the "sun rises and sets on Jessica," the baby her sister bore for her (1985:190). Linda and Glenn Merkel had a child he fathered with a surrogate, but when they heard that they could have a child genetically related to both of them, they decided to "try something a little more challenging" and hired a woman to gestate their embryo (Edmiston 1991: 236). Finally, "Elaina" and her husband, "Sam," had already adopted two children, but when she had the opportunity to gestate a child with an egg donated by her best friend, "Beth," she leaped at the chance: "In the labor room, all I did was cry, because I wanted the baby to be born, but I didn't want the pregnancy to end. I had had such a beautiful nine months—I had never felt so good in my life" (Liebmann-Smith 1989:177).

Pushed to the margins in these stories are the existing children—step, adoptive, and biological children with the "wrong" fathers or mothers. As they watch the nurturing women in their lives make the grueling journey to "genuine" motherhood, they must wonder about their own legitimacy. If their mothers are not already true mothers, how can they be true sons and daughters? Placing a hierarchy on motherhood places the same hierarchical values on childhood.

HEROIC ENDURANCE OR OBSESSION?

Hall's story illustrates well how the drive to accomplish motherhood regardless of the obstacles can create disturbing emotional results. Present at the birth of David, Hall seems to be unaware of the extreme nature of her desire to take possession of this child. She describes her actions in the delivery room: "As David came out I grabbed him, while Robin was saying, 'Take it easy!' He's still attached to me!' It was all so magical" (Radovsky 1993:38). Hall is not the only aspiring mother to nearly rip the baby from the womb of the woman she has hired to gestate for her: "Dr. Bates put the baby in Cynthia's arms. 'She was ready to bundle him up and walk away,' Bates recalls, laughing. 'But I said, "Wait, he's still attached!"'" (Edmondson Gupta 1989:216).

These women seem to forget that the mothers who are delivering babies into their arms are human, vulnerable, and even necessary. During Robin's second pregnancy, Hall wishes for something physically impossible: she wants to somehow remove Robin from the picture, even while she gestates. "Robin and I went shopping, ate lunch together and developed a real friendship. That's not to say that it was emotionally easy all the time. Once, at a visit to the obstetrician, I thought, Gee, it sure would be nice if Robin would leave so I could be alone with my baby" (Hall 1995:75).

Another woman, Helen Bransford, whose passion for a child also led her to hire a surrogate, demonstrates how completely she has divorced this woman from the fetuses she is carrying. She made the mistake of hiring a woman who was both overweight and a chain smoker, and when the pregnancy (twins) inevitably resulted in gestational diabetes, Bransford explains the problems in a "diary" account now available to her reader: "She also has a minor infection, and worst of all, she's still smoking. Combined with diabetes, smoking can cause insufficient blood flow to the babies, premature separation of the placenta from the uterus (i.e. death), low birthweight, and complicated circulatory problems. Damn her for doing a half-assed job" (1995:177).

The potential for harm to the woman carrying the children—death—warrants a parenthetical reference, while the potential problems for the babies are the clear focus of this woman's concern. Like Hall, Bransford wishes she could just dispense with the hired womb, especially because the woman is doing such a lousy job; because she cannot, Bransford writes the fetuses letters of apology for "picking such a lousy carrier" (1995:177). Neither Hall nor Bransford seems to recognize the detached way in which they view the two women who are risking their lives to create children for them.

GOD'S RIGHT HAND?

When a doctor who did not agree with the ethics of the procedure washed Del Zio's fertilized eggs down the drain, she accused him of playing God (1979). What she and her sister questers seem to have missed is that the doctors who facilitate reproduction can have less-than-altruistic motives. Financial gain and prestige are obvious draws to the fertility industry, but probably the most compelling motivation is that the fertility doctor gets to wave his magic wand over his patient and say, "Let there be life." Because the case history does not address human motivations, the antics of doctors like Cecil Jacobson, who was convicted of fraud for using his own sperm for inseminations (Scripps 1994:37A), come as a shock to the trusting readers of the women's magazine. (Jacobson was fond of telling his patients: "God doesn't give you babies, I do"; see Elmer-DeWitt 1991:27). A more recent scandal involving the University of California, Irvine's fertility clinic and Dr. Ricardo Asch, considered by the profession to be one of its leaders, produced one case history in which the woman tells how the doctor she trusted with her embryos betrayed her (Challender 1995). Asch and two colleagues were indicted on charges of insurance fraud and mail fraud in the egg "stealing" scandal, but Asch and one colleague left the country before being tried in the case (see Roberts 1995 and *Orange County Register* 1998). But such cases are rare in the women's magazine, and one need not read beyond the benevolent depiction of the grandfatherly Steptoe to find questionable motives the writers have not addressed. When Steptoe delivered Louise Joy Brown via a conveniently necessary cesarean section, her mother's missing fallopian tubes erased any doubt for observers that Steptoe had achieved in-vitro fertilization. One wonders whether he removed them because they were in the way of his medical procedures or his reputation.

REPRODUCTIVE BROTHELS

Unfortunately, the rosy picture of the fairy godmother-surrogate found in the case histories glosses over the worldly motivations of women who rent out their wombs. An example of how well the case history works to obscure the problematic nature of such arrangements is Bransford's narrative of her experience with "Hope," the chain-smoking woman she wishes she could fire halfway through the job. In an early diary entry, Bransford comments about the legal status of surrogacy: "The laws seem antediluvian, and the fear of creating a breeding class of women ludicrous" (1995:176). Yet Bransford tells her readers that Hope shares a cramped apartment with her mother, sister, and an assortment of children, and she earns $8,000 a year as a server in a restaurant (134). Hope lives below poverty level and is clearly engaging in surrogacy for the money. Bransford also reveals her class prejudice when she writes in a letter to the unborn fetuses, "Please know I'll do better by you when you come out. You won't have to breathe smoke, eat McDonald's, or *listen to country-music TV day and night*" (177; emphasis added). Despite her frustrations about Hope's unsuitability as a carrier (both physically and socially), Bransford, incapable of recognizing or unwilling to see the exploitative relationship she has participated in, still paints a happy ending: "Today Hope has a car, her debt is behind her, she has an expanded support system, and she plans to attend paralegal school" (178).

BROKEN HALOS

The babies edited out of these stories are those who arrive with birth defects. Instead readers meet the Arnotts' four little angels, who were presumably sent from heaven to answer their parents' prayers. In reality, the Arnotts' quadruplets arrived by cesarean section three months before term. Weighing in at between one and two pounds each, they spent the first three months of their lives in the neonatal unit at the hospital. The Arnotts were fortunate that their children have a 90 percent chance of developing normally (Simpson 1994). Medical statistics indicate that babies that are the product of multiple births are ten times more likely to be born prematurely and with low birth weights (Kershner 1996); two to three times more likely to suffer from spina bifida and heart abnormalities (Cohen 1996); forty-seven times more likely to have cerebral palsy (Brownlee 1994); and four times more likely to die (Kershner 1996). In the United States, the incidence of multiple births is 1 in 250 with in vitro, and 1 in 13 with GIFT (Fertility clinics 1996). Not surprisingly, the rate of multiple births in this country is on the rise, up 214 percent since 1980 (Cimons 1997).

THE FIVE HOLY GRAILS

Edited into the margins along with birth defects are the financial and management costs of multiple births. The case histories portray the day-to-day lives of these families as merely hectically humorous. When overwhelmed, the exhausted mothers simply "look back at being pregnant, worried and bedbound, and that puts it all into perspective" (Rock 1996:146). Faced with the kind of feminine heroism these women portray, how can the reader refuse to include reproductive technology in her repertoire of strategies for achieving motherhood? To do less would be to fail as a woman.

In fact, after reading her regular fare of gynecological case histories over the past twenty years, the checkout-stand reader has learned that to be a true woman she must have a child. She must be willing to pursue that child regardless of the costs—financial, physical, emotional, or social—to her, to the child, to her existing children, and to the women whose bodies she may be exploiting. She has learned that the doctors who perform these technological feats are benevolent wizards, whom she can and should trust with her reproductive power, that the technology is magical and potent, and that, if her quest demands it, other women's bodies and emotions are legitimately hers to exploit. The baby she may attain will be perfect and it will bring her the ultimate feminine fulfillment: the completeness of motherhood. Finally, the entire journey is one that has been mandated by the will of God.

A modern version of the nineteenth-century cult of true womanhood saturates every rhetorical aspect of the case history in the women's service magazine. The emotional and highly subjective language of the first-person narrative attracts the reader who, because she identifies with the storyteller, is more inclined to adopt the storyteller's unexamined belief in both motherhood at all costs and reproductive technology. This belief brings the childless woman into the fertility clinic and ensures her willing participation in a massive medical experiment that promises to change the way women reproduce but not how they are defined and valued in relation to reproduction. This redefinition of motherhood goes beyond reiterating and reproducing our existing "sexual caste system" (Daly 1978:227); it adds a new hierarchy of classifications that values women according to their reproductive function: as social nurturers, as suppliers of genetic material, or as providers of gestational environments. The "ordinary" woman who purchases the women's service magazine and reads about these technologies must recognize how she is collaborating in the revision of feminine value. Whether or not her progeny is being genetically engineered in the laboratory, she is being linguistically engineered into this newly extended sexual caste system. Whether she occupies the more valued position of social nurturer or the low-ranking position of human incubator, as a member of the reproductive brothel she is participating in a continuing devaluation of women that is both dehumanizing and destructive—to her and to the society in which she lives.

NOTES

This chapter appeared previously in Chloé Diepenbrock, *Gynecology and textuality: Popular representations of reproductive technology* (New York: Garland, 1998).

1. For an in-depth discussion of the history of the gynecological case history in the United States, and its portrayal in other media, see C. Diepenbrock, *Gynecology and textuality: Popular representations of reproductive technology* (New York: Garland, 1998).

2. See chapter 6 by Laura Shanner, "Bodies, Minds, and Failures: Images of Women in Infertility Clinics," for a nicely worked out discussion of cultural perceptions of male-female mind-body relationships and how they result in different conceptions about the amount of control we have over our reproductive capabilities.

REFERENCES

Baker, N. C. 1980. The secret of our very special baby. *Ladies' Home Journal,* August, pp. 46–54.

Bransford, Helen. 1995. Surrogacy: A mother's story. *Vogue,* July, pp. 134–37, 176–78.

Brownlee, Susan. 1994. The baby chase. *U.S. News and World Report,* December 5, pp. 84–93.

Burke, Kenneth. 1969a. *A grammar of motives.* Berkeley: University of California Press. Originally published in 1945.

Burke, Kenneth. 1969b. *A rhetoric of motives.* Berkeley: University of California Press. Originally published in 1950.

Challender, Debbie. 1995. Fertility fraud: Why one mother may never know her babies. *Redbook,* December, pp. 84–87.

Cimons, Marlene. 1997. Ratio of multiple births in U.S. has risen 214 percent since 1980. *Houston Chronicle,* January 29, p. 12A.

Cohen, Cynthia B. 1996. "Give me children or I shall die!": New reproductive technologies and harm to children. *Hastings Center Report* 26:19–27.

Corea, Gena. 1987. The reproductive brothel. In *Man-made women: How new reproductive technologies affect women,* pp. 38–51. Bloomington: Indiana University Press.

Daly, Mary. 1978. *Gyn/ecology: The metaethics of radical feminism.* Boston: Beacon.

Davenport, Christine, and Donna Freedman. 1995. Oh baby, baby, baby, baby! *McCall's,* April, pp. 82–83.

Del Zio, Doris, with Suzanne Wilding. 1979. I was cheated of my test-tube baby. *Good Housekeeping,* March, pp. 135, 200, 202, 203.

Edmiston, Susan. 1991. Whose child is this? *Glamour,* November, pp. 234–37.

Edmondson Gupta, Nelly. 1989. Brave new baby. *Ladies' Home Journal,* October, pp. 140–41.

120

Part One: Historical Bases of Reproductive Discourse

Elmer-DeWitt, Phillip. 1991. The cruelest kind of fraud. *Time,* December 2, p. 27.

Fein, Elaine. 1993. Love (times) five. *Family Circle,* August 10, pp. 96–98.

Fertility clinics: What are the odds? 1996. *Consumer Reports,* February, pp. 51–55.

Garvey, Mark, ed. 1995. *Writer's market.* Cincinnati: Writer's Digest Books–F&W Publications.

Hall, Deidre, with Dean Lamanna. 1995. What we did for love. *Ladies' Home Journal,* December, pp. 74–80.

Hanmer, Jalna. 1985. A womb of one's own. In Rita Arditti, R. D. Klein, and Shelley Minden, eds., *Test-tube women: What future for motherhood?* pp. 438–48. Boston: Pandora.

Hidlebaugh, D. A., I. E. Thompson, and M. J. Berger. 1997. Cost of assisted reproductive technology for a health maintenance organization. *Journal of Reproductive Medicine* 42:570–74.

Holmes, H. B., B. B. Hoskins, and Michael Gross, eds. 1980. *Birth control and controlling birth: Women-centered perspectives.* Clifton, N.J.: Humana Press.

Katz, Bill, and Linda Sternberg Katz. 1995. *Magazines for libraries.* 8th ed. New York: R. R. Bowker-Reed.

Kershner, Kelly. 1996. In vitro fertilization: Is conceiving a child worth the costs? *USA Today,* May, pp. 30–32.

Libman Block, Jean. 1979. God willed it. *Good Housekeeping,* January, pp. 62, 64, 66, 67, 70, 71.

Liebmann-Smith, Joan. 1989. Two friends with one dream. *Redbook,* March, pp. 122–23.

Margolis, Maxine. 1984. *Mothers and such: Views of American women and why they changed.* Berkeley: University of California Press.

Markoutsas, Elaine. 1981. Women who have babies for other women. *Good Housekeeping,* April, pp. 96, 98–100, 102, 104.

McDowell, Janet Dickey. 1993. Miracle babies. *First for Women,* May 17, pp. 30–34.

Milling, T. J. 1998. Eight born to Houston mom. *Houston Chronicle,* December 21, p. 1A.

Mills, Karen. 1985. I had my sister's baby. *Ladies' Home Journal,* October, pp. 20, 22, 190.

Nash, J. M. 1991. All in the family. *Time,* August 19, p. 58.

Neumann, P. J., Soheyla Gharib, and M. C. Weinstein. 1994. The cost of a successful delivery with in vitro fertilization. *New England Journal of Medicine* 331:239–43.

Orange County Register. 1998. Doctor points finger at colleagues in fertility scandal. *Sacramento Bee,* March 18, p. A5.

Radovsky, V. J. 1993. Special report: Overcoming infertility. *First for Women,* May 17, pp. 37–38.

Raymond, Janice G. 1987. Fetalists and feminists: They are not the same. In Patricia Spallone and D. L. Steinberg, eds., *Made to order: The myth of reproductive and genetic progress,* pp. 58–66. New York: Pergamon.

Raymond, Janice G. 1991. Women as wombs. *Ms.,* May–June, pp. 28–33.

Remsberg, Bonnie. 1982. She is a miracle. *Ladies' Home Journal,* January, pp. 75–77.

Roberts, John. 1995. U.S. doctors accused of misusing embryos. *British Medical Journal (International)* 311:585.

Rock, Andrea. 1996. The triplets club. *Ladies' Home Journal,* March, pp. 144–47.

Rowland, Robyn. 1992. *Living laboratories: Women and reproductive technologies.* Bloomington: Indiana University Press.

Schweitzer, Arlette, with Kathryn Casey. 1992. My children, my grandchildren. *Ladies' Home Journal,* February, pp. 125–27.

Scripps Howard News Service. 1994. Court upholds conviction of fertility doctor. *Denver Rocky Mountain News,* May 3, p. 37A.

Simpson, Kevin. 1994. Four little angels answered their prayers. *Woman's World,* July 12, pp. 12–13.

Spallone, Patricia. 1989. *Beyond conception: The new politics of reproduction.* Granby, Mass.: Bergin and Garvey.

Squire, Susan. 1994. Whatever happened to Baby M? *Redbook,* January, pp. 60–65.

Templeton, Allan, J. K. Morris, and William Parslow. 1996. Factors that affect outcome of in-vitro fertilisation treatment. *Lancet* 348:1402–6.

Travaglini, Kris. 1992. Our miracle daughter. *Ladies' Home Journal,* May, pp. 24–28.

Uchytil, Christa. 1993. I'm living with a miracle. *Ladies' Home Journal,* June, pp. 26–32.

Venn, Alison, Lyndsey Watson, Judith Lumley, and Graham Giles. 1995. Breast and ovarian cancer incidence after infertility and in vitro fertilisation. *Lancet* 346:995–1000.

Whitehead, Mary Beth, and Loretta Schwartz-Nobel. 1989a. *Family Circle,* February 21, pp. 101–2.

Whitehead, Mary Beth, and Loretta Schwartz-Nobel. 1989b. *Family Circle,* March 14, pp. 100–101.

Williams, M. S. 1988. A "quint-essential" Christmas. *McCall's,* December, pp. 107–9.

Woloch, Nancy. 1984. *Women and the American experience.* New York: Knopf.

Wood, J. P. 1956. *Magazines in the United States.* 2d ed. New York: Ronald Press.

Wright, Karen. 1998. Human in the age of mechanical reproduction. *Discover,* May, pp. 74–81.

PART TWO

REPRODUCTION, LANGUAGE,

AND MEDICAL MODELS

5

WOMEN'S REPRODUCTIVE

CHOICES AND THE GENETIC

MODEL OF MEDICINE

CELESTE M. CONDIT

U.S. taxpayers are slated to spend $3 billion on research on the Human Genome Project, designed to transcribe the entire genetic sequence of human beings and of related experimental animals. Spin-offs from the project are already producing notable health benefits for some people. However, this intensive focus on genes and health also harbors the potential for creating or exacerbating problems for many women with regard to reproductive health.

Problems for women arise because the Human Genome Project is promoting a "genetic" model of medicine to replace the well-established germ theory. Unlike the germ theory, the genetic model envisions particular human bodies as essentially and fatally flawed from the moment of conception. Advocates of the genetic model usually envision "treatment" through prenatal selection or genetic engineering. The model thereby places a greater and more direct onus for the health of children on women's bodies. This responsibility arrives in a context of choice that requires substantial absorption of technical information. Information-giving activities will therefore structure women's choices. Diverse groups of women need to influence these structures both within the medical establishment and outside it.

This chapter describes the development of the genetic model of medicine through a close analysis of an address by internationally renowned geneticist Paul Berg, supplemented by related genetic texts. It also discusses the implications of this model for women and reproduction. Finally, it uses a "public ethnography" to explore the ways the information-giving structure in a medical care system driven by advanced technology shapes women's "choices."

The Genetic Model of Medicine

Scholars often refer to the established model of medicine as the "germ theory." This theory specifies that human disease occurs when foreign organisms such as viruses, bacteria, worms, or fungi invade the body. Maintaining health therefore means avoiding germ agents, ridding the body of germs when they have successfully invaded, and ensuring the body's ability to resist germs through vaccines but sometimes also by ensuring good nutrition and environmental conditions.[1] In contrast, the genetic model of medicine specifies that inadequacies in the genetic configuration of individuals cause illness. According to this model, foreign invaders don't cause diseases, but failures in the body's own constitution do. In other words, viruses can invade and cause damage only if an individual's genetic configuration is such that the individual is unable to resist the viral invasion. Similarly, the genetic model of medicine specifies that cancer results from the failure of an individual's genes to regulate cell division properly, and manic depression occurs because one's genes produce the wrong balance of brain chemicals (or receptors for these chemicals).

Replacing the germ theory of medicine with the genetic theory is not an easy enterprise for crusading geneticists. The medical establishment is heavily invested in the germ theory, both materially and intellectually. The public is likewise accustomed to the germ theory and resistant in many ways to the genetic model, especially given its long-standing connection to eugenics. As a consequence of this resistance, those who seek to establish the genetic model must proceed carefully. In general, the elements of this model are addressed in fragments in a variety of locales. By establishing various fragments of the model independently of one another, the groundwork is laid for later presentation of the model as a whole. To reveal the argumentative structure upon which the transition to the genetic model is based, however, we can best turn to an instance where the rationale for the genetic model is developed in its entirety.

Rhetorical analysis of a single, complete text allows one to attend both to the specific argumentative components a rhetor deploys and to the ways in which discrete argumentative components build upon each other. Michael Leff has developed the rationale for and elements of this "dispositional" or "temporal" method of analysis (1988). He has clarified the ways in which many rhetorical texts that construct ideological transitions "move" the audience from one ideological terrain to another through a temporal progression. Each move a text makes establishes a position that disposes the audience toward the next move. Thus to understand the ways in which writers construct new models or world-views, one must examine, in order, the progressive series of positions an author takes in a text that seeks to move an audience by stages from one ideological "place" to another.

Paul Berg is a Nobel Prize–winning geneticist and an ardent crusader for funding for genetics research who speaks frequently about genetics. He has delivered, on multiple occasions, a speech that provides a paradigmatic exemplar of the rhetorical case for shifting from the germ theory to the genetic theory of medicine (Yee 1993; Siegfried 1993; Golden 1995). I focus here on one version of this address, which Berg gave at the University of Georgia on January 29, 1996, entitled "Understanding Our Genes: Opportunities and Concerns."

Speaking to an audience of University of Georgia scientists, humanists, and academic administrators, Berg began his rhetorical enterprise by stating his claim that genes are central to human health. He asserted that "these [genes] determine virtually every aspect of our physical nature. That is, our appearance, our metabolism, susceptibility to infection and diseases like diabetes, cancer, hypertension, lifespan, and very likely basic intellectual abilities. In short, we are in large measure the outcome of the 100,000 different genes that we inherit and, very importantly, the ways those genes act in response to the environment" (Berg 1996:2).

To establish the plausibility of this claim, Berg turned first to the cellular level, describing in shorthand fashion how genes function by coding for proteins. Beginning at the cellular level is a strong rhetorical move. Scientists in the audience will not find Berg's account problematic, for it is quite standard, and nonscientists will feel unauthorized to challenge him.

Berg's account of cell-level action is itself biased, however. Berg drew a stick figure diagram that indicated Genes → Protein. This is a correct statement but an incomplete one and therefore misleading. In this diagram and in all subsequent portions of his talk, Berg made the gene the central actor in the cellular drama by using two rhetorical strategies. First, he punctuated the series by starting his account with the gene. He would tell a different story if he drew a diagram that started with the environment, such that Environment → Activator Molecule → Gene → Protein. Both such diagrams would be technically correct. The former makes the gene the active and initiating agent; the latter makes the environment (defined in a variety of ways) an obvious participant in the process. Throughout his address Berg mentioned the environment but always referred to the gene as acting in response to the environment, rather than to the environment as acting on the human body. Thus this genetic model imagines the environment as fixed and immutable, whereas the genes are active and therefore must be controlled.

In his diagram, Berg was also centralizing the role of the gene through the rhetorical strategy of simplification. In reality, genes do not produce proteins unless the cell has available adequate supplies of basic chemicals, and this is an environmental and, for humans, a social locus of control. Thus the diagram should read Gene + Nutrition = Protein. By simplifying, however, Berg again portrayed the gene as the central and active agent, a singular locus of control.

Having constructed genes as the central active agents in cellular processes, Berg next moved to the level of the organism and disease. Here again, however, he made a strategic choice. He did not begin with complex diseases or with obviously organism-caused diseases (e.g., small pox or tuberculosis) but rather with diseases that are caused by mutations in single genes, most notably sickle cell and cystic fibrosis. Berg described in moderate detail the way in which a misconfigured gene can lead to faulty gene products and thereby cause these diseases. Once again, Berg's account is a true one. However, once again, his selection of these components as paradigmatic of the body and its relationship to disease represents a misleading bias. Berg claimed that these diseases are "very common" (7). This is a difficult claim to dispute, because he has not quantified it, but single-gene defect diseases account for much less than 5 percent of serious human illnesses globally. Berg intensified the sense that these single-gene conditions are "typical," however, through an additional device. He showed pictures of rats and flies with single-gene alterations; the rats had become obese, and the flies had legs growing out of their eyes. Berg thus generalized the control of the single gene beyond a few specific diseases, demonstrating the power of genes to control all facets of the individual and, by implication therefore, all disease. Berg noted at this point, "So what I've done over this series of a few slides is to focus your attention on the impact of mutations on physiological functions or development. The story being the gene-specifying proteins which have specific functions, metabolic, morphologic, developmental, signaling, whatever" (9). Having established single-gene disorders and interactions as paradigmatic, he was ready to promote the genetic model of disease at the most general level.

Berg's next slide was labeled COMMON INHERITED DISEASE. On this slide he listed diabetes, Alzheimer's, schizophrenia, manic depression, cancers, hypertension, cardiovascular disease, rheumatoid arthritis, and multiple sclerosis. After putting this slide up, he said, "What I wanted to focus on is cancer. In part because I think people have not generally viewed cancer as a genetic disease. It is a genetic disease by any definition which says that it results from mutations in genes which have essential functions in modulating or moderating cell division and growth" (10).

Berg's decision to focus on cancer is again a strategic one. Although still elusive in important respects, cancer is one of the best-studied diseases, and no one disputes that cell regulation, and therefore genes, have some role in cancer (the role of genes in most of the other conditions is much less well understood). Moreover, cancer is a disease that is clearly inadequately accounted for by the germ theory of medicine, and it is probably the disease that the general public fears most. Berg spent almost a quarter of his address detailing the ways in which cell division occurs and the ways in which genes play a role in that process. As in the earlier account at the cellular level, however, Berg again centralized the gene and decentralized environmental influences and other cell components. His account is accurate but partial. He showed a slide of a cartoon and said,

> So, we have met the enemy and he is us, paraphrasing the comic strip of *Pogo* for those of you old timers that might have read that. And my friend Francis Collins who has the human genome project essentially gave me a copy of this slide which essentially tries to make that message that in cancer it is our own genes, absolutely essential genes, and perfectly normal genes, which undergo damage, mutation, change in the protein, loss of function, or gain of function, and thereby leading to this abnormal *control*. (14; emphasis added)

In this rhetorical vision, cancer comes not from outside but is, rather, a defect in us, ourselves. We are our own enemy. Again, he indirectly acknowledged environmental agents but only in a nonspecific way. Genes "undergo" damage, the source of which he never specified. And ultimately, it is not the environment or nutrition but genes that "control" and must therefore be the focus of medical control.

· Given public beliefs about the importance of the environment, Berg was not quite bold enough to deny the role of environment completely, but he signaled his desire to do so. In his next oral paragraph he said,

> So, I draw from this a [*sic*] overarching and perhaps overambitious conclusion. And it is that all human disease is a consequence of the interaction of our genes with the environment. In my more guarded, or less guarded, moments, I would say, I would *usually* write that all human disease is a consequence of damage to our

> genes. And that changes or produces a new perspective on how
> we think about detecting human disease, managing it, and hope-
> fully curing it. (15; emphasis added)

Effacing the environment, or even the broader context of the cell, making it less consequential, less active than individual genes certainly does
change the notion of medicine, interiorizing it almost completely. As
Berg went on to specify, the focus of medical research then is not on
tracking down infectious agents, providing hygienic environments and
good nutrition, or even on producing antibiotic agents. Instead "we're
driven, compelled to try to identify the genes which are responsible for
human disease. If that's where we have to target our therapy we want
to know which genes are affected" (15).

Berg has thus argued for a new vision of medicine and appropriate
therapies based on a genetic model of human disease. A genetically ill
body is different from a body invaded by germs. A genetically ill body
needs not merely to have an alien invader run out, or merely to have a
part replaced, but to have an expert rewrite the fundamental "code" of
the body. The vision is not uncontested or incontestable. As Berg noted,
no substantially effective gene therapies for any major diseases have
arisen from this research. Berg attributed this failure, however, to a
"gap in time" that will eventually prove effaceable. In the meantime,
ironically, he is content to tout the spin-off products from genetic research that augment conventional medicine in some surprising and successful ways.

Berg's address is not an isolated piece of discourse. Although the full
argument for genetic medicine is not represented in most places, people
regularly repeat various components of the address, and many scientists argue that genetics brings "a new era in medicine" (Caskey 1993).
Francis Collins, head of the Human Genome Project at the National
Center for Human Genome Research, repeatedly appears on radio and
television programs and in various videos to tout the vision of genetics
as central to all diseases. He tells his audiences, "I would ask you in
your deliberations to think of genetic disease in broad terms, not narrow terms" (HuGem 1995). Genetic disease is "not a 'back corner'" disease, he insists; rather, "virtually every medical condition has a genetic
component." The same set of claims is evident in the pamphlet produced by the National Institutes of Health called *Understanding Gene
Testing* (n.d.). The pamphlet says, "All cancer is genetic, in that it is *trig-
gered* by altered genes" (12; emphasis added). These discourses, and
many others, obviously seek to centralize the gene and to assign it the
controlling, "triggering" role in human health.

Other supportive discourses as well as underlying social and scientific conditions promote Berg's view. In the first place, the state of the science of genetics and the character of the human condition encourage Berg's centralizing of single-gene disorders as the model of all genetic disease relationships. That is, single-gene disorders are the easiest to investigate. They have therefore been investigated first. As a result, they come "first" not only rhetorically in Berg's document but also first historically as a stage of scientific investigation. Therefore, the tendency to see these conditions as paradigmatic is strong. Whether the future will alter that status as more complex conditions become more central to scientific research remains to be seen.

Second, various social conditions also promote a paradigm of medicine directed at curing rather than preventing disease through nutritional and environmental measures. Not only does our concept of "medicine" remain focused largely on crisis cure rather than long-term health and well-being (though recent years have seen some movement in the broader direction) but broader social values encourage more attention to crisis response than to health management over the long term. Health management requires broad expenditures with indirect payoffs, both on the part of the society and on the part of individuals. Crisis response features direct, targeted payoffs—it cures visibly ill people. Thus narrowing the scope of disease concepts to focus on genes that are malfunctioning or will definitely malfunction has some inherent social appeal.

The genetic model of medicine thus has substantial forces supporting its rise to prominence. Nonetheless, some counterbalancing forces are at work too. The lack of successful gene therapies, and the genetic account's limited applicability (or efficiency) with regard to many disease conditions, may serve as effective brakes on the acceptance of this model. To this point, however, I have suggested only general reasons for finding the genetic model of disease to be insufficient. Women also should have very specific concerns about the implementation of this model.

The Womb as the Site of Genetic Medicine

The germ theory of disease identified germs as the target of medical control. Disease-control mechanisms clearly involved human bodies, but bodies were not the central demons of disease. Disease invaded and violated people. In contrast, in the genetic model of medicine, the people themselves are faulty. This model identifies one's genes as essentially deficient, and this is not an accidental characteristic of the person, for the model simultaneously identifies genes as the core of one's being. One's genes determine one's fundamental characteristics.

If germs are at fault for disease, one targets the germs. If a person's genes are at fault for disease, one targets the person's genes. Currently, no gene therapies for disease are available. This leaves open two possibilities for treatment in the genetic model of disease. First, one may deny the appropriateness of treatment at all. If one has faulty genes, one is destined for illness, and interfering with that destiny is inappropriate because it will violate natural selection and lead to the accumulation of greater disease propensity in the human genome. Few credible contemporary voices argue for that approach, though the argument has surfaced periodically throughout Western history.

The other approach to genetic medicine in the absence of gene therapies is genetic selection. Through in-vitro fertilization or abortion, parents can select against bringing children into the world who harbor faulty genes. Today this approach to genetic medicine is the central approach, and biotechnology companies are rapidly pushing an expanded array of genetic testing products. This approach puts the onus for health on individuals but more centrally on women. The genetic model of medicine assigns women substantial duties for ensuring the health of their children. Women are supposed to undergo the anxiety-producing process of prenatal testing (Rothman 1993). If testing finds the fetal genes are deficient, women are supposed to abort their pregnancies, facing both loss of a wanted child and the risks and discomforts of late-stage abortion. Alternately, women are supposed to conceive their pregnancy through preimplantation selection, which requires in-vitro fertilization—an expensive, largely ineffective, and emotionally draining experience (Condit 1996; Flores 1996).

Genetics professionals often argue that the emphasis on prenatal selection is undesirable and that it is only a short-term measure. They suggest that in the long term, gene therapies (or treatments derived from genetic knowledge) will replace genetic selection. But it is too early to know whether that will be so, and it is unclear how long this "interim" period will be. Undoubtedly, the interim era will vary widely for different diseases, and as long as any significant disease exists for which no genetic therapy is available, the model specifies that pregnant women should undergo genetic testing. With conditions like Down's syndrome, this promises to be a very long time indeed. Moreover, there are already indications that gene therapy may often be an in-utero procedure, thereby implicating women's bodies in yet another fashion. Finally, it is not at all clear that gene therapy will ever be economically feasible, given the relatively low financial costs of genetic selection (by abortion). Especially if people become accustomed to genetic selection, the society might well ask why it should bring into being flawed people, whose basic genetic flaws it will only need to correct, rather than insist on medically flawless people in the first place.

Obviously, women have strong reasons for resisting the transfer to the genetic model of medicine, with its increased obligations for women and its location of their wombs as the site of responsibility for disease. Women's opposition to this model can be effective in resisting it. The genetic model of medicine is not a comprehensive model but a narrow and partial one. It is not likely to be efficient or inexpensive. And many social agents, including family doctors, oppose this model.

Women ought, therefore, to promote a different vision for medical care. This would be a comprehensive model, one that recognizes the role of the gene but keeps it within place and within scale—integrated with active notions of germs, environment, and nutrition. Whether such a comprehensive model arises to resist the genetic model or not, women will probably have to continue to make genetic choices. Women will probably find that whether to undergo genetic testing, and what kind, are decisions now with us on a permanent basis. Whether the availability of genetic testing is desirable and useful for particular women or groups of women will vary widely, depending in large measure on the woman, her resources, her attitudes toward disease and disability, and her beliefs about the status of the fetus. Thus regardless of the situation of individual women, women of the future will have to make genetic choices at some levels; therefore exploring some of the vital components of these choices is important.

Information and the Structuring of Genetic Choice

Most research geneticists and genetic counselors are highly committed to the notion of individual choice with regard to reproductive genetics and other genetic issues (Wertz and Fletcher 1989). Society needs to maintain and support this insistence that women should be the decision makers on these vital personal issues. But the medical genetics community conceptualizes choice on a laissez-faire model.[2] This framework ignores the prestructuring by the medical community and society at large of the technical information necessary for making specific choices. Scientific and technical protocols and social agendas—rather than the value choices and personal preferences of the women involved—are the basis for the range of available choices and the informational support for those choices.

To illustrate the way in which medical institutions structure the information and options available to women for their choice making, consider the differences in the delivery of genetic counseling at public hospitals and in private hospital settings. The examples that follow come from a series of observations I made of genetic counseling sessions in diverse clinic settings with the financial assistance of a visiting investigator grant from the National Institutes of Health.

Three people sit in an examining room of a publicly funded hospital in a large urban area: the observer, the counselor, and the "client." Like most other clients who will pass through this door, the client is a pregnant woman receiving Aid to Families with Dependent Children, Medicaid, housing supplements, and food stamps. Because she is in the detoxification center, someone flagged her chart and told her to see the genetic counselor.

The client—let us call her Ms. Williams—complains that the section of the detox center that she is in provokes pregnancy-related nausea because of the state of the other clients, who are vomiting and unclean. She is considering leaving the detox center that day. She states that she wants to keep her child. This is her fifth pregnancy, and her mother and foster parents care for her four children. She is adamant that she doesn't believe in abortion.

The counselor begins to take the family history. Asked about her health, Williams states that she smokes cocaine every month as soon as her welfare check comes, spending it all immediately. She acknowledges high alcohol consumption, though she states she has tapered off during pregnancy. She says her marijuana use has dropped dramatically since she started on cocaine seven years ago. Taking the family history consumes most of the session. The counselor meticulously creates little squares and circles neatly aligned to construct a proper pedigree. The counselor's attention to her charting makes communication difficult. Williams anticipates and answers questions two or three ahead, but the counselor hears answers only to the immediate question that she is writing down. The client starts out cooperative but ends up a bit withdrawn. As the charting proceeds, the geneticist asks repeated questions about particular relatives, "Is he/she healthy?" In response, Williams volunteers information about extensive drug and alcohol abuse in the family—perhaps because she understands this session is a response to her own alcohol and drug use, given that her access to the genetics clinic is a result of her presence in the detox center.

Williams's third child was born with cerebral palsy—she downplays the child's limp and learning difficulties and portrays her as "doing very well." She is not the primary caregiver for the child. Williams cannot remember her own history very well. She seems to lose track of key personal events and has trouble dating the pregnancy. After an hour the counselor offers her the MSAFP screen (a blood screen that detects increased probability of major fetal differences such as Down's syndrome). Initially, Williams says, "Yeah, I want that. I want anything they got." However, she cools to the notion as the counselor explains in a rather ambiguous way that it "would help you prepare for the baby if there is anything wrong with it." The counselor does not discuss the characteristics of the diseases for which the MSAFP screens. Instead the counselor describes in detail how cocaine can cause premature labor and that this would be bad for the baby. She also describes in detail the risks of alcohol in pregnancy and describes the risks of cigarette smoking in very thorough detail. The counselor tries to get Williams a nicotine patch. When they approach a physician, however, he tells Williams, "You're strong; you can quit cold turkey like everybody else." Williams ultimately agrees to an appointment for an ultrasound, but she says she probably won't be able to keep the appointment because she will probably leave the detoxification center.

Williams is not a typical patient. In the two weeks that I spent as an observer at this location, I saw other women with very different lives; each of their sessions with the genetics counselor was its own puzzle and process. The counselor offered one woman the MSAFP because of advanced maternal age (older than thirty). A prison guard accompanied this client, and her statements about what she wants change depending on whether the prison guard is in the room or out of it. I see another woman, who carries one copy of a gene for a blood disorder. She appears to me to be mentally retarded, sucks her thumb, and wants to force her partner into a genetic screen in retaliation for his failure to call a nurse when she had trouble with an IV when she was in the hospital. I see another woman, who probably has fetal alcohol syndrome, who is homeless, and who is in the psychiatric hospital for depression and potential suicide. Lest class assumptions make the picture too neat, however, I also see a woman who works at the day care center in the hospital, who struggles valiantly to match the information the counselor provides with her own values with regard to her unplanned pregnancy.

Williams is not typical because the conditions and concerns of these women are radically different from each other. Each session goes differently in a dozen ways because each client faces such different concerns and problems. Nonetheless, Williams's session points to several recur-

136

ring factors that shape the conduct of genetics, and these serve as problems and limits on women's abilities to make free and informed choices. First, these women are here because the bureaucracy has told them to appear. They come not because they sought out information and assistance but because they are sent. Second, someone has sorted and categorized these women in advance by their "condition." The counseling they receive falls into categories: "drug and alcohol," "advanced maternal age," and "carrier status" counseling. The medical establishment and the state have decided that these women should receive information about how specific conditions may affect their unborn child and to make certain tests available to them (but not other information and tests). The perspectives of the state and the medical community, not the initiatives or interests of the women, structure the information and tests. Moreover, as we will see shortly, the information these women receive is different from that conveyed to women in other settings. The focus of Williams's counseling session is on drug effects, not on procedural risks or diseases identified by the standard genetic tests. Third, these women are rarely able to engage successfully with the scientific facts that are presented to them. When the counselor quizzes them after her explanations, they routinely demonstrate misunderstanding. Fourth, the women are apparently not affected by the counseling in positive ways. None of the women I observe seems to receive a service from the counseling that she wants to receive. The counselor seems to respect the norms of individual reproductive choice in these sessions— she does not coerce any of the women I see into a decision (the most frequent outcome is nonaction). But neither do the sessions serve the women's needs. The sessions seem mainly to be a minor annoyance that they endure along with the rest of the bureaucracies into which they find themselves inserted. It seems clear, therefore, that culture and class interact to make genetic counseling something that is imposed on them and of little use to them. This is a significant contrast to other women's experience.

Across town, at a major research hospital, a white, upper-income couple has sought out genetic counseling for their twins, who were conceived via in-vitro fertilization, undertaken twelve weeks earlier. Erica and Sam Jones sit around a conference table, in a large and tastefully decorated room, with the observer and the white female counselor. After the counselor describes amniocentesis, both its contributions and risks, Erica Jones states that they "never considered NOT having the procedure." They definitely want it. The counselor goes through the standard description of what the procedure will reveal, and Sam Jones asks, "What happens if it comes back not normal?" The Joneses conclude, "Then we have to make more decisions." The counselor says yes and adds, "We'll talk with you again and then you have more choices." She mentions "selective reduction" but is flushed and embarrassed. She gets halfway into sentences and can't finish them. She uses *termination* rather than *abortion* but is clearly embarrassed to suggest they might abort a fetus. She describes the risks of miscarriage to one twin if the other twin is "selectively reduced." She backs out of the discussion with, "We'll deal with it if we have to; I think you are going to get normal results."

The counselor then goes through the family history to see whether the couple has other risk factors and finds none. She then asks Erica Jones whether she "has any bad habits." The counselor giggles nervously, "Do you smoke?" "No." "Have you had any alcohol?" "No." "Any street drugs?" "No." She asks whether they have questions. Sam Jones asks whether there are any other tests that they can order. The counselor sidesteps this by saying that their family history shows no need for other tests. (Other tests exist—for cystic fibrosis, for Huntington's disease, for sickle cell anemia—but the counselor judges that these are not relevant and appropriate for them, making this judgment in line with the standard practices of the institutions with which she is affiliated.) The counselor reviews the consent form and the Joneses sign it.

The Joneses do not engage with the counselor, even when she tries talking about the baby. They refer to the counselor's "making her presentation." Sam Jones is a vice president for a medical group, and they have gone through rigorous in-vitro fertilization procedures. They are savvy. Their attitude toward the counseling is relatively patient, but they are not eager or particularly interested in what the counselor has to say. They have already determined that they want to use every tool that medicine has to offer. The counselor is reluctant to provide all the information they want as well as the implications of these tests.

This couple is no more typical of the research hospital patients than Williams is typical of the public hospital's. The research hospital's patients include a couple who are just seeking information about a family disease. The group includes a working-class couple who are highly distraught because their doctor administered an MSAFP, the results of which were outside the normal parameters. A woman who works as a nurse is here to decide between chorionic villus sampling (CVS) and amniocentesis for advanced maternal age.

Despite their important differences, these clients' stories also reveal key forces at work. Some people very much want to control their reproduction. They very much want the information that genetics provides. They are willing to abort fetuses that seem more likely than usual to have health problems. Although they sometimes have difficulty grappling with the information the genetic counselors provide, they are able to process the information well enough to use it for their own ends. At least some patients are able to use genetic counseling in the service of their own values and interests. Most noticeably, the counselor facilitated the decision of the nurse, who wanted to use amniocentesis but whose doctor was pointing her toward CVS. The counselor helped her to articulate her preference and enforce her decision against the doctor's predispositions.

These women are able to use this information in part because they have the financial resources to choose whether to attend the sessions and to use the technologies. But they are also able to use this information because their cultural values and background favor control over reproduction and favor information processing in the Enlightenment mode of rationality and statistical assessment. But the institutional presentation of the information and access to the tools limits the choices of even these women. The counselor serves as a gatekeeper. She does not pass judgment on the couple's choices, but she does control the information they receive and therefore the range of choices open to them.

These stories tell us that the effects of genetic information and technologies are likely to be highly variable. Even if taxpayers fund all the choices offered by genetics, some cultural and class groups will find the choices more useful and will be able to manipulate them for their own ends far more than others can. Part of the differences lies in the concerns, values, and interests of the women themselves, but an important part rests in the structuring of the information and choices that women receive. The current institutional arrangement is to counsel poor women to control their drug habits for the benefit of the genes of the children they conceive and gestate. Middle- and working-class women will experience genetics differently. To the extent that they more actively desire to enhance or control the outcomes of their pregnancy, they may welcome these tests and struggle more actively to engage the tests on their own terms. However, the perceptions of their needs by the medical and social authorities who finance and deliver this information will also structure the information and choices of middle- and working-class women.

A substantial part of the difficulties for women involved in genetic selection comes from the need to understand highly technical material in order to make informed choices. Genetics is not unlike much of the rest of medicine today in this respect. The problems that arise in producing free choice for women with regard to the use of genetic technologies are thus representative of the problems in the application of all high-technology–based medicine and reproductive health issues. These problems arise because technologically assisted choices require substantial technical information, as well as technical and social support. This produces a set of paradoxes: women cannot make fully informed choices without receiving technical information. However, because the information comes from a medical-technological establishment that operates on both technical and patriarchal biases, these biases, not the values of the women making the choices, structure the information. Consequently, the preferences of the medical establishment prestructure these apparently free choices. Similarly, the problem of tailoring choices to specific groups of women based on their own needs and interests has no immediate and simple solution. If no one edits the information, it will suit some women's needs and interests better than others, but if someone edits it first, the information provided to different groups could be discriminatory.

One way to try to ameliorate these difficulties is to ensure that diverse women's perspectives and concerns influence the formation of the technology and the structures for delivering the technology and the information about it. Genetic choices should not result solely from medical and technical protocols and frameworks. Medical personnel can, indeed, report incidence rates of diseases, risks and costs of various procedures, and treatment options. These factors do not have an exclusive role, however, in deciding which women should receive information about which options. These are not merely technical decisions but also valuative decisions. As with an increasing number of health decisions, genetic choice involves not merely knowing the medical facts but deciding what outcomes are preferable and what risks acceptable.

We cannot expect individual women to canvass all the available social and technical information in order to decide what information they need. The available information is simply overwhelmingly vast and often beyond the comprehension of some clients. Medical personnel are not competent to make these decisions for women. Another option is to involve diverse organized women's groups in creating the structures and options offered to women at different sites and locations. The women's groups involved should reflect the population of women served at that site, and their goals should not be to influence women's choices in a specific direction but to open up those choices as much as possible within the life contexts of the women being served. Failing this, women's groups need to develop extra-institutional sites at which they can share information and experience about these technologies.

Research into genetics offers both welcome possibilities and threatening potentials to differently situated women. It has the potential to improve the ability of many women to control their reproductive outcomes, and it may improve the health of women who have cancer, diabetes, cystic fibrosis, or other genetically influenced diseases. On the other hand, if the genetic model of medicine develops in a narrow fashion, genetic research also has the potential to make women the servants of the information structures that deliver genetic technologies and to place the major burden for the population's health on the wombs of women. The extent to which genetic information serves or hinders women depends not so much on its inherent character but on how we manage to shape both its meaning and the institutions that deliver its products. Women should be active and involved in these shaping processes.

NOTES

The author thanks the University of Georgia and the National Institutes of Health for financial support that made this chapter possible. She is also deeply grateful to Barbara Bowles Biesecker and Don Hadley for their assistance in gaining access to counseling settings and for their warm hospitality, and to the many counselors and clients who were willing to allow her to observe their counseling sessions (their names have been omitted or changed to ensure privacy).

1. Critics have found the germ theory itself has paid inadequate attention to environmental and social factors, but the gene theory intensifies the internal focus and essentializes it.

2. For an earlier analysis of reproductive choice, see Petchesky (1985). For more totalistic critiques of genetics from feminist perspectives, see Spallone (1992).

REFERENCES

Berg, Paul. 1996. Understanding our genes: Opportunities and concerns. Charter Lecture, delivered January 29 at the University of Georgia, Athens.

Caskey, T. C. 1993. Presymptomatic diagnosis: A first step toward genetic health care. *Science* 262:48–49.

Condit, C. M. 1996. Media bias for reproductive technologies. In R. L. Parrott and C. M. Condit, eds., *Evaluating women's health messages: A resource book*, pp. 341–55. Thousand Oaks, Calif.: Sage.

Flores, L. A. 1996. Options and risks with reproductive technologies. In R. L. Parrott and C. M. Condit, eds., *Evaluating women's health messages: A resource book*, pp. 327–40. Thousand Oaks, Calif.: Sage.

Golden, Frederic. 1995. On the frontier of the genetic revolution. *San Francisco Chronicle,* May 21, p. 8.

HuGem Project. 1995. *Opportunities and challenges of the Human Genome Project.* Washington, D.C.: National Institutes of Health. Videotape.

Leff, Michael. 1988. Dimensions of temporality in Lincoln's second inaugural. *Communication Reports* 1:26–31.

National Institutes of Health. n.d. National Cancer Institute. *Understanding Gene Testing.* Pamphlet.

Petchesky, R. P. 1985. *Abortion and woman's choice: The state, sexuality, and reproductive freedom.* Ann Arbor, Mich.: Northeastern University Press.

Rothman, Barbara Katz. 1993. *The tentative pregnancy: How amniocentesis changes the experience of motherhood.* 1986. Reprint, New York: Norton.

Siegfried, Tom. 1993. Advances in DNA knowledge complicate definition of gene. *Dallas Morning News,* October 18, p. 9.

Spallone, Patricia. 1992. *Generation games: Genetic engineering and the future for our lives.* Philadelphia: Temple University Press.

Wertz, D. C., and J. C. Fletcher. 1989. *Ethics and human genetics: A cross-cultural perspective.* Berlin: Springer-Verlag.

Yee, Laura. 1993. CWRU's starring lineup; Symposium includes leading scientists, doctors. *(Cleveland) Plain Dealer,* September 28, p. 3.

6

BODIES, MINDS, AND FAILURES

IMAGES OF WOMEN

IN INFERTILITY CLINICS

LAURA SHANNER

Women may experience infertility as a significant life crisis, which new reproductive technologies (NRTs) such as in-vitro fertilization (IVF) are designed to resolve. One might therefore assume that infertility clinics would be supportive and encouraging environments for women. The clinical experience for women seeking NRTs, however, is often disturbingly negative in ways that surpass physical discomforts and medical risks: common linguistic and visual images of women in North American, Australian, and British infertility clinics are often insulting, diminishing, and objectifying rather than supportive.

Clinical writings and interactions often speak of and present women as failures, girls, body parts, merely parts of an infertile couple rather than whole persons, and objects of pornography. Combined with powerful beliefs about gender roles, reproductive imperatives, and control of our bodies and bodily processes, these images create an internally coherent but damaging image paradigm for infertile women.

This paradigm of infertile women as less than whole persons also raises interesting paradoxes for the philosophical problem of mind-body interactions, which give us further reason to examine critically and change the view of women that underlies contemporary infertility medicine. The beliefs and images that constitute a paradigm are not mere abstractions, however, as the language and behaviors that convey beliefs can elicit powerful responses in both the object of the beliefs (in this case, female IVF patients) and in others who interact with them. Ignoring or perpetuating the harms that those beliefs cause is therefore morally negligent.

The images of women documented and examined in this chapter emerged over nearly a decade of reviewing literature from medicine, ethics, health policy, infertility self-help guides, patient information materials, and feminist writings. In addition, I have conducted extensive interviews with clinicians, researchers, patients, and counselors in the United States, Australia, Canada, and Great Britain. Several clinics in these countries have generously supported my research by allowing me to conduct site visits, while a few—the Jones Institute, Virginia; Royal Women's Hospital, Melbourne; Royal North Shore Hospital, Sydney; Lingard Fertility Centre, Newcastle, New South Wales; and Queensland Fertility Group, Brisbane—allowed me to engage in daily observations of patient consultations, examinations, surgeries, laboratory techniques, and other activities at the clinic for a cumulative total of nearly a year in residence. The interviews and participant-observer methodologies helped me come to understand both the science behind IVF and the lived experiences of infertility treatment. Unexpectedly, the patterns of language and behavior detailed here gradually emerged from the literature and daily clinical routines. Continuing review of clinical documents and practice in the United States, Canada, Australia, and the Great Britain—part of my ongoing research and contribution to health policy in genetic and reproductive technologies—has confirmed the pervasiveness of these images.

My work as a philosopher has been to attempt to make sense of the pieces I observe in the field or, more specifically, to explore the deeper meanings and ethical implications of the perpetuation of certain assumptions and images. I make no statistical claims here regarding the frequency of specific images or the ways in which these images have changed over time, nor do I wish to imply that clinicians are intentionally insulting or universally insensitive. This field has some truly wonderful, supportive clinicians who carefully choose their words and policies. I believe that the images I discuss here are consistent with larger social paradigms and beliefs about women and that the clinical use of undermining imagery is largely unintentional. However, I suggest that such images pose a subtle threat to the well-being of any female infertility patient who must confront them. We are therefore morally bound to challenge and change these taken-for-granted expressions wherever they are found.

Images in the Clinic

COUPLES

Clinicians have long emphasized that infertility is a "disease of couples," because it takes two to create a baby, and because many cases of infertility either involve physical factors in both partners or have no explanation. Partly because infertility and medical protocols may severely strain intimate relationships, clinicians have designed the treatment process to draw both partners into strengthening their bond. The clinicians' attempt to treat the couple rather than just infertile individuals is thus a compassionate, psychologically helpful response to the complex relationships involved in family formation and an attempt to involve both partners in a mutually supportive enterprise rather than in an alienating individual ordeal.

On the other hand, Marta Kirejczyk and Irma van der Ploeg (1992) rightly argue that reconceptualizing infertility as a "disease of couples" allowed clinicians to redefine IVF as a therapy for male infertility. If we are treating couples, we need not establish which partner has the physical abnormality or who receives the treatment, so long as the "couple" gets pregnant. The language of couples makes it seem reasonable rather than unjust to provide treatments whose risks are directed almost entirely toward women, even when some of these women are perfectly healthy, whereas their partners are infertile. The language masks the fact that couples do not receive hormone injections, laparoscopies, or surgery; individuals do. The terminology of "couples" conveniently allows women—and the risks that they disproportionately shoulder in new reproductive technologies—to disappear.

The diminishment of women in the "couples' disease of infertility" is a medical instantiation of the larger social phenomenon of women's disappearance in marriage. Historically, married couples became one person, and he was male. As William Blackstone (1765) noted regarding eighteenth-century British common law:

> By marriage, the husband and wife are one person in law: that is, the very being or legal existence of the woman is suspended during the marriage, or at least is incorporated and consolidated into that of the husband. . . . For this reason, a man cannot grant anything to his wife, or enter into covenant with her: for the grant would be to suppose her separate existence; and to covenant with her would be only to covenant with himself. . . . But though our law in general considers man and wife as one person, yet there

are some instances in which she is separately considered; as inferior to him and acting by his compulsion. . . . The husband also, by the old law, might give his wife moderate correction. For, as he is to answer for her misbehavior, the law thought it reasonable to intrust him with this power of restraining her, by domestic chastisement, in the same moderation that a man is allowed to correct his apprentices or children. (Kanowitz 1973:61–63)

The British common law tradition is the basis for the legal systems of all English-speaking nations, and its assumptions and historical influences have been difficult to eradicate. The diminishment of women in marriage lingers in the still-accepted symbolic norm for a woman to adopt her husband's last name rather than to keep her own; note how rarely men take their wives' names or couples adopt a new name together. Discrimination continues in many jurisdictions regarding inheritance, investments, credit reports, and other important financial aspects of marriage, divorce, and spousal death; society still largely ignores domestic violence, which men commit vastly more often against their wives than women do against their husbands; and the legal definition of rape may not include rape within marriage. The practical ability to leave a marriage reflects the relative strength of the partners: the rate at which husbands kill wives is highest after separation, and the standard of living for men still tends to rise after a divorce, whereas for women (and their children) it tends to drop substantially. Even health and longevity favor men over women in marriage: married men have a longer life expectancy than single men, but married women have a shorter life expectancy than single women. The IVF clinic exaggerates what is still often true in marriage: women are likely to fade from the picture as we speak of benefits to "the couple" rather than enumerate the inequitable distribution of risks and benefits to each member.

THE GIRLS IN THE CLINIC

Although it seems clear that women rather than couples receive most infertility treatments, perhaps we are not treating women after all: another subtly demeaning linguistic habit is that of using the word *girls* to refer to the women undergoing treatment. Physicians, nurses, and patients themselves often speak of the number of girls in the waiting room or the lovely girls with whom they have developed friendships in the course of treatment. When someone points out this linguistic habit, most people (of both genders) protest that it means nothing; North Americans and Australians commonly use *girls* as the informal reference to females, supposedly comparable to the word *guys* to refer to males. We thus commonly encounter "the girls in the office" and men who seek a date with a "pretty girl." Of course, the difference between the words *guys* and *girls* is significant: juvenile males are *boys* rather than guys, but juvenile females are properly called girls. Thus daily informal references to adult females equate them with children, both in the clinic and in the wider society.

In contrast, speakers rarely equate men with their juvenile selves, and most cases of such usage the speaker clearly intends it to be pejorative; "boys will be boys" and "a night out with the boys" are phrases that refer to playful, juvenile, or irresponsible behavior. I once heard members of an Australian semen analysis laboratory comment on male patients who nervously approach "the little boys' room" to produce the semen sample, but other than in jokes about masturbation, the routine terms for males are *husbands, partners,* or *men.* I have never in my clinical experience heard it said that someone should round up the boys to receive their hormone injections, for example, or that the boys who come through the program are really nice people. In the casual jargon of both clinicians and patients, the couples undergoing treatment seem to consist of men and girls.

Such a subtle linguistic habit may seem to carry little practical weight, as most people seem not to be offended by it. However, as Stephanie Ross (1981:197) argues, oppression need not be equated with offense, just as harm need not always be felt as hurt. That both women and men use the terms does not mean that the words carry no oppressive force but merely that both sexes have accepted the oppressive premise. Blackstone's comparison of wives to children, both of whom are rightly rebuked by the head of the household, echoes in our everyday conversation.

Discussing the similar linguistic habit of southern white Americans who refer to a black adult male as boy, Robert Baker suggests that "the terms we utilize to identify something reflect our conception of it. . . . [F]or a group to talk that way it must think that way" (1981:162). The example of racist diminution reveals two related motivations for the habit: the analogy of parental power over children implicitly justifies white social power over blacks, and it imparts the childlike traits of obedience, cheerfulness, and helplessness that are far less threatening to the power structure than are adult traits of autonomy, strength, and intelligence. Linguistic diminution has the same effect between genders that it has between races, and it springs from the same motivations. If clinicians and patients routinely refer to women as girls, all must (perhaps unconsciously) accept the premise that the women are—or should be—like children.

Referring to women as girls reinforces a stereotype of women as irrational, immature, unable to make decisions, and dependent upon others (especially men) to take care of them; speakers thus portray women as incompetent and not autonomous, and the message is that women's decisions do not merit the same respect accorded men's decisions. The speech pattern thus reinforces masculine power and feminine compliance. The linguistic demotion of women's status to that of children is especially problematic when women must be able to give full and informed consent about treatments that will affect their health, their lives, and the lives of their children.

PORNOGRAPHY

Infertility clinics routinely provide material that many women consider blatantly offensive: they make pornography available in most semen collection rooms. Presenting women as sexual objects is consistent with the language of *couples* and adult *girls* in depicting a woman as something less than her husband or partner, not fully adult, and thus by implication not worthy of the respect granted to men and to adults.

For this discussion, I define *pornography* as any objectifying, violent, or degrading depiction of bodies and sexual acts. *Erotica* is an explicit representation of bodies or sexual acts between or among persons who convey mutual respect and concern for the well-being of their partner(s) as complete people rather than as sexual objects. Under these definitions, commonly accepted explicit materials such as *Playboy* and *Penthouse* would be pornography rather than erotica. Unfortunately, very little nonobjectifying erotica is available in North American and Australian markets; we live in an odd time in which we still hesitate to discuss sex education, condoms, or loving sexuality, but we glorify violence and exploitative sexuality in our language, music, and media. The vast majority of sexually explicit materials emphasize the easy availability of a woman (or, less frequently, a child, animal, or passive male) as a sexual object for the pleasure of (usually) a male. It is significant that the English language has several words and metaphors for sex that also serve as metaphors for harm and anger (*screw, fuck, bang,* etc.), and that these words most often depict the male as the active partner and the female as the recipient of the angry/sexual act (Garry 1978; Lakoff

1987). English has no commonly used word to express joyous, loving, respectful sexual intercourse, and we have very few opportunities to view such encounters.

Men clearly face enormous pressure to "perform" on short notice for semen evaluation and to provide sperm when eggs are retrieved for IVF, and this distress deserves relief. The use of widely available explicit materials may therefore seem a reasonable activity. However, it is discomforting to realize that the standard IVF protocol for women involves encouraging their partners to view magazines (and, in the better clinics, videos) of women in typically subservient and objectified roles. Clinical insensitivity in this case often extends to both genders: the spaces set aside for men, especially in the early years of IVF clinics, were often horribly inadequate for the purpose of procuring a semen sample. I was told of one clinic in which the semen collection area was merely a curtained corner near the waiting room; the clinicians expected men to masturbate within yards of a room full of women, with people walking past the curtain posing the threat of opening it. Clinics still frequently send men to the restroom to masturbate. Writings by patients voice the embarrassing and, only in hindsight humorous, conditions that men face in these settings:

> While they wheeled me into surgery to aspirate the eggs, they put Gene in a little utility room by himself. He was right next door to the laboratory. . . . There was a washbasin with a wooden shelf above it that held a small plastic container and a piece of paper with instructions for keeping the sperm sterile. There was no chair or window in the room, but there were a mop and a bucket and a stack of *Playboy* and *Penthouse* magazines with a note that said, "If you require help." Gene said the instructions were rather vague about when to wash and how to dry your hands. He said the pressure was overwhelming—him sitting on the floor with his pants around his ankles in the gray cement room. He was supposed to knock on the door when he had the sperm. He told me he thought he was going to go crazy. It wasn't exactly romantic. He kept thinking, My wife's going to have surgery and what if I can't do this? (Radner 1989:34–35)

Even when the clinic has overlooked basic material and psychological comforts such as chairs and privacy, so that a man must sit miserably on a cement floor or can be overheard by the clinic staff and other patients, someone has remembered and provided pornography. When clinic facilities improve, the pornography selection also tends to improve: greater varieties of magazines, videos, and sometimes sex toys are available in upscale clinics.

Perhaps the problem of sperm collection has no ideal solution, except perhaps to allow men to bring their own erotic materials. Fresh semen is preferable to frozen, partly because of the lower lab costs but also because the quality or quantity of sperm often contributes to the infertility problem. Masturbation is clearly preferable to invasive sperm collection by urethral catheters, surgery, or electrical shock to the prostate. Having the female partner participate in the masturbation might seem less objectifying than pornographic images, but this raises practical difficulties if the woman needs to prepare for her own surgery. Retrieving sperm from intercourse before transvaginal egg retrieval would also cause added irritation to the vagina and is likely to increase the risk of infection during the procedure.

Having the woman assist her partner to masturbate may also create psychological hazards if she will undergo a gynecological procedure afterward, as confusion of sexuality and medical intervention in the mind of either the patient or clinician has great potential to be emotionally traumatic for the patient. Most infertility clinicians are male; in 1993 only 16 percent of the members of the American Fertility Society were female. As a result, a woman recently aroused or engaged in sexual activity with her husband would shortly thereafter have another man—a male clinician—sit between her legs and insert an ultrasound probe into her vagina.

Most clinicians take great care to separate sexuality from gynecological interventions, but the entire enterprise of assisting reproduction *itself* has sexual overtones that are hard to avoid. Our traditional ways of starting pregnancy involve active sexuality; infertility often challenges one's sense of gender identity or "wholeness" as a man or woman; infertility treatment may disrupt spontaneous marital relations. Gynecological exams and interventions frequently evoke distress related to sexuality for female patients, especially when conducted by male physicians. Psychologist Aline Zoldbrod (1993) notes that many women experience posttraumatic stress from infertility treatments that parallel women's experiences of rape: both involve pain, emotional distress, and loss of control over one's genitalia.

Instead of avoiding such sexual overtones, the infertility clinics reinforce them through the pervasive use of materials that depict women as objects for sexual pleasure. I find it difficult to believe that clinicians and patients of either gender can completely alter their responses, depending upon the immediate context, to the visual image of female genitalia in isolation. The lithotomy position, in which a woman's feet are in stirrups and the rest of her body is shielded by drapes, is nearly identical in visual presentation to the pornographic "beaver shots" of female genitalia frequently found in the explicit materials provided by the clinic. One is supposed to be purely clinical and arouse no emotion, whereas the other is intentionally sexual, creating a very uncomfortable dissonance.

FAILURE

The words *couples* and *girls*, as well as the pornography, depict women as something less than full, adult persons. Reinforcing this image of diminishment is a pervasive terminology of failure that both patients and clinicians adopt. Common refrains throughout infertility patient interviews and writings include "I feel like a failure," "defective," and "unworthy" (also see Menning 1977). Although common to both women and men, women use failure terminology more often and more globally, and others more frequently direct such terms toward women than toward men. Patients perceive themselves to have failed to produce children, to satisfy their partner's and parents' wishes, and to achieve that which "normal" people seem to do with ease. This sense of failure takes on both practical and moral dimensions and contributes greatly to the emotional turmoil and crisis of infertility. It is therefore cause for concern when medical terminology routinely reinforces the sense of personal failure by using the word *failure* and other value-laden, emotionally charged words to describe causes of infertility and steps of the treatment cycle.

Both medical and general readership discussions of infertility trace the "failure" to achieve pregnancy to the failure to produce eggs or sperm, the failure to respond to hormones, the failure of eggs to fertilize, the failure of embryos to implant in the uterus, or the failure of the uterus to sustain the pregnancy. Clinicians inform patients, often in so many words, that they may be removed from the IVF program if they "fail to respond" properly at any step of the treatment. In a lengthy review article on stress-induced infertility, Wasser and Isenberg (1986) attempt to support the normality of infertile persons by documenting how reduced fertility in nonhuman animals is considered a normal response to stress; however, it runs under the judgmental title, "Reproductive Failure Among Women: Pathology or Adaptation?" Note that the article does not focus on reproductive failure among *men,* who contribute to nearly half of all diagnosed cases of infertility.

The patient-as-failure image also pervades the presentation of clinical pregnancy rates. Information booklets and professional journals rarely speak of the IVF team's failure to help 80 to 90 percent of their patients but instead emphasize the clinic's success rates. Clinical language implies that the patients' failure to respond to treatment accounts for a low success rate, but the language does not credit patients with achieving successes. The clinic thus places patients in a no-win situation or double bind, which Marilyn Frye (1983) describes as a pervasive condition of oppressed groups. Even when it seems obvious that the patients succeeded when the clinical staff failed in several ways, wrong parties often receive the credit:

> After seeing many a Doctor after we got married and having a few operations to try to rectify the problems of my infertility . . . we were referred to Professor Carl Wood. . . . He said he would have a look at me himself to decide what could be done, thus an operation . . . [where he] removed one of my tubes. He then proceeded to tell me that *due to all my other operations,* my ovaries were hardly accessible, which made it ever so hard for David to fertilise an egg. But with all this bad news, he said that we could try IVF. . . . [A]fter 15 months our letter arrived to say we could start. We then had all the necessary tests and we were informed of some news that came as such a shock to us, especially David. We were told he had a very low sperm count and poor mobility. *We could not believe it as we always thought that it was me with the problem.* . . . Professor Wood kept our spirits up and said we could still try IVF. So over the next few years we had four attempts, all to no avail. . . . After much sole [sic] searching, David and I decided that we would get on with our lives. . . . David always wanted to renovate a home, so we bought one which needed a lot of work. . . . It was 16 months since our last try [at IVF]. Meanwhile I began to feel tired all the time . . . and then I missed my period. . . . To our astonishment the news was I was 6 weeks pregnant. *Even though we did it ourselves, we owe so much to Professor Carl Wood and the IVF staff, as we know that without IVF and the Professor's continual encouragement and not giving up on us, this might never have happened.* (Harvey 1990; emphasis added)

We should note in this case the surgery-induced scarring, the failure to diagnose sperm abnormalities, and an apparent disregard for artificial insemination before resorting to further surgery and IVF. Rather than expressing outrage at the clinic's compounding of her difficulties, the patient extends to the IVF team her deep appreciation and even credit for a spontaneous pregnancy.

PERSONIFICATION

Some terms common in infertility diagnosis and treatment replace the notion of failure with undesirable personality traits
attributed to body parts, which the patient and others may then perceive as reflecting her personality. Some clinicians blame pregnancy
losses resulting from structural aspects of the uterus on an "incompetent cervix." In a miscarriage, the woman failed to carry the pregnancy: she mis-carried it, or carried it badly or wrongly, and thus she
(perhaps like her cervix) may seem incompetent. When the cervical
mucous is too thick for sperm to penetrate, the common clinical term
is "hostile cervical mucous." Even guidebooks by former patients per-
sonify body parts: "Ideally, about two days before ovulation occurs . . .
the glands increase [mucous] production about 30-fold. . . . The pH of
the [mucous] becomes slightly alkaline, a 'sperm-friendly' solution that
serves as a buffer to the vagina's normally acidic environment" (Harkness 1987:123).

A "hostile cervical environment" might also refer to an antibody or
allergic reaction to semen. Because the sperm are foreign proteins in
the woman's body, though, it might be equally appropriate to speak
of "hostile semen" and "protective cervical fluid." It seems to be the
woman who has an attitude problem that confounds fertility; if only
she and her mucous were less hostile or more "sperm friendly," everything would be fine.

Interestingly, when a man's body produces antibodies to his own
sperm, as may happen following the reversal of a vasectomy, clinicians
do not refer to the condition as "hostile testicles" that cause "incompetent sperm"; rather, he has "male factor infertility" or an "antibody reaction." Different linguistic paradigms thus seem to be operating for
male and female patients. "Anovulation," "nonfertilization," "antibody
reactions" and "thick mucous" would adequately describe the female
patient's situation without personifying it or projecting blame on her
for causing it.

Philosophical Reflections

CONTROL AND BLAMEWORTHINESS

We might wonder why infertility terminology is problematic when we commonly speak of kidney failure or congestive heart
failure without such deep connotations of personal failure. One plausible explanation for the difference is that we tend to believe that we

exercise a higher level of control over our fertility than we do over most other bodily functions. Although lifestyle choices regarding diet, exercise, or smoking may lead to organ failure, we generally do not believe that we take active control over the state of our organs' functioning. Reproductive capacities are largely under our conscious control, however, and often play a significant role in our daily lives: we choose whether, when, and with whom to have sex; which, if any, contraceptive to use; whether to have an abortion; and when to plan to have children. Now we may also choose whether to use reproductive technologies to initiate pregnancy.

Many counselors suggest that the magnitude of the crisis of infertility parallels the amount of control that the patient has assumed over her or his reproductive capacity. Years of sexual restraint and/or contraceptive use constitute "birth control" and "family planning." As contraception has become increasingly convenient and reliable in recent decades, we have come to expect convenient and reliable conception as well. Infertility foils the family planning, though; birth control is now beyond control, and family planners are left wondering what they did wrong. When our control proves to be limited, we perceive this limitation as inadequacy, incompetence, or personal failure. It seems clear, though, that contraception has given us an unrealistic sense of control over our fertility and family planning; it is inaccurate and thus unfair to ourselves or others to cast blame for failing to live up to unreasonable expectations. Clinicians could reduce our overconfident sense of control by emphasizing bodily variations and the imperfections of medical interventions, and by eliminating the "failure" terminology.

The expectation of controlling fertility may create a secondary sense of failure, which is the patient's feeling of guilt for causing the infertility through unwise reproductive choices. It is true that some decisions may cause later infertility: sexually transmitted diseases, vasectomies or tubal ligations, scarring from IUDs or abortions, hormonal disruption after using birth control pills, poor egg or semen quality from delayed childbearing, and exposure to drugs and other toxins are all potential causes of infertility. The causal links between behavior and physiological conditions are usually difficult to establish, however, and about one-third of infertility cases have no identifiable physiological causes. Guilt or shame about socially unaccepted sexual behaviors, such as adultery or homosexual encounters, and even about normal sexual behavior such as masturbation or fantasies, may resurface as a feeling that the infertility is a deserved cosmic punishment for deviance. In these cases, the feelings of guilt and responsibility for infertility are clearly misplaced.

FUNCTION

The second link between the failure of personified reproductive organs and the perception of the person as a failure is not a matter of responsibility or blameworthiness but rests on deeper philosophical ideas about the role of reproduction and the functions of human living. In a teleological account of human life, the end or function of people is to behave in certain ways or to achieve certain goals. We perceive most other bodily processes as allowing personal existence, or *being;* reproduction is a function, or a human *doing.* Life-threatening conditions thus provide an odd sense of comfort: if I cease to be, at least I cannot be a failure. Infertility is not life threatening, however, and humans often perceive that failing to do what is expected is a failure of the existing self.

If people perceive reproducing to be a purpose or end of human living, as sociobiology and some religions assert, then the inability to do so seems to be a failure to meet one's basic ends. A watch that keeps inaccurate time fails at its primary task and therefore is a bad watch; similarly, people who hold this set of expectations perceive a person who does not bear children as a failed person and thus a "bad" person, or at least less than fully human. Being a bad or incomplete person might be the result of God or fate, just as we might blame the watchmaker for making a bad watch rather than blaming the watch itself for failing to keep time. Because we perceive fertility to be under our control to such a significant extent, though, we are more likely to perceive the failure to reproduce as a choice-based personal failure than merely an uncontrollable structural flaw.

BODIES, MINDS, AND TRANSCENDENCE

At a linguistic level, we find it easier to associate women with their bodies than we do men with their bodies. When an organ common to both sexes malfunctions, we usually describe the self as having a structural failure; thus we say that "you have congestive heart failure" rather than "you aren't circulating correctly," or "you have kidney failure" rather than "you didn't filter your toxins." When organs unique to women do not work, however, the language often implies that the woman herself has failed. The diagnostic phrase "ovarian failure" fits the standard medical language pattern of the failed organ rather than the failed patient, but this term may be used interchangeably with sentences directed toward the patient herself. Although we say to a woman, "You are menstruating" or "You aren't ovulating," we lack the vocabulary to say to a man, "You aren't spermulating." Some clinical observations do not refer to body parts at all; the failure of implantation usually does not specify embryos or the uterus but boils down to a simple incrimination: "You didn't get pregnant."

As several feminist philosophers observe (Spelman 1982; Lloyd 1984; Grimshaw 1986), philosophical writings have traditionally emphasized rationality over embodiment and characterized rationality as masculine. Plato postulated that reason rules the appetites and the passions as a chariot driver controls horses; Descartes distinguished the mind and body as separate substances and reaffirmed the mind as the human essence. Women, to the extent that classical philosophical texts mention them at all, tend to be identified with their bodies: by menstruating, giving birth, and attending to the physical details of daily life, they do not transcend their bodies as men do. Plato, Aristotle, Kant, and many others have suggested that women are therefore more like animals, children *(girls)*, or slaves who are primarily embodied rather than transcendent or rational.

To some extent, I agree that women may have a different experience of transcendence from their bodies than men do. This is not a metaphysically important difference but merely an *experiential* difference. The menstrual cycle (like pregnancy) is a uniquely feminine phenomenon that males can only observe and describe from the outside; the description of a bodily event not lived can be objective, rational, detached, and thus transcended. The woman who menstruates, however, experiences the process as a whole-body phenomenon, affecting everything from her size and weight to her appetites and moods. Even women who have few menstrual symptoms or who ignore them find it difficult to ignore bleeding.

The gender-specific menstrual rhythm differs from universal daily rhythms such as hunger, thirst, elimination, and sleep, which seem simply to be part of our basic somatic equipment; if reason is supposed to transcend the body, then these basic functions are precisely what dieting, toilet training, and alarm clocks ought to control. The universal limitations of the body thus *establish* the mind-body duality, because the mind is supposed to transcend them. When only *some* people exhibit a particularly dramatic and uncontrolled bodily cycle, we perceive the phenomenon as something that some people "transcend" and others do not. A man may therefore perceive himself as having transcended his body when he controls his daily appetites, but even when women perceive themselves as having transcended their bodies, intermittent bleeding reminds them otherwise.

Critics often suggest the male sexual response as a counterexample to the claim that men are not reminded of their bodily selves as women are, but the suggestion fails. Healthy men typically experience full or partial erections while sleeping, making this phenomenon more like a daily rhythm than a periodic event, and healthy males have erections from before birth through old age. Only *some* healthy females (non-pregnant women between puberty and menopause) menstruate. More important, healthy men are able to exert at least partial control over their sexual response: they may induce erections through imagery and/or masturbation—an assumption critical to justifying the clinical provision of pornography—and they can sometimes end unwanted erections by unpleasant imagery or the proverbial cold shower. A man's control of his sexual appetites and responses is, in fact, a commonly accepted indicator of his transcendent rationality or spirituality. Try as she might, however, a woman is simply unable to will her periods to start or end; control is possible only with massive hormonal or surgical intervention. Thus it is easy to perceive men as having transcended their bodies better than women, because women experience a dramatic and uncontrollable bodily process that men do not share.

WOMAN AS OBJECT

The images of women common in infertility clinics do not exist in isolation but are consistent with the images and expectations that pervade many aspects of women's lives. Our cultural emphasis on women's appearance reinforces the theoretical identification of women with their bodies. Feminist literature has long debated the role of fashion, makeup, dieting, cosmetic surgery, and other practices in the process of objectifying women. The pursuit of attractiveness echoes several themes of infertility treatment: preoccupation with appearance is dismissed as a silly enterprise suited to children (girls), and the Anglo practice of shaving legs and underarms makes women literally look like young girls. A man who succeeds in the adult worlds of politics or business may seek a beautiful young "trophy wife," but "trophy husbands" are rare. A trophy is not a person but an object. Beauty rituals may be considered forms of disciplining the female body; analogously, the temperature charts, hormonal control of ovulation, timed intercourse, and repeated surgeries of IVF are all forms of bodily discipline.

With so many cultural layers reinforcing the identity of women and their bodies, it is not surprising that a diagnosis of failure of a female body part is projected as, and perceived to be, a failure of the woman herself. Rather simple syllogisms can express the difference between male and female identifications with their bodies, and the resulting difference in perceptions of themselves as failures. Given the assumption that the mind/soul/essential self is metaphysically different from and transcends the material body (at least for men), the mechanical failure of the body implies no judgment about the person:

> The mind/self is distinct from the body.
> The mind/self transcends the body.
> The body has failed.
> Therefore, the mind/self transcends a failed body.

If society identifies women with their bodies, however, the syllogism is simple and incriminating:

> A woman is her body.
> The body has failed.
> Therefore, the woman is a failure.

He *has* a low sperm count, and she *isn't* ovulating. Men are thus traditionally perceived as full persons who *have* bodies, where bodies are defined as material things, or objects. If women *are* their bodies, then women are material things or objects that may then be used for sexual or reproductive purposes. A woman who fails to reproduce is therefore herself a failure that needs to be fixed or replaced.

Women, Men, and Paradoxes in the Mind-Body Problem

The view that women are "more embodied" or "less transcendent" than men raises a devastating paradox for the classic philosophical problem of mind-body interaction. If women and men do indeed bear significantly different relationships to their bodies, as so many philosophers have suggested, we need to explain the enormously complicated metaphysics of gendered mind-body dualities. That is, although plausible explanations of the interaction between material bodies and nonmaterial substances (souls, minds) are already difficult to develop, we would have to modify such explanations to include *two different types of interaction* for female and male human beings. We would have to explain whether males and females have different types of material and/or nonmaterial aspects or whether the same types of substances merely interact differently in the two sexes. Women and men would be vastly more different than alike, not just in terms of biology or psychology but at the fundamental metaphysical level of our composition. Reproduction between such essentially different creatures would have to be explained, and the metaphysical upheaval entailed by a sex-change operation boggles the mind. It is far more plausible to suggest that the mind-body relationship is metaphysically similar for the sexes and that the traditional view of women as "less transcendent" is misguided.

The perceived identity of the female self and body need not be negative, as classical philosophers would have us believe; instead, women's insights may reshape our thinking about the mind-body problem at a broader level, leading us to understand ourselves phenomenologically as embodied beings rather than analytically as a poorly defined interaction of mysterious substances.

A theme in much of the feminist criticism of reproductive technologies is the image of women as subhuman reproductive objects, "baby machines" (Scutt 1988; Corea 1979), incubators, or empty vessels waiting to be filled, rather than human beings with reproductive and other interests. Just as the perception of a woman as a sexual object can result in real harms in the form of rape, sexual harassment, and a sometimes ill-defined sense of frustration and personal inadequacy, the perception of women as reproductive objects may lead to the real harms of physical injury through improper medical intervention, coercion for reproductive or contraceptive purposes, and the devaluation of women in both reproductive and nonreproductive roles. As we have seen, the words *girls*, *couples*, and *failure*, and the use of pornography in the infertility clinic—combined with long-standing social norms regarding attractiveness, reproductive function, and rational control of our bodies—all contribute to an understanding of women as reproductive objects.

Historically, society has held women responsible for infertility, rather like malfunctioning incubators. Henry VIII divorced or beheaded five of his six wives for their failure to produce sons, yet his sperm determined Elizabeth's sex, and the odds suggest that Henry had the infertility problem all along. The wives of Henry VIII were literally disposable sexual and reproductive objects. Today, when we know that nearly half of all diagnosed cases of infertility are wholly or partly caused by male factors, clinicians still rarely discuss and inadequately study male infertility. While unlikely to be beheaded and literally disposed of, some healthy women today undergo IVF to compensate for their husbands' low sperm count. We should not forget that some women have died from IVF complications.

The image of women in infertility clinics is thus coherent and greatly disturbing: the *girls* in the program, who by failing to become pregnant have failed to demonstrate their womanhood, await surgery at the hands of primarily male physicians; meanwhile, these clinics encourage the male partners to masturbate to images of women in submissive, objectified, and unrealistic roles. These behaviors will help the "couple" get pregnant, unless the woman fails to respond to treatment. The image of women as less transcendent than men is consistent with the image of women as less rational and more childlike. Female embodiment is also compatible with the stereotype of women as more emotional and actively irrational than men; note that the etymological root of *hysterical* is *hyster*, the Greek word for *uterus*. If a woman does not transcend her uterus but is instead controlled or defined by it, society may perceive her as a reproductive object on par with the sexual object represented in pornography.

We should address immediately the specific images and language in clinical settings that project women as—and may easily make women feel—demeaned, childlike, and objectified. Whether blatant or subtle, whether intentionally or unintentionally perpetrated, and whether consciously or unconsciously recognized, such images cannot have a positive effect on women's self-esteem, self-image, and standing relative to men. These psychosocial effects undermine a woman's ability to give fully informed consent for invasive medical procedures that have enormous implications for her life, her health, and her children. When such undermining images are coupled with inadequate testing of new reproductive technologies (Royal Commission 1993) and a scarcity of other options for coping with infertility, the dangers of these images are very clear.

REFERENCES

Baker, Robert. 1981. "Pricks" and "chicks": A plea for "persons." In Mary Vetterling-Braggin, ed., *Sexist language*, pp. 161–82. Lanham, Md.: Littlefield, Adams.

Blackstone, William. 1765. *Commentaries on the laws of England,* book 1, chapter 15, pp. 442–45. In Leo Kanowitz, ed., *Sex Roles in law and society: Cases and materials,* pp. 61—63. Albuquerque: University of New Mexico Press, 1973.

Corea, Gina. 1979. *The mother machine.* New York: Harper and Row.

Frye, Marilyn. 1983. *The politics of reality: Essays in feminist theory.* Freedom, Calif.: Crossing Press.

Garry, Ann. 1978. Pornography and respect for women. *Social Theory and Practice* 4:395–421.

160

Part Two: Reproduction, Language, and Medical Models

Grimshaw, Jean. 1986. *Philosophy and feminist thinking.* Minneapolis: University of Minnesota Press.

Harkness, Carla. 1987. *The infertility book: A comprehensive medical and emotional guide.* San Francisco: Volcano Press.

Harvey, Jane, to *IVF Friends Newsletter* (Melbourne, Australia). 1990. July, pp. 10–11.

Kanowitz, Leo, ed. 1973. *Sex Roles in law and society: Cases and materials,* pp. 61–63. Albuquerque: University of New Mexico Press.

Kirejczyk, Marta, and Irma van der Ploeg. 1992. Pregnant couples: Medical technology and social constructions around fertility and reproduction. *Issues in Reproductive and Genetic Engineering* 5:113–25.

Lakoff, George. 1987. *Women, fire, and dangerous things: What categories reveal about the mind.* Chicago: University of Chicago Press.

Lloyd, Genevieve. 1984. *The man of reason: Male and female in Western philosophy.* London: Methune.

Menning, B. E. 1977. *Infertility: A guide for childless couples.* Englewood Cliffs, N.J.: Prentice-Hall.

Radner, Gilda. 1989. *It's always something.* New York: Simon and Schuster.

Ross, Stephanie. 1981. How words hurt: Attitude, metaphor, and oppression. In Mary Vetterling-Braggin, ed., *Sexist language,* pp. 194–213. Lanham, Md.: Littlefield, Adams.

Royal Commission on New Reproductive Technologies. 1993. *Proceed with care: Final report.* Ottawa: Minister of Government Services.

Scutt, J. A. 1988. *The baby machine: Commercialisation of motherhood.* Carlton, Australia: McCulloch.

Spelman, E. V. 1982. Woman as body. *Feminist Studies* 8:109–31.

Wasser, S. K., and D. Y. Isenberg. 1986. Reproductive failure among women: Pathology or adaptation? *Journal of Psychosomatic Obstetrics and Gynecology* 5:153–75.

Zoldbrod, Aline. 1993. *Men, women, and infertility: Intervention and treatment strategies.* New York: Macmillan.

7

THE POLITICS OF LANGUAGE

IN SURGICAL CONTRACEPTION

LYN TURNEY

Two unrelated events inspired this chapter: a column in the local newspaper, written by general practitioners, that provided information about female sterilization, and a conversation with a veterinary surgeon about the sterilization of my female cat.[1] At first glance, they have little in common except, taken together, they provide us with insights into the enabling capacity of language to create meaning and to direct social action, specifically in relation to surgical contraception.

The cultural and individual acceptance of surgical sterilization as contraception occurs at two levels. The broader level at which this occurs is within the meaning making "common sense" of everyday understandings—that is, within discourse—and the sociocultural activity, or discursive practices, that discourse enables. In a more direct manner it occurs at linguistic and textual levels in the interchange between clinicians and their patients. The focus of my analysis in this chapter is at the second level, the level of the clinic, where clinicians use language selectively, in both written and verbal form, to shroud and shift meaning in order to understate bodily intervention and to cast contraceptive surgery not only as a benign nonevent—a simple contraceptive method—but as also having the ability to recraft, enhance, and "resex" the body.

In examining the language of the clinic, I deconstruct the text of information sources for lay consumption (mainly women), in which simplified versions of this surgical procedure are described in language that is qualitatively different from that of medical texts (for the consumption of doctors). I look specifically at the language that typically appears in information brochures, pamphlets, and summary information sheets (or newspaper columns) to explain sterilization procedures and their effects to women consumers. I then take up in some detail one issue that these brochures almost universally discuss, that is, that sterilization will not only *not* affect a woman's sexual feelings but will actually enhance her sex life. Further, I reveal how value-laden cultural explanations often masquerade as scientific "truth."

In deconstructing the language of the clinic, I compare common assertions in clinical accounts with scientific findings from the medical literature and women's experiences in relation to sterilization, bodily intervention, and sexual pleasure. The latter are from open-ended questionnaires, letters, and in-depth interviews and are part of a larger study of women's experience of surgical sterilization (Turney 1996). The findings of this study and from the review of the medical literature generally dispute clinical claims of universality in relation to the efficacy of sterilization, of sterilization as a problem-free procedure, and as a suitable means of improving sexual enjoyment.

Theoretical Framework

I use a theoretical framework that brings to the center of analysis language that is dynamic and context based, because what we know and how we negotiate and engage in social interaction is possible only through language (Davies 1994). In this view, nothing exists or happens outside language—reality is constituted within language (Turner 1987). Conversely, because of the indeterminacies and failures of language, the "interference in meaning caused by language" (Davies 1994), we can deconstruct it. Although I have discussed elsewhere (Turney 1995) some of the limitations of accepting purely linguistic accounts of both experience and culture, language *is* nevertheless important to how we understand the world. Its enabling capacity, its ability to create meaning and to direct social action, makes it perhaps the most important medium of cultural transmission.

Language articulates ideas both by giving them meaning and by being the vehicle that makes possible everyday practices and social institutions. The French philosopher Michel Foucault (1973, 1977, 1980) first drew our attention to the power of *discourse*, which is centrally concerned with, but not reducible to, language (Schilling 1993). Discourses are like stories—narratives or accounts in which explanation has coherence, logic, and truth that come to be accepted as reality. Discourse is also a system of meaning created in social interaction through the mechanism of language and what language enables. It structures reality and determines what it is possible to know and do and at the same time can literally disqualify alternate accounts of social reality (Smart 1989). In this way discourses always privilege and preserve particular distributions of power (Abercrombie, Hill, and Turner 1988). What we are concerned with in relation to surgical contraception, in the broader sense, is medical discourse that structures much of our reality, not only in relation to fertility and sterility but also in terms of normative behavior around sexual practices and, more generally, in terms of the day-to-day activities of individuals.

If we are to understand power and how knowledges are both constructed and disqualified, we need to be concerned with language, the vehicle of transmission. In relation to sterilization, we need to deconstruct the clinical discourse that creates it as a normative practice by closely examining its language. Because language as a medium conveys meaning and reality imperfectly, we need to examine it to reveal what it masks and what it excludes, to expose it for its partiality and its failure by telling alternative accounts or providing different readings in order to "unsettle apparently closed systems and empires of meaning" (Douzinas and Warrington 1991:xiii).

Clinical Information

The esoteric knowledge of Western medicine has traditionally been shrouded with medical jargon that generally makes it inaccessible to laypersons. Consumerist and feminist demands for more information have led, in some cases, to the provision of "simplified" versions of medical procedures as consumer information. It is, however, important to examine this type of pseudoclinical description and, in particular, the language of explanation. Under the guise of simplifying language for the purpose of clarity, it often actually euphemizes surgical practice by using language to negate the seriousness, permanency, and intrusiveness of a particular procedure, such as surgical sterilization. Further, it dismisses women's accounts of the physiological effects of surgery as "nonscientific,"thus effectively erasing their experience in relation to any surgical procedure. In examining clinical information as provided in information brochures—and confirmed in women's accounts of what clinicians have told them—I use women's own words, supported by research findings from the medical literature, to challenge this expunction.[2] I do this specifically in relation to clinical claims in regard to the permanency, reversibility, and failure of surgical contraception as well as the assertions of procedural simplicity and the lack of side-effects. I argue that the sanitizing language associated with clinical accounts of surgical sterilization serves to mask the invasive nature of the procedure and trivialize and make invisible its complications and side-effects. In the second part of the chapter, I challenge clinical claims regarding enhanced sexuality as a result of sterilization.

"Closing" the Fallopian Tube and Problems with Reversibility

Information brochures typically begin with a brief explanatory paragraph on the mechanics of reproduction before going on to describe the surgical activity involved in sterilization as "closing" or "blocking" the fallopian tubes. Medical researchers and gynecological text for the consumption of doctors, in contrast, are not so neutral with language. They more accurately explain that the surgery crushes a section of each tube and the surrounding tissue. In fact, the surgeon *must* destroy part of the tube or rejoining of the tube (anastomosis) and thus failure of the procedure is a real possibility. For example, Mattingly's 1977 gynecological text describes how to electrocoagulate, or apply an electric current to, the tube in a manner that does the job "thoroughly": "The tube smokes and swells, and occasionally a popping noise is heard from fluid in the tubal lumen [the hollow part of the tube] and tissue. When the tube swells and then collapses, coagulation is sufficient to permit avulsion [a forcible tearing away] of a segment" (358).

In discussing the causes of sterilization failures in a medical journal, Soderstrom says that "complete vascular obliteration must be assured to arrive at the lowest failure rate" (1985:399).

The problem with using neutral or passive language—as the information brochures do—is that it misrepresents the procedure to women and in subtle ways implies that "closed," "blocked," "clamped," or "tied" tubes are easily opened, unblocked, unclamped, or untied (Clarke 1989; Parente 1984), when this is clearly not the case and there is sufficient evidence that this procedure should never be promoted as reversible.

Sterilization reversal for women is not a simple procedure but requires major microsurgery to rejoin the fallopian tubes, part of which were destroyed completely (by crushing, burning, strangulating, or cutting) to effect sterility in the first instance. The literature shows reversal has relatively low success rates, particularly as the rates given are for women who have been carefully prescreened for suitability (Gillett and Martin 1993; Rachagan and Jaafar 1993). The information brochures cite studies on the success rates, but these studies were of preselected and mostly small samples of women who have the best prognosis for reversal (see, for example, Langer et al. [1993], who studied 25 women; Rachagan and Jaafar [1993], who studied 26 women; and Gillett and Martin [1993], who studied 83 women). Also, the figures given for successful pregnancy after reversal are crude rates that typically include miscarriages and ectopic pregnancies, and they range from 28 percent (Langer et al. 1993) to 61 percent "successful" pregnancies (Gillett and Martin 1993). The reversal rate is much lower than is the desire for reversal. Henshaw and Singh (1986) report that more than a quarter of married U.S. couples who have opted for permanent methods might like to have another child and 10 percent want to have their sterilization reversed.

Even if the rejoining of the fallopian tubes is successful, many women have to undergo fertility treatment in order to become pregnant (see, for example, Langer et al. 1993) because of reduced ovarian function (Hakverdi et al. 1994). A study by Hakverdi and colleagues shows ovarian deficiency within twelve months after tubal ligation in 60 percent of women who had been carefully prescreened for "normal" ovarian function, whereas 30 percent of women in the study group were not ovulating after one year. This means that although the fallopian tubes after reversal may be technically viable in terms of providing a conduit for sperm and ova, hormonal deficiency and resultant inability of the ovary to produce ova severely reduce the possibility of pregnancy (see Young et al. 1993). As well, the chance of successful reversal decreases over time since sterilization because of normal age-related decline in fertility (Rachagan and Jaafar 1993; Calvert 1995). And the younger a woman is at the time of reversal, the more likely she is to achieve a successful pregnancy (Young et al. 1993).

Semantics and Reversibility of Surgical Sterilization

Although the brochures typically discuss reversal as an option of last resort, the very raising of the possibility of reversal can be, and is, misread and mistranslated in clinical exchanges as "until circumstances change," that is, as semipermanent rather than permanent. This is how some women express the meaning of reversal and what it conveys to them:[3]

> If I remember rightly [I was told] that the operation could be reversed if I changed my mind.

> [The doctor] just told me that the clips weren't as permanent.

> I had clamps put on because it is more easily reversible.

> [I] felt [tubal ligation] was safer than available contraceptions, because it was reversible.

> [The doctor told me the clips] could be removed if I wanted more children.

> [The gynecologist] was enthusiastic and positive about my sterilization, making it seem very simple and matter of fact. He encouraged me to have clamps instead of cutting or burning the tubes, claiming the clamps would be my ultimate contraceptive solution, given that I may change my mind about having children in the future. I agreed to the clamps because he claimed it was a much simpler procedure.

Summing up the illusions women have about reversibility and what it means in real terms, as a viable option, one woman I interviewed said:

> I realized [reversal] was such a long operation. . . . Everyone is there to help, to help you have [the tubal ligation] and it's such a quick operation. Such a quick procedure, and they say to you— the only thing that really in the end made me say yes, apart from everything else, was that it was reversible. They told me it was reversible, it's no big deal. And it was that that made the difference between the cutting and the clamp. So that word reversible was my only comfort. Even at that time when I said, "Yes, I'll do it," the word—not that I wanted more children at that point—but if something is reversible it's not such a . . . final step and it's not a serious thing. So I forgot everything I read because the word *reversible* was there. Right, so that was my comfort. But when I went into the "reversibleness" of it all, and realized what a big— well, it's microsurgery. . . . When I realized what a big operation it was, I thought, well, cutting me open and getting it is not going to—really—I'm stuck with it. I'm stuck with it, you know.

These women clearly demonstrate the failure of clinicians to convey accurate representations of surgical contraception as an essentially irreversible procedure. Arguably, in the context of the social trend to serial monogamy, it is a method of contraception that women should approach with great caution.

The Failure of Surgical Sterilization

Although studies report high proportions of women who were not sufficiently informed of the permanency of surgical sterilization (for example, Allyn et al. 1986; Gomel 1978), information brochures typically understate the failure rate of sterilization (resulting in pregnancy) as somewhere between 0.2 and 0.3 percent. However, studies report higher rates. For example, in two recent large studies the cumulative failure rates (or those recorded over time) were shown to be about 2 percent or 1 in every 50 women (Birdsall, Pattison, and Wilson 1994; Peterson, Xia, et al. 1996).[4] This is clearly an unacceptably high rate of failure for a surgical procedure that the medical establishment promotes for its permanency and *low* failure rates. The researchers who conducted the hospital audit that formed the basis of one study (Birdsall, Pattison, and Wilson 1994) overtly state that "sterilization is associated with a significant failure rate" (473).

Further, pregnancy after sterilization is highly likely to be ectopic with the embryo embedding in the fallopian tube rather than the uterus—a condition that, if undetected, is life threatening (Chick, Frances, and Paterson 1985; Peterson, Xia, et al. 1997).[5] Ectopic pregnancies are more likely when the method of sterilization is bipolar coagulation, still the preferred method in the United States (Peterson, Hulka, et al. 1993) where the rate of ectopic pregnancy is reported to be half (50 percent) of all failures (Pollack 1993). Most women who do become pregnant after sterilization have to decide whether to undergo an abortion (for example, 74 percent in Falfoul et al. 1993), but abortion is the only choice available to the ectopic pregnancy group.[6] Abortion for some of these women can be an emotionally traumatic experience, particularly for those who oppose it on moral grounds—often the reason many women decide on sterilization in the first place.

Surgical Sterilization as a "Simple" Procedure

In addition to using misinformation about the permanency of sterilization, brochures frequently negate the seriousness and intrusiveness of the surgery itself. They represent laparoscopic sterilization as a "common," "simple," and "quick" operation. However, no studies have provided evidence that quicker surgical procedures are less damaging than longer operations or that because an operation is common it is necessarily safe. Medical studies typically measure the safety of sterilization in terms of subsequent hospital admissions for treatment of side-effects, so the figures typically given when side-effects are discussed omit those women whose side-effects do *not* require hospitalization and who merely put up with their adverse effects or report them to a clinician. So, when individual women report menstrual problems, pain, and discomfort as a result of tubal sterilization, their problems are individualized, go unrecorded, and are dismissed, leaving the women to cope with side-effects they are told do not really exist. Because no one acknowledges, much less systematically records, their side-effects, there remains no space for women's voices to be heard in relation to their experienced pain and/or discomfort. The status of sterilization as a commonly used procedure thus ratifies its continuance simply because it is common, it is misrepresented as simple, and it is promoted as a natural choice at the end of a woman's "contraceptive career" (Thomas 1985). Women report in a variety of ways their unquestioning acceptance of sterilization as a "quick fix" and a safe and simple procedure:

> [Tubal ligation] just seemed to be the easiest way out I think—the safest way out.

> Basically I went into making the decision without even thinking about any consequences. All I wanted to do was to have the tubal ligation. I was under a very good gynecologist and I trusted him implicitly.

> I just never really gave it a thought, and I believed with every article that I had read that this procedure was a miracle cure.

> The opinions we're getting from doctors is [that there is] nothing to it, [it is a] simple operation, and you won't have to worry about contraception again.

> [I believed that] it was just a simple operation and that then I'd have no more problems. That's why I went ahead and had it done. . . . If I'd have known what I was going to be in for I would never have [agreed to have it done]—but it was just made to sound so simple.

> I feel that I didn't consider all my options. I wasn't given any information. I thought it was an easier way out.

Surgery as Noninterventive

Most brochures claim that tubal ligation itself is straightforward and has few complications. But it is a surgical intervention with all the risks and side-effects of any surgical procedure. Research on complications shows an overall rate of 4.0 percent at surgery alone (Chick, Frances, and Paterson 1985). This means that 1 in every 25 women who *elect* surgical contraception as a routine, simple procedure suffers from complications such as hemorrhage, burns, direct trauma to pelvic organs or blood vessels, and infection. Yet clinical accounts typically dismiss this reality as a nonevent or as producing only "minor discomfort." This is how three women, who did not experience contraceptive surgery as a simple straightforward event, describe their experience:

> Upon the anaesthetic wearing off after late afternoon surgery, I was in quite-extreme pain all night and only just managed to hobble, doubled-up and with help, out of the hospital when discharged the next morning. In discomfort and aching, I stayed in a curled-up position to ease further pain from erect posture for some days. A week later, I was still walking around at work in a hunched position from cramp-like pain.

> I was in severe pain and my body went into shock, my blood pressure dropped very low and I was given pethidine and a glucose drip to stabilize my blood pressure. By midday I was still in recovery with very low blood pressure, unbearable pain, and vaginal bleeding, which I was surprised to have. . . . The pain was terrible for four days, and I had purple-red bruising over my lower abdomen for almost two weeks after the procedure. The recovery took at least ten days and I was shocked and disappointed.

> Immediately after the operation I suffered for a week from bloating and terrible cramping—period-like pain. On returning to the gynecologist, he dismissed my complaints and told me to take a few panadol and it would go away. . . . I have since suffered from severe but unexplained and occasional pain in the right side of my groin. I believe this is related to my operation as I never experienced it before I had the procedure done.

Although the experiences of these women are not necessarily representative of the experience of all women, it seems that women *do* suffer more immediate, postoperative discomfort than they were told they would, particularly in accounts that minimize the surgical, and therefore invasive, nature of this method of contraception.

Negating Menstrual Disturbance

Information brochures generally claim that sterilization does not affect a woman's menstrual cycle in any way and go on to explain away any changes that women have reported as resulting from the return to normal bleeding after using the contraceptive pill or intrauterine device, or due to older methods of sterilization that were more destructive, or to normal aging. An examination of the medical literature, however, clearly refutes any claim about the nonexistence of menstrual disorders following sterilization. For example, Wilcox and colleagues (1992) found that by five years after sterilization, more than one third (35 percent) of 5,070 women reported high levels of menstrual pain, whereas almost half (49 percent) reported heavy bleeding (see also Shain et al. 1989). The researchers say that neither the usual effect of aging nor the amount of tissue damage caused by older methods such as diathermy (burning the fallopian tubes) explains these changes. In fact, women to whom surgeons applied spring clips (a modern method) were more likely to experience increased menstrual pain. Further, earlier research findings show that women who have *not* previously used the contraceptive pill also report menstrual disturbance (Lawson, Cole, and Templeton 1979). When I specifically asked the women in my study about menstrual pain, they rejected the idea that their periods were heavier and more uncomfortable because of the loss of the control offered by the pill. That is, they rejected the notion that they had forgotten what their "real" periods were like before they took the pill, a claim made in both the medical and consumer literature informing women that any increased bleeding they experience is simply a "return to normal." An editorial in the *Lancet* suggested that a woman contemplating sterilization should discontinue oral contraceptives "to discover whether she can now tolerate her normal periods" ("Late complications" 1976:574).

So, although clinicians provide an explanation of menstrual disturbance after tubal sterilization that may *seem* to be commonsensical, their explanation turns out to be simply a theory based on opinion rather than scientific fact. Women dispute this theory:

> By day two of each period I feel as if my body turns on a tap to drain the blood.

It was not like a normal heavy period. It was just like water gushing out in vast quantities. It was bright red. It was frightening, not normal. I always felt there was something wrong.

One day a month—I feel my insides are dropping out—[it is] not pleasant.

It just suddenly starts and it's like a gush of blood all down you and you think, "Oh, I've got my period," which can be quite embarrassing, it is embarrassing, it's extremely embarrassing.

Increased Incidence of Hysterectomy following Tubal Sterilization

Brochures also address the question of how often hysterectomy follows tubal ligation, claiming reports of its frequency are either a misconception or related to the use of older methods of sterilization (in which the fallopian tubes were burned to occlude them). However, research still shows that sterilized women are three to four times more likely than nonsterilized women to undergo hysterectomy (Kjer and Knudsen 1990). More recently, Goldhaber and colleagues (1993), in a study of 80,007 women, reported that sterilized women were significantly more likely than their nonsterilized counterparts to undergo hysterectomy and that relative risks of undergoing a hysterectomy varied *little* by method of tubal occlusion. But this study also reported that risks were highest when hysterectomy was performed for menstrual problems or pain and doubled for women who were younger than twenty-five when they were sterilized (see also Shy et al. 1992).
The language that sterilization providers use in clinical exchanges thus clearly sanitizes the actuality of surgical intrusion into the bodies of women for contraceptive purposes and negates the effects it has on some women. How can women give a proper informed consent to this procedure when, under the guise of providing *more* information, clinicians are actually perpetuating a mythical account of sterilization that obscures more than it reveals?

Enhancing Sexual Enjoyment?

Now we come to the overt claims that surgical sterilization enhances female sexual enjoyment. I discuss these by juxtaposing two surgical procedures that are linguistically constructed as entirely different but that are performed for the same expected outcome and are essentially the same practice. I thus address the ambiguities around human female sterilization and "desexing" or "neutering" in veterinary practice and the muddled ways in which issues of sexuality are linguistically manipulated in order to make surgery for contraception acceptable practice for humans.

Although language is never entirely innocent, some linguistic accounts appear more naïve than others where it matters less. People speak of the sterilization, neutering, or spaying of animals in quite realistic terms as they need not observe social niceties regarding surgical practice and domestic animals—among other things, society considers neutering pets to be environmentally responsible. At a lexical level, the terms *castration* and *neutering* are clearly separated from the medicalized terms *tubal ligation, hysterectomy,* and *vasectomy.* Yet culturally and physiologically, the terms overlap significantly at the levels of both cognition and embodiment.

The paradoxical status of sterilization in terms of sexuality is a dominant theme that emerges whenever sterility is considered, despite medicine's efforts *in this particular context* to subvert and sometimes exploit common cultural beliefs that view sterility in negative terms. Doctors, for example, *never* speak of human female sterilization or its expected outcomes by using veterinary terms such as *spaying, neutering,* or *desexing.* Yet sterility and the act of destroying fertility are intricately tied up with cultural understandings of sexual potency, the body, and the self. The discursive manipulation of such understandings becomes transparent when we compare the work of Shanner (see chapter 6) in which she explains how the medical establishment has pathologized infertility and intricately entwined it with sexual identity and sexual performance in the context of in-vitro fertilizaton (IVF) treatment. It characterizes IVF research, in turn, as a salvationist and heroic technology that promises the completeness of self and "coupledom" that fertility *here* endows. Despite what clinicians assert about sterilization's having a benign physiosexual effect,[7] sterilized women (and men) undergo a bodily alteration that remains socially and culturally ambiguous despite its widespread contraceptive use.

The Languages of Sterilization

When I took my female cat to the veterinary surgeon to be sterilized, I asked him to clarify exactly what he was going to do to her. He quite readily explained that he would need to totally remove the ovaries, tubes, and uterus of the cat because experience has shown that removing only the tubes or uterus inevitably causes further health problems. Total removal of the sex organs would, however, "stop the cat cycling" (that is, the fertility cycle would cease), thus removing feline desire and, presumably, "attractiveness" to her prospective male suitors—that is, she would no longer go into heat. As well, the veterinary surgeon carefully explained that, because the cat would no longer be interested in the joys of the night, she would not stray and would thus become a good docile pet.

However, in human female sterilization (hysterectomy and tubal ligation), the language expressing medical knowledges does not include any mention of ill health resulting from leaving the ovaries *intact*. In fact, clinicians make quite the opposite claim, that surgical removal of the uterus or destroying part of the fallopian tubes does not affect female hormones and desire, providing that at least one ovary is retained—that is, it is actually important to *retain* the ovaries. If ovarian failure occurs as a result of both tubal ligation (Hakverdi et al. 1994) and hysterectomy (Riedel, Lehmann-Willenbrock, and Semm 1986; Siddle, Sarrel, and Whitehead 1987), the difference between human sterilization and neutering would seem to be purely semantic. So, if sterilization does cause eventual ovarian failure that could render the uterus problematic because of excessive and prolonged bleeding, as discussed earlier, the veterinary surgeon may actually be providing the more accurate account in relation to subsequent problems and ill health.

Further, in terms of sexual functioning, the family planners and populationists promoting surgical contraception for women claim that it actually *improves* their sex lives rather than making them more docile. In purely materialist terms, how can the destruction of fertility actually increase interest in sex? Given the damage done by the procedure in terms of the interference with the endocrine system (Hakverdi et al. 1994), women are more likely to show a decreased interest in sex. However, I do not want to adopt such a biologically reductionist approach to sexuality, because human sexuality and desire are intricately entwined with the social and the psychological and are irreducible to biology and hormones. I merely wish to point out that, in biomedical terms, such claims are entirely without a scientific basis. When science fails, though, clinicians resort to a social explanation of this "increased interest in sex"; that is, removing "the fear of pregnancy" is said to improve a woman's sex life. So through surgery the act of desexing is articulated as a type of re-sexing that rescues the fertile woman (mother of two) from the inhibitory "fear of pregnancy" so that she can realize her full sexual potential. Upon examination, however, it is unclear just how the (surgical?) removal of fear of pregnancy, of itself, would make for better or more uninhibited sex or improved sexual satisfaction. Sterilization does not, for example, remove the inhibitory presence of demanding young children or the overtiredness from working a double day. Nor does it, of itself, improve relationships other than perhaps those based on coercion. What it *does* remove, though, is a good reason for refusing sex.

The Surgical Destruction of Fertility

Clinicians construct the phenomenon of the "fear of pregnancy" differently at different points in a woman's reproductive life. For women past childbearing age, the fear of pregnancy is constructed as problematic and detrimental to sexual enjoyment in a way that it is not in earlier stages, when it is arguably more of a problem, especially if the relationship is unstable or transitory. In terms of medicine, this phenomenon becomes a clinically acceptable explanation that justifies the surgical "fixing" of postchildbearing women as an appropriate means of increasing sexual satisfaction.

Elsewhere (Turney 1994) I have discussed my finding that the discursive linking of women's genitalia to reproduction rather than to sexuality has enabled them to be rendered unnecessary—and even dangerous and dispensable as functional units—once childbearing is complete. But, although the relationships between sexual organs and reproduction are somewhat explicable in terms of a medically constructed "contraceptive career" (Thomas 1985)—the end point of which is the termination of fertility—this particular construction does not explain the variable connections between fertility and femininity over the span of this "career." Permanent infertility or the absence of fertility in the sexually active period before childbirth is constructed not only as problematic but as rendering the unfortunate woman cursed, incomplete, "less of a woman," someone to be pitied and helped by the miracles of modern medicine, at whatever personal and material cost (see Shanner in chapter 6). In contrast, the voluntary permanent sterility effected by surgical methods after childbearing is considered to be nonproblematic and generally unconnected to femininity. The notion of a "sterile (or barren) mother" has no social meaning because sterility somehow becomes irrelevant. A woman's fertility becomes expendable once she has completed the socially prescribed function of child production in adequate number. The crucial link between femininity and fertility of the prechildbearing phase (albeit constructed) is rendered invisible in the postchildbearing phase of a woman's life. A powerful example of the enabling capacity of particular discourses to license the surgical destruction of fertility is demonstrated by 88 percent of women in my survey who responded that the "loss of femaleness" at sterilization was of "minimal importance"—a nonissue. What is the difference here— why has the crucial cultural link between fertility and femininity been negated? Does the ownership of children, rather than the biological capacity to bear them, now declare fertility? Perhaps femininity is irrelevant to the category of mothers, or maybe femininity now equates with the maternal, or perhaps femininity and fertility are not related at all. Whatever the case, we need to look at the issue in terms of whose interests are served by manipulating meaning and categories in this way.

Female Sexuality following Surgical Sterilization

What discussions of sterilization and sexuality generally omit is what women themselves say about how they experience this bodily alteration that has no external representation but that nonetheless is imbued with potent cultural meaning. Studies on sexual satisfaction and alteration of sexual practices following sterilization are relatively rare; most were conducted in the 1970s and 1980s. Most conclude that the majority of women's sexual relationships and libido are either not affected or improve (Chick, Frances, and Paterson 1985; Philliber and Philliber 1985). In all studies on sexuality, however, a small group of women reports "a deterioration in sexual functioning" (Chick, Frances, and Paterson 1985:93; see also Kjer 1990; Philliber and Philliber 1985). The most recent study by Kjer typically measured "sexual adjustment" after sterilization in terms of "coital frequency" and "perception of libido," which he reports were "improved or unchanged in the majority of women" (211). The emphasis in these studies is on performance and activity; the implication is that more sex means better sex. Such measures of sexual satisfaction are arguably masculinist and are uninformed by any real notion of female desire, pleasure, or enjoyment. Shanner (see chapter 6) similarly comments on the absence in the English language of terminology to describe sexual encounters in positive, affirmative ways.

Philliber and Philliber (1985) reviewed twenty-four studies that asked women about "sexual desire," again defined in terms of frequency of intercourse. They found a broad variation in responses, ranging from zero to 44 percent of women who experienced decreased sexual desire after tubal sterilization. In two-thirds (67 percent) of all studies included in the review, 10 percent or more women reported that their sexual relationships had deteriorated after sterilization. It would seem, then, given the confounding of desire and libido with frequency and women's inability to use the fear of pregnancy as a reason for refusing sex, we need to listen more carefully to the voices of those women who are reporting a decline in sexual satisfaction as a direct result of surgical sterilization.

What Women Themselves Say about Sexuality and Sterilization

My study of women's experiences of surgical sterilization found that a little more than one half (51 percent) of all women reported no change in sexual activity after tubal ligation, a clear refutation of the universality of claims of improved sexual enjoyment. Twenty-four percent of all women reported change of a positive nature, saying they had experienced increased sexual activity and "more relaxed" sexual activity. In contrast, 20 percent reported a decrease in sexual activity, desire, or urge to instigate sex.[8]

The women who reported positive changes in their sexual activity and feelings about sexuality and sex life ascribed those improvements to spontaneity and less worry about pregnancy rather than to enhanced desire. In fact, only five women (3 percent) in the entire study expressed an improvement in sexual pleasure that seemed to be related to a physiological enjoyment of sex (rather than pleasure as the absence of fear or anxiety about pregnancy). These few women talked of unrestrained and unrestricted enjoyment using such terms as *fun, pleasure, freedom,* and newly experienced orgasm. Perhaps satisfaction in terms of body awareness was best expressed by one woman in this comment: "I am now free to listen to my body and seek sexual contact when I (and my body) seek it—generally at or before ovulation—a natural sexuality I've had to ignore and use to determine my sex life in the past."

Another woman, however, expressed serious reservations about the "naturalness" of unlimited sex afforded by sterilization and, although she clearly was engaged in consensual sex, her observations raise issues in relation to the accessibility and "safety" of the sterile female body and the potential for coercive sex:

> The only plus [in relation to tubal ligation] is that my sex life, or our sex life was great. I mean you could have sex whenever you

want, without that fear. In the beginning it was a novelty you know. But then it was like, oh God, you know, even this isn't right. We live in this society of plenty plenty plenty, even sex, you know, you can have it on call any time, to a point that I was even starting to feel that that was wrong. . . . I've forgotten what it's like to say no we can't have sex tonight because—it's a bad time. . . . I never thought I would miss that. I mean, I can say no I don't want sex, I mean sex is whether you want it or not. But it was just that . . . I felt sort of like we were gorging on sex. I mean, not that there was anything wrong in that, but . . . I suppose in a way it was like, I don't know if, a moral issue, was right. Is it right to be able to have so much sex and enjoy it? No, moral's the wrong word. . . . You know, I mean we were given a body and to enjoy sex at certain times. I never sort of thought of that. . . . When you're young you have sex whether you've got your period or not. Whereas now it's like when I have my period it's my time, you know, with my body.

These two women highlight the alienation from the interior of their bodies that women may experience as a result of relying on medicalized contraceptives. Fertility and its cycles are now frequently controlled chemically or surgically so that sex is regular and rendered independent of natural female desire. The importance of natural cycles and rhythms of the female body are at issue here, and it becomes questionable whether surgical or chemical interference with either the body's physiology or its sociosexual engagement can ever be an enhancement to sexuality.

As I stated earlier, 20 percent of the women surveyed in my study reported an actual decrease in sexual activity since their operation, clearly refuting the claims that promise enhanced sexuality as an outcome of contraceptive surgery. The comments these women made ranged from loss of interest or lack of libido to loss of desire because of discomfort or pain. Some women also expressed an increased awareness of cyclic changes linked to levels of sexual desire. For example:

I have a very bad lack of libido. . . . In the first few days after menstruation my libido is quite good, then it sort of tapers out to virtually nothing until the next month. . . . Well, I mean I probably get angry at times because I sort of feel that now that we've got no kids at home, we should be able to enjoy that sexual relationship at any time during the day or night. . . . And that's when I sort of think, well, you know, really it's sort of ruined our little bit of sexual fun, if you'd like to call it that, where some days it's fine and other days it's like "Oh, do I have to?—just go away."

Some women reported a decline in sexual desire as sometimes grad-
ual and perhaps the result of age and a long-term relationship with the
same partner, whereas others reported the decline in interest to be immediate, noticeable, and therefore clearly linked to sterilization. For
example:

> [I view sex with] distaste, aversion, no interest. [I have a] lack of
> interest bordering on disgust. I was interested and active before
> and the change was immediate. . . . Before the operation I was a
> loving sexually active wife. After the operation I lost all interest
> almost immediately.

> [After tubal ligation] I felt different. I wasn't the same. I didn't
> have any sort of thing for sex or anything like that and I didn't
> really put it together at the time, I just didn't understand it. [It
> happened] fairly well straight away and I didn't think a lot of it
> at the time and I didn't really understand it.

> One other problem—I don't know whether this is relevant—I
> have become very unsexual and for the last six months or a year,
> I can't even achieve an orgasm.

The discomfort or pain that some women experience is the main con-
tributory factor in their lack of or decline in interest in sexual activity.
Thus if tubal sterilization causes damage to the ovarian artery (Berger,
Radwanska, and Hammond 1978; Cattanach 1985; Cattanach and Milne
1988; Radwanska, Berger, and Hammond 1978) or interrupts the direct
delivery of hormones to the uterus to maintain a healthy, lubricated
cervix and vagina (Ringrose 1974), these developments would seem to
directly implicate sterilization in the reduction of sexual enjoyment for
some women. Some women expressed discomfort from dry vagina:

> Two years down the track—my natural sort of lubricating glands
> as far as sex and that are concerned, they were definitely dried
> up. . . . And then I saw—I'd lost my libido.

> I like to be in control of my life and my body was always under
> control before. It was also very frustrating for my husband be-
> cause we had a very good sex life before and afterwards I was
> unable to have a sex life, it was either too dry, infected, or too wet.
> I found out the infections could be corrected by him using oint-
> ment, and lubrication helped the dryness, but it took eight years
> before we could have a normal sex life and by then I had lost
> interest.

Finally, if tubal sterilization causes some women to experience heavy and prolonged bleeding and/or midcycle, premenstrual, menstrual, or continuous abdominal pain, these surely are greater barriers to the promised uninhibited sex than is the fear of pregnancy. Some women report this to be clearly the case. One woman who had come to believe that the only solution to her poststerilization excessive menstrual bleeding and unbearable pain was a hysterectomy was not treated seriously in relation to her abdominal pain and excessive bleeding until she told the gynecologist that it was affecting her sex life.[9] He then immediately made arrangements for the operation, not because of her pain and suffering but because her pain and bleeding made her unavailable for sex. This clearly affirmed the status of her body as a receptive object of unfettered sexual pleasure.

Within this constructivity, sterilization enables a transformation of the dangerous reproductive body into an uncomplicated site of sexual pleasure. In veterinary terms, surgical de-sexing or neutering becomes a means of re-sexing mothers, promising to rescue them from their domesticity and their main reason for not engaging in sex (fear of pregnancy). Thus, in numeric terms, sexual activity can be increased, volume is translated as libido, and libido is equated with desire. At the same time, women's resistance to unlimited nonproductive sex, perhaps because of pain or discomfort, is cast as pathological.

In summary, this chapter has questioned the truth claims of clinical medical discourse and practice in relation to permanency, safety, and the surgical enhancement of female sexuality through sterilization. What is exposed in the process is the interpretative nature of science and how contemporary clinical practice both reflects and perpetuates broader societal attitudes toward women's reproductive bodies and effectively erases the experience of women in relation to any ill effects of sterilization. Because of the peculiar way in which the female body is constructed within clinical discourse and because women's reporting of side-effects associated with sterilization is trivialized, dismissed, or negated (Turney 1993), women learn that their reproductive bodies are inherently problematic, that suffering and discomfort are natural conditions of the female body, and that female reproductive equipment is distasteful and dispensable once childbearing is complete. With the interior of the female body thus defined, interpreted, and rendered unimportant by clinical medicine, internal mutilation of it remains unconsidered and uncontested.

Part Two: Reproduction, Language, and Medical Models

NOTES

1. The most commonly used term is *tubal ligation,* meaning to tie the (fallo-pian) tubes, but this term is somewhat misleading and largely outdated, be-cause the most common methods are to apply a spring (Filschie or Haulka) clip and/or burn the tubes. However, although I prefer to use the more correct (and less medicalized) term *surgical sterilization,* or simply *sterilization, tubal ligation* is still the term that women and doctors most commonly use. Medical researchers and some practitioners also use the terms *tubal sterilization, laparo-scopic sterilization,* and *female sterilization.*

2. I specifically refer to the following undated information sources: (a) bro-chures from the Royal Australian College of Obstetricians and Gynaecologists, the Family Planning Association of Victoria, and Leichhardt Women's Com-munity Health Centre; (b) a handout information sheet from the journal *Aus-tralian Family Physician;* (c) and the aforementioned newspaper column from the Royal Australian College of General Practitioners. Throughout the chapter I collectively refer to these as "information brochures."

3. All women quoted in this chapter are participants in my research on the experience of tubal sterilization (Turney 1996).

4. Birdsall, Pattison, and Wilson (1994) divide their group of failed steriliza-tions into "surgical" and "administrative" failures. The former are the result of mistakes such as misapplication of the clip or ring that occludes the tube (86 percent), and the latter refers to those women who were already pregnant at the time of surgery. In terms of the result for the women con-cerned and for the consent process, this technical division is meaningless. Peterson, Xia, and colleagues (1996) excluded thirty-four more women from their figures because of undetected pregnancy at the time of sterilization.

5. These women have a 25 to 75 percent chance that the pregnancy will be ectopic (Chick, Frances, and Paterson 1985). Falfoul and colleagues (1993) report 2 in 5 (40 percent) to be ectopic, whereas Birdsall, Pattison, and Wilson (1994) report 9.0 percent to be ectopic.

6. The Birdsall, Pattison, and Wilson study (1994) did not report the outcome for women in terms of how they managed their unwanted pregnancies.

7. See, for example, Murtagh (1993), Royal Australian College of General Practitioners (1994), and Royal Australian College of Obstetricians and Gy-naecologists (undated). As an example, the latter brochure, "Sterilisation in Women," in a typical example clearly states that "sterilisation does not ad-versely affect psychological or sexual feelings and may even have the effect of improving sexual enjoyment, because concern about pregnancy has been removed."

8. A further 4 percent reported a change but did not specify the kind of the change ($n = 128$; 3 missing values).

9. Upon seeking a second opinion, she learned that her pain was caused by a large overlooked "walnut sized cyst" on the ovary.

REFERENCES

Abercrombie, Nicholas, Stephen Hill, and Bryan Turner. 1988. *Dictionary of sociology.* London: Penguin.

Allyn, A. P., D. A. Lemon, N. A. Westcott, and R. W. Hale. 1986. Pre-sterilization counseling and women's regret about having been sterilized. *Journal of Reproductive Medicine* 31:1027.

Berger, G. S., E. Radwanska, and J. E. Hammond. 1978. Possible ovulatory deficiency after tubal ligation. *American Journal of Obstetrics and Gynecology* 132:699–700.

Birdsall, M. A., N. S. Pattison, and P. Wilson. 1994. Female sterilization: National Women's Hospital, 1988–1989. *New Zealand Journal of Medicine* 107: 473–75.

Calvert, J. P. 1995. Reversal of female sterilization. *British Journal of Hospital Medicine* 53:267–70.

Cattanach, J. F. 1985. Oestrogen deficiency after tubal ligation. *Lancet* 1:847–48.

Cattanach, J. F., and B. J. Milne. 1988. Post-tubal sterilization problems correlated with ovarian steroidogenesis. *Contraception* 38:541–50.

Chick, P. H., M. Frances, and P. J. Paterson. 1985. A comprehensive review of female sterilization—Tubal occlusion methods. *Clinical Reproduction and Fertility* 32:91–97.

Clarke, Adele. 1989. Subtle forms of sterilization abuse: A reproductive rights analysis. In Rita Arditti, Renate D. Klein, and Shelley Minden, eds., *Test tube women: What future for motherhood?* London: Pandora.

Davies, Margaret. 1994. *Asking the law question.* North Ryde, Australia: Law Book Co.

Douzinas, C., and R. Warrington. 1991. *Postmodern jurisprudence: The law of text in the texts of law.* London: Routledge.

Falfoul, A., R. Friaa, M. Chelli, and M. Kharouf. 1993. Pregnancy following female surgical sterilization: A study apropos of thirty-eight cases. *Journal of Gynaecology, Obstetrics, Biology, and Reproduction* (Paris) 22:23–25.

Family Planning Association of Victoria. Undated brochure. Sterilization.

Foucault, Michel. 1973. *The birth of the clinic: An archaeology of medical perception.* New York: Vintage.

Foucault, Michel. 1977. *Discipline and punish: The birth of the prison.* London: Allen Lane.

Foucault, Michel. 1980. The politics of health in the eighteenth century. In Colin Gordon, ed., *Michel Foucault power/knowledge.* Oxford: Harvester.

Gillett, W. R., and W. L. Martin. 1993. Reversal of female sterilization: Outcome of 210 referrals. *New Zealand Medical Journal* 106:173–75.

Goldhaber, Marilyn, Mary Anne Armstrong, Ira Golditch, Paul Sheehe, Diana Pettiti, and Gary Friedman. 1993. Long-term risk of hysterectomy among 80,007 sterilized and comparison women at Kaiser Permanente, 1971–1987. *American Journal of Epidemiology* 138:508–21.

Part Two: Reproduction, Language, and Medical Models

Gomel, Victor. 1978. Profile of women requesting reversal of sterilization. *Fertility and Sterility* 30:39.

Hakverdi, A. U., C. E. Taner, A. C. Erden, and O. Satici. 1994. Changes in ovarian function after tubal sterilization. *Advances in Contraception* 10: 51–56.

Henshaw, S. K., and S. Singh. 1986. Sterilization regret among U.S. couples. *Family Planning Perspectives* 18:238–40.

Kjer, J. J. 1990. Sexual adjustment to tubal sterilization. *European Journal of Obstetrics and Gynaecology and Reproductive Biology* 35:211–14.

Kjer, J. J., and L. Knudsen. 1990. Hysterectomy subsequent to laparoscopic sterilization. *European Journal of Obstetrics and Gynecology and Reproductive Biology* 35:63–68.

Langer, Martin, Pauline Hicks, Nora Nemeskeri, Barbara Schneider, and Marianne Ringler. 1993. Psychological sequelae of surgical reversal or of IVF after tubal ligation. *International Journal of Fertility* 38:44–49.

Late complications of female sterilisation. 1976. Editorial. *Lancet* 1:573–74.

Lawson, S., R. A. Cole, and A. A. Templeton. 1979. The effect of laparoscopic sterilization by diathermy or silastic bands on post-operative pain, menstrual symptoms, and sexuality. *British Journal of Obstetrics and Gynaecology* 86:659–63.

Leichhardt Women's Community Health Centre. Undated brochure. Female sterilization (Leichhardt, Australia).

Mattingly, R. F. 1977. *Te Linde's operative gynecology.* Philadelphia: Lippincott.

Murtagh, John. 1993. Tubal ligation. *Australian Family Physician* 22:611.

Parente, J. T. 1984. Tubal ligation: A misnomer. *American Journal of Obstetrics and Gynecology* 151:829.

Peterson, H. B., J. F. Hulka, J. M. Phillips, and M. W. Surrey. 1993. Laparoscopic sterilization: American Association of Gynecologic Laparoscopists 1991 membership survey. *Journal of Reproductive Medicine* 38:574–76.

Peterson, H. B., Z. Xia, J. M. Hughes, L. S. Wilcox, L. R. Tyler, and J. Trussell. 1996. The risk of pregnancy after tubal sterilization: Findings from the U.S. Collaborative Review of Sterilization. *American Journal of Obstetrics and Gynaecology* 174:1161–70.

Peterson, H. B., Z. Xia, J. M. Hughes, L. S. Wilcox, L. R. Tyler, and J. Trussell. 1997. The risk of ectopic pregnancy after tubal sterilization. *New England Journal of Medicine* 336:762–67.

Philliber, S. G., and W. W. Philliber. 1985. Social and psychological perspectives on voluntary sterilization: A review. *Studies in Family Planning* 16:1–29.

Pollack, Amy. 1993. Long-term consequences of female and male sterilization. *Contemporary OB/GYN* 38:41–54.

Rachagan, S. P., and Y. Jaafar. 1993. Fertility following reversal of female sterilization. *Medical Journal of Malaysia* 48:225–28.

Radwanska, G. S., G. S. Berger, and J. E. Hammond. 1978. Possible ovulatory deficiency after tubal ligation. *American Journal of Obstetrics and Gynecology* 132:699–700.

Riedel, H. H., E. Lehmann-Willenbrock, and Kurt Semm. 1986. Ovarian failure phenomenon after hysterectomy. *Journal of Reproductive Medicine* 31: 597–600.

Ringrose, C. A. D. 1974. Post-tubal ligation menorrhagia and pelvic pain. *International Journal of Fertility* 19:166–70.

Royal Australian College of General Practitioners. 1994. GP file: Two ways of tubal ligation. *Geelong Advertiser,* August 3, p. 9.

Royal Australian College of Obstetricians and Gynaecologists. Undated brochure. Sterilization in women (East Melbourne).

Schilling, Chris. 1993. *The body and social theory.* London: Sage.

Shain, R. N., W. B. Miller, G. W. Mitchell, A. E. C. Holden, and M. Rosenthal. 1989. Menstrual pattern change one year after sterilization: Results of a controlled, prospective study. *Fertility and Sterility* 52:192–203.

Shy, Kirk, Andy Stergachis, Louis Grothaus, Edward Wagner, Julia Hecht, Garnet Anderson. 1992. Tubal sterilization and risk of subsequent hospital admission for menstrual disorders. *American Journal of Obstetrics and Gynecology* 1:1698–1706.

Siddle, N., P. Sarrel, and M. Whitehead. 1987. The effect of hysterectomy on the age at ovarian failure: Identification of a subgroup of women with premature loss of ovarian function and literature review. *Fertility and Sterility* 47:94–100.

Smart, Carol. 1989. *Feminism and the power of law.* New York: Routledge.

Soderstrom, R. M. 1985. Sterilization failures and their causes. *Obstetrics and Gynaecology* 152:395–403.

Thomas, Hilary. 1985. The medical construction of a contraceptive career. In Hilary Homans, ed., *The sexual politics of reproduction.* Aldershot, U.K.: Gower.

Turner, Bryan. 1987. *Medical power and social knowledge.* London: Sage.

Turney, Lyn. 1993. Risk and contraception: What women are not told about tubal ligation. *Women's Studies International Forum* 16:471–86.

Turney, Lyn. 1994. Competing discourses around sterilisation: An analysis of embodiment and reproduction. In John Germov, ed., *Health papers,* pp. 71–89. Department of Sociology and Anthropology, University of Newcastle, Australia.

Turney, Lyn. 1995. Social theory and the female body. Paper presented at the the Australian Sociological Conference, "Tolerance, Diversity, and Social Inequality," December 5–8, 1995, University of Newcastle, Australia.

Turney, Lyn. 1996. Surgical sterilization: Medical power, women's knowledge. Ph.D. diss., School of Social Inquiry, Deakin University, Geelong, Australia.

Wilcox, Lynne, Beverley Martinez-Schnell, Herbert Peterson, James Ware, and Joyce Hughes. 1992. Menstrual function after tubal sterilization. *American Journal of Epidemiology* 135:1368–81.

Young, G. P., D. J. Ott, M. Y. M. Chen, J. A. Fayez, and D. W. Gelfand. 1993. Postoperative hysterosalpingography: Radiographic appearances and clinical results following tubal surgery. *Journal of Reproductive Medicine* 38: 924–28.

8 BABY TALK

THE RHETORICAL PRODUCTION

OF MATERNAL AND FETAL SELVES

EUGENIA GEORGES AND

LISA M. MITCHELL

A decade ago, Barbara Katz Rothman observed that many North American women "take pregnancy as a reading assignment" (1986:45). The proliferation of information pamphlets, magazine articles, and books about pregnancy written specifically for women bears out this claim, yet these texts appear to have escaped detailed critical feminist analysis.[1] This widespread "educating" of women, ostensibly to inform and empower them, raises questions about the assumptions of maternalism, authority, and choice encoded in these texts. We look at some of the pregnancy guidebooks popular in Greece and in Canada in order to illustrate the ways in which rhetorical constructions of pregnant women's bodies and experiences are culturally distinct. Our cross-cultural comparison thus provides a dual focus for the "lens" of language and rhetoric that forms the common approach to this book.

The dual focus is especially useful for highlighting the cultural inflections of medical and scientific discourse, which is commonly assumed to be, and represented as, culture free. This chapter examines how the language and images of these guidebooks reflect and rewrite scientific views of the body and reproduction even as they sideline maternal knowledge and practice and discipline women to become particular kinds of patients and mothers. In this respect our analysis builds upon the work of various feminist authors who have studied reproductive and fetal discourses in the North American context (e.g., Hartouni 1993; Martin 1987; Petchesky 1987; Rapp 1988, 1990). However, its unique cross-cultural comparative perspective enables us to discuss not only the commonalities but also "what is not shared in an emerging global culture of reproduction" (Rapp 1994:34). Drawing from our respective ethnographic studies of pregnancy and ultrasound fetal imaging (see Georges 1996 for Greece; Mitchell 1994 for Canada), we are able to focus our analysis on the ways in which these constructions of motherhood, the fetus, and pregnancy are culturally configured in Greece and in Canada and their connections to discourses on gender, abortion, nationalism, and modernity. In each case, we examine the ways in which culturally specific rhetorical strategies derive their persuasive force from distinctive historical and political contexts.

In the course of our in-depth interviews with pregnant Greek and Canadian women, we discovered the extent to which both consulted expert texts in the form of pregnancy guides. The most popular pregnancy source materials in Canada are, in fact, written by British and U.S. authors, yet Canadian women readily consume them as "essential information" with little or no cultural interference. We concentrate our analysis on one free booklet, *Nine Months for Life*, published by the physicians' association in Canada's second most populous province, and one best-selling book-length guide: *What to Expect When You're Expecting*, published in the United States and written by Arlene Eisenberg, Heidi Murkoff, and Sandee Hathaway. The women interviewed by Mitchell often used both guides. The materials available to Greek women are much less numerous, and many are translations of books originally published in other countries. Our discussion here focuses on the only complete book-length pregnancy guide written by a Greek, *Birth Is Love*, by Aleka Sikaki-Douka. Women interviewed by Georges most often used *Birth Is Love* as their guide. We base our analysis on close readings of these texts, informed by our long-term anthropological fieldwork in the two settings.

We begin with a reading of the English-language texts, presumably more familiar to the readers of this chapter, and examine both illustrations and text for their explicit and implicit meanings. We then turn to our analysis of *Birth Is Love* and provide a somewhat more extensive discussion of the less familiar Greek historical, cultural, and rhetorical context. Although the English and Greek texts display some stylistic similarities and often deploy similar visual images, they are nonetheless grounded in notably divergent cultural understandings and rhetorical strategies.

Reading Pregnancy in Canada

The two guides that Canadian women read are somewhat different in appearance and format. *Nine Months for Life* devotes most of its twenty-four large glossy pages to month-by-month descriptions of fetal development, maternal symptoms, and medical care. It presents each month (except the last two) on two facing pages headed with a single word or phrase: "Hope" (the first month), "Harmony" (the fourth), "Wonder" (the fifth), and so on. A list of physiological "warning signals" for each month appears against a soothing pastel color bar. The layout provides space for a woman to jot down "Questions for your doctor" and to record the dates of her medical appointments, her number of weeks of pregnancy, as well as her blood pressure, weight, weight gain, and urinalysis results for that month. For each of the first six months, the focal point is a close-up color photograph of the fetus in utero.

Except for a handful of simple black-and-white drawings, the 450 pages of *What to Expect,* now in its third edition, are text. The first of four main sections, "In the Beginning," covers such topics such as "Are you Pregnant?" "Choosing (and Working with) Your Practitioner," prenatal diagnosis, risks to the fetus, and dietary advice. In the second section are month-by-month descriptions of the physical and emotional changes and the tests and examinations a woman can expect during pregnancy. Part 3 covers maternal illness and chronic health conditions and, under "When Something Goes Wrong," a variety of problems such as miscarriage, fetal distress, and premature labor. The final section discusses the postpartum experience, breast feeding, fathers, and preparing for the next baby.

Intended to "answer a woman's questions" about pregnancy and childbirth, both publications adopt a conversational and friendly tone while carefully establishing that they are providing advice endorsed by physicians. *What to Expect* adopts the additional strategy of incorporating quotes from unnamed (perhaps fictional) women throughout the book. Highlighted in boldface or as sidebar quotes, women's queries, testimonials, and shared confidences contribute to the informal quality of the guide while implicitly reassuring readers that the authors are in tune with women's concerns during pregnancy.

The guides that Canadian women read differ not only in appearance and format but in rhetorical strategies. *Nine Months* emphasizes fetal subjectivity and individuality through visual images, whereas *What to Expect* focuses on maternal responsibility and avoiding risk; its advice also is more detailed than that in *Nine Months*. As we will show, these different rhetorical constructions are based upon shared cultural assumptions about motherhood and the fetus. Both guides are illustrative of the rhetorical construction of pregnancy in mainstream Canadian and U.S. discourse. In other words, these guides assume that the reading woman wants to be pregnant, has a heterosexual partner (although Eisenberg, Murkoff, and Hathaway give a nod to single women), has access to regular prenatal care, and will labor and deliver in a hospital under the care of a physician.

In describing these guides as *mainstream,* we are deliberately drawing attention to their having been based upon a widely accepted version of a broader North American medicoscientific narrative on pregnancy. Canadian schools use similar narratives, as do electronic and print media for the factual reporting of how humans are conceived and develop before birth and how pregnancy affects women. In this narrative, pregnancy is rationally ordered into trimesters (each about thirteen weeks long), forty weeks, or, as in the two guides discussed here, nine monthly segments. This rational ordering strategically deploys a grid by which women can chart how well they are "doing pregnancy." As we argue, the authors of both guides read by Canadian women assume that "being pregnant" is insufficient for having a child and becoming a mother; rather, women need instructions on how to participate in pregnancy. Moreover, these guidebooks assume that the key to a successful pregnancy is learning about the fetus.

Fetal Knowledge

Of the guidebooks we selected, *Nine Months for Life,* in particular, emphasizes fetal development and it does so primarily through visual rather than written strategies. The fetal images are the work of Lennart Nilsson, a Swedish photographer whose photographs of conception and embryonic and fetal development are reproduced widely in electronic and print media around the world, as well as in his own book, *A Child Is Born* (1990). Nilsson's photographs are strikingly clear and detailed, as if they were neutral recordings of in-utero events. However, the obvious or "natural" meanings of these images are carefully constructed (Condit 1990; Hartouni 1993; Petchesky 1987) by using a variety of culturally inflected strategies. For example, each image is greatly magnified so that from the first month, the fetus of potentially ambiguous personhood appears to be the size of a five- or six-month fetus, presumably of uncontested personhood. Culturally salient elements of personhood and individuality also figure prominently in Nilsson's photographs—fetal faces, hands, feet, and genitals. In some of the most widely reproduced images the fetus appears to be sucking its thumb. Nilsson's photographs, particularly those reproduced in the Quebec guide, bathe the fetus in a warm diffuse light, so that it appears golden or pink skinned, fragile, soft, and translucent. Yet we know from premature delivery that fetal skin is a deep red color until about the seventh month (Kantrowitz, Wingert, and Hager 1988). Through these strategies, what seems "obvious" to the viewer is that from even the earliest stages the fetus appears as a distinct and complex individual.

Textual strategies are also brought to bear on making the images tell a particular story. As Condit (1990:85) has shown in her analysis of fetal images, both the selection of visual elements and the textual commentary are essential to convincing the viewer that the fetus is human, visually appealing, and a person. In guides with few such images—*What to Expect,* for example, which includes only simple drawings of the outline of the fetal form—these narrative constructions of fetal subjectivity are especially important. In each guide, language choices strategically construct and highlight fetal individuality and awareness. *Nine Months for Life* tells its readers, for example: "The baby [at 20 weeks] measures 25 to 30 cm (10 to 12 in) and weighs about 500 g (1 lb). A few hairs have appeared on its head. Although its eyelids are still closed, the baby is starting to become aware of sounds coming from outside: your voice, and your partner's" (Corporation professionnelle 1990:12).

The authors of the North American guides describe the fetus in terms of the appearance or near appearance of certain physical parts, especially the heart, brain, spine, and developing arms and legs. They visually establish continuity from embryo through fetus to baby with a month-by-month series of images and by choosing words that draw attention to fetal features: "buds," "forming," or "will soon develop." They give special mention to small features, for example, the genitals, tooth buds, ankles and wrists, hair, eyelashes, nails. The appearance and development of these physical parts bestow human and, especially, babylike qualities on the fetus.

The authors of these guides give the fetus, whatever its physical appearance, a specific and unambiguous identity: it is "the baby." Although the terms *embryo* and *fetus* do appear in these guides, they usually restrict their use to definitions, captions, and topic headings. The authors use the term *baby* in most descriptive summaries of fetal development and whenever they imply a relationship or interaction between the fetus and someone else (the woman, her partner, or the physician). In addition, uncertainty about fetal subjectivity is erased. Described as active and intentional, able to swallow, yawn, suck its thumb, frown, and blink, the fetus has emotions and experiences distinct from those of the woman. "Fetuses are only human. Just like us they have 'up' days, when they feel like kicking up their heels (and elbows and knees), and 'down' days, when they'd rather lie back and take it easy," write Eisenberg and her colleagues (1991:201). The authors of *Nine Months for Life* combine smallness of size, complexity, or completeness of anatomy, potentiality, and existence of movements or functions to construct not only humanity but also personhood and sentimentalized babylike qualities in the fetus: "The baby [during the second month] is now 3 cm long (1¼ in.) and weighs a little more than a pea (1 g or ⅟₃₀ oz.). Facial features are starting to form, eyelids are sealed shut, and ears are semi-circular ridges. Arms and legs are clearly distinguishable, with little buds at the tips that will soon develop into fingers and toes. And the baby's heart has already been beating for four weeks!" (Corporation professionnelle 1990:6). In short, word choice and visual practice simultaneously construct a powerful message for pregnant women: what lies inside their wombs is not a mass of undifferentiated tissue or a fetus of incipient personhood but an appealing, sentient, and vulnerable baby.

Monitoring Motherhood

Although it includes several pictures of the fetus and one of a newborn, *Nine Months for Life* does not include a single image of a woman. Nilsson completely erases women's bodies from his images; he pictures the fetus against an opaque and dark background.[2] The illustrations in *What to Expect* do not so much erase the woman from pregnancy as they reduce her to a fetal environment or transparent fetal container. In this guide, descriptions of each month of pregnancy begin with a drawing of a headless, armless woman, her breast bared and her transparent torso containing only vagina, rectum, bladder, uterus, and fetus. The caption reads, "What You May Look Like."

These guides to pregnancy inscribe a path for women similar to the "One-Two Punch of the Technocracy," as described by Reynolds (cited in Davis-Floyd and Dumit 1998:9). Once conceptually separated from the fetus, women must be instructed about their relationship to that new individual. This bodily rupture of fetus and woman surfaces in the statements of those Canadian women interviewed by Mitchell who referred to reading guide books as "a way of getting involved" in the pregnancy. Maternal attachment, formerly considered "natural," a ubiquitous "instinct," can no longer be left to nature but must be consciously initiated and actively managed. Specifically, women are instructed to participate in pregnancy by constantly monitoring their bodies, emotions, relationships, and lifestyles. Excretion, digestion, bodily appearance and sensation, and mood swings, as well as diet, sleep habits, exercise, employment, leisure time, clothing, shoes, sexual activities, skin and hair care, medications, interactions with others, even the air that the women breathe require careful attention and surveillance. In this way, the guides read by Canadian women fashion their identity as altruistic mother, nurturing and sensitive to the nuances of her body and thus the needs of her baby.

The authors of these materials encourage their readers to "get used to" and "adapt" to the discomforts of pregnancy and cast women's sensations of pregnancy as "reminders" of their new role and their responsibilities. The authors of *Nine Months for Life* write, "After the first few days of euphoria, once your pregnancy has been confirmed . . . [there] are moments of inner questioning. . . . Will you make a good mother? . . . As soon as you think you're pregnant, even before your doctor confirms it, get comfortable with the idea that you are going to have a baby" (Corporation professionnelle 1990:4). Two pages later they advise: "[At two months] the tiny human being attached to you is beginning to make demands on your body. These are harmless, but can cause you some discomfort. It will take time for your body to adjust to these new conditions, to the new being living inside of you. But you'll see. In just a short time your body will adapt and you'll be pleasantly surprised to find out how easily the two of you can live in harmony" (6).

Assuming that women need to be reminded of their responsibilities during pregnancy, the authors of *What to Expect* offer this advice:

> One of the major obstacles to changing habits is forgetting what your goals are; they can easily slip from your mind when temptation is near. So tape pictures of babies (cute, healthy-looking babies) on the refrigerator, inside kitchen cupboards, on the outside of the liquor cabinet, on your desk at work. If skipping breakfast is your vice, put a sign inside your front door that asks, "Have you fed your baby breakfast today?" (Eisenberg, Murkoff, and Hathaway 1991:63)

In summary, the imagery and language of the guides read by Canadian women articulate the fetus as a distinct self, an active and intentional being. The guides dramatize its size and complexity of appearance in statements and images in order to create a physical and, ultimately, a moral resemblance between the fetus and a baby. They also give women a particular self, the rational and informed mother, nurturing and sensitive to the nuances of her body (her baby). These two normative constructions rationalize the existence of guides to pregnancy in Canada: they are intended to tell women how to become mothers, how to read their bodies for evidence of fetal needs, and how to take care of the fetus. These guides enjoin Canadian women to actively participate in their pregnancy, not as medical experts but as caring, devoted, informed, and rational mothers.

Reading Pregnancy in Greece

Birth Is Love has long been the only full-length pregnancy guide available in Greece that is written by a Greek. The author, Aleka Sikaki-Douka, is a nurse-midwife who lived for a while in Canada and practiced in Athens for many years. Introduced by two prologues, the book's 240 pages are divided into twenty chapters, generously illustrated with dozens of anatomical drawings, electron micrographs, reprints of Nilsson's fetal photographs, as well as many full-page pictures of fathers holding babies, women in leotards exercising, and women in the various phases of hospital birth. The style is informal, with the author adopting an intimate woman-to-woman tone and often addressing the reader as "we." The text is thoroughly monological, however: women's "voices" in the form of quotes are almost completely absent, as is the question-and-answer format characteristic of the more dialogical presentation of the North American materials. Throughout, Sikaki-Douka speaks with the authoritative voice of a member of a medical profession whose beneficently paternalistic and authoritarian model of relations with patients remains largely intact.

Stylistic differences aside, *Birth Is Love* appears to have much in common with the texts discussed in the preceding section—from the full-page captioned reprints of Nilsson's photographs of the developing fetus that launch the text to their shared objectives of increasing women's participation in their pregnancies. On closer reading, however, the texts are grounded in strikingly different cultural understandings and deploy distinctive symbolic codes, idioms, and rhetorical strategies to often divergent ends. In this section we describe some ways in which pregnancy and maternal and fetal subjects are rhetorically constructed in this popular Greek book. We begin by examining how the book's sometimes implicit, sometimes explicit, and often imperative, mandate—that women become "informed" regarding the physiological functioning of their bodies in medicoscientific terms—is inflected by specifically Greek story lines, rhetorical conventions, and cultural understandings.

Authorizing Modernity

As in *Nine Months* and *What to Expect*, the author's credentials and authority are established from the outset in the guide's first prologue, which is written by a well-known Athenian professor of obstetrics and gynecology who is also the director of the maternity clinic at the country's major public maternity hospital (his titles follow his byline). As a physician-professor, this doctor occupies the highest rung in his profession's hierarchy and belongs to the category of physician that patients regard as the most prestigious, authoritative, and desirable. After praising the book and assuring the reader that it will become "an essential aid for every Greek woman," the doctor devotes the remainder of the half-page prologue to a critique of the state of contemporary Greek women's scientific literacy:

> One large part of the problem faced by Greek women who await a child is unfortunately due to misinterpretations, old superstitions, and mistaken prejudices. It is time for the younger generation of Greeks, properly informed, to face more responsibly and scientifically the subject of pregnancy, birth, postpartum and also contraception.
>
> Today's Greek woman has no reason to envy other women of the civilized world, and for that reason she is entitled, but also obligated, to follow the spirit of her times, as this is expressed in the up-to-date development of science. To this end, I am sure, this book will contribute. (7)

Thus, from the very first page of *Birth Is Love*, the doctor authoritatively sets the terms for discussing a major recurrent theme: the need to remedy the "problem" of Greek women's scientific illiteracy.

We can understand the peculiar rhetorical force of terms such as *civilized, up-to-date, superstition,* and *science,* used repeatedly in *Birth Is Love,* only within the specificities of the Greek historical and political context. These terms are part of an ongoing and long-standing debate about national identity, and they are embedded in a network of associations with which Greeks are intimately familiar and which they themselves use strategically in daily discourse. Each, furthermore, is part of a con-

catenated set of binaries such as traditional/modern, East/West, other/
Europe, conservative/progressive, and the like, which have become
"paradigms of analysis of the modern Greek condition" (Panourgia
1996:28). Within this set, fraught with implicit hierarchies that privilege the second term of each pair, *Europe* and *European* are tropes that
carry particular rhetorical force.

Today, as in the nineteenth century, the idea of Europe is closely related to what has been called a "perennial crisis" in Greeks' sense of
identity (is Greece part of the East/Orient or of the West/Europe?). In
the nineteenth century, Greece's independence from Ottoman rule was
contingent on the interests of the then-powerful nations of the West.
Support for the nascent project of Greek nationhood was also grounded
in the European master narrative that located the origins of European
civilization in the genius of Greek antiquity. The Greek elite courted
this crucial support and actively sought to align itself and the emergent
Greek national identity with the powerful nations of the West and
against the "oriental" realities of everyday experience (Herzfeld 1986,
1995; Jusdanis 1992). This conundrum of a "flawed" Greek identity has
perhaps deepened in recent years as a consequence of Greece's "full"
membership in the European Union (EU), which Greece has in general
actively embraced. However, in practice the more powerful EU states
often regard Greece as a marginal, unruly, and "semi-oriental" junior
partner, whose capability of applying such Western values and institutions as rationality and efficiency remains an open question. With
an acute awareness of themselves as historical beings, Greeks today
attempt to negotiate these terms in order to situate themselves more
favorably within the larger narrative of powerful outsiders that has already assigned them a place—at the so-called margins of Europe.

Against this historical and political context, we can read the doctor's
exhortation to young Greek women to actively position themselves
on the symbolically privileged side of these binaries (progressive, civilized, Western, modern science)—an exhortation that Sikaki-Douka repeats at many points in the book—as a call to take responsibility for
their role in favorably representing themselves and the Greek nation
to the "civilized" world—in other words, Europe and the West. Thus,
unlike the North American texts, which portray scientific knowledge of
the pregnant body primarily as a means to reduce risks to the fetus,
Birth Is Love presents this knowledge as an essential part of the project
of becoming a modern pregnant subject:

> How is it possible for a person to grow up correctly without
> knowing how the body works? (33)

> Embryological knowledge offers you the joy and satisfaction of learning, of seeing, and of living, even if in your imagination, what is happening in your insides, in your uterus, in the pregnant woman's organism. (6)

> Most women arrive at the clinic in complete ignorance about what is to follow. . . . It must be our goal to become personally informed regarding the functioning of our reproductive organs and of our biological systems. (11)

Although the text abounds in exhortations ("it is essential, yes, essential, for each woman to be informed about her physiological functioning," as Sikaki-Douka stresses in her prologue [11]), the author is seldom explicit about the specific objectives of acquiring this bioscientific knowledge. When she is, the objectives include such ends as the ability "to actively participate, to control our behavior, our demonstrations, expressions of our feelings," "to plan," "to behave in a conscious, rational and logical manner, to remain controlled," "to be active, logical, calm" (154). Nowhere does Sikaki-Douka suggest that such knowledge is essential for reducing risks to the fetus or the worries a woman may have concerning the health of the fetus. In fact, she takes only about two or three pages of the 240 pages in the book to discuss the risks posed by such maternal behaviors as smoking and drinking coffee (the first seven editions never mentioned alcohol, which appears only briefly in the eighth and most recent), and she sandwiches these sections between a discussion of women's nail care and a two-page history of maternity clothes. Rather, scientific knowledge is represented as valuable symbolic capital and as a means for pregnant women to acquire the qualities long associated with the ideal of modernity: planning, rationality, control, logic.

In this respect, the dominant themes and rhetorical constructions found in *Birth Is Love* display some striking parallels and continuities with those that characterize the historical Greek debate about women's education in general. In the nineteenth century, Greek intellectuals argued that women's literacy and education were doubly essential if Greece was to move progressively toward the West/Europe, on the one hand, and to symbolically disassociate from its stigmatized Eastern/ Ottoman past on the other (Bakalaki 1994; Herzfeld 1986). *Birth Is Love* deploys women's *scientific* illiteracy, like their illiteracy in earlier times, as a metonym for the more general "backward" and "premodern" features of national identity that Greeks must overcome if their country is to be identified with a more civilized West and in particular with

Europe. In both instances, the Greek woman functions "as an apt trope for the condition of Greeks generally" (Herzfeld 1986:232).

Using another rhetorical strategy also common to the nineteenth-century reformers (see Bakalaki 1994:78), Sikaki-Douka invariably buttresses the legitimacy of her claims and recommendations by referring repeatedly to European authorities and practices. As Sikaki-Douka tells the reader in her prologue, she "often refer[s] to how the system works outside of Greece, because," she remarks somewhat cryptically, "this is something that bothers me" (10). These references are most often textual, but on occasion Sikaki-Douka also refers to her own firsthand experiences in Canada and England. The guide is in fact studded with references to an astonishing number and variety of European and North American physicians, researchers, and writers, as well as to specific European and North American practices. Within a quarter page on page 134 of the seventh edition, for instance, Sikaki-Douka mentions Europe twice, as well as Denmark, Belgium, Finland, and France. Among the scores of references to experts, she cites Greeks only four times; after the prologue the first reference to a Greek appears halfway through the guide (115).

At several points Sikaki-Douka also uses these rhetorical strategies and the binaries so familiar to the discourse on Greek national identity to mount a muted, partial, and sometimes contradictory critique of the Greek medical system in general and of the delivery of obstetrical care in particular. Although as a nurse-midwife Sikaki-Douka is part of this privileged system, to some extent she speaks from the margins of a profession that has progressively restricted the scope of her professional practice and authority (urban midwives play a strictly auxiliary role in contemporary Greek obstetrics). Thus Sikaki-Douka tags particular beliefs and practices as European and Western not only to persuade women to adopt them but also to critique the Greek system and customary practices, most often in an oblique manner. Invariably, when the juxtaposition "in our country/abroad" appears in the text, it is to critique the Greek practice and implicitly to recommend an often idealized and essentialized Western model as a replacement. For example, speaking of prenatal blood tests, Sikaki-Douka writes, "You have to go to the microbiology lab, as is customary in our country. In the exterior, the tests are done in the obstetrician's office. That way, the pregnant woman doesn't have to be troubled running around from one doctor to another" (54).

Or, when recommending the participation of fathers-to-be in the labor process:

> In our country, the father's participation in birth is limited to
> taking his wife to the obstetrician when she is ready to give birth
> and handing her over with a perfunctory kiss. . . . I remember in
> England a father warmly and positively holding a woman's hand
> the moment of her contractions, trying to breathe with her to help
> her with the rhythm and to encourage her. Even to wipe her
> perspiring face, to comfort her. The woman is calm and relaxed,
> allowing herself his care, and time rushes by in this warm atmo-
> sphere. (57–58)

Here Sikaki-Douka uses the ethnographic authority implicit in the eye-
witness account of Western practices in an attempt to persuade her
reader of the desirability of allowing men to accompany their wives
during labor. This is also a rare instance in which Sikaki-Douka exhorts
women and men to confront forcefully their doctors to effect change
in standard obstetrical practice. Assuring them that "there exist many
doctors with a new mentality, who've studied abroad," who would
concur with this practice, she fires a volley of imperatives: "Fathers,
then, take action, read, inform yourselves, lay claim to your right" (58);
"Women, you would do well to . . . try to cultivate, incite, urge, expect
your husband's presence and participation. . . . Don't hide behind un-
justified excuses" (59). The author does not mention a woman's mother,
or other female kin, as appropriate companions during labor. Implicit
in Sikaki-Douka's preference for the husband is an idealized paradigm
of egalitarian "Western" nuclear conjugal relations over both a patriarchal "Greek" model and the extended networks of female kin that usually rally around the birthing woman.

Throughout the text Sikaki-Douka's profuse reliance on the tropes of
Europe and the West partakes of a practical rhetorical strategy that has
been called "occidentalism." Like the more familiar concept of orientalism (Said 1978), occidentalism is a simplified and stylized construction
of the "West" deployed for social, political, and economic ends that depend on the context (Carrier 1995). Perhaps as a consequence of the
contradictions in her own position—she is a cosmopolitan member of
an elite and powerful profession that has increasingly devalued the
status of midwives—Sikaki-Douka uses occidentalist strategies at different places in the text, *both* to lay claim to the moral authority instrumental in educating and disciplining modern medicalized pregnant
subjects *and* to mount a critique (albeit of a partial and sometimes veiled
nature) of selected aspects of Greek obstetrical practice.

Fetal Subjectivity as Process

Rhetorical constructions of the fetus in the Greek text also differ notably from those in the North American guides. Unlike the latter, *Birth Is Love* does not highlight fetal subjectivity. Sikaki-Douka uses both *fetus* and *baby* throughout the text; however, she uses the term *fetus* far more frequently (the Greek term, *emvrio,* encompasses both embryo and *fetus*; it is derived from the word meaning 'to swell'; compare the Latin-derived *fetus,* which means 'young one' [Berlant 1997: 108]). This preference for biomedical terminology is not surprising, if a major objective of Sikaki-Douka's guide is to increase women's scientific literacy. What is of greater interest are the differences in the North American and Greek textual strategies used to represent the fetus.

These differences are particularly striking for the early months of gestation and fade somewhat in descriptions of the latter part of pregnancy. As noted earlier, *Birth Is Love* begins with some dozen full-page reprints of Nilsson's fetal photographs. While these pictures appear in warm hues in *Nine Months,* the images are a grainy black and white, and far from cuddly, in *Birth Is Love.* The accompanying captions either negate, or simply do not highlight, the personhood and humanness of the fetus. Instead, captions focus primarily on physiological developments such as "the ossification of the skeleton" (26). Thus, for instance, the caption to the third Nilsson photo reads, "Bird or tadpole? No, it's neither. It's a 30-day-old embryo. The embryologists who first studied the early stages of human life have confirmed that: in the beginning of its life the embryo doesn't have any human characteristics!" (20). In another description, Sikaki-Douka more lyrically compares the fetus to a "flower in a crystal vase" (61). Comparisons with nonhuman animals are also common. The caption under the photo of a three-month-old fetus describes its somersaults as being executed "with the ease that aquatic creatures have" (25), and elsewhere Sikaki-Douka writes that "the fetus looks like it has wings" (61). Potentiality is also muted when future arms and legs are described not as "buds," as they are in the North American texts, but as "protuberances," and "swellings," or when the future heart, so charged a symbol of humanity, is represented as "rudimentary, not at all like the shape it will have later" and as "a projection behind a small excrescence in the shape of a tail" (60).

The contrasting rhetoric of the captions for the Nilsson images in the North American and Greek texts points to the dependence of photographic "realism" on culturally inflected narrative strategies. As Benjamin observed, "All the relations of life [are turned] into literature" particularly in medical photographs, "whose shock will bring the mechanism of association in the viewer to a complete halt" and that therefore require captions (quoted in Berlant 1997:106). In the cases at hand, these distinctive (national) literatures are predicated on differentially emphasized attributes of personhood and subjectivity. Thus instead of an already separate human person that is trying to communicate its needs to a woman who must be educated to become a sensitive translator of her bodily symptoms, the unity of woman and fetus, as portrayed in the Greek text, is still intact. "The fetus depends completely on the woman and the woman depends completely on the fetus" (51). Eventually, Sikaki-Douka continues, the protuberances and swellings "will grow into an admirable extension of ourselves" (60). Sikaki-Douka's description of the ninth month of pregnancy explicitly asserts that becoming human is a process rather than an either-or state: "It is now a complete newborn, if not, however, a complete person. Another state begins. . . . Only after some years will its development, its flowering, be complete" (68).

Occasionally, an antagonism exists between the fetus's needs and the woman's. Revealing a view of the fetus-as-parasite, also commonly held by North American embryologists until a couple of decades ago, Sikaki-Douka writes that "the fetus during all its intrauterine life only demands and takes, it gives absolutely nothing" (71) (cf. Franklin 1991). Thus women are well-advised to "make time for yourselves, don't neglect yourselves" (144). Far from promoting a model of selfless motherhood, Sikaki-Douka even quotes approvingly from the Italian writer Oriana Fallaci's imaginary dialogue with her fetus: "I'll give you my body, I'll get fat for you. But not my soul, not my reactions. These I'll keep to myself" (98).

Not surprisingly, the discourse on bonding, so central to the North American texts, is entirely absent in *Birth Is Love*. Instead, there is the exhortation to separate, if only to a limited extent. (One point of "making time for yourself," Sikaki-Douka continues, is that such self-care makes a woman "a strong and happy mother" [144].) Maternal altruism is more or less taken for granted in the Greek text; it is part and parcel of Sikaki-Douka's representation of "traditional" Greek motherhood (55). Because of the association of maternal sacrifice with tradition, a degree of separation and self-care come to be constructed as a vehicle and sign of the more up-to-date and modern mother.

In the North American guides the reader is enjoined to "pamper yourself" (Corporation professionnelle 1990:17) or to "do something . . . that has nothing to do with childbirth or babies" (Eisenberg, Murkoff, and Hathaway 1991:250). Significantly, the "something" turns out to be paying attention to her husband. Elsewhere in *What to Expect,* the authors do say that a woman is permitted to occasionally and briefly escape the regime of self-discipline by indulging in an anniversary glass of wine or a slice of her own birthday cake (78). However, the authors of the guides read by Canadian women predicate this attention to one's self not on the idea of a woman's empowering herself or keeping something of herself separate from her role as wife and mother. Rather, they assume that Canadian women need occasional incentives and rewards for engaging in their regime of self-discipline.

The Cultural Rhetoric of Pregnancy in Greece and Canada

In recent decades the Canadian patient-practitioner model in prenatal care has shifted from one based on assumptions of passive patients and authoritarian physicians to one more closely aligned with a consumer-provider relationship. Driven in part by obstetrics' response to public demand for more "natural" childbirth and by the appearance of alternative birth models (e.g., LeBoyer, Lamaze) and alternative specialists (midwives, doulas), the consumer-provider model seems to offer women and their partners greater decision-making power regarding pregnancy care and more control over the experience of pregnancy and childbirth.

Many women in Canada today do have some choice about labor and delivery practices (e.g., type of pain management, music during labor, squatting or reclining during delivery, using a mirror during crowning) and, for some women, type of practitioner (physician and/or midwife) and place of delivery (traditional delivery room, labor-birth-recovery room, hospital-affiliated birth center, home) (Levitt and Hanvey 1995). Although changes in obstetrics resonate with a Canadian ethos of self-determination, personal preference, and tolerance of difference, having access to these choices remains contingent on medical definitions of "normal" pregnancy. Furthermore, women are making choices about childbearing in a social environment that increasingly and publicly places responsibility for pregnancy outcome on women. In Canada daily national coverage of a court battle about the rights of a pregnant woman with a history of substance abuse and her fetus is only the most recent of frequent electronic and print media stories that cast public scrutiny on maternal practices and construct the fetus as endangered (Gee 1996).

This trope of endangered fetus and ir/responsible mother deeply in-
fuses the guides to pregnancy read by Canadian women. Each guide
portrays pregnancy as a time of risk, uncertainty, and potential harm
to the fetus. Women reading the guides learn about the randomness
of genetics, the impossibility of avoiding all environmental hazards,
and the unpredictability of fetal development as potential sources of
problems during pregnancy and childbirth. Gambling and risk-taking
metaphors are particularly apparent in *What to Expect*, which tells pregnant women about "the best odds diet," "tempting fate" with a second
pregnancy, and playing "baby roulette" (Eisenberg, Murkoff, and Hathaway 1991:80, 26, 76). Even as the book acknowledges that risks—specifically, risks to the fetus—are everywhere, it locates many of those
risks in the bodies, histories, and activities of pregnant women (see also
Daniels 1997). Choices made long before pregnancy, activities engaged
in before pregnancy was suspected, and behaviors throughout pregnancy may all pose a risk to the fetus. Yet the guidebooks repeatedly
reassure women that they can reduce these risks. Thus by "choosing"
self-monitoring, self-control, and self-sacrifice, women redefine themselves as active participants *in* pregnancy and publicly demonstrate
that they are doing what is best for the baby.

Ironically, although the language of choice, personal preference, and
women's control over the experience of pregnancy permeates guidebooks in Canada, these books advocate a self-monitoring that increases
maternal anxiety, self-doubt, and compliance with medical regimes of
prenatal care. In addition, by individualizing risk and responsibility,
these guidebooks divert women's attention from the social causes of
discomfort, suffering, and risk during pregnancy (poor working conditions, the double shift at work and home, environmental toxins, pov-
erty, and, for many low-income women, lack of quality health care).
Thus instead of the trope of modernity, guidebooks read by Canadian
women are infused with a powerful rhetoric that individualizes maternal responsibility for what is constructed as an endangered, vulnerable,
and sentimentalized fetus.

In Greece a more authoritarian and paternalistic patient-practitioner
model in prenatal care remains largely in place. Although the Greek
women's movement was instrumental in effecting significant social and
legal changes in the 1970s and 1980s, reforming the reigning obstetrical
model was not among its pressing concerns. As of today, there are few
challenges to the hegemony of obstetricians and a rigid and technologically intensive protocol of hospital-based care. Thus, although *Birth Is
Love* deploys the rhetoric of choice, the purview of options in prenatal
and obstetrical care actually described in the text is quite limited.
Rather, *Birth Is Love* suggests that one of the most important choices

women can (and must) make in pregnancy is to become biomedically knowledgeable about their bodies. In making this choice, women are represented as actively identifying themselves as modern pregnant subjects. The version of modernity presented in the Greek text is not primarily about separation, risk, and maternal responsibility. Rather, it is about breaking with "traditional" local knowledges of the body (with "ignorance") and becoming scientifically literate. By pursuing this new literacy, the guide suggests, women may acquire not only the symbolic capital but also the specific desiderata of modernity: rationality, logic, discipline, and the like.

Acquiring this literacy belongs to the category of strategies that Greek anthropologist Alexandra Bakalaki has described as "aimed at realizing 'European' fantasies," part of the everyday experience of Greeks whose "most introverted self-perceptions entail what they consciously or unconsciously construe as a 'European' gaze upon themselves" (1994:100). Internalization of this gaze is evident from the very first page of *Birth Is Love,* and it drives the many insidious comparisons Sikaki-Douka makes between the Western and Greek practices. Repeatedly tacking between the two, *Birth Is Love* also reinforces the necessity of women's continual self-monitoring. But, although the normative mother implicit in the North American texts is one who does all she can to reduce risks to the fetus, in the Greek guide she does all she can to be educated in Western/European practices and knowledge as these are stylized in Sikaki-Douka's occidentalist representations.

Comparing the rhetorical constructions of pregnant woman and fetus in guidebooks popular in Greece and Canada reveals both commonalities and differences. Modeled on what each culture takes to be the medicoscientific "facts" of conception, fetal development, and pregnancy, the guides deploy images, instructions, and advice to refashion the thinking and behavior of women. Encouraged to replace their own interpretations of pregnancy with those of the expert voices in these guides, women in both Greece and Canada read that a successful pregnancy depends upon how well they transform themselves. Yet the different cultural understandings, distinctive symbolic codes, idioms, and rhetorical strategies of these guides lead to divergent ends. In the Greek case, the point of women's detailed self-monitoring is not to individualize responsibility for a privileged fetal "super-subject" (Bordo 1993:88), as it is in Canada. It is, rather, to fashion oneself as a modern pregnant subject against a grid of meaning that we can understand only in the context of Greece's current and past identity. In one location, fetal literacy signifies the "good mother," in the other, modernity. Yet, in both sites, women are directed and controlled in the service of the Other.

Part Two: Reproduction, Language, and Medical Models

NOTES

1. Baby and child care guides have received some feminist historical analysis. See, for example, Arnup (1990) and Strong-Boag (1982).
2. Hartouni (1993) and Petchesky (1987), among others, have discussed the masculinist technocentric bias of these fetal spacemen.

REFERENCES

Arnup, Katherine. 1990. Educating mothers: Government advice for women in the interwar years. In Katherine Arnup, Andrée Levesque, and Ruth Roach Pierson, with the assistance of Margaret Brennan, eds., *Delivering motherhood: Maternal ideologies and practices in the nineteenth and twentieth centuries,* pp. 190–210. New York: Routledge.
Bakalaki, Alexandra. 1994. Gender-related discourses and representations of cultural specificity in nineteenth-century and twentieth-century Greece. *Journal of Modern Greek Studies* 12:75–111.
Berlant, Lauren. 1997. America, "fat," the fetus. In *The queen of America goes to Washington City: Essays on sex and citizenship,* pp. 83–144. Durham, N.C.: Duke University Press.
Bordo, Susan. 1993. *Unbearable weight: Feminism, Western culture, and the body.* Berkeley: University of California Press.
Carrier, James. 1995. Introduction. In James Carrier, ed., *Occidentalism: Images of the West.* Oxford: Clarendon.
Condit, C. M. 1990. *Decoding abortion rhetoric: Communicating social change.* Urbana: University of Illinois Press.
Corporation professionnelle des médecins du Québec. 1990. *Nine months for life.* Montreal: author.
Daniels, Cynthia. 1997. Between fathers and fetuses: The social construction of male reproduction and the politics of fetal harm. *Signs: Journal of Women in Culture and Society* 22:579–616.
Davis-Floyd, Robbie, and Joseph Dumit, eds. 1998. *Cyborg babies : From techno-sex to techno-tots.* New York: Routledge.
Eisenberg, Arlene, Heidi Murkoff, and Sandee Hathaway. 1991. *What to expect when you're expecting.* 2d ed. New York: Workman.
Franklin, Sarah. 1991. Fetal fascinations: New dimensions to the medical-scientific construction of fetal personhood. In Sarah Franklin, Celia Lury, and Jackie Stacey, eds., *Off-centre: Feminism and cultural studies,* pp. 190–205. New York: HarperCollins.
Gee, Marcus. 1996. The issue that won't go away. *(Toronto) Globe and Mail,* August 17, p. D1.
Georges, Eugenia. 1996. Fetal ultrasound imaging and the production of authoritative knowledge in Greece. *Medical Anthropology Quarterly* 10:1–19.

Hartouni, Valerie. 1993. Fetal exposures: Abortion politics and the optics of allusion. *Camera Obscura* 29:130–49.

Herzfeld, Michael. 1986. *Ours once more: Folklore, ideology, and the making of modern Greece.* New York: Pella.

Herzfeld, Michael. 1995. Hellenism and occidentalism: The permutations of performance in Greek bourgeois identity. In James Carrier, ed., *Occidentalism: Images of the West.* Oxford: Clarendon.

Jusdanis, Gregory. 1992. *Belated modernity and aesthetic culture: Inventing national literature.* Minneapolis: University of Minnesota Press.

Kantrowitz, Barbara, Pat Wingert, and Mary Hager. 1988. Preemies. *Newsweek,* May 16, pp. 62–67.

Levitt, Cheryl, and Louise Hanvey. 1995. *Survey of routine maternity care and practices in Canadian hospitals.* Ottawa: Health Canada and Canadian Institute of Child Health.

Martin, Emily. 1987. *The woman in the body: A cultural analysis of reproduction.* Boston: Beacon.

Mitchell, Lisa M. 1994. The routinization of the other: Ultrasound, women, and the fetus. In Gwynne Basen, Margrit Eichler, and Abby Lippman, eds., *Misconceptions: The social construction of choice and the new reproductive and genetic technologies,* pp. 86–98. Prescott, Ontario, Canada: Voyageur.

Nilsson, Lennart. 1990. *A child is born.* New York: Delacorte.

Panourgia, Neni. 1995. *Fragments of death, fables of identity: An Athenian anthropography.* Madison: University of Wisconsin Press.

Petchesky, R. P. 1987. Foetal images: The power of visual culture in the politics of reproduction. In Michelle Stanworth, ed., *Reproductive technologies: Gender, motherhood, and medicine,* pp. 57–80. Minneapolis: University of Minnesota Press.

Rapp, Rayna. 1988. The power of "positive diagnosis": Medical and maternal discourses on amniocentesis. In Karen Michaelson, ed., *Childbirth in America: Anthropological perspectives,* pp. 103–16. South Hadley, Mass.: Bergin Garvey.

Rapp, Rayna. 1990. Constructing amniocentesis: Maternal and medical discourses. In Faye Ginsburg and Anna Lowenhaupt Tsing, eds., *Uncertain terms: Negotiating gender in American culture,* pp. 28–42. Boston: Beacon.

Rapp, Rayna. 1994. Commentary on American Anthropological Association panel "Reproducing Reproduction." *Anthropology Newsletter,* November, p. 34.

Rothman, B. K. 1986. *The tentative pregnancy: Prenatal diagnosis and the future of motherhood.* New York: Viking Penguin.

Said, Edward. 1978. *Orientalism.* Harmondsworth, U.K.: Penguin.

Sikaki-Douka, Aleka. n.d. *Birth Is love.* 7th ed. Athens: author.

Strong-Boag, Veronica. 1982. Intruders in the nursery: Childcare professionals reshape the years one to five, 1920–1940. In Joy Parr, ed., *Childhood and family in Canadian history,* pp. 160–221. Toronto: McClelland and Stewart.

PART THREE

REPRODUCTION

AND LEGAL/POLICY ISSUES

9

MEDICAL INSURANCE

AS BIO-POWER

LAW AND THE NORMALIZATION

OF (IN)FERTILITY

ELIZABETH C. BRITT

I just want to be normal again. I don't think I'll ever be normal again.

Susan, infertility patient

A normalizing society is the historical outcome of a technology of power centered on life.

Michel Foucault, *The History of Sexuality*

In 1987 Massachusetts passed An Act Providing a Medical Definition of Infertility.[1] The broadest legislation of its kind in the country, the statute mandated insurance coverage for infertility by defining it as a medical condition. As a result, almost any Massachusetts resident with both medical insurance and a medical diagnosis of infertility can obtain virtually unlimited access to infertility treatment, including reproductive technologies. For this reason, the Massachusetts mandate has important implications for feminists interested in the material circumstances within which women make reproductive decisions. This chapter, as a cultural studies approach to rhetoric, illustrates that these material circumstances are inextricably intertwined with the symbolic systems with which we make meaning.

I argue here that the Massachusetts mandate, as an example of what French philosopher Michel Foucault calls "bio-power" (1990:140), is an expression of law's interest in the management of life, both at the level of individual bodies and at the level of populations. Medical treatment for infertility has normalized the experience, that is, it has created standards for judging individuals as "normal" or "abnormal" and has developed techniques for reforming those identified as abnormal. The mandate participates in this normalization by authorizing a medical model for the treatment of infertility, providing symbolic and economic encouragement for women and couples to pursue this avenue of resolution to the often life-altering experience of infertility.

At its heart, normalization is a deeply rhetorical issue. Norms operate through persuasion (for example, you "should" go to church, or you "ought" to be at a certain weight for your height), a feature often hidden by the norm's roots in statistics. By using the language of mathematics, statistics has claimed the objectivity ascribed to that language. Yet, like mathematics itself, the norm can be thought of as an argument: an argument about what qualities or characteristics should be measured, about what units of measurement should be used, about the dividing line between the "normal" and the "deviant," and, in a more general sense, about the importance of ranking and comparing individuals in a population.

I have based this chapter on ethnographic data gathered in the Massachusetts infertility community in 1995–1996. The stories are those of white, middle-class women (single and married, lesbian and heterosexual) who were using (or had used) reproductive technologies to overcome "medical infertility" (a diagnosis given to heterosexual couples who are unable to become pregnant), which is covered by the Massachusetts mandate, or "social infertility" (a diagnosis given to single women and women in same-sex couples who are unable to have a child because of a lack of sperm), which is not covered. I focus on this group for several reasons. For the larger project of which this chapter is a part, I sought to talk to anyone involved in or affected by the Massachusetts mandate, including those using the reproductive technologies that it made more accessible. However, of the group using reproductive technologies, most of those who responded to my study were white, middle-class women, a phenomenon seen by others studying infertility (see, for example, Becker and Nachtigall 1994:515). Although it is vitally important that research be done on why people of color, the working class, and the working poor might use (or might not use) reproductive technologies, I argue that the focus on middle-class white women for this study was appropriate for two reasons. First, the state mandate came about largely because it was sponsored and lobbied for by RESOLVE, the infertility support and advocacy organization, which was (and continues to be) mostly white and middle class (Simons 1988:155).

Second, women are the primary patients and the partner (in hetero-sexual couples) most likely to seek, make decisions about, and prefer to continue medical treatment (Becker and Nachtigall 1994), even though the cause of infertility is just as often found with a male partner as with the female (RESOLVE 1990).

Each of these women took part in an open-ended interview (lasting between half an hour and two and a half hours), during which she related her experience of infertility and discussed how she had arrived at certain decisions and insights. Their stories illustrate the multiple ways in which the infertile do not adhere to societal norms. Unable to do what most people appear to do effortlessly, the infertile may experience a profound sense of alienation from their bodies, families, friends, co-workers, and communities. Their reproductive systems are not functioning as they should. They are unable to proceed in their lives as they, and others, may have expected. To use no medical intervention or to stop trying to become pregnant is to face a set of questions about the normalcy of their desires. Is it abnormal not to seek help from a doctor? Are we a family if we don't have children? The decision to seek medical intervention brings with it another set of uncertainties. The infertile might struggle with questions about whether the use of reproductive technologies is "natural" and therefore a normal way to have a child. They may wonder about the extent to which an adoptive family might be perceived as normal within their circle of reference. If they decide to pursue adoption, they must decide whether to try to adopt a child who matches their physical characteristics and whether a child of another race or nationality would fit within their definition of a normal family.

In this chapter, I examine how normalization operates through the medical treatment of infertility, how some infertile people come to interpret their status, and the role of the Massachusetts mandate in these processes. After briefly introducing the concept of normalization, I use women's stories to illustrate how normalization operates through the medical model of infertility. I then argue that the pursuit of medical treatment for infertility seems all the more normal when people interpret adoption as an abnormal way to have a family. After using the example of infertility to illustrate that normalization is most successful when not all abnormals are "cured," I conclude by arguing that the Massachusetts mandate normalizes both infertility and fertility. That is, it both places the infertile within the realm of standard medical practice (thereby helping the infertile feel less isolated and more normal) and authorizes a system that differentiates the infertile from the fertile (thereby reinforcing their abnormal status).

Normalization: A Brief Introduction

Although it is tempting to look back on the history of childlessness and ask such questions as, "Did childless colonial Americans feel abnormal?" evidence exists that normality itself is a relatively recent concept that we cannot universalize. We have come to think of comparing ourselves to a norm as natural, as something that humans must have always done. From our intelligence to our height and weight, we measure and compare ourselves to "average" values. These values influence our daily routines, our educational opportunities, our work compensation, and our medical care. Cultural critic Leonard J. Davis, however, notes that words surrounding the idea of the norm, as it is thought of today, did not come into use in Western languages until 1840 to 1860 (1995:24), the period of the industrial revolution. Before that period, the Western human imagination conceived of the "ideal," which was markedly different from the "normal." The ideal represented perfection, which only the divine could attain. Because all human beings fell short of that ideal, no humans expected to conform to it (24–25).

The norm, a standard to which humans *did* expect to conform, came about with the advent of industrialization. During industrialization, human productivity became a central concern (Davis 1990; Foucault 1979). Ranking and comparing individuals to increase the usefulness of a population was a vital part of industrialization. A population's usefulness could be maximized by making the individual body a productive component of other social systems, and the process of normalization was a vital part of this endeavor. Attention focused "on the body as a machine: its disciplining, the optimization of its capabilities, the extortion of its forces, the parallel increase of its usefulness and its docility, its integration into systems of efficient and economic controls" (Foucault 1990:139). On the most obvious level, factories needed workers who produced at optimum efficiency. This way of conceiving of the usefulness of human bodies permeated not only factories, however, but a variety of institutions, including hospitals, schools, the military, and prisons (Foucault 1979).

The discipline of statistics, a result of the "probabilistic revolution" of the nineteenth century (Ewald 1991:142), both created the modern notion of the norm and established the link between the individual body and social systems. From astronomy, statisticians borrowed the idea of averaging errors (a procedure for locating a star) and applied this idea to humans to construct "averages" of physical and moral attributes (Davis 1990:26). Statisticians measured and plotted human attributes just as the astronomers had measured and plotted data from observation of the stars. They could describe an entire population by using a graphical representation (what has come to be known as the bell curve, or the "normal distribution") that depicted norms (those toward the center of the bell curve) and deviations (those at the extremes). The ability to describe human characteristics in scientific terms was a boon to social engineers and commentators of divergent political stripes, providing scientific justification both for the "middle way of life" of the bourgeoisie and a standard by which economist and social theorist Karl Marx could level his critiques of the distribution of wealth (Davis 1990:27, 29). By recasting a political problem in the "neutral language of science" (Dreyfus and Rabinow 1983:196), politicians could transform it into a technical problem with an attainable technical solution.

The norm, according to Foucault, became one means by which bodies could be made more docile, that is, "subjected, used, transformed, and improved" (1979:136). In a disciplinary system, bodies are individually and minutely observed, their activities measured, and their measurements compared and averaged. Those individuals who fall outside desirable values are subjected to rehabilitation. The result is a process that is both individualizing (in that it describes particular characteristics in minute detail) and homogenizing (in that it is part of a general collective of information used to create categories and distributions of populations, and in that it is used to help the individual conform to the norm) (Foucault 1979:184). The techniques of normalization are essential to the process of discipline because they help organize, classify, and control anomalies. On the surface, these techniques seem designed to eliminate anomalies. However, the techniques are designed at the same time that the anomalies are themselves "discovered." In other words, the techniques of normalization do not so much identify and correct the abnormal as they create and perpetuate the distinction between the normal and the abnormal. The normal and the abnormal, therefore, do not exist as discrete entities to be observed but as "functions" that "stimulate modification" (Canguilhem 1991:77).

The categories of "fertile" and "infertile" operate in this way. In practice, the ability to procreate is a continuum rather than a set of binaries; this continuum operates throughout populations as well as within an individual's lifetime. For example, two women who start trying for a pregnancy may not become pregnant at the same time. One may become pregnant after a month, the other after two years. Similarly, a woman might become pregnant after six months with her first child but might not become pregnant with her second child until she has tried for three years. Frequency and timing of intercourse also affect the number of months it will take before a pregnancy occurs. The categories of "fertile" and "infertile" are therefore not labels of conditions that reproductive endocrinologists have discovered. Instead, reproductive endocrinologists created the categories (by deciding how much time passes before the "average" person can be expected to become pregnant) so that they can intervene.

Normalization and the Medical Model of Infertility

Central to this chapter is Susan, whose story highlights some of the major issues and dilemmas for white, middle-class infertile women in Massachusetts.[2] When we first met, Susan (then thirty-seven and working in finance) had been undergoing medical treatment for infertility for three years. Her husband, Paul (who also took part in the study), was a forty-five-year-old physician. Both had been previously married, and Paul had three children (all conceived without assistance) with his former wife.

SUSPECTING INFERTILITY

Like many women, Susan had an idea that it often takes a while to become pregnant. She did not expect it to happen immediately and did not suspect anything abnormal until several months had passed. She recalls:

> I wasn't that naive, you know, it's going to happen instantly the first month, so for the first five, maybe six months, I was just like any other woman who is trying to get pregnant, disappointed when you get your period but not devastated. . . . It never even occurred to me that there was something wrong. I was thirty-four at the time, and after about six or seven months, maybe, eight months, . . . we said, well, maybe there's something wrong, maybe we should talk to somebody, and still thinking, . . . we know sometimes it takes a little while when you're older.

Most women in this study expressed a similar understanding. After nine months of unprotected intercourse, for example, Monica, also thirty-four, began to suspect that something was wrong. Others thought that they might have difficulty because of a general awareness of infertility or from knowing someone who had had difficulty getting pregnant. Betsy, thirty-one, and her husband, who had immediate family members who had had difficulty, discussed adoption as an option even before they began trying. Several women said that a history of irregular periods (or other conditions, such as endometriosis) led them to believe that they might not conceive easily.

Single women and women in same-sex relationships, on the other hand, can self-diagnose themselves as socially infertile as soon as they decide to have a child. This diagnosis is not the result of failed attempts at conception but of a (usually) long decision-making process that takes into account the money available for insemination and second-parent adoption (for those with partners), the strength of the couple's relationship or of external support structures, and the social and cultural context in which the child would be born. Of course, physicians may also diagnose medical infertility in single women and women in same-sex relationships after a certain number of unsuccessful attempts at artificial insemination, or after finding (through the charting process used by many women undergoing artificial insemination) an irregular cycle or other condition that would make conception difficult.

Textbook definitions of medical infertility, and the definition adopted by the Massachusetts mandate, place the boundary between normal and abnormal fertility at one year. However, at least one other definition (that of the World Health Organization) places this boundary at two years, suggesting that the criteria for infertility are neither clear-cut nor the result of consensus (Heitman 1995:91). Some critics argue that both definitions allow people to be misdiagnosed, citing data from the U.S. Office of Technological Assessment that show that only 16 percent to 21 percent of couples who are infertile by the twelve-month definition will remain infertile throughout their lives (Wagner and Stephenson 1993:3). Still, most women in this study began to suspect a problem with fertility sometime before one year had passed or twelve attempts at insemination had occurred.

DIAGNOSIS

A family physician or gynecologist is often the first professional a woman seeks out when she suspects impaired fertility. Using the twelve-month definition, some physicians might advise patients to continue to try until that point (perhaps advocating that the woman begin charting her menstrual cycle in order to time intercourse optimally), or they might advise preliminary tests. In Susan and Paul's case, a noted fertility specialist informed them in an early phone consultation that they were still within normal limits but that initial testing could do no harm. Following this advice, Paul had a sperm analysis and Susan had a series of tests designed to assess the health of her reproductive system.[3] Paul's sperm analysis was normal.[4] Testing showed that Susan's fallopian tubes were clear, that her uterine lining was healthy, that the hormone levels in her blood fell within normal limits, and that her reproductive organs were normal. Susan and Paul's diagnosis was "unexplained" infertility, meaning that thorough investigations had not yielded a reason for their inability to conceive.

Rather than starting a battery of tests, physicians might advise women younger than Susan to use an ovulation predictor kit or to chart their ovulation. When charting her menstrual cycle, a woman takes her temperature at the same time each morning on a basal body thermometer, which measures in tenths of degrees, and records each measurement on a chart. During ovulation the temperature rises slightly. It falls again at the onset of menstruation. Charting her menstrual cycle gives the woman an indication of when (and if) she is ovulating, so that she can time intercourse or artificial insemination. She can also bring the charts to her physician to help diagnose ovulatory problems.

The charting of the menstrual cycle is a technology of normalization. Clinicians will compare the data that the woman collects and records to the menstrual cycle of the "average" woman; a physician uses these comparisons to help determine a course of treatment. Through this technique the woman becomes an object of knowledge, something that can be described and about which arguments, in the form of hypotheses or diagnoses, can be made (for example, "The patient has luteal phase defect"). Like other technologies of normalization, the knowledge created about the woman is both individualizing and homogenizing. She is known as a discrete entity and as a member (and data point) in a certain population. Because variation is typical in all women, the twenty-eight-day cycle rarely exists. Therefore, we can see efforts to regularize the menstrual cycle according to this norm as homogenizing (Ellison 1996).

The collecting and recording of menstrual data is one striking example of the role of writing in normalization. Charting the menstrual cycle "situates [individuals] in a network of writing; it engages them in a whole mass of documents that capture and fix them" (Foucault 1979: 189). A cycle is no longer just a bodily experience that a woman knows viscerally. Instead the menstrual cycle takes visual shape with each temperature reading a woman records. These data points become a way of knowing the menstrual cycle as a graph of highs and lows that a clinician can compare in an objectified way to that of the average woman.

A woman who charts her own menstrual cycle is participating in self-observation and providing information to health care providers who will help her to become more normal, if necessary. It is important to remember that in this participation, the woman becomes a subject as well as an object of knowledge. For women using artificial insemination by donor (often single heterosexual women and lesbians with no indications of reproductive impairments), charting is part of the standard practice of becoming pregnant. For single heterosexual women and lesbians in particular, charting is part of the routine of baby making, much like frequent intercourse is for heterosexual couples when they first attempt to conceive. Because sperm is expensive, women using artificial insemination by donor need to be able to have inseminations when they are most likely to conceive.

For Sarah, a married heterosexual woman, having a normal chart gave her both a sense of control and a sense of frustration. Before attempting to get pregnant with her first child, she charted for two months, then became pregnant. "It all happened the way it was supposed to," she said. "It was great." But when she tried unsuccessfully to get pregnant for the second time, her "perfect" charts were a source of frustration:

> A couple of months went by and nothing happened. Which isn't that unusual, but I was charting things very carefully and it really seemed to me like it should be working and they weren't. . . . The charts were working right, everything was doing exactly what it was supposed to do. It just wasn't happening. And it was very frustrating because it would seem like it was happening, you know, I had been reading, that it's two weeks between ovulation and when you get your period. This has got to be it. You know all this stuff was happening, and it wasn't happening. It was devastating, a couple of times.

For Sarah, the normal charts were good news when she conceived but frustrating when she did not. The discrepancy between results confounded her sense of how her body worked. Other women do not always interpret their charts as physicians or "how to get pregnant" books might. They might define their body temperature (even if it is not 98.6) as normal or create their own charts to correspond to their cycles, reflecting a willingness to redefine the normal.

TREATMENT

Susan had a gut-level feeling that "there was nothing wrong" with her. She "stonewalled" against some of the procedures, afraid of the pain or angry that she might have to undergo them only to prove what she felt she knew all along. Still, when she and Paul were diagnosed with unexplained infertility, Susan kept hoping that their doctor would find something wrong so that they could fix it. She says:

> I was mad that I had had to have all these things and . . . at the lab they kept saying that I was normal. But I started saying, well, I want them to find something wrong so they can fix it, 'cause I've heard so many stories, "Well, I've had a blocked tube, but they opened it up and then I got pregnant," "Oh, I did have endometriosis, but they gave me such and such and I got pregnant." You know, it's like, Jesus, if they can't find anything wrong they can't fix it, so it was just really a Catch-22. Unexplained infertility is really, really hard.

Susan's frustration grew out of the sense that if her reproductive system were working normally, she would conceive. Because she was not conceiving, she believed that some identifiable cause must exist and that, once located, modern medicine could correct it. Like Susan, many other women expressed belief in a technologically inspired view of the human body as a machine (Greil 1991:53) with interdependent, fallible parts (Whiteford and Gonzalez 1995:29). Several women used mechanical metaphors to describe their bodies, referring to their reproductive systems as "plumbing." Using this metaphor, they perceived their bodies as systems that could be evaluated, diagnosed, and repaired. Sarah, for instance, felt that she was an ideal candidate for in-vitro fertilization because "it was a very clear-cut situation where the plumbing wasn't working."

Susan's new physician, an infertility specialist, recommended a conservative course of treatment: medicated intrauterine insemination (IUI), a procedure in which she would take drugs to regulate her menstrual cycle and he would inject sperm past the cervix into the uterus at the appropriate time in the cycle. Although some people question whether unexplained infertility should be treated at all (because many people will become pregnant on their own), the philosophy of the director of a leading Boston-area infertility clinic is to bring this population back into the range of the normal. In other words, with treatment those in the unexplained category have the same chances of conception, per cycle, as the general population, about 20 percent (Tan, Jacobs, and Seibel 1995:30). For those with unexplained infertility, he says, IUI is the least invasive procedure that will get results, so he prefers to try six medicated IUI attempts (varying the medication with each one) before moving to more invasive procedures such as in-vitro fertilization (IVF). Susan's physician took a similar approach (although he did not vary the medication). Although Susan and Paul asked to start with a more aggressive approach, such as IVF, their physician was reluctant, saying that it made no sense to start with a more invasive and expensive procedure when Susan might get pregnant through IUI.

By the time Susan was ready for her first IUI treatment, she and Paul had been trying to have a child for two years. She was excited and optimistic, saying, "This is what we had been waiting for." Although their sex life had disintegrated during the infertility testing, the IUI procedure gave them a chance to try to fit this experience within the realm of normal procreation. He held her hand during the insemination, and she remembers thinking, "Okay, we're making our baby." During the time of the first IUI attempt, they also rejuvenated their sex life as they began to separate love making from baby making. At that point, she says, their sex life returned to some semblance of normalcy, only to descend again when the IUI failures took their toll. Within a few months they had done three IUI cycles, none of which had worked.

Susan's case illustrates how current infertility practice operationalizes the norm. As recently as the late 1970s, doctors spent more time trying to find and fix the particular anomaly that was causing the infertility. For example, a woman might undergo repeated surgeries to open blocked fallopian tubes (an abnormal condition) so that she could then become pregnant normally. Today the goal of practitioners is to bring a couple's chances of conception back to that of a normal couple, regardless of whether they correct the underlying anomaly. Clinicians originally designed the technique of in-vitro fertilization, for example, to bypass blocked fallopian tubes so that the woman could become pregnant; they now use IVF for a wide variety of conditions, including male factor infertility. Physicians also consider in-vitro fertilization a less invasive, less risky, and more successful treatment than surgery for infertility resulting from blocked fallopian tubes.

After three IUIs and no pregnancy, Susan and Paul were more adamant about wanting to try IVF, and their physician finally agreed. They switched to a different facility and to a different physician, and Susan became pregnant on the first attempt. After several weeks, however, an ultrasound showed that the fetus was not viable. After a dilation and curettage (a procedure in which the physician scrapes and removes the contents of the uterus) and a few weeks' rest, Susan tried two more cycles, each one canceled after the initial ovary stimulation because not enough egg follicles had been produced. Blood tests showed that her ovaries were probably slowing down, and her doctors were not optimistic about her ability to become pregnant without using an egg from a donor. For Susan, the knowledge that she had begun the normal transition into menopause made her feel old beyond her years. She says:

> While it's not technically premature ovarian failure, it's the kind of thing that [for] women my age, that's happening all the time, but if they're not having infertility problems, they don't know it, and it's just that slow decline towards menopause. It could take ten years, and [for] women who've had their children, or don't want children, or aren't considering, it's irrelevant. You don't feel this at all. And now that I know that this is happening to my body, I feel a hell of a lot older than thirty-seven. I'm going to be thirty-eight next month, but I feel forty-eight, I feel fifty-eight some days.

So, although Susan understood that the processes her body was undergoing were normal for women her age, she still felt "betrayed." Being normal, in this instance, was not comforting because it conflicted with her unfulfilled desire for pregnancy. Approaching menopause made it hard for Susan to fulfill accepted "life course norms "(Greil 1991:133). In this instance, being normal was not comforting because it conflicted with her unfulfilled desire for pregnancy.

Adoption and the "Normal" Family

When I interviewed Susan, she and Paul were assessing whether to stop treatment, live without children, or adopt. Like many prospective adoptive parents, Susan was anxious about the process. First, the expense seemed exorbitant; according to 1995 figures from the Open Door Society, an adoption advocacy group, an international adoption can run $6,000 to $18,000 and a domestic adoption twice that. In addition, because of "shortages," Susan was afraid of not being able to adopt a healthy white infant. She did not know whether she and Paul would look enough like normal parents for a birth mother to choose them. She reasons, "You may never be chosen by a birth mother, they might say, 'Oh, god, you're as old as my parents, I'm sixteen, I don't want you. On the other hand, they might say, 'Oh, I was raised by my grandmother, older people are good.' You just never know if you're going to get chosen." She had similar worries when she considered international adoption. The age limits for adopting children from other countries vary, but Susan was afraid that most of them would see her husband, at forty-five, as too old.

Susan had other fears about international adoption. In some adoptive situations, agencies make an effort to select a child that physically resembles the adoptive parents (while in domestic adoptions, agencies at the time were reluctant to match children with adoptive parents of a different race). Physical likeness allows adoptive parents some measure of privacy and control over how and when their children learn about their origins. A child that does not look markedly different from its adoptive parents will not draw the attention, or often invasive questions, of strangers and acquaintances.

For Susan, having a child of a different nationality would invade her privacy, telling the world about her infertility and labeling her family as different. So, even though adopting a girl from China had appeal for her, she was bothered by how strangers would react.[5] She remembers the story of a woman with a daughter from China. When the girl was with only one of her parents, people sometimes asked whether the girl was her daughter, or whether the other parent was Asian. But when the child was with both parents, Susan says, "It's right there in your face, all the time, it's right there for the world to see." Having a child of the same race, therefore, was part of looking normal and having more control over disclosure of her reproductive life. She says: "I want to be as damn normal as I can be at this point. I think I would prefer to have a child of the same race, because then I was in control of who knew, when they knew, and how they knew, not because I want to hide it, but because I want more control in my life, and I want to present it to the child in a certain way."

At a much deeper level too, Susan did not know whether adoption was the right choice, simply because it didn't seem normal. She says, "I just want to be normal again. I don't think I'll ever be normal again, because adopting or child free are not considered normal. Only biological children are considered normal."

Susan is acutely aware of the hierarchical ordering of familial relations. Whereas in colonial America, "fluid and flexible arrangements" made the raising of children "more communal, less private, and less biologically or legally defined" (May 1995:31), contemporary American family life centers around the ideal of two parents living with their own offspring in a private dwelling. The preference for parenting biologically related children runs deep, and the bias against adoption is part of everyday culture. The adoptive relationship is widely seen as inferior and as the last resort when other options fail (Bartholet 1993). The preference for biologically related children extends to the single women and women in same-sex relationships in this study. Although some considered adoption as well as artificial insemination, the pull of a genetic link was strong. Ellen, single and undergoing insemination, intensely wanted a "little me," a desire she called "almost like a male ego thing." Anne, though she did not believe that she experienced the ticking of the "biological clock," did experience a strong urge to carry a child; she and her partner are now considering a second child, which her partner now wants to carry. Other women in same-sex relationships offered very practical reasons for wanting biological children. Lauren and her partner felt that a biologically related child would stand a better chance of being accepted by their families. Another couple, Janice and Theresa, each secured their biological (and therefore legal) ties to their son through an unusual procedure: donor sperm fertilized Theresa's egg, which was transferred to Janice, who gave birth. This procedure also satisfied Theresa's desire for someone who looked like her (she had been adopted) and helped to alleviate Janice's menstrual disorder.

Failure and the Success of Normalization

As mentioned earlier, normal fertility does not mean that all couples will conceive every time they try. For a practitioner of infertility medicine, normal fertility (based on an average age of twenty-five) means that a couple has a 20 percent chance of conceiving in any given cycle (Tan, Jacobs, and Seibel 1995:30). In addition, because fertility is a continuum rather than a binary, about 5 percent of individuals within a population will never be able to conceive (Heitman 1995:19). In other words, it is normal for a certain number of people within a population to be unable to conceive. For the individual or couple, however, being normal means being able to have a child. The goal, when using techniques and technologies designed to produce pregnancy, is to become pregnant, not to have the average chances of becoming pregnant.

The reality that some people will never conceive a desired child helps to sustain the distinction between the fertile and the infertile. Foucault notes that this is a key feature of normalization: for the process to continue, rehabilitation must sometimes fail. Writing of the failure of the prison to reform hardened criminals, a goal claimed by prison advocates, Foucault notes that the high rate of recidivism leads to the conclusion that prisons do not really work. Instead of judging prisons by this stated criteria, Foucault argues that we have to look at what else their failure achieves: "One would be forced to suppose that the prison, and no doubt punishment in general, is not intended to eliminate offenses, but rather to distinguish them, to distribute them, to use them: that it is not so much that they render docile those who are liable to transgress the law but that they tend to assimilate the transgression of the laws in a general tactic of subjection" (1979:272). In other words, "prisons, and perhaps all normalizing power, succeed when they are only partially successful" (Dreyfus and Rabinow 1983:195).

In the treatment of infertility, failure to remove the stigma can take at least two forms. In the first instance, an individual or couple may be in the percentage of the population that will never conceive. When Susan's physician described the statistical probabilities for pregnancy, she never imagined she would be in the small minority of those whom medicine cannot help. She says, "Nobody told us how bad it would be if we failed. And nobody told us how wonderful it was to be successful by a different option, earlier, and we didn't realize that we could have walked away."

Her trust in the "medical miracle," she says, prevented her and Paul from exploring other options sooner, when she might have had more mental, psychological, and physical reserves. Coming from a "medical family," they believed that medicine would have the answer.

The stigma of infertility can also remain after an individual or couple has "resolved" their desire for a child. After giving birth to or adopting a child, parents may struggle not to be too protective or too lenient with their "miracle" children. They may want to further expand their families, and they may face both subtle and overt pressure from those who believe that an only child grows up to be spoiled and selfish. Sarah, having had one child without assistance and then twins through IVF, was grateful not to have to answer questions about having more children. With three children, she felt safe in answering that she desired no more. Susan and Paul, eleven months after our first interview, were beginning to deal with this issue. They had adopted an infant girl, a procedure that was much easier and less traumatic than Susan had imagined. She was now wondering whether they might someday want to have a sibling for their daughter. Despite their good experience with adoption, Susan thought that another adoption would be impossible because the first adoption, which cost more than $30,000, had depleted their financial reserves. Their only option, she said, would be to go back to medical treatment, this time using an egg from a donor.

Infertility Insurance as Bio-Power

Foucault (1990) notes that in a disciplinary society, power is not merely prohibitive; it is also productive. That is, power is now less concerned with taking life and more concerned with making life more efficient, more productive, and more useful. The Massachusetts mandate for insurance coverage for infertility, as a device that allows a greater percentage of the population access to reproductive technologies, might be thought of as a way of making women's bodies more useful and productive (Sawicki 1991:83). Although the mandate has widened the accessibility of reproductive technologies, it symbolically and materially encourages women in some social and cultural positions to reproduce. Although women in other groups (particularly, those without health insurance) are not (as a group) prohibited from having children, the end effect is what Ginsburg and Rapp call "stratified reproduction" (1995:3). The mandate excludes the working poor and those on Medicaid, and only the middle-class and wealthy socially infertile can afford to subsidize the treatment that the mandate excludes. Further research is needed in two keys areas: to determine how those in excluded groups interpret the processes of normalization accompanying the medicalization of infertility; and to understand more fully how middle-class white women might interpret or transform these processes in empowering ways.

The mandate's financial provisions give couples an incentive to adhere to the norms of parenthood in general and biological parenthood in particular. In the middle of treatment Susan addressed the strength of its pull: "I'm leaning toward adoption, but I feel like I should try another time, and it's paid for. They're willing to spend the money, I should try another time. How can I let go of the possibility of being successful that way? Success may be right around the corner. And it's free."

This incentive can make it hard, as Susan says, to know when "enough is enough." Combined with this financial incentive, the mandate symbolically authorizes the medical definition of infertility and medical treatments for it, constructing adoption as an inferior choice (Bartholet 1993:212–14). The financial impetus to adhere to biological norms may be more appealing to heterosexual women with partners than to single women or women in same-sex relationships. While partnered heterosexual women tend to expect normal procreation to cost nothing, those with social infertility have a different set of starting assumptions. Lauren and her partner, for example, budgeted $10,000 to become pregnant (plus an additional $20,000 to do a second-parent adoption). If they were unable to conceive with $10,000, they still had the money to adopt a child. Having considered the expenses of insemination, none of the single women or women in same-sex couples in this study expected insurance to cover it completely (although they may have wanted it to).

Authorizing a medical definition of infertility, however, has made the experience of infertility a more normal condition. Whereas infertility was once seen as caused by a woman's moral failure or unconscious desire to avoid motherhood (Sandelowski 1990), infertility is now seen as more central (though not completely so) to mainstream medicine.

Because most infertility treatment is practiced on women, we can view the mandate as helping to place women's bodies on the medical map, whereas once they stood on the periphery. It has also created new norms for women to aspire to, which can be used by women in empowering ways (Sawicki 1991:83). With more individuals and couples seeking treatment, and with organizations such as RESOLVE encouraging the infertile to come out of the closet, those experiencing infertility are more likely to know other normal people similarly affected. At the same time, the medicalization of infertility has "transformed infertility from an acute, private agony that was accepted as fate, into a chronic, public stigma" (Whiteford and Gonzalez 1995:29). That is, because the treatment of infertility is more visible, the abnormal status of the infertile is more fully in the public eye.

NOTES

I would like to thank the Wenner-Gren Foundation for Anthropological Research for generously funding the fieldwork for this project (Gr. 5873). I also owe an enormous debt to those who took part in this study, most of whom must remain nameless.

1. The statute provides, in part: "Any blanket or general policy of insurance . . . shall provide, to the same extent that benefits are provided for other pregnancy-related procedures, coverage for medically necessary expenses of diagnosis and treatment of infertility to persons residing within the commonwealth. For purposes of this section, 'infertility' shall mean the condition of a presumably healthy individual who is unable to conceive or produce conception during a period of one year" (Commonwealth of Massachusetts 1987).

2. Not her real name. Throughout this chapter, first names used alone are pseudonyms.

3. Because a sperm analysis (which measures count, shape, and motility) is quick and easy, most infertility clinics now perform this test as early as possible. Testing men for infertility is a relatively recent practice, however. U.S. clinicians routinely neglected male infertility until at least the 1960s (May 1995:158–59).

4. Although semen analysis once comprised only counting sperm, clinics now also consider whether the sperm are moving (motility) and examine the shape of the sperm heads (morphology), as these factors appear to influence whether a sperm is capable of fertilizing an egg. A reproductive endocrinologist at a major Boston-area clinic considers a semen analysis normal if it shows at least twenty million sperm per sample, if at least 60 percent of the sperm are moving, and if at least 5 percent of the sperm have perfectly oval heads.

5. Because of China's one-child policy and because of the cultural and so-

224

Part Three: Reproduction and Legal/Policy Issues

cial preferences for sons over daughters, girls fill Chinese orphanages. See Anagnost (1995) for a cultural analysis of this policy.

REFERENCES

Anagnost, Ann. 1995. A surfeit of bodies: Population and the rationality of the state in post-Mao China. In F. D. Ginsburg and Rayna Rapp, eds., *Conceiving the new world order: The global politics of reproduction*, pp. 22–41. Berkeley: University of California Press.
Bartholet, Elizabeth. 1993. *Family bonds: Adoption and the politics of parenting.* Boston: Houghton Mifflin.
Becker, Gay, and Robert D. Nachtigall. 1994. "Born to be a mother": The cultural construction of risk in infertility treatment in the U.S. *Social Science and Medicine* 39:507–18.
Canguilhem, Georges. 1991. *The normal and the pathological.* Cambridge, Mass.: Zone Books.
Commonwealth of Massachusetts. 1987. *Acts and resolves.* Chapter 394, §1.
Davis, Leonard J. 1995. *Enforcing normalcy: Disability, deafness, and the body.* London: Verso.
Dreyfus, Hubert L., and Paul Rabinow. 1983. *Michel Foucault: Beyond structuralism and hermeneutics.* 2d ed. Chicago: University of Chicago Press.
Ellison, Peter. 1996. Reproductive ecology and "local biologies." Paper presented at the 95th Annual Meeting of the American Anthropological Association, November 20, San Francisco.
Ewald, Francois. 1991. Norms, discipline, and the law. In Robert Post, ed., *Law and the order of culture*, pp. 138–61. Berkeley: University of California Press.
Foucault, Michel. 1979. *Discipline and punish: The birth of the prison.* Translated by Alan Sheridan. New York: Vintage.
Foucault, Michel. 1990. *The history of sexuality: An introduction.* Vol. 1. Translated by Robert Hurley. New York: Vintage.
Ginsburg, Faye D., and Rayna Rapp, eds. 1995. *Conceiving the new world order: The global politics of reproduction.* Berkeley: University of California Press.
Greil, Arthur. 1991. *Not yet pregnant: Infertile couples in contemporary America.* New Brunswick, N.J.: Rutgers University Press.
Heitman, Elizabeth. 1995. Infertility as a public health problem: Why assisted reproductive technologies are not the answer. *Stanford Law and Policy Review* 6:89–102.
May, Elaine Tyler. 1995. *Barren in the promised land: Childless Americans and the pursuit of happiness.* New York: Basic.
RESOLVE, Inc. 1990. *When you're wishing for a baby: Getting started or how do I know if I'm infertile?* Arlington, Mass.: author.
Sandelowski, Margarete. 1990. Failures of volition: Female agency and infertility in historical perspective. *Signs: Journal of Women in Culture and Society* 15:475–99.

Sawicki, Jana. 1991. *Disciplining Foucault: Feminism, power, and the body.* New York: Routledge.

Simons, Harriet. 1988. *RESOLVE, Inc.: Advocacy within a mutual support organization.* Ann Arbor: UMI.

Tan, S. L., H. W. Jacobs, and M. M. Seibel. 1995. *Infertility: Your questions answered.* New York: Birch Lane.

Wagner, Marsden G., and Patricia Stephenson. 1993. Infertility and in vitro fertilization: Is the tail wagging the dog? In Patricia Stephenson and Marsden G. Wagner, eds., *Tough choices: In vitro fertilization and the reproductive technologies,* pp. 1–22. Philadelphia: Temple University Press.

Whiteford, Linda M., and Lois Gonzalez. 1995. Stigma: The hidden burden of infertility. *Social Science and Medicine* 40:27–36.

10 THE LEGAL STATUS

OF DIRECT-ENTRY MIDWIVES

IN THE UNITED STATES

BALANCING TRADITION

WITH MODERN MEDICINE

MARY M. LAY

Within the United States, current legal response to direct-entry midwives ranges from encouragement to prosecution. Direct-entry midwives, also called traditional or lay midwives, enter directly into midwifery education and practice, rather than through the discipline of nursing, and often are the only health care providers willing to attend home births. Their legal status varies widely from state to state, a reflection of the difficulty that legislatures and state agencies have in reconciling midwifery practice and philosophy with current medical knowledge systems about birth.

For example, New Mexico's health department regulations, which govern direct-entry midwives there, formally recognize the state's midwifery guild by referring to the *New Mexico Midwives' Association Policies and Procedures* manual. Florida's late governor, Lawton Chiles, proclaimed October 10–14, 1994, as Licensed Midwife Week. Chiles believed that half of all babies could be born with midwives in attendance (Gaskin 1994:6), and by 1999 five Florida schools of midwifery were graduating direct-entry midwives. On the other hand, in September 1995 Karen Webster, a direct-entry midwife in Maryland, received a criminal summons for practicing nursing without a license; Webster was the fifth such midwife that Maryland charged in less than two years. Also, on December 13, 1995, after an undercover investigation in which employees of the New York State Education Department posed as potential clients, police arrested direct-entry midwife Roberta Devers-Scott; she was charged with the felony of practicing midwifery without a license. In New York, the only licensed midwives are those who complete a program in midwifery whose admission requirements include a nursing degree. Devers-Scott entered into a plea bargain and was sentenced to three years' probation and fined $1,000 (Schlinger 1996:25; Webster 1997:5).

The legal status of direct-entry U.S. midwives in the late twentieth century reflects complex relationships among individual women's rights, the professional and legal jurisdictions of medical communities and state agencies, and cultural attitudes toward birth and motherhood. The language that defines midwifery and sets the scope of practice and contraindications for midwifery and home birth often conflicts with the self-definitions, philosophy, and standards of care expressed by direct-entry midwives' guilds and organizations. Most particularly, direct-entry midwives must balance their belief that birth is a safe and natural process with their moderate use of reproductive technologies—procedures and drugs that many direct-entry midwives feel make home birth safe but that state and medical discourse communities believe should remain within the jurisdiction of formal, institutionalized medicine. This uneasy relationship between midwifery tradition and modern medicine, as reflected within the legal language that defines midwifery practice, forms the rhetorical basis for this chapter.

I briefly describe the regulatory status of direct-entry midwives throughout the United States to characterize the overall climate for the midwives and their home-birth clients. Then I examine closely certain stylistic features of the licensing rules that address direct-entry midwives, for example, definitions of midwifery practice and of such terms as *high risk* and *low risk, abnormal* and *normal*, and definitions of pregnancy conditions that set the legal boundaries of direct-entry midwifery. I organize this examination along three lines:

- The contrast between the self-definitions of the midwives and the state and medical definitions of their practice
- The tension between the midwives' desire to have access to medical technologies and pharmaceuticals and their need to remain autonomous
- My analysis of how, in the case of home birth and direct-entry midwifery, state regulatory agencies' obligation to protect citizens from the results of uninformed choices may outweigh individual rights

228

Part Three: Reproduction and Legal/Policy Issues

I assume the social construction of knowledge and the relationship of knowledge, discourse, and power as described by such scholars as the philosopher Michel Foucault. A society's discourse—in particular, oral debates and written texts—creates knowledge about topics, and those who are assigned the task of creating that knowledge experience and exercise power as they identify cultural truths about these topics. These truths work to normalize cultural practices as citizens internalize such truths and allow these truths to direct their self-image and choices. A rhetorical analysis of the discourse of direct-entry midwifery reveals how U.S. society in the 1990s considers birth a risky business best handled in a hospital setting. Therefore, this discourse considers the choice to birth at home, an experience that most mothers describe as empowering, to be not only unusual but also potentially irresponsible. Rhetorical analysis also reveals how direct-entry midwives must trade their autonomy for even limited access to medical knowledge and technologies and how state agencies and medical experts generate hegemonic knowledge systems about birth in a way that defines and may restrict women's experiences.

Legal Status of Direct-Entry Midwives in the United States

The current legal status of direct-entry midwives in the United States and the various discourses about midwifery reveal the extent to which legal access to reproductive technologies involves a sacrifice of autonomy and freedom for midwives and their clients. Although home-birth and midwifery communities do not consider certain medical procedures, particularly those exercised during an emergency, incompatible with the traditional tools of midwifery, legal discourse distinctly assigns control of these tools to state-identified medical experts. Licensed direct-entry midwives often have access to these reproductive technologies only under the supervision of a physician.

As of 1999, seventeen states license, register, or certify direct-entry midwives: Alaska, Arkansas, Arizona, California, Colorado, Delaware, Florida, Louisiana, Montana, New Hampshire, New Mexico, Oregon, Rhode Island, South Carolina, Texas, Washington, and Wyoming. In 2000, Minnesota joins this list; a bill passed in 1999 establishes licensing for direct-entry midwives. In eleven states, direct-entry midwifery practice is legal through judicial interpretation or statutory inference; in the seven states that do not legally define direct-entry midwives, they are not specifically prohibited from practicing. In six states, direct-entry midwives are legal by statute, but licensure is not available; the remaining nine states prohibit direct-entry midwives through statutory restriction or judicial interpretation. However, legal status alone does not determine the climate for direct-entry midwifery in any particular state. For example, in 1999 in Minnesota, Alabama, New Jersey, and New York direct-entry midwives were legal by statute, but the means to licensure was not available. However, at the same time (1991–1995) that the Minnesota Board of Medical Practice struggled to find a way to examine and regulate its direct-entry midwives, Alabama, New Jersey, and New York subjected direct-entry midwives to investigations, injunctions, and arrests. Moreover, within the seventeen states that licensed, registered, and certified direct-entry midwives in 1999, some state statutes so restricted the practice of the direct-entry midwifery that the midwife who practiced underground had much more freedom and autonomy than her legally sanctioned sister.

Many direct-entry midwives, in contrast to physicians, nurses, and nurse-midwives, are not graduates of formal educational institutions; instead they learn their craft through self-education, apprenticeship, and shared birth stories, and their practices include such measures as herbal remedies and the power of intense communication and human touch. For example, Ina May Gaskin tells readers of *Spiritual Midwifery*, "Great changes can be brought about within the passing of a few words between people or by the midwife's touching the woman or the baby in such a way that great physical changes happen" (1990:277). However, regardless of state recognition, midwifery guilds and organizations confer upon their members professional status. For example, the Midwives' Association of North America established the North American Registry of Midwives, which became a separate but affiliated organization to examine and certify direct-entry midwives, called Certified Professional Midwives, in 1994.

Although they still rely on midwifery experiential and embodied knowledge, many direct-entry midwives turn to reproductive technologies to screen out high-risk mothers and to respond to emergencies. At the same time, they may challenge the boundaries of risk as defined by medical communities—expressing confidence in handling multiple births, breech presentations, and other such conditions at home. Thus Gaskin's book teaches midwives how to cut an episiotomy and to suture, administer the drugs pitocin and methergine to control postpartum hemorrhage, and turn a breech baby.

Finally, the public discourse generated on direct-entry midwifery and home birth within the United States comes from several communities: state midwives' guilds such as the Minnesota Midwives' Guild and the New Mexico Midwives' Association and national organizations such as the Midwives' Alliance of North America; professional medical organizations, such as the American Medical Association, state boards of nursing, and the American College of Nurse-Midwives; and legal groups and agencies, such as legislatures, justice departments, departments of health, and boards of medical practice. As the next section shows, state statutes and agency documents often distinguish the boundaries of medical science and technology from those of women's art or craft, and state surveillance abetted by medical expertise frequently limits private rights and free trade.

Defining Midwifery and Normal Birth

Legal definitions, as rhetorician Paula Treichler states, set limits and determine boundaries: "Unlike meanings, which are bound up in what people *think* and *have in their minds,* and *intend,* definitions claim to state what *is.* A definition is a meaning that has become official and thereby appears to tell us how things are in the real world" (1990:123). However, a definition may describe one discourse community's knowledge system much more than it may another's.

Licensing statutes and rules and regulations generally open with a set of definitions, designed to set boundaries on the practitioners and practices to be regulated. In the case of direct-entry midwifery, these definitions often contrast to those created by practitioners themselves, which attempt to reflect rather than restrict the various philosophies and meanings within the practice. Unlike the documents created by direct-entry midwives, which describe the experience of birth and the relationship between the birth mother and her midwife, state regulations often define midwifery according to how it must differ from the norm of medical care. The construction of regulatory definitions therefore contains barriers for the direct-entry midwives who wish to combine both traditional practice and modern reproductive tools.

For example, the Midwives' Association of North America (MANA) defines direct-entry midwifery as follows:

> Midwives work as autonomous practitioners, collaborating with other health and social services providers when necessary. . . . Midwives recognize that a woman is the only direct provider for herself and her unborn baby; thus the most important determinant of a healthy pregnancy is the mother herself. Midwives recognize that empowerment inherent in the childbearing experience

and strive to support women to make informed decisions and take responsibility for their own well being. (1994:31)

This definition stresses the autonomy of the midwife, the equality of her relationship with the birth parent, the variety of traditional and modern tools at her disposal, and the empowerment of the woman during the experience of birth.

In contrast, state statutes define direct-entry midwifery not by what it encompasses but by what it does not and birth not by the empowerment but by the risk it might bring to the woman and her infant and how and by whom that risk must be handled. State statutes then define direct-entry midwifery as something other than the norm—medical care in a hospital facility or birthing clinic. Arkansas state law, for example, defines midwives as "any person other than a physician or certified nurse midwife who shall manage care during the pregnancy of any woman or of her newborn during the antepartum, intrapartum, or postpartum periods; or who shall advertise as a midwife by signs, printed card or otherwise."

Similarly, South Carolina health regulations define midwifery services as those "provided by a person who is not a medical or nursing professional licensed by an agency of the State of South Carolina, for the purpose of giving primary assistance in the birth process either free, for trade, or for money." In 1999 Minnesota statutes defined midwifery as "the furthering or undertaking by any person to assist or attend a woman in normal pregnancy and childbirth" but excluded forcible, artificial, pharmaceutical, and mechanical practices:

> [Midwifery] shall not include the use of any instrument at a childbirth, except such instrument as is necessary in severing the umbilical cord, nor does it include the assisting of childbirth by an artificial, forcible, or mechanical means, nor the removal of adherent placenta, nor the administering, prescribing, advising, or employing, either before or after any childbirth, of any drug, other than a disinfectant or cathartic.

In defining direct-entry midwives as Other, these states designate, in essence, medically attended births as the standard to which home births are contrasted. Although the language of the state statutes designates midwives as attending normal births, the abnormal birth or the birth needing medical attention and the practitioners who attend such births set the standards for midwifery practice—and set the boundaries of what the state considers normal birth. The normal and the abnormal, the standard and the Other, are thus inextricably bound, and medically attended hospital birth actually represents the norm. As Lois McNay, in her study of Foucault, states, "The other is not always a marginal figure; rather its construction as such is always central, in a mundane way, to the maintenance of any hegemonic system of norms" (1994:6). Again, the discourse of direct-entry midwives and their clients focuses on the empowering experience of birth and the equality of the relationship between the birth mother and her midwife, whereas legal discourse defines midwifery as something other than the norm of medical care.

To support the definition of a normal birth, then, state statues further contrast direct-entry midwifery to medical practice. Using conditions involving medical risk as the standard, state statutes further restrict midwifery care to so-called low-risk births. For example, Montana's regulations are typical in prohibiting the direct-entry midwife from treating high-risk pregnancies: "The practice of direct-entry midwifery does not constitute the practice of medicine, certified nurse-midwifery, or emergency medical care to the extent that a direct-entry midwife advises, attends, or assists a woman during pregnancy, labor, natural childbirth, or the postpartum period when the pregnancy is not a high-risk pregnancy."

Regulations set by the Arizona Department of Health Services define low risk as "the expected outcome of pregnancy, determined through physical assessment and review of the obstetrical history, [which] shall most likely be that of a healthy woman giving birth to a healthy infant and expelling an intact placenta." Finally, Oregon's state regulations define "absolute risk" as "the conditions or clinical situations whereby a client is evaluated to determine obstetrical or neonatal risk which would preclude being an acceptable candidate for an out of hospital birth."

State statutes make clear, then, that medical diagnosis and assessment, as reflected in state agency guidelines, determine risk and set the boundaries for midwifery care and home birth. For example, South Carolina health regulations say that "medical evaluation" determines which cases are "prospectively normal for pregnancy and childbirth." Louisiana law states that "the licensed midwife may provide care to low risk patients determined by physician evaluation and examination to be essentially normal for pregnancy and childbirth ... criteria generally accepted as normal as defined by the board."

Therefore, although MANA and midwifery guild definitions stress the equality between the mother and midwife and the empowerment that is possible during home birth, state statutes assign the medical profession the task of judging what is normal or low risk. The medical profession, then, is the normalizing profession, which differentiates, hierarchizes, compares, and excludes, to use Foucault's terms (1979: 182–84). In empowering medical professionals to establish the cultural truth about birth, the normal or low-risk home birth becomes the abnormal or the unusual birth. Hospital birth is the usual choice, regardless of how many of those babies could arrive safely at home. For example, only one half of 1 percent of babies born in Minnesota are planned home births (Illg 1991:2). The numbers are small even in states that sanction midwifery; for example, in 1994 Arkansas reported 172 births attended by licensed direct-entry midwives (Penn 1995:10).

States that regulate direct-entry midwives, then, often rely on medical authority to determine what characterizes a normal birth and what physical factors define low versus high risk in pregnancy. Home births attended by direct-entry midwives must be nonmedical births.

Midwifery and Reproductive Technologies

Direct-entry midwives practicing today must reconcile their ideology of practice with the increasing cultural use of reproductive technologies. For example, many modern midwives want legal sanction to perform an episiotomy in an emergency or to administer drugs such as pitocin or methergine to stop a postpartum hemorrhage. Also, an infant might require oxygen for resuscitation. If perineal tissue tears slightly during delivery, many direct-entry midwives would rather suture the mother at home than transport her to the hospital.

Some conditions that medical knowledge systems consider high risk for home birth can be assessed before an emergency occurs—such as a mother who desires a vaginal birth after a previous cesarean section (VBAC), a woman who is carrying twins, or a baby who is persistently in a breech position. However, twins and breeches can come as a surprise during labor, and some women elect to stay home even after they become aware of these conditions, if their midwives feel confident in helping them. For example, midwife Valerie El Halta states: "I have caught more than 20 sets of twins, assisted with more than 100 successful VBACs, and have caught more than 100 babies who happened to choose a breech position. I remain adamant in my belief that these deliveries, while demanding great respect, do not necessarily portend greater risk to either mother or her baby" (1996:22).

Although a few states grant direct-entry midwives certain autonomy in making decisions about the risk in these conditions, state regulation carefully limits the midwives' legal access to reproductive technologies and prohibits their legal handling of high-risk conditions at home.

234

Moreover, state-sanctioned access to medical tools can become a trade-off—in some states direct-entry midwives eliminated attending breech, VBAC, and multiple gestations at home from their practice to gain the legal right to carry pitocin, suture, and perform episiotomies. This trade-off represents to many midwives such as El Halta not only a loss of autonomy but also a loss of knowledge—information that, for example, midwives such as Ina May Gaskin have passed on to each other regarding successful ways to turn breech babies without medical intervention.

The difficulty that direct-entry midwives have in gaining access to even limited medical tools during emergencies is part of traditional midwifery's centuries-long relationship with medical procedures and technologies (for general reviews of the medical profession's historical relationship to midwifery and reproductive rights, see Starr 1982; Corea 1988; Oakley 1989; Rothman 1989; Martin 1991; Rowland 1992; Theriot 1993; Borst 1995; Wilson 1995; Moore and Clarke 1995). In chapter 1, Jeanette Herrle-Fanning describes the period within the history of midwifery when male midwives and physicians gained access to the birth room by way of their anatomical knowledge and reproductive tools (see the mention of the importance of the invention of the forceps in the Introduction; see also Donegan 1978; DeVries 1985; Donnison 1977; Litoff 1978; Roush 1979; Gaskin 1988). We still hear today, from both the midwifery and medical communities, many of the arguments made against midwives' using reproductive technologies when they were first invented. Therefore, the significance of the invention of the forceps—one of the first reproductive technologies used in birth—to the status of midwives is as complex as modern midwives' relationship to technology. For example, Wertz and Wertz speculate that the midwives Herrle-Fanning describes might not have used forceps for several reasons: "Legal restrictions stemming from the power of surgeon's guilds may have prevented it, and the simple force of custom, which associated men with instrumental interferences, may have limited women's use of forceps. Men may have also refused to sell forceps to women, or women may have found that using early versions required a degree of physical strength they did not have" (1977:39). However, many midwives themselves also responded negatively to any attempt to include such technologies in midwifery practice: "Their work, they insisted, was 'contrary' to that of Chamberlen [inventor of the forceps]. They did not use instruments, nor had they any desire to do so, having 'neither parts or hands for that art'" (Donegan 1978:27). Use of the forceps simply did not belong in midwives' practice of natural or normal childbirth.

Equally complex is the cultural message that accompanied such medical procedures and tools as the forceps. Women sought the relief from pain, the shortened labor, and the potential of such tools to save their lives and that of their infant during a problematic labor. As Leavitt (1986) explains, when William Shippen introduced such tools to the birth room in 1762 in America,

> Shippen's practice of allaying painful and lengthy labors by bleeding, giving opium, and occasionally using forceps illustrates why women wanted physicians to attend them. The prospect of a difficult birth, which all women fearfully anticipated, and the knowledge that physicians' remedies could provide relief and successful outcomes led women to seek out practitioners whose obstetric armamentarium included drugs and instruments. (40)

Those practitioners who brought relief were medical men, who displaced female midwives. However, although women gained relief from some lengthy and dangerous labors, they lost control and empowerment. As Robbie Davis-Floyd says: "The application of forceps shows the mother beyond all doubt that her machine is indeed defective, and brings home the message that the lives of the mother and her baby are truly dependent on the institution and its technology" (1992:130). The birth experience became hierarchical, with the physician in control: "In the development of obstetrics, the metaphor of the uterus as a machine combines with the use of actual mechanical devices (such as forceps), which played a part in the replacement of female midwives' hands by male hands using tools. . . . The woman's body is the machine and the doctor is the mechanic or technician who 'fixes' it" (Martin 1992:54). Although the forceps were generally replaced by the cesarean section in the twentieth century, modern direct-entry midwives and the state agencies that regulate midwifery still define direct-entry midwifery's relationship to medical procedures and technologies.

Again, although modern direct-entry midwives and their home-birth clients wish a nonmedical birth, many also want legal access to medical procedures and tools that make home birth safe in an emergency. In fact, some direct-entry midwives feel so strongly about this issue that they obtain drugs such as pitocin from friendly physicians and carry the drugs despite any legal admonition against doing so. Thus midwifery guild documents attempt to confirm that direct-entry midwives can handle both emergency situations that require certain procedures and drugs and have the knowledge to handle certain conditions that medical experts consider high risk. For example, the Minnesota Midwives' Guild's *Standards of Care and Certification Guide* (1995) affirms that "the midwife shall have the knowledge and ability to recognize and control postpartum hemorrhage and perform emergency resuscitation of the mother and/or newborn" (20). A member of the New Mexico Midwives' Association may administer pitocin during a postpartum hemorrhage and needs to consult with a physician only if this treatment fails (n.d.:90). Midwives who belong to the Minnesota guild may handle a known multiple gestation when the woman wants a home birth if they consult with other senior midwives (Minnesota Midwives 1995:appendix D).

Therefore, use of medical procedures and tools is no longer inconsistent with the self-image of many direct-entry midwives. One direct-entry midwife, contemplating Texas's licensing rules, decided that access to medical science and technology was appropriate within her personal boundaries for safety:

> I do not believe my ability to start an IV, draw blood, or suture a tear defines me as a midwife. I do believe these skills could be helpful to me and my clients. They could allow me to keep a client out of the medical system when she didn't need to be there, as well as provide opportunities for education and knowledge—and this, for my clients, is power. I also reject the idea that having these skills somehow makes me less a midwife and less pure a practitioner. A midwife can look at these skills as either barriers or bridges; I choose to see them as bridges. (Patsdauter 1996:74)

Some Arizona midwives, restricted by licensing rules from carrying antihemorrhagic drugs, either carry them illegally or ask their clients to get a prescription from a physician for self-administration during an emergency (Sullivan and Weitz 1988:153).

Overall, the language within state laws is more restrictive than within documents produced by the direct-entry midwives themselves regarding how and when the midwife can handle high-risk or emergency situations. For example, Montana regulations specify that the midwife can administer pitocin (for hemorrhage) and xylocaine (for suturing) "only if prescribed by a physician." The Montana midwife may not "perform any operative or surgical procedures except for an episiotomy or simple surgical repair of an episiotomy or simple second-degree laceration." Moreover, in Montana, no direct-entry midwife can accept as a client a woman who "has a fetus in any presentation other than vertex at onset of labor" or "multiple gestation."

Yet many other states, such as Arkansas, Florida, Arizona, and New Hampshire, allow direct-entry midwives to perform episiotomies and to repair first- and second-degree lacerations (women suffering third-

and fourth-degree lacerations must be transported to a medical facility for suturing). Some states allow midwives to administer specific drugs; for example, Alaska, one of the most liberal in its regulation of direct-entry midwives, permits midwives to administer xylocaine hydrochloride and cetacaine for the postpartum repair of tears, lacerations, and episiotomy and pitocin and methergine for postpartum hemorrhage. However, Colorado state law states that "a direct-entry midwife shall not dispense or administer any medication or drugs except for required eye prophylactic therapy," and in Wyoming a midwife may attend home births but cannot offer any prenatal or postpartum care at all. Almost all state statutes pertaining to direct-entry midwifery require that a midwife transfer a woman to a physician's care (if before the onset of labor) or transport her to a medical facility (during labor if time permits) if she is carrying twins, presenting in the breech, or ever had a cesarean.

Although many twentieth-century direct-entry midwives in the United States see certain medical procedures and tools as compatible with their practices, particularly during an emergency, and they often have confidence in their ability to handle conditions ruled high risk by medical authority, their legal access to these aspects of science and technology is limited. Those midwives who are legally recognized by state agencies often trade autonomy for this limited access to medical tools as they give up the right to help clients who want to birth twins and breech presentation babies at home.

Individual Rights and State Obligations

State legislatures charge such agencies as departments of health and boards of medical practice with protecting their citizens, mandating, for example, that the Arkansas Health Department "regulate and ultimately protect the health of the public." Balanced against that charge is the freedom of citizens to birth where and with whom they please (see, for example, Montana's midwife licensing rules). Some states, such as Texas, also consider their tradition of midwifery care, and others, such as Arkansas, consider a shortage of medical providers for handling birth, particularly among poorer citizens. Florida state law expresses this balance of needs and rights as follows:

> The Legislature recognizes the need for a person to have the freedom to choose the manner, cost, and setting for giving birth. The Legislature finds that access to prenatal care and delivery

> services is limited by the inadequate number of providers of such services and that the regulated practice of midwifery may help to reduce this shortage. The Legislature also recognizes the need for the safe and effective delivery of newborn babies and the health, safety, and welfare of their mothers in the delivery process. The Legislature finds that the interests of public health require the regulation of the practice of midwifery in this state for the purpose of protecting the health and welfare of mothers and infants. Therefore, it is unlawful for any person to practice midwifery in this state unless such person is licensed pursuant to the provisions of this chapter.

Central to this balance of rights and protections is the issue of who determines whether and when the "health and welfare of mothers and infants" are jeopardized or enhanced by home birth and direct-entry midwifery care. Whose voice counts in the discourse that creates the authoritative knowledge about birth? Given the autonomy that direct-entry midwives may sacrifice to gain limited access to medical tools and procedures, do they gain a greater voice in the public discourse about birth?

With few exceptions, through informed consent the state citizen must legally acknowledge the risks rather than the benefits of home birth and direct-entry midwifery care to, in essence, retain the right to birth where and with whom she chooses. With few exceptions, to protect their citizens from poor choices or unqualified practitioners, state agencies rely on medical knowledge systems to assess the risks of home birth and midwifery care in each case. Again, the direct-entry midwife has limited ability to contribute to the knowledge about birth within the legally sanctioned and public discourse. In contrast, direct-entry midwifery ideology assumes that the woman takes responsibility for her decision. For example, the Minnesota Midwives' Guild's *Standards of Care* (1995) states: "Healthy childbearing women and their families have the right and responsibility to seek information on birth and thus make an educated evaluation of their place of birth. . . . Each birthing woman shall assume responsibility for her birth, and the safety of the environment according to her emotional, physical and spiritual needs" (v).

However, most state regulatory laws require that the birth parents sign an informed consent form before a direct-entry midwife may attend them. For example, Alaska's state licensing division states: "A certified direct-entry midwife shall inform a woman seeking home birth of the possible risks of home birth and shall obtain a signed informed consent, including the recommendation for a physical examination required . . . before the onset of labor." Colorado state law declares: "The general assembly hereby finds, determines, and declares that the authority granted in this article for the provision of unlicensed midwifery services does not constitute an endorsement of such practices, and that it is incumbent upon the individual seeking such services to ascertain the qualifications of the registrant direct-entry midwife." The parents must acknowledge that they know the risks of home birth and direct-entry midwifery care.

A few states allow the direct-entry midwife to assess that risk. For example, Oregon regulations state:

> The midwife provides health care, support and information to women throughout pregnancy. She determines the need for consultation or referral as appropriate. The midwife uses a foundation of knowledge and/or skill [e.g., "methods of diagnosing pregnancy" and "identification of, implications or and appropriate treatment for various infections, disease conditions and other problems which may affect pregnancy"].

However, the majority of states that regulate direct-entry midwives require a screening exam by a physician and referral or transfer of care when the midwife or the physician perceives high-risk conditions. For example, Arkansas requires that each "patient" be "evaluated by a physician practicing obstetrics at or near the time that care is initiated and again at or near the 36th week." Florida law requires direct-entry midwives to "risk screen potential patients" and "if the risk factor score reaches 3 points the midwife shall consult with a physician who has obstetrical hospital privileges." If the physician and midwife "jointly" determine that the woman can expect a normal delivery, the midwife can continue to attend her. VBACs and women who have had five or more pregnancies receive an automatic risk score of 3. In most states, multiple gestation and breech presentation require physician referral and consultation. For example, Colorado law states:

> A direct-entry midwife shall not provide care to a pregnant woman who, according to generally accepted medical standards, exhibits signs or symptoms of increased risk of medical or obstetric or neonatal complications or problems during the completion of her pregnancy, labor, delivery, or the postpartum period. Such complications include but are not limited to signs or symptoms of diabetes, multiple gestation, hypertensive disorder, or abnormal presentation of the fetus.

Thus state legislatures and agencies use medical knowledge systems, particularly in assessing risk, to survey and normalize birth. Again, in the words of Foucault (1979), normalization and surveillance are "instruments of power" by "indicating membership in a homogenous social body but also playing a part in classification, hierarchization and the distribution of rank. In a sense, the power of normalization imposes homogeneity; but it individualizes by making it possible to measure gaps, to determine levels, to fix specialties and to render differences useful by fitting them one to another" (184). Under state regulation, although each case of pregnancy can be individualized according to medical standards, such as Florida's three-point risk standard, all pregnancies and births seem to carry inherent risk unless proved the exception.

"Power is exercised rather than possessed," proposed Foucault (1979: 26). Strategic positions—often rhetorical strategies—link power and knowledge. "Power is everywhere; not because it embraces everything, but because it comes from everywhere. . . . Power is not an institution, and not a structure . . . it is the name that one attributes to a complex strategical situation in a particular society" (1990:93). But in the case of direct-entry midwives, the medical communities upon which state agencies rely do not seem to be exercising power simply because they can. In fact, the legal status and defining language of direct-entry midwifery and home birth reflect a greater complexity. Contemporary culture finds birth risky outside the hospital setting. A pregnant woman must pass an examination, conducted frequently by a physician, and sign a waiver before a licensed direct-entry midwife can stay home with her. Although the midwife may be confident about her knowledge about birth, as acquired through experience and apprenticeship within her own discourse community, medical knowledge continually questions home birth. A midwife *might* refuse a client for any number of reasons—her own family needs, the number of clients she has at the moment, whether the client's philosophy fits her own—but she *must* refuse a client whose condition is considered high risk by her licensing board. Even though the contemporary direct-entry midwife relies primarily on her heart and hands to "catch" her clients' babies, she wants legal access to all medical procedures and tools that would make home birth safe.

As Joseph Rouse, the scholar of philosophy and science, would say in his study of Foucault,

> Knowledge is established not only in relation to a field of statements but also of objects, instruments, practices, research pro-

grams, skills, social networks, and institutions. . . . Taken by itself, a statement, a technique or skill, a practice, or a machine cannot count as knowledge. Only in the way it is used, and thereby increasingly connected to other elements over time, does it become (and remain) epistemically significant. (1994:110)

A rhetorical analysis of the regulatory discourse about direct-entry midwifery in the United States reveals that, although the licensed direct-entry midwife gains limited legal access to medical tools and procedures, she and her client lose some aspects of their freedom to choose how and where to birth. The official truth about birth is that it is often risky, requiring medical intervention, and that home birth should be available only to those subscribing to essential aspects of medical knowledge systems about birth. In the United States at the close of the twentieth century, the empowering experience of birth within the woman-centered environment of the home is available to the very few.

REFERENCES

Borst, C. G. 1995. *Catching babies: The professionalization of childbirth, 1870–1920.* Cambridge, Mass.: Harvard University Press.
Corea, Gena. 1988. *The mother machine: Reproductive technologies from artificial insemination to artificial wombs.* London: Women's Press.
Davis-Floyd, Robbie. 1992. *Birth as an American rite of passage.* Berkeley: University of California Press.
DeVries, R. G. 1985. *Regulating birth: Midwives, medicine, and the law.* Philadelphia: Temple University Press.
Donegan, J. B. 1978. *Women and men midwives: Medicine, morality, and misogyny in early America.* Westport, Conn.: Greenwood.
Donnison, Jean. 1977. *Midwives and medical men.* London: Heinemann.
El Halta, Valerie. 1996. Normalizing the breech delivery. *Midwifery Today* 38:22–24, 41.
Foucault, Michel. 1979. *Discipline and punish: The birth of the prison.* Translated by Alan Sheridan. New York: Vintage.
Foucault, Michel. 1990. *The history of sexuality: An introduction.* Vol. 1. New York: Vintage.
Gaskin, I. M. 1988. Midwifery re-invented. In Sheila Kitzinger, ed., *The midwife challenge,* pp. 42–60. London: Pandora.
Gaskin, I. M. 1990. *Spiritual midwifery.* 3d ed. Summertown, Tenn.: Book Publishing Co.
Gaskin, I. M. 1994. Regional reports: Region 3, South. *MANA News* (Midwives' Alliance of North America), November, pp. 6–7.

Illg, Susan. 1991. A recommendation regarding the legal and regulatory status of traditional midwives in Minnesota. Unpublished master's thesis, Humphrey Center for Public Affairs, University of Minnesota.

Leavitt, J. W. 1986. *Brought to bed: Childbearing in America, 1750 to 1950.* New York: Oxford University Press.

Litoff, J. B. 1978. *American midwives, 1860 to the present.* Westport, Conn.: Greenwood.

Martin, Emily. 1991. The egg and the sperm: How science has constructed a romance based on stereotypical male-female roles. *Signs* 16:485–501.

Martin, Emily. 1992. *The woman in the body: A cultural analysis of reproduction.* Boston: Beacon.

McNay, Lois. 1994. *Foucault: A critical introduction.* New York: Continuum.

Midwives' Alliance of North America (MANA). 1994. Core competencies: Guiding principles of practice. *MANA News* (Midwives' Alliance of North America), November, pp. 31–33.

Minnesota Midwives' Guild. 1995. *Standards of care and certification guide.* Minneapolis: Genesis Midwives' Writing Collective.

Moore, L. J., and A. E. Clarke. 1995. Clitoral conventions and transgressions: Graphic representatives in anatomy texts, c. 1900–1991. *Feminist Studies* 21:255–301.

Oakley, Ann. 1989. *The captured womb: A history of the medical care of pregnant women.* New York: Basil Blackwell.

Patsdauter, Vicki. 1996. In my opinion. *Midwifery Today* 40:73–74.

Penn, MariMikel. 1995. Regional reports: Region 9, South Central. *MANA News* (Midwives' Alliance of North America), July, p. 10.

Rothman, B. K. 1989. *Recreating motherhood: Ideology and technology in a patriarchal society.* New York: Norton.

Rouse, Joseph. 1994. Power/knowledge. In Gary Gutting, ed., *The Cambridge companion to Foucault*, pp. 92–114. New York: Cambridge University Press.

Roush, R. E. 1979. The development of midwifery—Male and female, yesterday and today. *Journal of Nurse-Midwifery* 24:27–37.

Rowland, Robyn. 1992. *Living laboratories: Women and reproductive technologies.* Bloomington: Indiana University Press.

Schlinger, Hilary. 1996. New York state: Witch-hunt or political strategy? *MANA News* (Midwives' Alliance of North America), January, pp. 1, 24–25.

Starr, Paul. 1982. *The social transformation of American medicine.* New York: Basic.

Sullivan, D. A., and Rose Weitz. 1988. *Labor pains: Modern midwives and home birth.* New Haven, Conn.: Yale University Press.

Theriot, N. M. 1993. Women's voices in nineteenth-century medical discourse: A step toward deconstructing science. *Signs* 19:1–31.

Treichler, P. A. 1990. Feminism, medicine, and the meaning of childbirth. In Mary Jacobus, E. F. Keller, and Sally Shuttleworth, eds., *Body/politics: Women and the discourses of science*, pp. 113–38. New York: Routledge.

Webster, Karen. 1997. Regional reports: Region 2, North Atlantic. *MANA News* (Midwives' Alliance of North America), January, p. 5.

Wertz, R. W., and D. C. Wertz. 1977. *Lying-in: A history of childbirth in America.* New York: Free Press.

Wilson, Adrian. 1995. *The making of man-midwifery: Childbirth in England, 1660–1770.* Cambridge, Mass.: Harvard University Press.

11 HOT TOMALLEY

WOMEN'S BODIES AND

ENVIRONMENTAL POLITICS

IN THE STATE OF MAINE

BEVERLY SAUER

On February 2, 1994, the Maine Department of Human Services (DHS) issued a Joint Health Advisory that concluded: "Preliminary analysis of data from tests conducted on lobsters taken off the coast of Maine indicates unacceptably high concentrations of dioxin in lobster tomalley (the lobster liver) but not in lobster meat. These results have prompted state officials to issue a health advisory against the consumption (eating) of tomalley by pregnant women, nursing mothers and women of child bearing age." The department warned, however, that "others should limit their consumption of tomalley, as dioxin found in tomalley will contribute to the overall intake of this chemical, and to cancer risk generally."

The controversy over dioxin in Maine pitted opponents of regulation against environmentalists, sportfishers, and Native Americans with tribal rights to fish in clean waters. Maine's legislature had been considering an act to establish a numeric water quality criterion for dioxin—a carcinogen and known toxic substance produced as a by-product of paper mills in Maine. Dioxin in Maine rivers polluted more than local water supplies: Maine's rivers carried the toxin downstream to estuaries and rich Atlantic fisheries. The threat of cancer from lobster tomalley would bankrupt coastal communities dependent on summer tourism. Increased regulation, on the other hand, could drive industry to close outdated facilities or seek friendlier regulatory climates. As testimony reveals, the issues were muddied by competing interests: weekend fishers worked for the paper companies, which were the direct source of dioxin in the Penobscot River, and tourists liked clean rivers as well as lobster (Margolin and Bailey 1992; Lachter 1993; Jones 1993; Georgia-Pacific 1993; Collins 1993; Banks 1993; Amaral and Carr 1993; Otis 1993; Marriott 1993; Pardilla 1993; Walsh 1993).

From an environmental perspective, the dioxin debate in Maine raises interesting and problematic questions about the ways that risk communicators foreground the reproductive value of women's bodies in the public debate about a chemical that is potentially toxic in quantities that are too small to measure by ordinary means. Given the wide range of populations at risk, for example, why did the Maine DHS target women of childbearing age in its lobster dioxin advisory? What are the consequences of excluding other populations at risk? If the risk were indeed significant, why exclude other special populations—particularly Native Americans and sportfishers. If, on the other hand, the risk were founded on improbable uncertainties or overenthusiasm on the part of environmentalists, why didn't the DHS simply ignore risk warnings and encourage the ordinary cultural practices of enjoying and preparing lobster? Such a conclusion would argue for a more rational or balanced approach to regulation that is consistent with the distanced objectivity of what feminists have called "male-stream science" (Code, Mullett, and Overall 1988; Code 1991; Harding 1991; Keller 1985, 1990; Merchant 1989).

This chapter combines the descriptive methods of recent research in risk and decision science (Dawes 1988; Fischhoff 1996; Morgan et al. 1996) and the analytical methods of feminist rhetorical theory to examine the ways that risk communicators foreground the reproductive value of women's bodies in risk assessment and public policy (Sauer 1993, 1994; Frank and Treichler 1989; Treichler 1989; McConnell-Ginet 1989; Hacker 1990). This analysis suggests that risk communicators construct two different rhetorical frameworks to define the problem of risk. In the scientific reports that preceded the DHS advisory (including a "comprehensive, scientific reassessment of dioxin and related compounds since 1991" by the U.S. Environmental Protection Agency [EPA], an external review of drafts of the reassessment documents, and public comment and review by the EPA's Science Advisory Board [EPA 1994:1], as well as related correspondence in the Maine Department of Agriculture), scientists acknowledge the uncertainty of their findings and focus instead on the relative risks to special populations. In this arena, women's bodies are clearly marked (identified) as gendered. Other androgynous classes like "sportfishers" conceal the gender markings that categorize individuals within the class. In the public arena, characterized by reports in the *Bangor Daily News* and testimony in the

Maine legislature, on the other hand, writers redefine the problem of risk as a question of scientific uncertainty in which conflicting scientific evidence and interpretation reflect the economic interests of well-defined and well-funded political opponents (Beal 1994; Porter 1994; Kloehn 1994; Kekacs 1993, 1994). In this arena, the DHS advisory is "good news" to the extent that it suggests that dioxin risk is limited to one clearly marked segment of the population (Astbury 1994).

The Maine DHS advisory used data from an EPA draft assessment to justify its warning to women, but the agency selectively filtered data that would suggest potential risks to (predominantly male) sport-fishers, members of the Penobscot Nation, and other special populations (USEPA 1994; "EPA Analysis" 1993). As this chapter argues, the presumed naturalness of the reproductive value of women's bodies enabled the DHS to argue for the presumed naturalness of a policy restricted to women. This argument resolved the problem of risk in both arenas: The DHS advisory provided the missing argumentative premise (in rhetorical terms, the enthymeme) in the DHS's rhetorical leap from scientific data (high levels of dioxin) to its consequent conclusion ("therefore, women must limit their consumption of dioxin") without engaging the public controversy that would surround a general limit on lobster consumption. (In chapter 12 Mary Thompson shows how arguments in favor of women's rights can also be used to shift the focus of the policy debates away from issues of safety and health.)

While the marginalization of women's bodies in the public domain supports feminist theories that argue that science policy has traditionally silenced, omitted, or excluded women's voices and experiences, analysis of the DHS advisory suggests that policy makers may also foreground the reproductive value of women's bodies in order to manage the public opposition to risk management policies that would threaten a more general (and public) notion of economic and social well-being. In examining the silences and omissions in a public policy targeted specifically at women, my analysis reveals the tensions between science as *public* policy and science as situated knowledge addressed toward deliberately gendered populations at risk.

Marked Women and Female Lobsters: The Maine Health Advisory

According to the DHS advisory, the agency targeted "pregnant women, nursing mothers, and women of childbearing age" because developing children were at "highest risk" for injury from exposure to dioxin. The advisory warned "others" to limit their consumption because "dioxin found in tomalley will contribute to the overall intake of this chemical" and thus to "cancer risk generally." The advisory notes that Maine had been sampling dioxin in fish since 1988 but had not included lobsters until 1993, when tests revealed "unexpectedly high" concentrations of dioxin in the tomalley (13.4–30.7 parts per trillion or ppt) but not in the meat. The advisory adds that the Maine advisory is "similar" to a Massachusetts advisory and to other "cautionary statements issued by the seafood marketing industry."

In advising women of childbearing and reproductive age to limit consumption of tomalley, the Maine DHS "marked" childbearing females as a special population at risk and defined other special populations as "others." From a feminist perspective, such marking is both biological and political. Biological markings distinguish male and female within a species and thus can be argued to be "natural" or "objective" indicators of physiological and biological difference. Political markings, on the other hand, create and construct difference. From a rhetorical perspective, biological markings enable writers to argue for a natural distinction between members of a race or species. Political markings, on the other hand, are neither natural nor objective, although they may be used to argue for the naturalness of particular ideologies and cultural distinctions.

Maine's environmental policies literally mark female lobsters to protect an endangered and declining population. When egg-bearing females are trapped, lobster fishers notch the tail fin of the female with a small *V* and return the lobster to the water as a "breeding female." It is illegal to sell or eat a "marked female" in Maine. Because male lobsters can theoretically impregnate more than one female, their presence is presumed not as important—statistically—in the reproductive health of lobster populations in general. Rather than address the larger political and economic causes that affect lobster populations (including overfishing and poorly regulated markets), Maine targets an easily recognizable population.

The analogy between marked human females and marked lobsters suggests that the Maine DHS used a similar policy to address the problem of dioxin. But the analogy does not reflect differences in mating habits of the two species. While human males can also theoretically impregnate more than one female—and thus by analogy might be excluded from the advisory—individual human males might argue for a more inclusive approach to population policy and environmental health on the ground that social conventions prescribe a more restricted notion of sexual activity.

The lens of gender suggests a more important flaw in the DHS advisory, however. If policy makers value all members of a species equally, male and female, adult and child, they must mark all members of the species. If the risk were indeed significant, for example, the DHS should have issued advisories for all consumers—or at least affected subpopulations (including primarily Native Americans and fishermen). Such a conclusion is logically linked to the scientific findings in the EPA draft assessment that was the basis for the advisory and argues for an ethical or more broadly conceived "humanist" solution to the problem. As the EPA draft assessment suggests, however, special populations with more direct exposure face different kinds of risk.

Marking Special Populations at Risk

In April 1994, the EPA presented its long-delayed findings in a draft reassessment of the dioxin controversy. A summary of the EPA draft reassessment, published as "Dioxin Facts," clearly articulates the uncertainties inherent in regulating a hazard that is potentially toxic in parts per trillion (USEPA 1994). The summary concedes that "the levels of dioxin and related compounds in the environment and in food in the US are based on relatively few samples and must be considered quite uncertain" (1). Each section of the report defines a different problem of certainty and uncertainty in science: the controversial nature of scientific findings; the problem of detecting clearly adverse effects; the relationship between animal and human biochemistry and physiology; the problem of generalizing about data drawn from occupational exposures; the wide spectrum of human response; and the nature of the linear and mechanical relationships that can be inferred from the data.

Two features of risk complicate the uncertainty of the EPA findings. First, the report notes, it is impossible to predict the level of "background exposure" in the general environment. This background exposure is not readily identifiable, although the report notes that "body burden levels among industrial nations are relatively similar" (2). In addition to "general population exposure," the report notes, "some individuals or groups of individuals may also be exposed to dioxin-like compounds from discrete sources or pathways locally within their environment" (2). These "special exposures" create significantly higher risks than daily exposures to the general population. As a result, the report notes, "simply evaluating these exposures as average daily intakes pro-rated over a lifetime might obscure the potential significance of elevated exposures for these sub-populations, particularly if exposures occur for a short period of time during critical times during growth and development of children" (2). Examples of these "special exposures" include "occupational exposures, direct or indirect exposure of local populations to discrete sources, exposure of nursing infants from mother's milk, or exposures of subsistence or recreational fishers" (2). The report describes the adaptive and adverse changes that occur in both male and female reproductive systems in these special populations:

> These facts and assumptions lead to the inference that some more highly exposed members of the general population or more highly exposed, special populations may be at risk for a number of adverse effects including developmental toxicity based on the inherent sensitivity of the developing organism to changes in cellular biochemistry and/or physiology, *reduced reproductive capacity in males* based on *decreased sperm counts,* higher probability of experiencing *endometriosis in women,* reduced ability to withstand an immunological challenge and *others.* (4–5; emphasis added)

Although the DHS advisory does not recommend specific consumption limits for other special populations at risk, a memo from the Maine Department of Agriculture, Food, and Rural Resources (Hicks n.d.) reveals the large number and highly local character of these special populations. According to this memo, tests on eight uncooked lobster samples revealed levels of TCDD (tetrachloro-p-dibenodioxin) equivalents in the muscles (claw and tails) that were less than 1.3 ppt. The level in the tomalley, however, ranged from 13.4 ppt to 30.7 ppt.

Based on these findings—and in the absence of a long-delayed EPA reassessment—the Department of Agriculture cautions that it is difficult to develop a "realistic estimate of the number of lobster (meat only) meals or tomalley meals per year" (2). The researchers thus advise pregnant women to limit their consumption of lobster tomalley meals per month to three. For the general population, they note, the number of lobsters that might produce a cancer-risk level of 1 per 100,000 ranges from 31 to 71 tomalley meals per year. At these levels of risk, pregnant women could eat approximately 15 lobster (meat) meals per month; others could eat approximately 150 lobster meat meals per year without significantly increasing their cancer risk.

For most readers, who might find even one lobster meal per month— or even per year—a luxury, such estimates may suggest that the advisory grossly overstates the problem of dioxin. As the Department of Agriculture memo notes, however, pregnant women could exceed safe limits "if the person was with a group eating lobster and ate the tomalley from the available lobster" (2). While few midwesterners might consume 31 to 71 lobster tomalley meals per year, Maine lobster fishers, residents in coastal communities, and sportfishers—male and female— could also exceed the recommended number of meals per year.

In specifying safe limits for lobster consumption, neither the DHS advisory nor the Department of Agriculture memo addresses the problem of "background sources" of dioxin from food sources like inland fish, environmental pollutants, coffee filters, and tampons (which are regulated by the U.S. Food and Drug Administration, not the EPA). In calculating the risk for lobster consumption, for example, the Department of Agriculture memo assumes "one 1 lb. lobster meal/month @94.1 g meat and 19.3 g tamale [*sic*] per meal, and no 'background' exposure." Given the relative increase in fish consumption in the United States, however, figures based solely upon lobster consumption may underrepresent the amount of dioxin from carp, eel, sunfish, and catfish—particularly in fish caught downstream from major point sources of dioxin like paper mills (Margolin and Bailey 1992). Even without background pollution, the figures suggest, ten Mainers will die each year from dioxin-related cancer deaths in a state with a population of only one million.

The problem of dioxin exposure is particularly critical for "unique classes of resource uses" like the Penobscot Indians, who consume large quantities of fish and wildlife. In testimony before the Maine Committee on Energy and Natural Resources, Jerry R. Pardilla, governor of the Penobscot tribe, notes the increased risk for children and sportfishers and, more important, members of the Penobscot Nation with tribal rights to fishing in the Penobscot River: "Most data is generated by surveying the holders of state fishing licenses. Sustenance fishing by tribal members does not require a state license nor does fishing by children. . . . My people are at greater risk because of their high consumption of wild food and fish. This factor must be given due consideration in any deliberation of the topic" (1993:2).

As the banner headlines in the *Bangor Daily News* on February 3, 1994, suggest, any limits on lobster consumption could threaten the livelihood and recreation of "other" unmarked populations at risk. Fortunately, the news broke in February, when few tourists visited the state and the lobster catch was low.

Good News: Marked Women in an Unmarked Environment

The *Bangor Daily News* (BDN) covered the advisory in a series of three related reports—with three distinct headlines—as the lead story on February 3, 1994: "State Issues Advisory for Lobster Eaters"; "Lobstermen React to Health Warning"; and "Dioxin Enters Rivers as Mill Waste." Two subheadings reveal the focus of the *BDN*'s report: "Tomalley Dioxin Level 'Unacceptably High'" and "Anger Mixed with Relief Meat Is OK."

Given the conflicting interests in the dioxin debate, the *BDN* faced a difficult problem (Kloehn 1994). A sidebar on the front page directs readers to a comic commentary about the problem of putting the proper "spin" on a story replete with political, environmental, and social overtones. In "Hot Tomalley, Science and Green Stuff," Steve Kloehn, a columnist for the *BDN*, jokes about a particularly stupid (female) tourist who complained that restaurant owners had given her a bad lobster because she didn't know what the green stuff (tomalley) in her lobster was.

The *BDN*'s spin turns a potentially disastrous news story into "good news": in three front-page news stories the *BDN* constructs a narrative that vindicates lobster meat, emphasizes the uncertainty and relativity of scientific findings, and celebrates the focus on women of reproductive age because the advisory shows that "others" can continue to consume lobsters in moderation. Only the tomalley is affected, thus vindicating the lobster body meat. In covering the issue from the perspective of competing interests in Maine economy, the *BDN* clearly did not see the DHS's focus on women as an indication of larger problems in the environment.

As the carefully balanced layout of the *BDN* demonstrates, the controversy over dioxin pitted opponents of regulation against environmentalists, fishermen, and Native American tribes with tribal rights to fishing in clean waters. Each article puts a positive spin on the DHS advisory.

In "State Issues Advisory for Lobster Eaters: Tomalley Dioxin Level 'Unacceptably High,'" for example, Ned Porter of the *BDN* staff cites Lani Graham of the DHS, who argues that the DHS warning is "a conservative approach. . . . A woman could eat a 1¼ pound lobster and its tomalley three times a month without adverse risk" (Porter 1994:1).

Porter acknowledges that the warning was confined to women because infants, newborns, and fetuses are considered to be at the highest risk for possible injury from dioxin, which has been linked to cancer and birth defects in animals. Although Porter cites the advisory's warning that "others" should limit their consumption of tomalley, he does not identify these others. Instead, Porter frames the debate as a familiar and ongoing antagonism between industry and environmentalists over the significance of scientific findings. Porter notes, "The announcement set to boiling the simmering feud between environmentalists and the paper industry over dioxin" (1). This political controversy frames the discussion of the significance of the advisory and suggests that scientific data inevitably reflect the competing economic and ideological interests of interpreters.

Porter cites expert informants to a positive spin on the DHS advisory. Floyd Rutherford, president of the Maine Paper Industry Information Office, for example, argues that the wide range of dioxin levels in lobsters taken from different sites suggests that the control group was insignificant (Porter 1994:1). Robert Bayer, a lobster specialist at the University of Maine, cautions that "any measurements that have to be taken in parts per trillion have to be suspect" (Astbury 1994:1). Susan Barber of the Maine Lobster Promotion Council transforms the "bad news" into good news: she suggests that the state's advisory was, in fact, a "reassuring indication of the lobster's natural defense system at work, keeping lobster meat wholesome, nutritious, and delicious" (Porter 1994:2). No experts question the significance of findings that focus on women; none describes the health effects on local populations at risk.

In a second article, "Lobstermen React to Health Warning: Anger Mixed with Relief Meat Is OK," Carroll Astbury repeats the notion that the warning means good news: lobster meat is OK; the warning simply means that the tomalley is doing its job (1994:1). Astbury's lead clearly puts a positive spin on the Maine advisory: "Some [lobstermen] were angry. Others were skeptical. But most of all, Maine's lobstermen were glad the state's warning about lobster tomalley came in the middle of winter when consumption is at a low point. They also were thankful that the warning was limited to tomalley and didn't include the delicious meat."

In the final article in the series, "Dioxin Enters Rivers as Mill Waste," Andrew Kekacs attempts to address more specifically the scientific and technical issues that surround the dioxin debate in Maine. Kekacs emphasizes that dioxin is produced "in *tiny amounts* by seven paper mills that use chlorine to bleach wood pulp. The chemicals pass through waste treatment systems and eventually are released into Maine rivers" (1994:1; emphasis added). According to Kekacs, the EPA considers dioxin to be one of the most dangerous manmade substances, but controversy surrounds testing programs that cost about $1,000 per test. Kekacs notes that a forthcoming EPA report will "resolve the dispute" between "scientists for the paper industry"—who dispute the health risks attributed to dioxin—and "other researchers [who] claim the chemical is more dangerous than originally feared." Like other *BDN* writers, Kekacs does not address the scientific and technical issues relating to women as the focus of the advisory.

Together, these three articles frame the issues in controversy in the debate: (1) the scientific uncertainties inherent in studying a chemical toxic in parts per trillion; (2) the significance of research results based upon small, local samples; and (3) the lack of agreement between scientists representing different interests. (In popular terms, these issues are reframed as (1) "overreaction to scientific findings"; (2) the "spin" put on these findings; and (3) the political and economic sellout of science in the service of economic and political interests.) These issues become critical in defining a responsible *public* policy, but they do not address the needs of special populations at risk who are unmarked in the DHS advisory.

Invisibly Marked Men in a Market Economy: Testimony in the Maine Legislature

As the articles in the *BDN* and testimony in the Maine legislature suggest, Maine faced political and economic pressure not to mark these other invisibly gendered populations at risk. As the debate in the Maine legislature suggests, any limits on the consumption of fish would violate the Penobscot Nation's sovereign rights under the Maine Indian Land Claims Settlement Acts and stigmatize "Native American populations" as "a special population at risk." If Maine marked the (predominantly male) category of sportfishers of reproductive age, on the other hand, the DHS would alienate unions, paper companies, and tourists who contributed to the state's fragile economic tax base. Neither solution would be tenable in Maine's fragile economic climate.

As testimony in the Maine legislature suggests, these men recognize themselves as a population at risk in the economic environment. To justify the state's environmental health, they point to visible signs in the environment—spawning salmon—as indices of clean water and low emissions. Defined as "others" by the DHS advisory, they do not "see" measurable signs of dioxin in the environment.

In his 1993 testimony before the Maine Legislature's Committee on Energy and Natural Resources, Doug Jones reveals the close link between unions, paper companies, sportfishermen of reproductive age, and local politics when he introduces his testimony opposing stricter water quality standards. In identifying himself as "fisherman, hunter, and canoer," Jones appeals to a strong Maine tradition that links hunting to the preservation of "native" Maine values and traditions of independence—values that distinguish native Mainers from flatlanders (people "from away") (1).

For men like Jones, the issue of survival is economic rather than environmental. They see themselves—and their lifestyle—at risk if paper mills leave the state. As a former employee of Georgia-Pacific and chairman of the Baileyville Town Council, Jones recognizes the link between tighter standards and the economic security of Maine towns dependent on paper companies as the sole source of employment. He testifies: "Although we're concerned about the recent cutbacks in employment and the loss of expansion that has occurred in our town, we firmly believe that the environment and industry are compatible, and in woodland and Maine, Georgia-Pacific has been the leader in environmental issues—having spent well over $200 million to prove it in the last 20 years" (2).

Jones's maleness marks him as a population at risk in Maine in two senses. Like women and female lobsters, his economic and biological survival depends upon the "Margin of Exposure" standards (guidelines for dioxin release) set by policy makers in Augusta and Washington, D.C. From Jones's perspective, the risk to his reproductive and immunological health is speculative and uncertain. The risk to his economic survival, on the other hand, is highly visible in the closed factories, abandoned storefronts, and unemployed men who must find new lifestyles in Maine's delicate economy.

Jones thus defends his employer's stance toward the environment and opposes increased regulation: according to Jones, state testing on bass below the Georgia-Pacific mill showed "no signs of dioxin." Georgia-Pacific's emissions are below current EPA standards. Jones praises his employer's attempts to lower dioxin emissions and points to visible signs in the environment—salmon spawning in the St. Croix River—to demonstrate the visible signs of a cleaner environment. For Jones, increasing the standards would create an "uneven playing field" that would jeopardize Georgia-Pacific's success in reducing dioxin in the environment. Jones testifies: "E.P.A. has already checked and tested Georgia-Pacific's bleach process and *could not* find any dioxin in any discharge except once in the course of exhaustive testing which Georgia-Pacific Woodland volunteered as part of a nationwide volunteer study. That measurement was below E.P.A. standards" (1).

Jones's testimony points to the problem of regulating a substance toxic in quantities too small to measure with ordinary means. If we add the lens of gender to this analysis, however, the presence of marked females within a population may also serve as powerful and visible evidence of the reproductive health—or sickness—of both human and lobster species.

Marked Populations as Signs of Risk

Mainers like Jones interpret and give meaning to events, objects, and experiences in the environment in order to give meaning to signs like spawning salmon in a stream. These signs—in the ordinary meaning of the term—construct a body of past commonplaces that provide guidelines and standards to guide interpretations and decisions in the present: "Plant your corn when the maple leaf is the size of the ear of a mouse." "Red sky at dawning, sailors take warning. Red sky at night, sailor's delight." As the environment responds to new toxins, Mainers have developed a new set of signs to indicate new risks: Red skies at night now mean high levels of atmospheric pollutants. Fishkills in harbors mean low levels of oxygen. Dead firs mean acid rain.

Rhetoricians like Perelman and Olbrechts-Tyteca (1971) distinguish between *signs*—deliberate acts that contain meaning—and *indices*—events and conditions in the environment that humans interpret. An open window may be a sign if a person opened the window as a signal or an index of the temperature signifying a continuing heat wave.

Indices make visible underlying problems in a system that are too small to see with ordinary human senses. They provide visible sensory data that allow decision makers to assess risk and hazard in a changing system. Decreasing barometric pressures, for example, predict stormy weather. Ozone measurements provide an index of air quality; pH levels indicate acid levels in streams and rivers. To measure risk and hazard in the environment, scientists construct indices based upon a body of past experiences in order to predict consequences in the future.

When lobster fishers mark female lobsters, they create signs—deliberate acts—to signify a female of reproductive age. Other lobster fishers recognize (literally, "see") these signs and agree to return marked females to the breeding population. But the number of marked females can also provide an index of the reproductive health of a system. The greater the number of marked females, the greater the ability of the species to reproduce.

Indices are not deliberate human acts like signs. To create an index, interpreters must construct categories and define the meaning of particular phenomena within a system. A particular index—the number of marked females, for example—may be related to the number of other variables—the number of lobster licenses issued in a year, the temperature of coastal waters, the number of algae present in the water, the increase in seal populations in coastal harbors as well as more serious underlying problems in the environment. As the EPA draft assessment recognizes, scientific indices contain a high level of uncertainty. A decline in the number of marked females, for example, may signify a decline in the number of lobster licenses or a particularly hard winter.

Writers at the DHS faced a difficult rhetorical problem when they constructed the advisory—how to communicate risk to the public without disrupting the political and economic environment of the state and how to talk about a problem that is measurable in quantities too small to detect by ordinary means. Although environmentalists saw the DHS advisory as an index of larger problems in the environment, industry analysts interpreted the advisory as one more attempt to regulate a declining economy. It is easy to discount indices, especially when they challenge cultural habits like eating lobster or when solutions to the problem might threaten the economic survival of other populations in the system.

Postscript: Tomalley in the Feminine Domain—Lobsters as an Index of Culture

Lobster is an index of culture. Mainers grow up eating lobster. They learn what parts to eat and how to deconstruct the bony shell without lobster crackers (which are similar to nutcrackers). Tourists, however, need instruction when they encounter their first lobster in a restaurant or attempt to cook this highly touted delicacy at home.

The DHS warnings raised questions in the public area but did not affect local cookbooks, restaurant place mats, and publicity from the Maine Lobster Promotion Council (1995). Like cigarette warnings and warnings on shellfish consumption, restaurants and fish markets faced difficult ethical and economic decisions in the face of scientific and political uncertainty.

Two publications from the Maine Lobster Promotion Council reveal this difficulty. Following the release of the DHS advisory, the Maine Lobster Promotion Council issued a press release acknowledging that the state Department of Environmental Protection had tested seafood and found dioxin in the tomalley of lobsters. The council noted that "finding the dioxins in the lobster tomalley is regrettable, and certainly a sign of the times in which we live." But the council concluded that the presence of dioxin in the lobster liver is "also a reassuring indication of the lobster's natural defense system at work, keeping the lobster meat wholesome, nutritious and delicious." In the face of the DHS advisory, the Maine Lobster Promotion Council issued the following "advice to consumers and concerned citizens": "(According to the *Advanced Seafood Handbook*) there is no known safety considerations [*sic*] when it comes to eating lobster meat. However consumers are advised not to eat the tomalley, the light green substance found in the lobster's carapace" (Barber 1994).

An information sheet from the Maine Lobster Promotion Council on how to cook a lobster, published one year after the advisory, however, states that both the tomalley (liver) and coral (eggs) make delicious eating:

> All of the MAINE LOBSTER is edible except for the bony shell structure, the small crop or craw in the head of the lobster, and the dark vein running down the back of the body meat. The green material is the liver or tomalley. This is excellent eating, as is the red or coral, which is the lobster's undeveloped spawn.

Eating lobsters is a cultural practice deeply embedded in New England culture and foreign to "others" far from the coast, where it is often perceived as a luxury or an index of high culture. While one might expect Maine publications to praise the virtues of lobster, several national cookbooks also provide recipes for lobster that extol the flavor of tomalley. Julia Child (1996) states: "The creamy green-gray substance in the chest cavity of a cooked lobster is known as tomalley. The female also contains the pink roe. . . . These are prized parts of the lobster, giving flavor and color to sauces and stews" (105). The *Joy of Cooking* (1997) tells readers: "The creamy green [substance] is tomalley (or liver), which is wonderful spread on toasts and served with the lobster" (Rombauer, Becker, and Becker 1997:492).

In targeting women the DHS advisory cannot change cultural practices in those private arenas where it is likely to be most effective—especially when the scientific debate marginalizes the voices of women in the public arena. We are accustomed to holding manufacturers liable for harmful products; we label cigarettes and alcohol; yet we take for granted the instructional quality of cookbooks without examining how these domestic texts help men and women implement policies defined as "public."

The texts I have examined range from popular reports and cookbooks to a scientific assessment of data. In each case, writers attempt to make meaning from scientific statistics and to describe exposure limits and levels of toxicity that can adequately protect the public. In adding the lens of gender to the public debate, we can draw conclusions about the ways in which policy makers construct categories of difference to protect special populations at risk.

The EPA draft assessment marks persons who suffer occupational exposure and sportfishers as populations at risk. Men and women of reproductive age represent subcategories of these special populations at risk. Within these categories, men and women suffer different adverse effects—the result of physiological and anatomical differences between male and female. The EPA report describes the different adverse effects on men and women: "reduced reproductive capacity in males based on decreased sperm counts, higher probability of experiencing endometriosis in women, reduced ability to withstand an immunological challenge and others" (1994:5). In some cases, adverse effects have been detected in studies. In other cases, however, scientists must extrapolate from animal studies and knowledge of the human metabolism in order to predict the probability and severity of noncancerous effects in humans. Thus, the EPA concludes, children may be at greatest risk from direct exposure (through breast milk, for example) because of the assumed increased sensitivity of growing tissues to the effects of dioxin.

Based upon EPA's assumption that children are at greatest risk, the DHS marks women as the sole special population at risk and constructs a category of "others" who must limit their lobster tomalley consumption. The DHS thus marks breeding women, just as lobster fishers mark breeding females to protect the lobster population. The analogy breaks down, of course, in its desired outcomes: the DHS seeks to protect the health of individual children whereas lobster fishers seek to increase the numbers of children in order to increase the population as a whole. If the health of individuals in the species is an issue, then DHS should logically protect both men and women in special populations.

As the testimony in the Maine legislature suggests, issues of reproduction are perceived as outside the debate between environmentalists and industry. The survival of the human population in Maine depends upon adequate resources. Those resources depend upon jobs threatened by environmental regulation. In this context, gender becomes invisible as categories like "sportfishers" take on specific (and gendered) cultural meanings for men like Doug Jones, who see themselves as distinct from both women and Native American populations at risk. Uncertain science has little persuasive power in the face of visible threats to the survival of a culture. In the DHS advisory, men become literally "other" to women. Native Americans are invisible.

Whether DHS writers deliberately targeted men or simply imitated warnings on alcohol and smoking, the DHS advisory ultimately reflects an underlying system of values that targets women as the site of reproduction and reproductive responsibility. These values shape the (1) kinds of information that policy makers consider important in communicating risk to the public; (2) the policies they construct; and (3) the arenas in which they disseminate them. These policies do not adequately protect special populations at risk. They balance the tension between visible economic loss and invisible indexes of risk in the environment. Ultimately, however, risk communicators must learn to address public skepticism about uncertainty without undercutting concern for safety.

REFERENCES

Amaral, Michael, and Kenneth Carr, to George Papadopoulos, Wastewater Management Branch, U.S. Environmental Protection Agency. 1993. January 14 letter regarding meeting summary: Lincoln Pulp and Paper/Dioxin/Bald eagles. Presented to the 116th Maine Legislature's Joint Standing Committee on Energy and Natural Resources. April 28.
Astbury, Carroll. 1994. Lobstermen react to health warning. *Bangor Daily News,* February 3, p. A1.
Banks, Joseph, to Douglas Walsh, Lincoln Pulp and Paper Company. 1993. April 15 [letter regarding] Dioxin in LP&P's effluent.
Barber, Susan. 1994. Memorandum to Consumers and Interested Citizens, Re: Lobster Tomalley. February 2.
Beal, Robert. 1994. Trapped by faulty logic. *Bangor Daily News,* February 3, p. 7.
Child, Julia. 1996. *The way to cook.* New York: Knopf.
Code, Lorraine. 1991. *What can she know? Feminist theory and the construction of knowledge.* Ithaca, N.Y.: Cornell University Press.
Code, Lorraine, Sheila Mullett, and Christine Overall. 1988. *Feminist perspectives: Philosophical essays on method and morals.* Toronto: University of Toronto Press.
Collins, Edward. 1993. Testimony of Edward Collins regarding L.D. 49. Presented to the 116th Maine Legislature's Joint Standing Committee on Energy and Natural Resources. April 28.
Dawes, R. M. 1988. *Rational choice in an uncertain world.* San Diego: Harcourt, Brace, and Jovanovich.
EPA analysis finds fish-eating wildlife may be at risk, identifies uncertainties. 1993. *Water Policy Report,* April 14, p. 10.
Fischhoff, Baruch. 1996. Unpublished manuscript.
Frank, F. W., and P. A. Treichler, eds. 1989. *Language, gender, and professional writing: Theoretical approaches and guidelines for nonsexist usage.* New York: Modern Language Association.
Georgia-Pacific Corp. 1993. Testimony for L.D. 49, An Act to Set Reasonable

Dioxin Levels. Presented to the 116th Maine Legislature's Joint Standing Committee on Energy and Natural Resources. April 28.

Hacker, Sally. 1990. *"Doing it the hard way": Investigations of gender and technology.* Edited by D. E. Smith and S. M. Turner. Boston: Unwin Hyman.

Harding, Sandra. 1991. *Whose science? Whose knowledge? Thinking from women's lives.* Ithaca, N.Y.: Cornell University Press.

Hicks, Lebelle. n.d. Memo to Lani Graham, M.D., Department of Human Services; Barry Mower, Department of Environmental Protection; Hal Winters, Department of Marine Resources, regarding preliminary results in the Dioxin in Lobster Meat and Tomalley Study.

Jones, Doug. 1993. Testimony. Presented to the 116th Maine Legislature's Joint Standing Committee on Energy and Natural Resources. April 28.

Kekacs, Andrew. 1993. BEP fails to set standard for dioxin: Results of EPA study awaited. *Bangor Daily News,* March 25, p. 17.

Kekacs, Andrew. 1994. Dioxin enters rivers as mill waste. *Bangor Daily News,* February 3, pp. 1–2.

Keller, E. F. 1985. *Reflections on gender and science.* New Haven, Conn.: Yale University Press.

Keller, E. F. 1990. From secrets of life to secrets of death. In Mary Jacobus, E. F. Keller, and Sally Shuttleworth, eds., *Body/politics: Women and the discourses of science,* pp. 177–91. New York and London: Routledge.

Kloehn, Steve. 1994. Hot tomalley: Science and green stuff. *Bangor Daily News,* February 3, p. 5.

Lachter, Barry. 1993. Louisiana-Pacific Corporation. A Proposal Regarding Inclusion of Totally Chlorine-Free Pulp in the Federal Government Guidelines for Paper Procurement. Testimony. Presented to the 116th Maine Legislature's Joint Standing Committee on Energy and Natural Resources. April 28.

Maine Department of Human Services. 1994. Joint health advisory, February 2.

Maine Lobster Promotion Council. 1994. *Lobster tales* 5 (spring–summer).

Margolin, Allan, and David Bailey. 1992. "Toxic fish risk much higher than EPA admits," says EDF. Weak EPA warnings leave pregnant women and others at risk. Press Release. Environmental Defense Fund.

Marriott, D. C., to state senator Mark Lawrence, co-chair, and state representative Paul Jacques, co-chair, Joint Standing Committee on Energy and Natural Resources. 1993. April 28 letter regarding L.D. 49, An Act to Set Reasonable Dioxin Levels. Presented as testimony to the 116th Maine Legislature's Joint Standing Committee on Energy and Natural Resources.

McConnell-Ginet, Sally. 1989. The sexual (re)production of meaning: A discourse-based theory. In F. W. Frank and P. A. Treichler, eds., *Language, gender, and professional writing: Theoretical approaches and guidelines for nonsexist usage,* pp. 35–50. New York: Modern Language Association.

Melnicove, Mark, and Kendall Merriam. n.d. *The uncensored guide to Maine.*

Merchant, Carolyn. 1989. *The death of nature.* San Francisco: Harper.

Morgan, Morgan G., Baruch Fischhoff, Lester Lave, and Paul Fishbeck. 1996. A proposal for ranking risk in federal agencies. In J. C. Davies, ed., *Comparing environmental risks: Tools for setting government priorities.* Washington, D.C.: Resources for the Future.

Otis, D. E. 1993. Testimony. Presented to the 116th Maine Legislature's Joint Standing Committee on Energy and Natural Resources. April 28.

Pardilla, Jerry R. 1993. Comments on L.D. 49, An Act to Set Reasonable Dioxin Levels. Energy and Natural Resources Committee. April 28.

Perelman, Chaim, and Lucie Olbrechts-Tyteca. 1971. *The new rhetoric.* Translated by John Wilkinson and Purcell Weaver. Notre Dame, Ind.: University of Notre Dame Press.

Porter, Ned. 1994. State issues advisory for lobster eaters: Tomalley dioxin level—"unacceptably high." *Bangor Daily News,* February 3, pp. 1–2.

Rombauer, Irima S., Marion Rombauer Becker, and Ethan Becker. 1997. *Joy of cooking.* New York: Scribner.

Sauer, Beverly. 1993. Sense and sensibility in technical documentation and accident reports: How feminist interpretation strategies can save lives in the nation's mines. *Journal of Business and Technical Communication* 7:63–83.

Sauer, Beverly. 1994. Sexual dynamics of the professions: Articulating the *ecriture masculine* of science and technology. *Technical Communication Quarterly* 3:309–12.

Treichler, P. A. 1989. From discourse to dictionary: How sexist meanings are authorized. In F. W. Frank and P. A. Treichler, eds., *Language, gender, and professional writing: Theoretical approaches and guidelines for nonsexist usage,* pp. 51–79. New York: Modern Language Association.

U.S. Environmental Protection Agency 1994. Communication, Education, and Public Affairs. Dioxin facts: Scientific highlights from draft assessment. September.

Walsh, Douglas, to George Papadopoulos. 1993. April 12 letter regarding Lincoln Pulp and Paper Co. NPDES Permit #Me002003.

12 THE CONSTRUCTION

OF PUBLIC HEALTH

IN THE FDA HEARINGS ON

SILICONE BREAST IMPLANTS

MARY THOMPSON

In 1991, amid growing public concern, the General and Plastic Surgery Devices Panel (GPSDP) of the U.S. Food and Drug Administration (FDA) met in Gaithersburg, Maryland, to hear public testimony on silicone gel–filled breast implants. The panel's objective was to review testimony concerning silicone implants and to advise the FDA on whether the implants were meeting a "public health need" (not on the safety of the devices), which would determine their continued availability in the marketplace. After listening to members of consumer and medical organizations, health professionals, and breast implant recipients, the panel recommended that the FDA formally label silicone implants "experimental" but authorize their continued use in controlled studies. This recommendation arose from the panel's unanimous finding that silicone breast implants do indeed serve "public health" interests. Although I align myself with those groups that oppose silicone implants because of the lack of available information on silicone, in this chapter I am more interested in the strategies used to defend the devices during the hearings.[1]

Using transcripts of the 1991 hearings, I examine how defenders of silicone breast implants successfully convinced the panel of the devices' importance to "public health" by strategically relying on testimony from breast cancer survivors, by acclaiming breast implants' role in safeguarding women's femininity, and by arguing that the FDA must defend women's "right to choose" what goes into their bodies.[2] The proponents of silicone implants, I argue, shifted the focus of the debate away from the safety of the devices and onto the preservation of the rights and naturalized gender of the humanist subject. As a feminist cultural studies critic, I read against the grain of this strategy to consider how liberal humanism works to maintain the heterosexist sex/gender system. My aim in this chapter is not to reject completely rights-based humanist ideologies but rather to demonstrate how the appropriation of liberal humanism for women in legal and public arenas can in some contexts work against feminist purposes. I rely on work by feminist critic Mary Poovey for a model of how humanism, when invoked in the public arena in regard to issues of gender, can be used in disturbing ways to hold women responsible for their oppression.

I argue that testimony by breast cancer survivors preserved the rights only of those individuals whose bodies performed hegemonic notions of gender; the testimony of defenders of silicone implants downplayed augmentation patients, however, because their implants—despite their seeming to perform normalized gender roles even more aggressively—denaturalize gender by exposing it as a social construction. The value of this study is in showing why feminist jurisprudence needs to remain critical of humanist discourse in order to be effective on behalf of women in the context of postmodernism, specifically when confronting issues of the technologically gendered body.[3]

Rhetorical Strategies of Opponents and Defenders of Implants

Silicone gel–filled breast implants have been on the market for more than thirty years. Until the early 1990s, approximately two million women received these implants. Although many implant recipients are happy with the devices, some women complain of serious symptoms of autoimmune system disease that they attribute to silicone leakage from the implants. In 1988 dissatisfied patients and doctors, working with Ralph Nader's Public Citizen Health Research Group, called for a ban on silicone breast implants (Haiken 1997). As a result, the GPSDP held a series of hearings in November 1991 and February 1992 that had a threefold purpose: to hear the views of the public, consumers, health professionals, and others on silicone gel–filled breast implants; to consider premarket approval applications from four firms; and to advise the FDA on whether the continued availability of the devices was necessary for the public health (Reams 1991, 1992).

The first meeting of the FDA panel on November 12, 1991, was devoted to an open public hearing. Members of consumer organizations, medical organizations, health professionals, manufacturers of medical devices, and individuals sharing their personal testimony spoke for and against silicone implants during this session. Groups represented at the hearing included the American Silicone Implant Survivors and the Command Trust Network (two organizations providing information on the safety of silicone implants) and Keep A Breast, My Image After Breast Cancer, and the Y-Me National Breast Cancer Organization (groups that support women diagnosed with breast cancer). Representatives of various health organizations were also in attendance, including members of the Organization for Obstetric, Gynecological, and Neonatal Nurses and the American Society of Plastic and Reconstructive Surgeons.

Those groups and individuals opposed to silicone implants based their arguments on the lack of information about silicone implants and implant patients. During the course of the hearings, manufacturers and medical professionals demonstrated a frightening lack of knowledge about the durability of the implants, the effects of ruptured implants and silicone gel leakage on the immune and other bodily systems, the extent of interference from implants in mammography examinations, and the actual number of women who had received implants and how to track this population. As a result of these discoveries, in 1992 the FDA formally labeled silicone implants "experimental," to be used only in tightly controlled studies involving reconstructed cancer patients and a limited number of women seeking breast augmentation. Although silicone implants remain available only for these limited purposes, it is astonishing and noteworthy that defenders of the devices were able to secure this access, given the lack of information about silicone and the severity of the charges leveled against the makers of the devices. How did the defenders do it?

Most of those testifying in favor of silicone implants were breast cancer survivors, an important fact in shaping how the issue was represented to the FDA panel. Eighty percent of breast implant surgeries are for cosmetic augmentation (women who want larger breasts); only 20 percent of implant surgeries are for the purpose of reconstruction after mastectomy. Yet of the sixty-seven recipients of silicone implants who testified in favor of implants at the public hearings, forty-seven were reconstruction patients. This number seems even further skewed considering that only 1 in 10 mastectomy patients decides to have breast implants as part of her reconstructive surgery (Mellican 1995).[4]

The defenders of silicone implants addressed their arguments primarily to the panel's third objective. Their strategy was to emphasize the role breast implants play in maintaining and/or restoring women's physical and psychological health, either as reconstruction following a mastectomy or as augmentation. They based this defense on four recurrent rhetorical points. First, they argued that some women will not be tested for breast cancer and/or will refuse to have mastectomies if they know reconstructive surgery is not available. Second, this group reasoned that insurance companies may refuse to cover women with implant-related complications if implants are banned. Third, defenders repeatedly claimed that implants are necessary for many women's emotional well-being; they argued that women with implants are happy, have high self-esteem, and high self-confidence. Fourth, defenders of silicone breast implants appropriated the discourse of liberal humanism, claiming that women have a right to choose implants as part of their treatment for cancer or for cosmetic reasons.

These last two points are of particular interest because of the tension created by representing women simultaneously as beings whose emotional state is controlled by their physiology and as humanist subjects whose entitlement to rights is based on beliefs in human rationality and autonomy. The contradiction between these two defenses of silicone implants went unnoticed during the hearings. I want to explore this tension, however, by looking first at some examples from the FDA hearings of how some of those who testified invoked humanist discourse in defense of women's right to choose silicone implants and then at examples of how they discussed implants as necessary to women's emotional well-being. Examining the intersection of humanist beliefs with gender issues can tell us how women are perceived, treated, and judged in the public arena.

Humanist Discourses
in Defense of Implants

The defense of silicone breast implants did not originate solely within medical discourses. In *Venus Envy* (1997) Elizabeth Haiken observes that in the 1970s many feminists supported the use of breast implants as part of women's recovery from breast cancer. During this period of the second wave of the women's movement, feminists fought to gain for women more say in the medical decisions made about their bodies. This included preventing unnecessary radical mastectomies, rethinking the practice of immediately removing the breast following a biopsy indicating cancer (giving the woman no time to prepare for losing a breast), and offering women more reconstructive options (258–62). Haiken observes that the medical profession's dismissal of women's concerns about mastectomies as mere vanity became one battle in a larger feminist attack on the medical subordination of women's interests (258).

At the 1991 and 1992 FDA hearings, defenders of silicone breast implants appropriated the rhetoric used by second-wave feminists to critique the medical profession's subordination of women. Because humanist discourse informs much of liberal feminist thought and language, the arguments used by witnesses at the FDA hearings defending women's right to choose silicone implants sounded like scenes from the second wave of the women's movement. The following pieces of testimony illustrate how proponents of silicone implants invoked liberal humanist discourse and imagery of the women's movement in defense of breast implants in order to redefine the debate and polarize support for the devices:

> The right to choose and freedom of choice are at the very core of this issue. Our rights as citizens should be protected and promoted. The decision needs to be left with the individual and her doctors. (Kay Barnes in Reams 1991:87)

> If you ban breast implants you are taking away women's freedom to choose what to do with their own bodies. When the government starts taking away our rights this is no longer a democracy. (Mary Follin in Reams 1991:359)

> I advise the FDA not to base their decisions in terms of hysteria, but rather in terms of facts of some of us who are very happy with our breast implants, where they have made a difference in our lives. . . . Do not put us through another situation where we have to continually fight for our rights. I invite you to take a look at the broad spectrum of women who have benefited from this. Also, our sisters have a right to augment if they want to. This is a woman's issue. (Keep A Breast representative in Reams 1991:370)

Strategic references to "continually fight[ing]," "rights," "freedom to choose," "sisters," and "woman's issue" represented the silicone breast implant debate as aligned with earlier causes in women's liberation—such as voting or abortion. Defenders of silicone implants argued that cancer survivors must have the freedom to choose implants and that doctors cannot deny women this right to reconstruct their bodies and, more important, their femininity. Furthermore, the Keep A Breast representative's dismissal of decisions based in "hysteria" serves to distance the defense of silicone from the historically discredited category of emotional irrationality and reposition it within the category of impartial rationality, which has traditionally defined the liberal humanist subject.

In order to represent the choice to have implant surgery as a rational one, defenders of silicone implants minimized accusations that women get breast implants because of irrational reasons, such as vanity or a desire to conform to social pressure. To ward off implied charges of vanity, proponents of implants downplayed the significance of cultural forces on their decisions and asserted their autonomy in making their decision to seek breast implants. Several women made a point of saying that their husbands or boyfriends did not encourage them or else actively discouraged them from getting breast implants. This oversimplified understanding of women's oppression worked during the FDA hearings to represent women seeking breast implants as autonomous agents exercising their freedom of choice. A statement made by Sharon Green of Y-Me exemplifies how defenders of silicone sought to position women's choices about their bodies outside the control of society: "This is not a debate on whether society puts too much emphasis on breast and physical beauty, [nor] will it become one. If the issue were about the availability of a device that would make a man like Magic Johnson feel better about himself, we would not be here today. Do not take away from women the freedom to choose this option" (Reams 1991:133).

Green foregrounds the role of society in gender discrimination even as she seeks to downplay the role of society in influencing women's decisions to get breast implants. The belief in each person's autonomous consciousness, individuality, and self-awareness underlies liberal humanism's construction of the subject. Liz Bondi (1993) describes the certainties of liberal humanism as

> the Cartesian cogito and its autonomous, sovereign subject, and also . . . the more general notion of an irreducible, stable, unalienated essence at the core of, and giving coherence to, every human individual. The idea of a self-sufficient unity within the human individual creates the basis for people to identify with one another as equals. Consequently, the liberal humanist view of the human subject has often been drawn upon to argue for such emancipatory necessities as the equal value of all human beings, and to endorse calls for equal rights. It remains the dominant hegemonic view in Western liberal democracies. (86)

Bondi's last point about the enduring power of humanist beliefs is a good one. Despite psychoanalytic theories of an influential unconscious and Marxist theories of false consciousness, both of which inform a postmodern sense of an alienated or fragmented consciousness, humanist notions of the self-aware subject persist—although tensions and conflicts characterize this coexistence. During the FDA hearings witnesses used the belief in the subject's autonomous, unalienated self-consciousness to support women's choices to have breast augmentation or reconstruction. At the same time, however, they represented women's choices to have silicone implants as arising from their emotional needs.

To promote silicone implants as meeting a public health need, witnesses argued that implant recipients feel empowered, have higher self-esteem, are more confident, feel whole again, and so on. This theory is contradicted, however, by research suggesting that women who are content with their bodies and never seek plastic surgery are in fact happier than women who do (Haiken 1997:276).[5] Nevertheless, several doctors who testified in the defense of implants were psychiatrists and psychologists who argued that implants are beneficial for women's mental health. Other witnesses illustrate some of these beliefs:

> I am here today on behalf of those two million women whose physical, emotional and psychological well being will be greatly impacted by your decision concerning breast implants. (Patrick McDonough of Komen Breast Cancer Foundation in Reams 1991:91)

> The psychological benefits to women from breast enhancement procedures have been well documented in the scientific literature. Women who have undergone breast reconstruction or augmentation report increased feelings of self-confidence, self-esteem and an improved body image that reinforces their feelings of femininity. (M. A. Braun, R.N., of Obstetric, Gynecological and Neonatal Nurses in Reams 1991:301)

> Breast cancer and the loss of my breast was trauma enough. Thanks to implants and skillful doctors I did not have to lose my feminine, sensual, sexual body image. (Joyce Ward, cancer survivor, in Reams 1991:403–4)

These arguments represent women's mental stability as determined by their emotions, which are in turn determined by their physiology. While seeking to add to women's claim to their right to rational choice, this strategy contradictorily reinscribed women in the hegemonically familiar role of being associated first and foremost with the body.

Susan Bordo (1993) has argued that historically Western culture has associated women with the body and emotions, whereas it has most closely linked men with the mind and rationality. These beliefs reasserted themselves throughout the FDA hearings. An example is the response made by a Dr. Freedman, a member of the panel, to Barbara Herzog, a woman whose implants ruptured while she was nursing her daughter, leading her to believe the silicone is responsible for her daughter's autoimmune disease:

> Ms. Herzog, you are in the unique position today to have discussed lactation, which is the primary function of breasts and we have heard very little about that today. You are also in the position to have nursed a child with breast implants that apparently had ruptured. How do you feel psychologically about having done that? (Dr. Freedman in Reams 1991:353)

It is interesting that out of any number of questions that Freedman could have asked Herzog—such as, does she have proof that silicone made her daughter sick?—he chooses instead to ask her how she feels. Additionally, Freedman apparently feels compelled to reiterate that the real purpose of breasts is lactation. In his testimony Freedman attempts to reestablish a "natural" link between gender (social beliefs and values) and sex (the biological makeup of the body) by shifting the discussion of breasts away from their appearance and onto the biological (more "natural") function of breasts. In his invocation of biology and motherhood, he is able to relocate the female subject in nature, which is traditionally related to the body and emotions, thus his question, "How do you feel?"

The perception that women need implants to help their self-esteem places the cause for their insecurity solely on them rather than on larger cultural factors. Like the discourse of the self-help movement more generally, this strategy of "empowering" women who feel they don't measure up—by insisting that they change themselves—fails to critique social attitudes that instill women with a sense of inadequacy to begin with. This notion of self-empowerment asks individual women to change themselves to adapt to problems in their lives, a strategy that may foreclose the explanation for women's dissatisfaction as being cultural even as it elides the possibility for social change through mass organization.[6]

Gender Ideology and Humanism in Public/Juridical Contexts

During the hearings, the women making choices about their bodies illustrated publicly the tension between contradictory associations of women with rationality and emotionality. I want to explore this contradiction in the perceptions of women (and how they present themselves) in public/juridical contexts by considering cultural critic Mary Poovey's argument that "even though the humanist subject seems to be without gender, it is always already gendered as masculine, for, within this tradition, the self-determining, rational subject always stands opposed to the subject-in-nature, which is gendered feminine" (1992:37).

In her work, "Postmodernism, Another View," Poovey looks at the construction of the humanist juridical subject in relation to gender in several recent legal cases dealing with sex and reproduction. Poovey argues that humanism's logic relies (uneasily) upon naturalized gender roles, which are presumed to arise from the stable core of the humanist subject. The problem of this reliance, she points out, is that the postmodern condition exists as "challenges to the most basic of humanist understanding—the individuality of the subject and the bodily integrity of the person" (39). The conditions of postmodernism have also caused shifts in gender roles (because more women are entering male-dominated fields out of economic necessity) in addition to our sense of what it means to be human (given the extension of technology into the body) and to be self-aware (for example, the increasingly acceptable view that recognizes the subject's consciousness as unreliable—including memory loss, loss of consciousness, susceptibility to coercive forces).

Despite an increasingly postmodern juridical view of the human subject, Poovey argues that conservatives often rely upon humanist views to bolster their notions of gender. She gives the example of the 1991 case, in which a university student was raped at a fraternity by men she knew socially. The jury found the accused men innocent—despite the woman's claim that she did not consent to have sex with them and that she was only intermittently conscious during the rape. The jury interpreted her presence at the fraternity as conveying her willingness to have sex with the men and believed that her defense—that she was unconscious—was only an excuse for the gaps and contradictions in her story. Poovey argues that the jury's inability to accept the notion that the woman lost consciousness as a result of being traumatized by the rape arises from the conservative cultural attitude that perceives rape as sex, not violence. The jury contradictorily judged the woman as irrational (she said no to sex but meant yes) and as rational (her story must be coherent in order to be believable).

Poovey's consideration of women's sexual and reproductive rights is a very different feminist issue than breast implants, but her analysis of how in juridical contexts gender ideology and humanism work together against women is useful for my analysis. Invoking humanism in the defense of silicone implants, therefore, was paradoxical, and it resulted in the panel and public's contradictory judging of the women seeking the devices (implant patients are either irrationally vain women or women making rational choices). As a result, the discourse of liberal humanism structured the debate about breast implants in a way that ultimately did not benefit women for two reasons. First, the strategy worked to secure the devices for women but at a price. The reliance upon the notion of the humanist subject's autonomy and self-awareness obfuscates coercive cultural pressures on women to conform to normalized beauty ideals and makes it appear that women's decisions to have implants occur completely outside of cultural influences. Moreover, the discourse can be turned against women and used to hold women personally accountable, not only for the decision to have implants but also for the success or failure of those implants. The following bits of testimony illustrate how implant recipients—not the implants—were criticized when the devices failed:

> I wonder how many more times we are going to allow so few to affect so many. Subject all of us to their individual beliefs and condemn us to their personal failures. (Ms. Richardson in Reams 1991:391)

> Women are going to have to learn to accept responsibilities for their actions, today, in the future and unfortunately those we have made in the past. (Ms. Ridgeway in Reams 1991:393)

Humanist beliefs enable the culture to judge women in a way that holds them responsible for their own oppression. Throughout the hearings manufacturers of silicone implants held themselves to be innocent because, they claimed, they were simply making devices that women demanded—a strategy by which the implant makers sought freedom from responsibility for the devices' safety.

Social Implications
of the Technologically Gendered Body

Another issue raised by the use of humanism in the context of the FDA hearings concerns who benefits from humanist beliefs. A dilemma within humanism is its basis in a logic of oppositions and exclusion; that is, it has traditionally defined the humanist subject in opposition to the nonhuman world, which is denied humanist rights and/or freedoms. During the hearings on silicone breast implants, no one ever addressed who might in fact be denied the "right to choose" implants. The decision to have implants is not a right but a function of privilege. Because the choice to have implants is largely dependent on means, it is not a "choice" for many people. The expense of such an operation renders it an option primarily for white women of the middle and upper classes.

Eclipsed by the discussion of rights is the underlying anxiety in the hearings regarding which bodies should have breast implants. The bodies of white women of the privileged classes have traditionally functioned as the cultural signifiers of femininity. The threat that breast cancer poses to these bodies became the unspoken focus of the FDA hearings. The structure of the debate about the significance of silicone implants to "public health" therefore did not relate to the threat that silicone could pose to women's bodies but rather to the threatening possibility of bodies failing to repeat the performance of their gender. In these hearings "public health" became a matter of maintaining and reconstructing bodies that perform femininity according to hegemonic notions of gender. Bodies not considered in the debates were those whose breast implants denaturalize the idea of gender—this includes most women who augment their breasts for improved self-esteem or for improved business (sex workers, topless performers/waitresses, models, actresses, etc.) and transsexuals.

The technologically gendered body problematizes humanism not only by challenging the integrity of the human body but also by calling into question the supposedly stable gendered core of the humanist subject. Breast implants signal the arrival of the technologically gendered body. On first consideration, breast implants seem to be about conformity to gender roles, but looked at in another way the ability to technologically construct gender denaturalizes reified notions of gender. Judith Butler in her 1990 analysis of drag performances argues that feminists have typically separated gender (culturally prescribed roles) from sex (biological traits), but this separation presupposes a materiality of the body before signification, which in fact masks the socially hegemonic construction of the body. The heterosexist imperative attempts to make it appear that we perform a gender that arises from an already gendered core, but drag (performing a different gender) calls this assumption into question. Failure to repeat the performance of one's gender challenges the notion of an abiding gendered self.

The implications of this theory for silicone breast implants is that it explains in one way the anxiety during these hearings regarding who gets to receive implants. For reconstructed cancer patients, implants safely mean that their bodies are "stylized" once again in a way that permits the repeated performance of their gender and that safeguards the notion of an abiding gendered core. Augmentation patients, on the other hand, highlight the performativity of gender, which implicitly suggests a failure to repeat itself and the absence of a gendered core. That is, on one level the existence of the technology for building gender works to remind us that gender is a performance of sorts.

The idea that gender is a social or technological construction was not only too disturbing for the witnesses and the panel to discuss but also subverted the basis of their humanist arguments by denaturalizing the sex/gender system. My contention is that breast implant technology denaturalizes the gendered human body, thereby challenging the culturally constructed and discursively maintained foundations of humanist values. When we consider that breast implant surgery is not a right but a matter of privilege, we can see the discourse of rights and freedoms served only those women whose gender works to maintain humanist beliefs.

In this chapter I have looked at how a common plastic surgery device was defended in a public medical/juridical arena by using humanist discourse. This defense relied upon cultural beliefs of the inner self as inherently gendered. Breast reconstruction patients' testimony supported the continued availability of silicone breast implants because the witnesses represented the devices as aiding women's "natural" desire to perform femininity, which cancer unnaturally interrupts. On the other hand, testimony at the FDA hearings underplayed the most popular use of silicone implants, for breast augmentation surgeries, because these surgeries challenge the idea of femininity as "natural." Therefore, I argue, the "public health need" met by silicone breast implants was in fact a cultural imperative for female bodies to perform hegemonic notions of gender.

A feminist rhetorical study of the defense of silicone breast implants raises this question: What is a feminist politics of plastic surgery? Such a feminist politics would need to honor the choices of women who want breast reconstruction while simultaneously remaining critical of the rapidly growing cosmetic surgery industry that relentlessly tells women that their bodies and faces are imperfect. The second wave of feminists used the discourse of liberal humanism to attack the medical profession for objectifying mastectomy patients' bodies and dismissing their concerns and their right to make choices about their bodies. In the 1991 FDA hearings, this rhetorical strategy returned in continued support of reconstruction patients but also in support of the plastic surgery profession's mass marketing of cosmetic breast implants. It seems that for third-wave feminists, breast implant politics cannot be easily defined.

In her work, *Technologies of the Gendered Body* (1996), Anne Balsamo develops and implements a feminist theoretical lens for understanding postmodern technologies and gender. She disputes postmodern theories that announce the "disappearance" of the body and gender in postmodern culture. Gender, she observes, remains a submerged discourse in such studies of technology, while these technologies are used to perpetuate oppressive cultural narratives of gender. In a chapter examining the imaging technology that cosmetic surgeons use to project to prospective patients what they might look like after surgery, Balsamo discusses how the cosmetic surgery profession repositions the female body as unruly and in need of intervention. She argues, "New imaging technologies are articulated with traditional and ideological beliefs about gender—an articulation that keeps the female body positioned as a privileged object of a normative gaze that is now not simply a medical gaze (the 'clinical eye') but also a technologized view" (57).

Although Balsamo criticizes the normalizing power of this technology, she maintains a critical space for its feminist understanding and use. She concludes by writing, "I am reluctant to accept as a simple and obvious conclusion that cosmetic surgery is simply one more site where women are passively victimized. . . . Like women who get pierced-nose rings, tattoos, and hair sculptures, women who elect cosmetic surgery could be seen to be using their bodies as a vehicle for staging cultural identities" (78). Balsamo's work offers a useful lens for considering the discourses of the body, gender, and identity in the context of postmodern technologies. Her work suggests compellingly that feminists cannot uncritically dismiss or embrace new technologies like breast implants; rather, her work enables feminists to consider new technologies as discursive sites for the deployment of power.

As such, feminists may understand breast implant technology as imbued with cultural discourses of humanity, the body, gender, and identity, which individual female patients and medical and cosmetic surgery professionals all draw upon in order to make meaning out of these devices. What I have sought to accomplish in performing a feminist rhetorical analysis of the defense of this technology is to map the intersection of these cultural discourses in order to highlight the need for a feminist politics of plastic surgery. Such a politics is needed, I believe, because the increasing popularity of plastic surgeries will presumably lead to more situations in the public arena similar to the FDA hearings.

NOTES

1. Despite the compelling reasons motivating women to seek breast implants, I believe that the durability of silicone implants and the effects of silicone in the human body have been and continue to be underresearched. Therefore I believe the devices should not be available to any women until the safety of silicone implants (not the demand for them) has been determined.

2. I have placed this phrase in quotes because I want to cast doubt on the notion that procuring the expensive procedure of breast implants constitutes a right that all women have. Moreover, I agree with the argument that women who choose to receive silicone implants when the information about the devices' safety is inadequate are not being allowed to make informed choices.

3. I define *postmodernism* three ways: as an artistic or architectural style characterized by the appropriation and fragmentation of conventional forms and by the lack of closure and unity; as a cultural moment characterized by the breakdown of consensus and metanarratives—such as humanism, progress, and rationalism—and the expansion of capitalism globally; and as a critical approach that works from a multiplicity of perspectives, including but not limited to issues of race, class, gender, and sexuality. See, for example, Jean François Lyotard's *The Postmodern Condition* (1984), Fredric Jameson's *Postmodernism, or the Cultural Logic of Late Capitalism* (1991), and Donna Haraway's essay, "The Cyborg Manifesto" in *Simians, Cyborgs, and Women* (1991).

4. Part of the reason for the (over)representation of cancer survivors in favor of implants at the FDA hearings is that this population of women is well organized and thus easily mobilized—they belong to the networks of support groups for women surviving breast cancer.

5. Elizabeth Haiken describes a 1977 study of 370 women in the Midwest that compared women seeking breast augmentation to women who were content with their breast size. The results showed that women with small breasts who were not seeking augmentation scored higher on the California Psychological Inventory than women who were average sized and not seeking implants and scored higher than women who were seeking augmentation. The satisfied group of women generally appeared more assertive and independent (1997:276). Haiken concludes that, "while altering one's body may be an act of self-assertion, this study seems to suggest, the qualities we might expect to see in an 'authentic feminist hero' are more commonly shared by those who see no need for surgery" (1997:278).

6. For more detailed critiques of women's self-help groups and literature in relation to feminism, see Susan Bordo (1993), Carol Spitzak (1990), Susan Faludi (1991), and especially Elayne Rapping (1996).

REFERENCES

Balsamo, Anne. 1996. *Technologies of the gendered body: Reading cyborg women.* Durham, N.C.: Duke University Press.
Bondi, Liz. 1993. Locating identity politics. In Michael Keath and Steve Pile, eds., *Place and the politics of identity,* pp. 84–101. New York: Routledge.
Bordo, Susan. 1993. *Unbearable weight: Feminism, Western culture, and the body.* Los Angeles: University of California Press.
Butler, Judith. 1990. *Gender trouble: Feminism and the subversion of identity.* New York: Routledge.
Faludi, Susan. 1991. *Backlash: The undeclared war against American women.* New York: Crown.
Haiken, Elizabeth. 1997. *Venus envy: A history of cosmetic surgery.* Baltimore, Md.: Johns Hopkins University Press.
Haraway, Donna. 1991. *Simians, cyborgs, and women: The reinvention of nature.* New York: Routledge, 1991.
Jameson, Fredric. 1991. *Postmodernism, or The cultural logic of late capitalism.* Durham, N.C.: Duke University Press.
Lyotard, Jean François. 1984. *The postmodern condition.* Translated by Geoff Bennington and Brian Massumi. Minneapolis: University of Minnesota Press.
Mellican, R. Eugene. 1995. Breast implants, the cult of beauty, and a culturally constructed "disease." *Journal of Popular Culture* 28:7–12.
Poovey, Mary. 1992. Feminism and postmodernism—another view. In Margaret Ferguson and Jennifer Wicke, eds., *Feminism and postmodernism,* pp. 34–52. Durham, N.C.: Duke University Press.
Rapping, Elayne. 1996. *The culture of recovery: Making sense of the self-help movement in women's lives.* Boston: Beacon.
Reams, Bernard, ed. 1991. *Transcripts of the panel meeting on November 12, 13, 14, 1991, on the topic of breast implants/Food and Drug Administration, General and Plastic Surgery Devices Panel* (Gaithersburg, Md.). Buffalo, N.Y.: W. S. Hein.
Reams, Bernard, ed. 1992. *Transcripts of the panel meeting on February 18, 19, 20, 1992, on the topic of silicone gel–filled breast implants/Food and Drug Administration, General and Plastic Surgery Devices Panel* (Gaithersburg, Md.). Buffalo, N.Y.: W. S. Hein.
Spitzak, Carole. 1990. *Confessing excess: Women and the politics of body reduction.* Albany: State University of New York Press.

AFTERWORD

TECHNOLOGIES OF THE EXTERIOR,

TECHNOLOGIES OF THE INTERIOR—

CAN WE EXPAND THE DISCOURSE

OF REPRODUCTIVE STUDIES?

ROBBIE DAVIS-FLOYD

In their introduction to this book, the editors note that the new reproductive technologies (NRTs) "raise conflicts about how technology might be used in relation to human birth; yet often, what gets reported and thus communicated to society at large is a mix of technological determinism and wonder, with very little critical perspective." The chapters in this book do an excellent job of providing that perspective. They call into question the dilemmas and paradoxes presented by the NRTs but so often skimmed over in both technoscientific and popular discourse. They also highlight the gender biases and pitfalls that pervade the design, application, marketing, and implementation of these reproductive technologies.

So often, language that appears to be gender neutral, even compassionately humanistic, disguises hidden patriarchal agendas. Foucault says that power is not possessed but performed; these chapters point up the performance of hegemonic ideologies and agendas even through such apparently feministic rhetoric as "informed choice." How informed can our choices be when the information we receive reflects only one way, the technomedical way, of looking at the world and at our bodies? From the new genetic model of medicine now taking hold to the older germ theory of disease, this technomedical approach is mechanizing, fragmenting, deconstructive, and expensive, and its widespread cultural credibility, while opening new options, is closing down others at a rapid pace.

Body-Talk Taboos

As the chapters in this book clearly point out, the way we talk about our bodies and our reproductive activities has been transformed in the last thirty years. In 2000, we talk about these things differently because we do them differently than we did in 1970. Turn-of-the-millennium women routinely go to work and stay there for years, postponing childbearing until their midthirties or early forties. They rely on various birth control methods so they can develop their careers, then find that the combination of age and the side-effects of these methods may have rendered them unable to conceive. Environmental pollution lowers sperm counts, contributing to the problem. But not to worry, says the advertisement for the infertility clinic! The problems we create with technology can be solved with more technology. And thus women step onto the discursive and performative conveyor belt of the NRTs.

In her excellent book *Embodied Progress: A Cultural Account of Assisted Conception*, Sarah Franklin (1997) describes the addictive nature of the in-vitro fertilization process: each step successfully achieved promises the possibility of going one step further the next time. Women who start out thinking, "The clinic is there, why not try it?" end up spending years of their lives and thousands of dollars trying to get to that next step, despite the statistics that warn them that only 10 percent will succeed. Assisted conceptive technologies have a pincer-like effect, trapping women between technodazzle promises and the slight statistical possibility that they will be the one for whom those promises will come true.

Taking the larger view, we can see that the NRTs whose rhetorical strategies are so cogently analyzed in this collection aptly demonstrate what anthropologist Peter C. Reynolds (1991) has called the "One-Two Punch of the Technocracy." In our introduction to *Cyborg Babies: From Techno-Sex to Techno-Tots* (1998), Joe Dumit and I describe this process as follows:

> Take a highly successful natural process, like salmon swimming upstream to spawn. Punch One: In the name of progress and improvement, render it dysfunctional with technology—dam the stream, preventing the salmon from reaching their spawning

grounds. Punch Two: Fix the problem created by technology with more technology—take the salmon out of the water with machines, make them spawn artificially and grow the eggs in trays, then release the baby salmon downstream near the ocean. This One-Two Punch—destroy a natural process, then rebuild it as a cultural process—is an integral result of technocratic society's supervaluation of science and technology over nature. Reynolds articulates this technoscientific de- and re-construction of nature as a process of mutilation and prosthesis. (10)

Elsewhere (Davis-Floyd 1994; Dumit and Davis-Floyd 1998), I have suggested that the cultural management of birth in the United States is a significant example of this One-Two Punch. For example:

Biomedicine mutilates the natural rhythms of birth by multiple interventions in every phase (withholding food and drink from laboring women, which weakens them; administering pain-relieving drugs that slow labor; making the woman lie flat on her back during labor and birth and thereby reducing the flow of blood and oxygen to the baby), then prosthetizes the skewed results (inserting IVs to administer the fluids the woman is not allowed to drink; injecting into the IV drugs to speed up labors slowed by drugs that relieve pain—which further inhibit blood and oxygen supply to the baby; electronically monitoring the baby's level of distress, which will rise as its blood and oxygen supply drop; delivering the iatrogenically distressed baby by forceps or cesarean section). (Dumit and Davis-Floyd 1998:10)

In cyborgifying childbirth, technomedicine creates problems with technology, then solves them with more technology in true One-Two Punch fashion. When the outcome is a healthy mother and a healthy baby, technomedicine claims the credit; when not, the blame is placed on nature or God because, clearly, all that humanly *could* have been done to prevent a bad outcome, *was* done.[1]

Like the birth activist I often am, I am personally inclined to deplore this situation. Yet like the good anthropologist I try to be, I am only too aware that it is very much in line with the desires and expectations of the majority of American women. Seventy of the one hundred women I interviewed for my first book, *Birth as an American Rite of Passage* (1992), either actively sought or were generally comfortable with technobirth. Technological interventions tend to give women a sense of safety, reassuring them that the best the technocracy has to offer—its highly sophisticated technology—is being applied to ensure a healthy baby. Of course, in reality technology can offer no such assurance; nevertheless, its application gives women the *feeling* that all that can be done is being done. This is the same feeling of covering all the bases sought by infertile women who want children and by those who accept prenatal testing. It's their personal variation on what I call the technocratic imperative: *if it can be done, it must be done.*

And so, as Barbara Katz Rothman (1989) has cogently pointed out, the range of our choices, while appearing to expand, in fact narrows down to what *technology* can do. If genetic tests exist, women feel they must use them; otherwise they would not be giving their babies "the best care" (Browner and Press 1995, 1997). If technoconceptive procedures are developed, we must try them; otherwise, we will not be doing everything we can to meet our cultural and personal imperatives to have children of our own. If a machine is available to monitor our baby's heartbeat electronically during labor, we must use it; otherwise, we will not be taking every possible precaution. Choices come and choices go: as we gain the choice to travel the promising but perilous paths of biotechnology, seeking to conceive, to bear babies that we know in advance to be healthy, to give birth to babies that remain so, we lose the choice to travel other paths.

What might those other paths be? The question is worth asking, because the answers are so non-normative (in the Foucauldian sense) that they are not obvious. The gym teachers studied by Verbrugge (chapter 3) came up with another way to approach menstruation, one based on their lived experience as women and their bottom-line view that women's bodies are fundamentally normal and healthy. Going further, in *The Woman in the Body*, Emily Martin (1987) asked what kind of creativity we might unleash were we to conceptualize menstruation as a time during which we might turn our attention inward to hear and to honor the rhythms of our bodies, acting on our physical needs—be they for sleep, for activity, or for quiet meditation. Normative behavior has long driven women to ignore such needs and rhythms to meet the demands of family and career—what if, like First Nations women who retreated to moon lodges to honor this special time (Buckley and Gottlieb 1989), we learned to respect our bodily needs and rhythms instead?

I know some women who have suffered from premenstrual syndrome (PMS) for years, only to find that it vanished when they began to respond to their monthly cycles by taking time off to listen to their bodies. They came to realize that the rage that had come bubbling up and been named "PMS" was both sign and symptom of a deep dissatisfaction with the way they were living their lives.[2] If some women can alleviate PMS not by medicalizing but by normalizing it—that is, by declaring that their symptoms are normal bodily responses to an overly harried lifestyle and then changing that lifestyle—what of the other situations addressed by the chapters in this book? What other ways than technomedicalization—the path through which our culture seeks to channel us—might we find to reconceptualize our approaches to the size of our breasts, infertility, the health of our fetuses, labor, and birth?

For example, if you are infertile, what other options are open to you besides the primrose path of the NRTs? One is obvious—adoption. Another, increasingly less obvious (because less normative) possibility is acceptance of childlessness. Such acceptance can involve filling one's life with other meaningful activities, or what Jane English (1988) has called "childlessness transformed." Another nonobvious choice might be to address the larger environmental problems of the area in which one lives, as these might be affecting the chances to conceive not only of oneself but also of many other women. Nutritional factors are another nonobvious choice; sometimes the lack of even one essential nutrient can dramatically affect the ability to conceive. Less obvious still are possibilities that exist completely outside the norm, such as taking a journey of personal discovery deep into the unconscious, looking for the reason that conception has not occurred. Such reasons, should they exist, might have to do with anything from excessive stress and tension in one's life to childhood sexual abuse that resulted in a soul decision never to bear children to face such pain.

I have interviewed women who uncovered these sorts of deeply unconscious reasons for their infertility. Working with therapists or friends, they were able to identify the psychological factors underlying their acceptance of unacceptable stresses and/or (what they called) their "unconscious programming." Empowered by this information, they proceeded to create conscious change in their lives and conceived within months. Along similar lines, I have on many occasions heard midwives and other health professionals comment on women who underwent years of fertility treatment yet conceived only after they gave up on the process and surrendered to being infertile—as if, somehow, letting go of desire is a necessary prerequisite to its fulfillment. Yet whenever I dare to mention such experiences, I find that most women react instantly and negatively—they feel it is "blaming the victim" to suggest that their psyches may have anything to do with their inability to conceive. "Don't go there," they tell me. "Don't tell us that our lifestyles or our psychology have anything to do with our infertility—it's a physiological reality over which we have no control."[3] And so a new kind of taboo emerges, and another set of choices vanishes, and we are left only with the exterior options of fixing our broken body-machines through medicine and its technologies. And we perpetuate this situation through our analytical discourse, as the One-Two Punch of body-talk taboos channels us to critique technomedical discourse and, in so doing, to keep the focus on it, rendering other sets of possibilities invisible.

And yet some infertile women do conceive as a result of interior exploratory journeys that lead to major lifestyle and attitude changes. Even if the success rate of such ventures is only the same 10 percent as the success rate of the infertility clinics, should they not form at least as large a part of our discursive field as the NRTs? But they do not. Instead, they are ridiculed as "New Age" and denied as fantasy and wishful thinking. Nevertheless, the idea that consciousness can play some role in affecting biology is one that is gaining more and more scientific credibility. Is there not more personal empowerment in exploring our abilities to heal ourselves than in giving our bodies over to the medical system? Where is that discussion in relation to infertility? It exists, as best I can tell, only on the countercultural fringe (see, for example, Parvati-Baker 1986a, 1986b, 1991, 1992; Payne 1997).

Baby-Talk Taboos

The same goes for fetal diagnosis during pregnancy. The health care system and prevailing values and opinions push tests like alpha-feto-protein (AFP, a diagnostic test) and amniocentesis and expound upon the benefits of fetal surgery in utero. But few talk about the consciousness side of that equation. Some women whom I and others (Westra 1996; Miller n.d.) have interviewed have powerful experiences of psychic connection with their unborn children. For example, Kristin told me, "When I was about two months pregnant . . . suddenly, from somewhere inside of the front of my head I heard these words, 'I'm here, I'm a girl, and my name is Joy Elizabeth.' . . . One night [much later on], I had a Braxton Hicks contraction and I heard a voice inside say, 'I'm scared.' I told her I was scared too and that everything would be okay because we were partners and we would do this thing together" (Davis-Floyd 1994:1134).

Elizabeth described her experience of active communication with her unborn baby:

> Two weeks before he was born, he was still breech. My midwives felt confident about a breech delivery, but I . . . very much wanted him to turn. I went to a therapist who was good at visualization

and asked her to help me get in touch with him. We did the visualization. . . . I could see him so clearly . . . and I asked him to
turn. By the time I woke up the next morning, he had completely
turned, and he stayed that way until he was born! (1994:1134)

I come to my own sense of fetal consciousness through deeply embodied experience that I have never before found a way to talk about in an
academic forum. Fifteen years ago, pregnant with my second child, at
the suggestion of my midwives I used visualization to get in touch with
my baby two weeks before his birth. He was posterior and the midwives wanted him to turn so that I would have an easier labor. My
friend Rima Star guided me as I traveled down through my body with
my consciousness, which I visualized as a tiny person. Entering my
womb, I swam slowly around my baby, noting the male genitals and
rejoicing that my intuition that he was a boy was correct! I saw that he
could not turn because the cord was lying across his neck and would
wrap around it and choke him if he turned. Consciousness to consciousness, I suggested that he try but received a wave of fear in response. I got scared too, but Rima suggested to me verbally that he seize
the cord with his hands and pull it down over his shoulder as he turned.
I communicated that to him with an image and in response received a
wave of relief. A day or so later he did turn; two weeks later he was
born holding the cord down over his shoulder with both hands.

Fantastic? Impossible? Not at all—just non-normative. The idea that
babies may be conscious, or that we can actually communicate with
them psyche to psyche, is one that has no credibility in the larger society. I never hear it talked about except among midwives, home birthers,
and those involved in the field of pre- and perinatal psychology.[4] Even
those women interviewed by Rayna Rapp (1999) about their non-
normative choices *not* to undergo prenatal testing never named fetal
consciousness or concern about the baby's experience as a reason for
refusing the tests. Yet the chapter by David Chamberlain (1998) in *Cyborg Babies*, "Babies Remember Pain," describes an incident viewed on
ultrasound of a baby in utero slapping and batting against the ultrasound needle as it penetrated the amniotic sac. Do we ever ask how
babies might feel about needles that invade the wombs they inhabit,
about electrodes stuck into their scalps during birth, about forceps
pressing into their temples, about injections and heel pricks right after
birth, about being taken away from their mothers and put into a plastic
box? Some people do but, again, it's not the dominant discourse. Doing
all these things to babies is what is normative; treating them as conscious beings is not.

Of course, part of feminist resistance to the idea of fetal consciousness comes from the possibility of its co-option by the patriarchy—it is pretty much a given in feminist understanding that conceptualizing the baby as a separate individual can all too easily be co-opted into rendering the mother unimportant or invisible; she becomes the fetal environment and is treated accordingly. When the baby is placed first, judges lock women up to keep them from taking drugs during pregnancy and states pass laws restricting abortion. Feminists want to keep abortion rhetoric focused on women's freedom to choose, but when the right-to-lifers get hold of the idea of fetal consciousness, watch for a new challenge to this discursive strategy. They will accuse us of killing babies that are not only autonomous but also conscious. So for good reasons, another taboo arises in feminist body talk: let's not talk about the baby's consciousness or experience because that can put the mother at risk, in multiple ways. And so another set of choices vanishes from view.

But several years ago I interviewed twenty women who both fiercely defend women's right to choose *and* believe that babies are conscious. If they choose to carry their babies to term, they protect them from hurtful procedures. They are open to the possibility of psychic connection with what they believe is a conscious being yet remain free to choose to abort. They talk to their babies through meditation or visualization before the abortion, asking forgiveness and understanding; sometimes after such conversations, they miscarry spontaneously. After miscarriage or a planned abortion, they often have powerful experiences of psychic connection with the child's spirit, which may accompany them throughout their lives as guardian and guide. All these women hold a deeply spiritual and religious belief that the womb is a gateway for the soul: as they understand it, when a baby is aborted, its soul does not die but simply returns to the other side to await its next chance at life. Billions of people around the world hold similar beliefs in reincarnation—why are they discounted in the abortion debates? I never tried to publish that research because I didn't know what to do with it; it didn't seem to fit within the dominant analytic modes. Since then, I have seen almost no social science research on this subject—it is as if we have silently decided that such experiences do not count because they do not exist in the feminist or social science lexicon.

The same can be said about birth. Although most women I have interviewed about pregnancy and birth took a somewhat mechanistic view of their bodies, of birth, and of the process of fetal development, a few of my interviewees did believe that their babies were conscious and that their bodies had the innate wisdom to give birth. Thus if a problem arose during labor, they would instinctively turn inward, communicating with the baby and/or accessing their own intuition to determine what was wrong. Maybe the mother is unconsciously resisting letting the baby out because of an unspoken fear that she won't be able to mother it well. Maybe the baby has its own reasons for wanting to stay put or for refusing to get out of a breech position. Maybe it's the father's anxiety, or that of the mother-in-law, that is impeding the birth. Home-birth midwives tend to be experts in technologies of the interior, sensing just the right moment to ask the key question, "Sarah, why don't you want this baby to come?" Here is Susan's story:

> Nikki [the midwife] kind of got worried towards the afternoon, because it just kept going on and nothing was changing. And she took me to the shower and said, "Just stay in there till the hot water goes away." And then Nikki asked my friend Diane, "What's the deal with Susan? Is she stressed out about work?" And Diane said, "Well, yeah, I think she's afraid to have the baby . . . that she's not going to be able to go back to her job." So when I came back out, Nikki said, "Right now your job is not important. What you have to do right now is have this baby. This baby is important." And I just burst into tears and was screaming at her and crying and I could feel everything just relax. It all went out of me and then my water broke and we had a baby in thirty minutes. Just like that. (Davis-Floyd 1994:1135)

Many of the home-birth midwives I have interviewed are willing to rely on intuition even when it contradicts external indicators, so long as their intuition about the baby's condition matches the mother's. They reject the technomedical notion that birth is safer when machines monitor it externally, citing the complications often caused by making the woman lie still in one position for long periods of time, the improvement in labor quality when women are up and walking around, the benefits of allowing women to eat and drink on their own during labor to keep up their strength, the beauty and magic of the look on their faces when they give birth on their own. Sometimes, the midwives say, when they try to get a sense of the baby during a long and difficult labor, they can see the baby "glowing" and they know everything is fine. But if there is darkness, a cloud, an emotion of disquiet, they will pack up and transport even if exterior diagnostic tools indicate that things are fine (Davis-Floyd and Davis 1996; Roncalli 1997). Where is the social science discourse about that? In recent years the cultural space for valuing such interior ways of knowing has grown along with the holistic health movement, but beyond *Women's Ways of Knowing* (Belenky et al. 1986), feminists have paid little analytical attention to intuition and the rich and empowering possibilities it entails for enhancing women's reproductive opportunities and experiences.

I am making no claim that such technologies of the interior will work every time, or even most of the time, but, then, neither do the technologies of the exterior, which cost more and do more harm. My point is that we have as much to learn from exploring the interior relationships between our consciousness and our physiology as we do from probing the exterior mysteries of the objective world. As a society we are already massively committed to the exterior path, from probing outer space to deconstructing the chromosome, and need no encouragement to pursue it. But most of us are leaving the interior paths, the paths of consciousness and intuition, untrodden. Why not explore them all? Yet the feminist analysis of the NRTs, although it is largely constituted as a critique, nevertheless takes the same exteriorizing approach, focusing on the variables of race, class, gender, and power to expose the hierarchical and patriarchal application of the new reproductive technologies—what Ginsburg and Rapp (1995) have called "stratified reproduction."

In such analyses, consciousness matters only when women narrate their own embodied experiences; otherwise, it does not seem to play a role. Certainly it is essential to reclaim and revalue women's experiences—indeed, I have sought to do just that in much of my work, but I suggest that we not stop there but rather work to develop a fully holistic approach, both to the analysis of the NRTs and to their application. We should not abandon exploration of reproductive technologies of the interior simply because such options are seldom available to the poor; the NRTs of the exterior are usually not available to the poor either, yet we pursue them avidly, writing analyses of how they exclude minorities while we exclude interior technologies, defining them out of existence by paying them no attention at all.

Cyborg Talk: Expanding Our Rhetorical Range

Should such a reconceptualization of what is talk-about-able in our scholarly reproductive discourse become a more visible part of our larger research agenda, I think we will find the concept of the cyborg to be just as analytically productive as it has been to date in our analyses of the external NRTs. It was a revelation to me, as I worked on my chapter for _Cyborg Babies_ (1998), that nothing in the concept or the reality of the cyborg precludes holism, consciousness, or organicity. Cyborgs can be just as organic as technological, just as holistic as technologically deconstructed, just as fringe as mainstream. For illustration one need look no further than Steven Mentor's chapter in *Cyborg Babies,* in which he describes how his wife, Margann, underwent technoconception through IVF, then gave birth to their cyborg baby in the most organic of ways, at home attended by direct-entry midwives (in line with only 1 percent of the U.S. birthing population).

The very ambiguity and malleability of the cyborg is what makes it so useful. I was helped to understand its analytical flexibility by Joe's and my identification of four different uses of the concept of cyborg that can and often do inform its reporters and analysts. They are the cyborg as positive technoscientific progress; the cyborg as mutilator of natural processes; the cyborg as neutral analytic tool and metaphor for all human-technological relationships; and the cyborg as signifier of contemporary postmodern times in which human relations with technoscience have changed for better and for worse (Davis-Floyd and Dumit 1998:8).

As the editors of this book point out in the introduction, the first use of the cyborg, which they refer to as "technological determinism," characterizes much of what gets reported and communicated to society at large and thus is also characteristic of prevailing public opinion. Indeed, the reification of technology has become, in my view, the defining feature of the American core value system. (Just look at where the money is spent. Money itself is certainly highly valued in the United States, but what we spend it on—which is usually more and better technology—tells the deeper story.) My commentary on hospital birth, which appears earlier in this afterword, exemplifies the second use, the cyborg as mutilator of natural processes, as do the chapters by Diepenbrock, Turney, and Sauer. The third use, the cyborg as neutral analytic tool and metaphor for human-technological relationships, and the fourth use, the cyborg as signifier of postmodern times, for better and for worse, are implicit in many of the other chapters, for ambiguity and multiplicity are the true message of these cyborgian technologies.

Just as epidurals free women from the pain of labor but increase the rate of cesarean sections, silicone breast implants can partially alleviate for some women the devastation of losing their breasts while generating terrible health problems in others. Just as IVF can give some women the babies of their dreams, it can wreak havoc for years on the bodies and lives of the same and other women. All these cyborg technologies both imprison and free, opening some options while closing others. It is my hope that one day the range of choice such technologies encompass will include not only ecological awareness but also the interior technologies I have described in this afterword, and that the full spectrum of that range will be just as open to the poor and socially disadvantaged as to the wealthy and socially privileged. I also hope that the research and writings of feminist social scientists will play a large part in achieving that goal.

Further Expansions from Outside to In: Writing the Birthing Body, Analyzing the Books

Indeed, to some extent they already have. In the introduction to _Childbirth and Authoritative Knowledge_ (1997), Carolyn Sargent and I issued the following call for new directions in research, finding even as we wrote that some of what we were envisioning was already being achieved:

> What is the experience of childbirth like for individual women embedded in their larger cultural systems? We must let women's voices be heard—a primary focus of anthropological research should be women's birth narratives. We must also pay attention to the somatic aspects of birth (Alma Gottlieb, 1996), as experienced and described by women and as studiable by researchers. What can women's bodies tell us about childbirth? How can we learn to listen? Now that the connection between hormones and emotions has been made clearer, can we return to biology to uncover the physical effects on labor and birth of cultural expectations and individual dreams and fears? Can we develop a language that expresses the deep physiology of birth as well as its cultural overlay? What would it be like to speak in the language of the birthing body?[5]
>
> And what effect does language itself have on women's perceptions of their biological experiences? Language is the filter through which experiences are interpreted and expressed. Some contemporary theorists insist that it is the medium through which social life is constructed. In the U.S., that medium is hegemonically technomedical; the richly organic alternative discourse of home-birthers is beginning to be studied as well (Cosslett, 1994; Davis-Floyd, 1994; Miller, 1994; Miller n.d.). But multiple folk discourses on birth and the body remain unrecorded. How do women talk about birth and their birthing bodies in other ethnic groups and

cultures? Our field would benefit from finely textured discourse analyses of women's reproductive speech. . . .

Inspired by the interactions of postmodernism and feminism, we suggest the need for special attention to: (1) conflicts and tensions in systems of authoritative knowledge (Davis-Floyd & Sargent, 1996, [1997]); (2) the language of birth (see for example Rabuzzi, 1994; Kahn, 1995; Cosslett, 1994) and the affective flow between the public discourse about birth and women's private experience (see Rapp, 1984; Rapp, 1988a; Rapp, 1988b; Duden, 1993); (3) the intense subjectivity and reflexivity of studying a process that so directly concerns women as a gender, and is, for many of us, profoundly experience-near (see Rapp, 1987; Davis-Floyd, [In press]; Kahn, 1995); (4) the multiple voices and divisive agendas within feminism concerning issues of the female body and the non/primacy of its reproductive role (Treichler, 1990; for the beginnings of this debate, see Ortner, 1974; Mathieu, 1978); (5) the agency and self-conscious choices of birthing women and birth practitioners (see Sargent & Stark, 1989; Browner & Press, [1997], Georges, [1997]; (6) the multiplicities of discourse, ideology, and treatment with which birthing women in many cultures must now cope (see Pigg, [1997]; Szurek, [1997]); (7) the ideological and cultural factors that work to channel women's choices along hegemonically-approved routes (see Rothman, 1989); (8) the politics of birth as cultural representation and expression (see Aijmer, 1992; Davis-Floyd, 1994; Daviss, [1997]). (15–17)

To this list and the excellent beginning the studies referenced in it have made, I would add my hope that future directions in research into the new reproductive technologies will stretch from macro to micro— from, for example, government and industry policies and trajectories to women's tactile, sensory, and embodied experiences, the kind that are so hard to write about. This stretch in fact is partially encompassed in Herrle-Fanning's work (chapter 1) on the two eighteenth-century British midwifery texts, which vividly show us the differences between knowledge as embedded in women's lifeworld experiences and the abstracted scientific knowledge of the (male) experts. That same difference is visible in late nineteenth-century midwifery writings because those same emphases are still carried forward by different kinds of midwives: for example, compare Ina May Gaskin's *Spiritual Midwifery* (1990), which encodes a home-birth midwife's knowledge inside a series of amazing birthing tales full of the rich hippie idioms that characterize residents of the Farm, with *Varney's Midwifery* (1997), which is written by a nurse-midwife and presents information in a purely abstract way using medicalized language. These two books represent opposite ends of the philosophical and linguistic spectrum that defines the range of contemporary American midwifery and point up the need for compassionate and thoughtful rhetorical analyses of their differences and similarities—indeed, an increasing number of fascinating works written by various kinds of midwives would benefit from comparative analysis.

For example, just as anthropologist Robert Hahn (1987) has traced the evolution of obstetrical thought through multiple editions of the authoritative *Williams' Obstetrics,* so might some enterprising social scientist take a similar approach to the various editions of Varney's tome or trace the evolution of home-birth midwifery knowledge and approach through the two editions of Elizabeth Davis's groundbreaking *Heart and Hands* (1997). A similarly fascinating enterprise would be to compare *Varney's Midwifery* with another abstract midwifery text, this one by home-birth midwife Anne Frye, who has been the first to attempt to comprehensively codify the full body of out-of-hospital midwifery knowledge in *Care during Pregnancy,* the first volume of *Holistic Midwifery* (1995). Such a social scientist would do midwifery a great service, as many midwives would benefit from a careful dissection of the differences between the rhetorical styles and strategies of nurse- and direct-entry midwives, and between the particular systems of authoritative knowledge about birth they are encoding in these works.

Direct-entry midwives have by now done what their early seventeenth-century counterparts could not do: they have created an abstract body of midwifery knowledge about holistic approaches to out-of-hospital birth and encoded it in textbooks, but in doing so they have not lost its embodied and experiential nature and flavor. They retain that flavor not only in their books, like those by Davis and Frye, but also through stories, the same kind of stories the early seventeenth-century midwife told. They tell those stories to each other all the time, and they write them down and publish them in magazines of their own, most especially *Midwifery Today* and Gaskin's *Birth Gazette.* Nurse-midwives in general are trained in a more abstract and medicalized body of knowledge than direct-entry midwives, like the late seventeenth-century Martha Mears. But unlike Mears, they tend not to buy into the knowledge of the male experts but rather to practice out of what both groups call "the midwifery model" of care. They too retain a rich tradition of storytelling, a strong respect for the knowledge encapsulated in such stories, and a willingness to publish their stories in various forums, including the magazines mentioned.

Nurse-midwives' stories tend to be filled with examples of the conflicts and contradictions they experience daily between the medical model dominant in the hospitals where they practice and the midwifery model they are taught and do their best to apply. The stories of direct-entry midwives who practice outside of hospitals show little ambivalence about models of care but do reveal the tension such midwives experience when they must transport their clients and cope in the hospital with a worldview radically different from their own. No social scientists have analyzed this large published corpus of informal midwifery stories; they form a rich data source that could be complemented with recorded oral narratives, and they lie waiting for the researcher who will take them up.[6]

My own present research addresses contrasts in the politics and philosophies of nurse- and direct-entry midwives as they professionalize; I have presented some of the results in "The Ups, Downs, and Interlinkages of Nurse- and Direct-Entry Midwifery: Status, Practice, and Education" (1998a) and "Types of Midwifery Training: An Anthropological Overview" (1998b), both of which appear in *Getting an Education: Paths to Becoming a Midwife.*[7] A major goal in writing those articles was to offer what I had learned about midwifery education to aspiring midwives who are wondering which path to take, in the hope that my research might more fully inform their choices. Those articles were perhaps the most difficult challenge I have undertaken to date, as they brought me smack dab into the postmodern researcher's dilemma—how do we write about our subjects when they are reading (and critiquing) rough drafts of our work before they are even out of the computer? How do we present the sometimes unpleasant truths we learn about them in ways that are fair and responsible but not hurtful and offensive? And, most important, how can we develop creative methods of collaborative scholarship in which our subjects are also our colleagues and coauthors? These are features of the postmodern world, the cyborg society in which the boundaries are increasingly permeable. Our world is transnational, our work interdisciplinary, our methods eclectic, our results available to all.

Ultimately, I ran those articles by twenty midwives (ten nurse-midwives and ten direct-entry midwives), in a very deliberate effort to be responsive to my subjects and inclusive of their (multiple!) points of view while still speaking the truth as I saw it in ways they could agree were honest and fair. It was an emotionally trying time, but I believe worth it in the end, and in the interests of developing a more collaborative anthropology. Likewise, rhetoricians who study the discourse and speech communities of various groups may wish to find their own creative ways to include the opinions and perspectives of those they study in the writings they produce.

A final suggestion, one that stems from my overarching desire to help create a useful social science of reproduction, one that makes a positive difference in women's lives by most fully informing their choices. I wonder: what about those women who have read social science analyses of the NRTs even as they are facing the choices these new technologies create? Does our careful analytic work make a difference? If a woman thinking about undergoing IVF, for example, reads Sarah Franklin's *Embodied Progress* (1997), how might it affect her decision about undergoing the process and, if she undertakes it, what her experience of that process is? I would really like to know—do we make a difference? How can we overcome our own body talk and baby talk taboos and work to make our research more relevant to the needs, desires, concerns of the women we study?

NOTES

1. To be sure, birth carries its own set of risks. In societies in which women are malnourished and overworked, rates of both maternal and infant mortality are high. But when women are healthy, well nourished, and receive adequate social support, the percentage of complications in childbirth is very low—well under 10 percent. And the majority of complications that may occur can be screened for in advance. Even the most conservative obstetricians will agree that 90 percent of all pregnancies and births in healthy women will be normal and uncomplicated. The problem is that far too often, technomedical interventions are not reserved for the small percentage of births that actually need them; rather, they are performed on most laboring women. By interfering with the normal process of labor, such interventions often generate the very complications they are designed to prevent. (For more information, see Davis-Floyd 1992; Goer 1995; Wagner 1994; Rooks 1997).

2. Victoria Hall (1998), a researcher at the University of Central Lancashire, United Kingdom, has found elevated levels of testosterone during the menstrual cycle in women with self-diagnosed mild PMS compared to a group of women with no PMS symptoms. Can social scientists address the implications?

3. These issues are just as salient in other disciplines. Ros Bramwell is a reproductive health psychologist and research director of the Midwifery Faculty at the University of Central Lancashire. Her current research project addresses one aspect I am calling attention to here: how do the stresses in people's lives affect their reproductive health? Her particular focus is on the menstrual cycle: Will stress at work result in more premenstrual distress? During a recent research seminar we both attended, Bramwell noted that

her colleague Ann Walker, in collaboration with other psychologists, held a symposium on the topic that got press coverage and then analyzed the coverage, which moved from saying that PMS could be seen as socially constructed to "it's all in your head." The papers immediately got letters to the editor asking, "How dare you say what I experience isn't real?" Of course, Bramwell noted, the psychologists involved were not saying, "You don't feel this way," but were asking instead, "Why do you feel this way?"

Bramwell noted that as soon as a problem is not directly physiological, society translates it to "it's all in your head," meaning it's not real. Because the phrase "social construction" is always subject to misinterpretation, Bramwell said, we have to ask how we can extend knowledge in a way that a range of audiences can hear correctly. She said she wants to develop a more quantitative model that will allow her to combine the social, personal, and psychological, but finding funding for such a project or any research like it is difficult. According to Bramwell, hardly any research exists on the causes of infertility and almost none on the psychosexual causes of infertility. She only half-jokingly noted that if she wanted to do research on whether yak milk could reduce infertility, she'd be funded because some company could make money from selling yak milk, but nobody can make money from learning whether conflict at work increases premenstrual tension or contributes to infertility.

4. For up-to-date information about this field and an extensive bibliography, see www.birthpsychology.com.

5. For an extraordinary and passionate writing of the birthing body, see Robbie Pfeufer Kahn, *Bearing Meaning: The Language of Birth* (1995).

6. And just as I have called elsewhere for careful analyses of the differences in how home-birth midwives, hospital-based midwives, and obstetricians use technology, so I call here for rhetorical analyses of the differences in the ways nurse-midwives, direct-entry midwives, and obstetricians think about and talk about birth technologies.

7. Both articles are also available at www.davis-floyd.com.

REFERENCES

Aijmer, G., ed. 1992. *Coming into existence: Birth and metaphors of birth.* Gothenburg, Sweden: Institute for Advanced Studies in Social Anthropology.
Belenky, M. F., B. M. Clinchy, N. R. Goldberger, and J. M. Tarule. 1986. *Women's ways of knowing: The development of self, voice, and mind.* New York: Basic.
Bramwell, Ros. 1999. Remarks made during a research symposium. February 12, Department of Midwifery, University of Central Lancashire, Preston, Lancashire, England.
Browner, C. H., and N. A. Press. 1995. The normalization of prenatal diagnostic testing. In Faye Ginsburg and Rayna Rapp, eds., *Conceiving the new world order: The global politics of reproduction,* pp. 307–22. Berkeley: University of California Press.

Browner, C. H., and N. A. Press. 1997. The production of authoritative knowledge in American prenatal care. In Robbie Davis-Floyd and Carolyn Sargent, eds., _Childbirth and authoritative knowledge: Cross-cultural perspectives,_ pp. 113–31. Berkeley: University of California Press.

Buckley, Thomas, and Alma Gottlieb. 1987. _Blood magic._ Berkeley: University of California Press.

Chamberlain, David. 1998. Babies remember pain. In Robbie Davis-Floyd and Joseph Dumit, eds., _Cyborg babies: From techno-sex to techno-tots,_ pp. 169–89. New York: Routledge.

Cosslett, Tess. 1994. _Women writing childbirth: Modern discourses of motherhood._ Manchester, U.K.: Manchester University Press.

Davis, Elizabeth. 1997. _Heart and hands: A midwife's guide to pregnancy and birth._ Berkeley, Calif.: Celestial Arts.

Davis-Floyd, Robbie. 1992. _Birth as an American rite of passage._ Berkeley: University of California Press.

Davis-Floyd, Robbie. 1994. The technocratic body: American childbirth as cultural expression. _Social Science and Medicine_ 38:1125–40.

Davis-Floyd, Robbie. 1998a. The ups, downs, and interlinkages of nurse- and direct-entry midwifery: Status, practice, and education. In Jan Tritten and Joel Southern, eds., _Getting an education: Pathways to becoming a midwife,_ pp. 67–118. Eugene, Oreg.: Midwifery Today.

Davis-Floyd, Robbie. 1998b. Types of midwifery training: An anthropological overview. In Jan Tritten and Joel Southern, eds., _Getting an education: Pathways to becoming a midwife,_ pp. 119–33. Eugene, Oreg.: Midwifery Today.

Davis-Floyd, Robbie. n.d. Knowing: A story of two births. Unpublished manuscript.

Davis-Floyd, Robbie, and Elizabeth Davis. 1996. Intuition as authoritative knowledge in midwifery and home birth. _Medical Anthropology Quarterly_ 10:237–69.

Davis-Floyd, Robbie, and Carolyn F. Sargent. 1996. _The social production of authoritative knowledge in childbirth,_ a special issue of the _Medical Anthropology Quarterly_ 10 (2).

Davis-Floyd, Robbie, and Carolyn F. Sargent, eds. 1997. _Childbirth and authoritative knowledge: Cross-cultural perspectives._ Berkeley: University of California Press.

Davis-Floyd, Robbie E., and Joseph Dumit, eds. 1998. _Cyborg babies: From techno-sex to techno-tots._ New York: Routledge.

Daviss, B. A. 1997. Heeding warnings from the canary, the whale, and the Inuit: A framework for analyzing competing types of knowledge about childbirth. In Robbie Davis-Floyd and Carolyn Sargent, eds., _Childbirth and authoritative knowledge: Cross-cultural perspectives,_ pp. 441–73. Berkeley: University of California Press.

Duden, Barbara. 1993. _Disembodying women: Perspectives on pregnancy and the unborn._ Translated by Lee Hoinacki. Cambridge, Mass.: Harvard University Press.

Dumit, Joseph, and Robbie Davis-Floyd. 1998. Cyborg babies: Children of the third millennium. In Robbie Davis-Floyd and Joseph Dumit, eds., *Cyborg babies: From techno-sex to techno-tots,* pp. 3–18. New York: Routledge.

English, J. E. 1988. *Childlessness transformed: Stories of alternative parenting.* Mt. Shasta, Calif.: EarthHeart.

Franklin, Sarah. 1997. *Embodied progress: A cultural account of assisted conception.* New York: Routledge.

Frye, Anne. 1995. *Holistic midwifery: A comprehensive textbook for midwives in homebirth practice,* vol. 1: *Care During pregnancy.* Portland, Oreg.: Labyrs Press.

Gaskin, I. M. 1990 (1977). *Spiritual midwifery.* 3d ed. Summertown, Tenn.: Book Publishing Co.

Georges, Eugenia. 1997. Fetal ultrasound imaging and the production of authoritative knowledge in Greece. In Robbie Davis-Floyd and Carolyn Sargent, eds., *Childbirth and authoritative knowledge: Cross-cultural perspectives,* pp. 91–112. Berkeley: University of California Press.

Ginsburg, F. D., and Rayna Rapp. 1995. *Conceiving the new world order: The global politics of reproduction.* Berkeley: University of California Press.

Goer, Henci. 1995. *Obstetric myths versus research realities.* New Haven, Conn.: Bergin and Garvey.

Gottlieb, Alma. 1996. Personal communication.

Hahn, R. A. 1987. Divisions of labor: Obstetrician, woman, and society in *Williams' Obstetrics,* 1903–1985. *Medical Anthropology Quarterly* 1:256–82.

Hall, Victoria. 1998. Effects of cycle phase and sex hormone levels upon physiological and psychological functioning in healthy women: an exploration and comparison of natural and oral contraceptive regulated cycles. Ph.D. diss., University of Central Lancashire, U.K.

Kahn, R. P. 1995. *Bearing meaning: The language of birth.* Champaign: University of Illinois Press.

Martin, Emily. 1987. *The woman in the body: A cultural analysis of reproduction.* Boston: Beacon.

Mathieu, Nicole C. 1978. Man-culture and woman-nature? *Women's Studies International Quarterly* 1:55–65.

Mentor, Steven. 1998. Witches, nurse-midwives, and cyborgs: IVF, ART, and complex agency in the world of technobirth. In Robbie Davis-Floyd and Joseph Dumit, eds., *Cyborg babies: From techno-sex to techno-tots,* pp. 67–89. New York: Routledge.

Miller, Janneli. 1994. Stop bleeding! Symbolic and physiologic effects of ritual and nonritual speech at birth. Paper presented at the 93d Annual Meetings of the American Anthropology Association, November 20, 1993, Washington, D.C.

Miller, Janneli. n.d. Whole births, whole selves: Identity and resistance in homebirth narratives. Unpublished ms.

Ortner, Sherry. 1974. Is female to male as nature is to culture? In M. Z. Rosaldo and Louise Lamphere, eds., *Woman, culture, and society,* pp. 67–88. Palo Alto, Calif.: Stanford University Press.

Parvati-Baker, Jeannine. 1986a. *Conscious conception: Elemental journey through the labyrinth of sexuality.* Monroe, Utah: Freestone.

Parvati-Baker, Jeannine. 1986b. (1974). *Prenatal yoga and natural birth.* Rev. ed. Monroe, Utah: Freestone.

Parvati-Baker, Jeannine. 1991. *The deep ecology of birth: Healing birth is healing our earth.* Monroe, Utah: Freestone.

Parvati-Baker, Jeannine. 1992. The Shamanic dimension of childbirth, *Pre- and Perinatal Psychology Journal* 7:5–20.

Payne, Niravi. 1997. *The language of fertility.* New York: Harmony Books.

Pigg, S. L. 1997. Finding, knowing, naming, and training traditional birth attendants. In Robbie Davis-Floyd and Carolyn Sargent, eds., *Childbirth and authoritative knowledge: Cross-cultural perspectives,* pp. 233–62. Berkeley: University of California Press.

Rabuzzi, K. 1994. *Mother with child: Interpretations of childbirth.* Bloomington: Indiana University Press.

Rapp, Rayna. 1984. XYLO: A true story. In Rita Arditti, Renate Duelli Klein, and Shelley Minden, eds., *Test-tube women,* pp. 313–28. Boston: Pandora.

Rapp, Rayna. 1987. Moral pioneers: Women, men, and fetuses on a frontier of reproductive technology. *Women and Health* 13:101–16. (Reprinted in M. D. Leonardo, ed. 1991. *Gender at the crossroads of knowledge: Feminist anthropology in the postmodern era.* Berkeley: University of California Press.)

Rapp, Rayna. 1988a. Chromosomes and communication: The discourse of genetic counseling. *Medical Anthropology Quarterly* 2:143–57.

Rapp, Rayna. 1988b. The power of positive discourse: Medical and maternal discourses on amniocentesis. In Karen Michaelson, ed., *Childbirth in America: Anthropological perspectives,* pp. 103–16. South Hadley, Mass.: Bergin and Garvey.

Rapp, Rayna. 1999. *Testing women, testing fetuses.* New York: Routledge.

Reynolds, Peter C. 1991. *Stealing fire: The mythology of the technocracy.* Palo Alto, Calif.: Iconic Anthropology Press.

Roncalli, Lucia. 1995. Standing by process: A midwife's notes on storytelling, passage, and intuition. In Robbie Davis-Floyd and P. S. Arvidson, eds., *Intuition: The inside story,* pp. 177–200. New York: Routledge.

Rooks, J. P. 1997. *Midwifery and childbirth in America.* Philadelphia: Temple University Press.

Rothman, B. K. 1989. *Recreating motherhood: Ideology and technology in patriarchal society.* New York: Norton.

Sargent, Carolyn, and Nancy Stark. 1989. Childbirth education and childbirth models: Parental perspectives on control, anesthesia, and technological intervention in the birth process. *Medical Anthropology Quarterly* 3:36–51.

Szurek, Jane. 1997. Resistance to technology-enhanced childbirth in Tuscany. In Robbie Davis-Floyd and Carolyn Sargent, eds., *Childbirth and authoritative knowledge: Cross-cultural perspectives,* pp. 287–314. Berkeley: University of California Press.

Treichler, P. A. 1990. Feminism, medicine, and the meaning of childbirth. In Mary Jacobus, Evelyn Fox Keller, and Sally Shuttleworth, eds., *Body/politics: Women and the discourses of science,* pp. 113–38. New York: Routledge.

Varney, Helen. 1997. *Varney's midwifery.* 3d ed. Sudbury, Mass.: Jones and Bartlett.

Wagner, Marsden. 1994. *Pursuing the birth machine.* Camperdown, Australia: ACE Graphics.

Westra, Terri. 1996. An exploration of the transpersonal dimensions of pregnancy. Ph.D. diss., Institute of Transpersonal Psychology, Palo Alto, Calif.

CONTRIBUTORS

INDEX

CONTRIBUTORS

Elizabeth C. Britt is an assistant professor in the English Department at Northeastern University, where she teaches courses in writing and rhetoric. She has published in *Science as Culture; Journal of Business and Technical Communication;* and *Studies in Law, Politics, and Society* and is completing a book-length cultural study of mandatory insurance coverage for infertility in Massachusetts.

Celeste M. Condit is a professor in the Department of Speech Communication at the University of Georgia. Among other works, she has written *Decoding Abortion Rhetoric: Communicating Social Change* (1990) and *The Meanings of the Gene: Public Debates about Human Heredity* (1999). She coedited *Evaluating Women's Health Messages* (1996) and coedits the journal *Women's Studies in Communication.* She was the winner of the 1998 Douglas Ehninger Distinguished Rhetorical Scholar Award.

Robbie Davis-Floyd is a research fellow in the Department of Anthropology at the University of Texas at Austin. A cultural anthropologist specializing in ritual, gender, and reproduction, she lectures nationally and internationally in these and related areas. She is the author of *Birth as an American Rite of Passage* (1992); coauthor of *From Doctor to Healer: The Transformative Journey* (1998); and coeditor of *Childbirth and Authoritative Knowledge: Cross-Cultural Perspectives* (1997), *Intuition: The Inside Story* (1997), and *Cyborg Babies: From Techno-Sex to Techno-Tots* (1998). She is studying the politics and knowledge systems of what she calls "postmodern midwifery" in the United States and Mexico, writing one book on ritual and another on the organic body. She also is conducting oral history interviews with NASA pioneers (inner space and outer space do correspond, after all).

Chloé Diepenbrock is an assistant professor of literature and communications at the University of Houston–Clear Lake, where she teaches courses in composition and rhetoric and writing. Her book, *Gynecology and Textuality: Popular Representations of Reproductive Technology* (1988), is a rhetorical study of media representation of reproductive technology.

Contributors

Kathleen Marie Dixon is an associate professor of philosophy at Bowling Green State University. She is a medical ethicist with teaching and research interests in the history of the health sciences, feminist analyses of medicine, and death studies. Her articles have appeared in medical and medical ethics journals and anthologies.

Eugenia Georges is an associate professor of anthropology at Rice University. Since 1990 she has been conducting research on gender, health, and the politics of reproduction in Greece.

Clare Gravon is regional field manager of the YWCA of the United States and was formerly associate director of the Center for Advanced Feminist Studies and Center on Women and Public Policy at the University of Minnesota. Her work includes activism on behalf of women's reproductive rights; from 1989 to 1992 she chaired the Minnesota Chapter of the National Abortion and Reproductive Rights Action League (NARAL), and she cofounded and chaired the Minnesota Alliance for Choice, a statewide reproductive rights coalition. Her evaluation research addresses neighborhood revitalization programs in the City of Minneapolis as well as gender and diversity programs within philanthropy.

Laura J. Gurak is an associate professor in the Department of Rhetoric at the University of Minnesota. Her research focuses on the rhetorics of technology, specifically, the way discourse about technology reshapes concepts of community, intellectual property, and gender. She has published articles in a variety of rhetoric and technical communication journals, including "Making Gender Visible: Applying Feminist Critiques of Technology to Technical Communication," (*Technical Communication Quarterly* 3 [1994]) and has written and spoken on issues of gender and the Internet. She is the author of *Persuasion and Privacy in Cyberspace* (1997), two forthcoming textbooks, and a forthcoming book called *Cyberliteracy.*

Jeanette Herrle-Fanning is working on a dissertation, "Of Forceps and Folios: Eighteenth-Century British Midwifery Publications and the Construction of Professional Identity," in the doctoral program in history at the Graduate Center of the City University of New York. She teaches at Lehman College.

Sally Gregory Kohlstedt is a professor in the Program of History of Science and Technology as well as past director of the Center for Advanced Feminist Studies at the University of Minnesota. She works on the intersection of science and culture, studying scientific institutions and popular science, as well as aspects of women, gender, and science. She has written and edited a number of works, including (with Helen Longino) *Women, Gender, and Science: New Directions* (1997) and *Women in the History of Science* (1999).

Mary M. Lay is a professor of rhetoric and past director of the Center for Advanced Feminist Studies at the University of Minnesota. She is past president of the Association of Teachers of Technical Writing and was elevated to Fellow of that association in 1995. She is coeditor of *Collaborative Writing in Industry: Investigations in Theory and Practice* (1991), *Technical Communication* (1995), and *Encompassing Gender* (tentative title, 2000). She has published on gender and scientific and technical communication in such journals as the *Journal of Advanced Composition, Quarterly Journal of Speech,* and the *Journal of Business and Technical Communication.* For the past several years, she has studied the licensing efforts of traditional midwives in Minnesota and has a book, *The Rhetoric of Midwifery,* forthcoming from Rutgers University Press.

Helen E. Longino is a professor of philosophy and women's studies at the University of Minnesota. She is the author of *Science as Social Knowledge* (1990) and coeditor (with Evelyn Fox Keller) of *Feminism and Science* (1996) and (with Sally Gregory Kohlstedt) of *Women, Gender, and Science: New Directions* (1997).

Lisa M. Mitchell teaches anthropology at the University of Victoria, Canada. Her current research explores biomedical and parental narratives of fetal anomaly and perinatal loss.

Cynthia Myntti is a consultant anthropologist and visiting senior lecturer on the faculty of health sciences at the American University of Beirut, Lebanon. She formerly served as codirector of the Center on Women and Public Policy at the University of Minnesota. She teaches and writes on reproductive health and international population policy and consults regularly for the World Health Organization and other international agencies. She has recently been in Lebanon studying several reproductive issues.

Beverly Sauer is an associate professor of English and rhetoric at Carnegie Mellon University, where she teaches Renaissance rhetoric and advanced professional and technical communication. She worked on the ethics and rhetoric of documentation and mining disasters in the United States and England. She has published numerous articles on risk and safety in technical communication, ethical consequences of language in the workplace, and the rhetorical construction of scientific and technical expertise at the dawn of early modern science.

Laura Shanner is an associate professor at the John Dossetor Health Ethics Centre and Department of Public Health Sciences at the University of Alberta, Canada. She previously taught philosophy and bioethics at the University of Toronto. Her publications on feminist bioethics, reproductive and genetic technologies, and women's health have appeared in books and journals in medicine, law, health policy, philosophy, and women's studies.

Mary Thompson teaches English and women's studies at Bowling Green State University. She recently completed her dissertation, "Women and Technologies of Body Modification," and is coediting a collection of essays from the Feminist Generations Conference.

Lyn Turney is a research fellow at the Australian Research Centre in Sex, Health, and Society, La Trobe University, Australia. She has conducted feminist research in women's experiences of surgery and the health of rural women. She has taught in health sociology and women's health, and is engaged in health services research.

Martha H. Verbrugge is a professor of history at Bucknell University, where she teaches the history of science and medicine. She is the author of *Able-Bodied Womanhood: Personal Health and Social Change in Nineteenth-Century Boston* (1988) and articles about the history of women's health and fitness. Her current research focuses on female physical educators in twentieth-century America.

INDEX

abortion, psychosomatic: data on, 58–59; Javert's theory of, 49–64; reasons for, 61–64

adoption, 114, 209, 218–20, 281

amniocentesis, 46

Asch, Ricardo, 116

assisted reproduction. *See* reproduction, assisted

babies, test-tube. *See* reproductive technologies

Berg, Paul, 125–31

Better Homes & Gardens, 101

bio-power, 4–6, 14, 20, 32–33, 45, 207, 221

Birth Is Love, 185, 191–201

Bransford, Helen, 98, 115–17

breast implants: breast cancer and, 265, 273; calls for ban on, 263; and class, culture, 272, 274; defense of, rhetoric used in, 265–74; defense of, strategies in, 263–74; feminist critique of, 270, 273–74; and harm to women, 271–72; hearings on safety of, 262, 264; opponents of, 264–74; and public health issues, 262–63, 268–69, 272–73

Brown, Leslie, 98, 106, 108–9, 114

Brown, Louise Joy, 99, 112, 116

cesarean section, 46

childbirth: in England, eighteenth century, 33–38; female suffering and, 38; "lying-in" ritual, 33, 38–39, 43; management of, by professionals, 45; rhetoric used to describe, 10; social and cultural attitudes toward, 45–46

Chukwu, Nkem, 109–10

Chukwu octuplets, 4, 109–10

Commentary, 101

Complete Practice of Midwifery, 38–41, 44

Cosmopolitan, 101

Del Zio, Doris, 98, 106, 109, 114, 116

Denman, Thomas, 42

Devers-Scott, Roberta, 227

El Halta, Valerie, 233–34

Family Circle, 101, 111

fetal monitoring, internal, 46

Food and Drug Administration, 262–68, 271–75

forceps, 12, 35, 47, 234–35

Foucault, Michel, 4–5, 14, 32, 45, 162, 207, 210–11, 221, 228, 232–33, 240–41, 277, 280

Franson, Claudia, 107

Gaskin, Ina May, 229, 234

genetic counseling, 45

genetic theory, in medicine: criticism of, 128; defined by Berg, 125–27; effects on women, 132–40; and genetic testing on women, 133–36; rhetoric used to support, 128–31; social class and, 137–38; state intervention and, 136

germ theory, in medicine, 125–26, 131

Glamour, 101

Good Housekeeping, 101, 103

gym teachers, female. *See* teachers, female gym

Hall, Deidre, 107, 111, 115

Human Genome Project, 125, 130

infertility: age and, 217–18; case studies, 212–17; class and, 221–22; definitions, 213; insurance coverage and, 207, 221–22; medical intervention and, 209; normalization process and, 20, 208–11, 217–20; rates, 98, 102; reproductive technologies and, 106–7, 278–82; and rhetoric of reproduction, 3; social, 208, 222; spending on, 98

infertility clinics: couples and, 144; data on, 151; and family planning, 153; feminist critique of, 157–59; images of women and, 142, 150, 154–56; language used to support, 142–46, 150–52, 154; literature, 142–46, 150–52, 154; pornog-

RHETORIC OF THE

HUMAN SCIENCES

Language and Historical Representation: Getting the
Story Crooked
Hans Kellner

Body Talk: Rhetoric, Technology, Reproduction
*Mary M. Lay, Laura J. Gurak, Clare Gravon, and
Cynthia Myntti, editors*

Therapeutic Discourse and Socratic Dialogue:
A Cultural Critique
Tullio Maranhão

The Rhetoric of Economics
Donald N. McCloskey

The Rhetoric of Economics, Second Edition
Deirdre N. McCloskey

Tropes of Politics: Science, Theory, Rhetoric, Action
John S. Nelson

The Rhetoric of the Human Sciences: Language and
Argument in Scholarship and Public Affairs
*John S. Nelson, Allan Megill, and Donald N. McCloskey,
editors*

What's Left: The Ecole Normale Supérieure and
the Right
Diane Rubenstein

Understanding Scientific Prose
Jack Selzer, editor

The Politics of Representation: Writing Practices
in Biography, Photography, and Policy Analysis
Michael J. Shapiro

The Legacy of Kenneth Burke
Herbert W. Simons and Trevor Melia, editors